CONSUMPTION AND GENDER IN SOUTHERN EUROPE SINCE THE LONG 1960s

CONSUMPTION AND GENDER IN SOUTHERN EUROPE SINCE THE LONG 1960s

Edited by Kostis Kornetis, Eirini Kotsovili and Nikolaos Papadogiannis

Bloomsbury Academic
An imprint of Bloomsbury Publishing Plc

B L O O M S B U R Y
LONDON · OXFORD · NEW YORK · NEW DELHI · SYDNEY

Bloomsbury Academic
An imprint of Bloomsbury Publishing Plc

50 Bedford Square	1385 Broadway
London	New York
WC1B 3DP	NY 10018
UK	USA

www.bloomsbury.com

BLOOMSBURY and the Diana logo are trademarks of Bloomsbury Publishing Plc

First published 2016

© Kostis Kornetis, Eirini Kotsovili, Nikolaos Papadogiannis and Contributors, 2016

All rights reserved. No part of this publication may be reproduced or transmitted in any form or by any means, electronic or mechanical, including photocopying, recording, or any information storage or retrieval system, without prior permission in writing from the publishers.

No responsibility for loss caused to any individual or organization acting on or refraining from action as a result of the material in this publication can be accepted by Bloomsbury or the author.

British Library Cataloguing-in-Publication Data
A catalogue record for this book is available from the British Library.

ISBN: HB: 978-1-4725-9627-7
PB: 978-1-4725-9626-0
ePDF: 978-1-4725-9628-4
ePub: 978-1-4725-9629-1

Library of Congress Cataloging-in-Publication Data
A catalog record for this book is available from the Library of Congress.

Typeset by RefineCatch Limited, Bungay, Suffolk

CONTENTS

List of Illustrations	vii
List of Contributors	viii
Acknowledgments	x
Transliteration	xi
Foreword *Guya Accornero*	xii

Introduction   Kostis Kornetis, Eirini Kotsovili and Nikolaos Papadogiannis   1

Part I   Consumption and Gender in Dictatorship and Disciplined Democracy

1 Gendering Touristic Spain, 1950s–70s   *Moritz Glaser*   29

2 Basque National Identities, Youth Culture and Gender in the 1960s: Beyond the Farmhouse and the *Ye-yé*   *Amaia Lamikiz Jauregiondo*   43

3 Consumerism, Gender Diversity and Moralization of Sexuality in the Iberian 1960s   *Rosa María Medina-Doménech and Richard Cleminson*   59

4 Gender and Consumer Behaviour: A Portrait of Portugal in the 1960s   *Inês Brasão*   85

5 Tourism, Body and Seaside Recreational Practices in Postwar Greek Society Until 1974   *Michalis Nikolakakis*   103

Part II   Consumption and Gender through the Moment of Transition

6 Representations of Sexuality and Gender in Portuguese Cinema During the late *Estado Novo* and the Carnation Revolution   *Érica Faleiro Rodrigues*   121

7 The Spanish Housewives in Transition (1959–80)   *Elena Díaz Silva*   137

8 Documenting Post-Authoritarian Subcultures in the European South: The Cases of Pedro Almodóvar's *Pepi, Luci, Bom* and Nikos Zervos' *Dracula of Exarchia*   *Kostis Kornetis*   153

9 'Naked Piazza': Male (Homo)sexualities, Masculinities and Consumer Cultures in Greece Since the 1960s   *Kostas Yannakopoulos*   173

Contents

Part III Consumption and Gender Between the Transition to Democracy and the Financial Crisis of the 2010s

10 Television Culture and Social Change in Post-revolutionary Portugal *Luís Trindade* 193

11 Leafing through the 1980s in Portuguese Fashion Magazines *Giulia Bonali* 209

12 Consuming the Past as a Televisual Product: Gender and Consumption in *Cuéntame cómo pasó/Tell Me How it Was* *Abigail Loxham* 227

13 Audio-visual Consumption in the Greek VHS Era: Social Mobility, Privatization and the VCR Audiences in the 1980s *Ursula-Helen Kassaveti* 241

14 Revisiting the Greek 1980s through the Prism of Crisis *Panagiotis Zestanakis* 257

Index 275

ILLUSTRATIONS

3.1	Distovagal (The secretary).	67
3.2	Miltown.	71
3.3	$ Perich *La Vanguardia*.	73
3.4	*Coimbra Médica*, XV, June 1968.	76
11.1	'Viva Azul', from *Marie-Claire* n. 3, 1989.	218
11.2	'Viva Azul', Cristo Rei, Lisbon, from *Marie-Claire* n. 3, 1989.	220
14.1	Photo showing children running carefree on a sidewalk.	268

CONTRIBUTORS

Guya Accornero (CIES-IUL) is a political sociologist working on democratic transitions and social movements. Her publications in this field include (with Olivier Fillieule) the book *Social Movements Studies in Europe: the State of the Art* (2016).

Giulia Bonali holds a masters degree in history of design from the Royal College of Art and the Victoria and Albert Museum. She is currently a PhD candidate at Birkbeck, University of London, at the Department of Cultures and Languages.

Inês Brasão holds a PhD in historical and economic sociology. She is a lecturer in the field of sociology. Her research focuses on work, leisure, subaltern studies and gender studies.

Richard Cleminson is Professor in Hispanic studies at the University of Leeds. He works on the history of sexuality and the history of anarchism in Iberia. His most recent book is *Catholicism, Race and Empire: Eugenics in Portugal, 1900–1950* (2014).

Elena Díaz Silva received her PhD in history from the Autonomous University of Madrid. She is a research fellow in the Department for Iberian and Latin American History at the University of Cologne, where she is currently participating in a project funded by the European Research Council about gender and exile.

Érica Faleiro Rodrigues is a film historian and filmmaker, researching gender and politics in film, with a focus on the years surrounding the Portuguese revolution of 1974 and the wider international context of screen representation of desire, sexuality and sexual freedom. She is currently a PhD candidate at Birkbeck, University of London, in the Department of Iberian and Latin American Studies.

Moritz Glaser is a doctoral student (under the supervision of Gabriele Lingelbach) and graduate teaching assistant at the University of Kiel, Germany. His dissertation encompasses the consequences of European mass tourism in Spain roughly from 1950 to 1980.

Ursula-Helen Kassaveti holds a PhD in film theory, sociology and cultural studies (University of Athens). She is a research fellow at the Aristotle University of Thessaloniki and her research interests revolve around popular film genres, visual culture, visual ethnography and cultural studies.

Kostis Kornetis holds a PhD in history and civilization from the European University Institute, Florence. From 2007 to 2012 he taught at the History Department at Brown University. Currently he is an assistant professor/faculty fellow at the University Carlos III de Madrid.

Eirini Kotsovili has studied history (McGill University) and literature (University of Oxford). She was an Onassis Foundation teaching fellow and is currently a lecturer at the Hellenic Studies Program, Simon Fraser University. Her research interests fall under the thematic spheres of identity and gender.

Amaia Lamikiz Jauregiondo holds a PhD from the European University Institute, Florence (2005). She has worked as a lecturer at the University of the Basque Country and is currently working as a history teacher in San Sebastian (Spain).

Abigail Loxham is a lecturer in Spanish cultural studies at the University of Manchester. She is the author of *Cinema at the Edges: New Encounters with Julio Medem, Bigas Luna and José Luis Guerín* (2014).

Rosa María Medina-Doménech is *profesora titular* at the University of Granada (History of Science Department), Spain. She works on the history of knowledge, emotions and subjectivity, from a postcolonial science perspective. Her most recent book is *Ciencia y Sabiduría del amor. Una historia cultural del franquismo* (2013).

Michalis Nikolakakis holds a PhD in sociology from the University of Crete. He is a sociology graduate from Panteion University, Athens and has an MA in social and political thought (Warwick University). The title of his PhD thesis is 'Tourism and Greek Society from 1945 to 1974'.

Nikolaos Papadogiannis obtained his PhD in history from the University of Cambridge in 2010. He is currently a teaching fellow at the University of St Andrews. His research focuses on youth culture, tourism, sexuality and gender in contemporary Europe.

Luís Trindade is Senior Lecturer in Portuguese studies at Birkbeck, University of London. In 2008 he published *O Estranho Caso do Nacionalismo Português*, on the relations between Salazarism and literature. In 2013 he edited *The Making of Modern Portugal*, an introduction to Portuguese modern history. His current research focuses on Portuguese revolutionary and post-revolutionary culture.

Kostas Yannakopoulos is Social Anthropologist and Associate Professor at the Department of Social Anthropology and History, University of the Aegean. His research interests focus on gender, sexuality, health, the relation between anthropology and psychoanalysis, politics of difference, urban space and queer history in post-war Greece.

Panagiotis Zestanakis is a historian. His research interests focus on everyday life history in post-dictatorship Greece, the history of media and representations and the uses of history in participative web cultures. Currently he is completing his PhD research project 'Lifestyles, Gender Relations and New Social Spaces in 1980s Athens' at the University of Crete.

ACKNOWLEDEGMENTS

We would like to cordially thank Guya Accornero, Alejandro Gomez del Moral, Luis Trindade and the two anonymous reviewers for their extremely useful remarks. We would also like to express our gratitude to Efi Avdela, Jo Labanyi, Luisa Passerini and Duncan Wheeler for having encouraged us to proceed with the preparation of this volume. We also need to mention the fruitful exchange of ideas we have had with Achilleas Hadjikyriacou, Dimitris Papanikolaou and Sofia Sampaio. The support of Rhodri Mogford and Emma Goode from Bloomsbury Academic has also been precious. Of course, the contributors and editors are solely responsible for any errors and the analysis herein. We would also like to note that the names of the volume's editors as well as the Introduction's authors are listed in alphabetical order.

TRANSLITERATION OF GREEK CHARACTERS INTO LATIN CHARACTERS

Greek	Latin
α	a
β	v
γ	g
δ	d
ε	e
ζ	z
η	i
θ	th
ι	i
κ	k
λ	l
μ	m
ν	n
ξ	x
ο	o
π	p
ρ	r
σ	s
τ	t
υ	y
φ	f
χ	ch or h, depending on pronunciation
ψ	ps
ω	o
αυ	av or ay, depending on pronunciation

FOREWORD
Guya Accornero

Collective books are always arduous and lengthy work, sometimes quite exhausting. Fortunately, Kostis Kornetis, Eirini Kotsovili and Nikolaos Papadogiannis rose to the challenge of editing such a book and what they have created is a brilliant, innovative and indispensable volume which will fill in a void on the dictatorships of Southern Europe (Greece, Spain and Portugal) and the changes swept in by democratization processes.

Indeed, in general the studies addressing the transition processes place more emphasis on the political changes than on the social and cultural transformations that preceded the fall of these regimes and followed democratization. In their investigation of political dynamics, in most cases the studies concentrate more on institutional processes than on the development of less conventional forms of participation and on 'popular politics'.

The fact that various aspects of cultural and consumer changes are addressed – in the sphere of cinema, television, magazines, leisure habits, to give but a few examples – in connection with the gender issue, before and after the fall of the Southern European dictatorships, adds value to the project. A further relevant merit of the book is its gathering of both young and well-established researchers, whose investigations arise from 'fresh' research, in many cases based on sources as yet unexplored. This major empirical work underlying each chapter, combined with innovative interpretative instruments, frequently places in question consolidated ideas about Southern Europe's societies under the dictatorships. It is surprising, for instance, to learn of the landscape of 'total freedom' for homosexual encounters in Athens in 1968, described in the chapter by Kostas Yannakopoulos. Or, in an opposite sense, the paradoxical effects of tourism – usually considered an element accelerating processes of 'modernization' – in reproducing conservative and traditional gender roles in Spain, where, as described by Moritz Glaser: 'stereotypes were commercialized and exploited' in order to 'increase the distinctiveness' of the country.

The issue of changes in consumption models is not secondary, but is central to understand the transformations which occurred in these societies during the enforcement periods of authoritarian and conservative regimes and after their fall. In spite of what might be thought, the dictatorships did not completely block the diffusion of 'modern' models of behaviour. In some cases, the influences of these models in the social and political processes of change were as strong as the diffusion of radical political ideas. The adoption of – or the aspiration to – 'modern' consumption models may thus be seen as a dynamic which entered into conflict with the structures of the regimes, contributing to their corrosion. The Portuguese case is particularly significant from this point of view. Promoter of an *ante litteram* 'austerity', Salazar's regime was characterized by the motto of 'mild manners' and the modesty of aspirations. As emphasized by Luís Torgal and

Amadeu de Carvalho Homem, Salazarism was dominated by 'ethics of the exercise of will with a firm grip on passions' which was converted into the 'exaltation of humility'. Thus, 'Salazarism reveals its aversion to capitalist development', albeit attempting to avoid, with some strategic intelligence, frontal confrontation with industrial and urban development as of the 1960s.[1] For instance, even if this contradicted his strong ruralism, Salazar could do nothing against the process of urbanization, portrayed in a magisterial fashion by Paulo Rocha in his film *Os Verdes Anos*. In the same way, he was not able to invert the growth of the service sector, at the expense of employment in agriculture and the consequent development of a middle class, that is, the main actor of the new mass consumption era.

In this regard, the words written by Pier Paolo Pasolini a few months after the Carnation Revolution are of particular interest:

> The mass culture cannot be an ecclesiastic, moralistic and patriotic culture: rather it is directly linked to consumption, which has its internal laws and its ideological self-sufficiency, such as automatically creating a power which no longer knows what to make of the Church, the Fatherland, the Family [. . .]. Thus, Portugal should no longer be a severe, tight-fisted, archaic nation: it should be immersed in the great universe of consumerism.[2]

For Pasolini, it was therefore and above all the power of affirmation of a massified culture, characterized by new models of 'homologated consumption that corrupted the societal bases and structures which kept the regime alive'. This homologation means the gradual disappearance of 'class' values and the 'old' divisions between 'fascist' and 'anti-fascist'. In his opinion, thus, 'The consequent cultural homologation refers to all: people and bourgeoisie, workers and sub-proletariat'.[3] Luís Trindade vividly describes in his chapter this process of depoliticization – in this case with respect to programmes broadcast by public television – since the end of the 1970s, and its consolidation during the 1980s.

The present book explores whether the affirmation of a mass culture – that characterized the post-authoritarian periods, and, to some extent, led to the fall of the dictatorships – appears to transcend any element of class. This approach, above all if carried forward with a critical vision and not merely an encomiastic view of the 'benefits' of modernization, can offer very interesting and unexplored pathways for the study of democratic transitions. In fact, one of the principal elements of originality of the present book is its attempt, in the words of its authors, to create a bridge between 'transitology' and the study of the so-called 'sexual revolution'. Indeed, as noted above, most of the studies on transition processes have a primarily political, and political-institutional focus.[4]

The focus on models of female consumption is convincing in this sense, since it helps to delimit the arena of the phenomenon. On the other hand, although with different inflexions in different countries, it is clear that it is in the feminine universe that changes and perceptions of new possibilities have occurred in a more radical manner. In the three countries, feminist movements appear relatively late – and in an explicit way only after the end of the authoritarian regimes – since the urgency of political liberalization was much stronger and predominant. In the meantime, if we look more directly into the world of the imaginary, of habits and consumption models, we understand that before the instances of change had appeared as claims, they were already present as a change of behaviour, and not always in a conflictual form. In this sense, when looking at the issue of gender in the dictatorships of Southern Europe it could be interesting to employ the concept of 'discrete sexual revolution' created by Isabella Cosse and also used by Valeria Marzano for the Argentinean case. As she says: 'the recent historical research focusing on youth and sexuality in the immediate post-war period and the 1960s has engaged in a revision of the ways of addressing "sexual revolution"'. Thus, 'from the exclusive attention to the most vocal groups (such as women's liberation and gay's right movements) and from the calls to "free love" to emphasize an often unacknowledged "discrete sexual revolution".'[5] It would appear that the panorama drawn by the various contributions on Greece, Spain and Portugal in this book goes in the same direction.

I would like to highlight two further aspects characterizing the existing research – apart from some relevant cases[6] – on these societies during the period under review. In the first place, the lack of studies on the role of processes of changes of consumption and habits in major dynamics of macro-structural transformation at a political level, and especially in transitions. Moreover, the hesitant use of the analytical instrument of the 'Long 1960s' for countries living under dictatorial regimes. It has to be stressed that both these aspects have successfully been overtaken by the present book.

Finally I would like to add that the joint study of processes of political change in connection with social movements and changes of consumption, with a focus on gender issues, is a key which enables the creation of a very convincing link between many processes that normally appear as disconnected in the studies carried out. In this way, it is also possible to overcome the classic separation between agent and structure, between the top-down dimension and the bottom-up dimension, between institutional politics and popular politics and, above all, between 'civil society' and 'state'. Following some innovative currents of French political sociology of interactionist foundations, there would be no specific top-down movement in opposition to a bottom-up movement. The two processes would be intrinsically interlinked and would be reciprocally and constantly influencing one another, such that it is practically impossible to separate them.[7] This dichotomy is instead reproduced in studies on transition processes, both in those employing an 'institutionalist' focus and those which concentrate on social movements and other forms of popular politics.

Although in the words of the authors of the present book this dichotomy between the top-down moment and the bottom-up moment is also declared, it is my opinion that in the specific accomplishment of the book this is 'in fact' surpassed. It is surpassed by the evidence of the empirical cases analysed, where all the components are obviously strongly interlinked and act simultaneously.

And moments of changes of regime are particularly indicated to place in evidence this question. Political crises are not only moments of institutional change but also imply a certain level of cognitive shock. In this sense, they are moments when the redefinition of political structures is accompanied by a temporary suspension of the structural reference points and it is in this space of 'non-definition' and uncertainty that innovative elements frequently emerge in political, social and cultural terms and in terms of habits. These are moments when the possibilities appear to multiply and, hypothetically, any path can be travelled. The Portuguese revolutionary period (1974–5) is an almost 'textbook' case of these phases, although I believe that this phenomenon is also observed in non-revolutionary contexts and in the case of transitions through reforms, although perhaps with less intensity.

These moments are analysed in a rigorous manner by the French political scientist Michel Dobry[8] in his book *Sociologie de crises politiques*, where the classic division between state and civil society is surpassed, adopting the concept of 'sectors', that is, social arenas which are under permanent interconnection and whose existence and legitimation depends on reciprocal recognition. At moments of political crisis, in a transition for example, this recognition might be missing and the consequent loss of legitimation and significance of the different sectors throws open, in addition to a moment of great uncertainty, a series of unexpected possibilities. This approach was used brilliantly by Diego Palacios Cerezales, in his pioneer study on the Portuguese revolution.[9]

And the present book, in my opinion, goes in the same promising direction. The strong interconnection between changes in habits and consumption, gender issues, societal structures and political processes which emerges in each chapter, and the acceleration that each of these elements could transmit to all the others is a demonstration of this.

Notes

1. Luís Reis Torgal and Amadeu de Carvalho Homem, 'Ideologia Salazarista e cultura popular. Análise da biblioteca de uma casa do povo', *Análise Social* 1982–83.4–5, 1439.
2. Pier Paolo Pasolini, *Scritti corsari* (Milano: Garzanti, 1st ed. 1975). Excerpt from the interview with Pier Paolo Pasolini published in the newspaper *Il Mondo*, 11 July 1974 (translation by the author).
3. Ibid.
4. This approach has consolidated and contributed to the affirmation of what is known as 'transitology' which has developed above all through the enormous collision of studies such as those by O'Donnell, Guillermo, Philippe C. Schmitter and Laurence Whitehead, *Transitions from Authoritarian Rule: Comparative Perspectives* (Baltimore, MD, Johns Hopkins University Press, 1986); Linz, Juan and Alfred Stepan, *Problems of Democratic Transition and Consolidation: Southern Europe, South America, and Post-Communist Europe* (Baltimore, MD: The Johns Hopkins University Press, 1996); Howard J. Wiarda (ed.), *Development on the Periphery: Democratic Transitions in Southern and Eastern Europe* (Lanham: Rowman & Littlefield, 2006). For an analysis of the evolution of this sub-discipline of political science see Philippe C. Schmitter, 'Reflections on "transitology" – before and after', in D. Brinks, M. Leiras and S. Mainwaring, *Reflections on Uneven Democracies: The Legacy of Guillermo O'Donnell*

Foreword

(Baltimore, MD: Johns Hopkins University Press, 2014). In general, the paradigm of transitology is placed in a neoliberal approach, i.e. it considers democracy as, above all, a question of formal procedures and rules, viewing issues of social justice and economic equality – therefore, the result of democratic decisions – as secondary. For a critical analysis of the transitology approach, see Donatella della Porta, 'Mobilizing for Democracy. The 1989 Protests in Central Eastern Europe', in G. Accornero and O. Fillieule (eds), *Social Movements Studies in Europe. The State of the Art* (NY-London: Berghahn, forthcoming); and Michel Dobry, 'Les voies incertaines de la transitologie: choix stratégiques, séquences historiques, bifurcations et processus de path dependence', *Revue française de science politique* 50.4–5, 2000, 585–614.

5. Valeria Manzano, *The Age of Youth in Argentina. Culture, Politics and Sexuality from Pérón to Videla* (Chapel Hill, NC: The University of North Carolina Press, 2014).

6. Among others, Nigel Townson (ed.), *Spain Transformed: The Late Franco Dictatorship, 1959–75* (Houndmills, Basingstoke: Palgrave Macmillan, 2007); Miguel Cardina, *A tradição da contestação. Resistência Estudantil em Coimbra no Marcelismo* (Coimbra: Angelus Novus, 2008); Kostis Kornetis, *Children of Dictatorship. Student Resistance, Cultural Politics and the 'Long 1960s' in Greece* (New York-Oxford: Berghahn, 2013); Nikolaos Papadogiannis, *Militant Around the Clock? Youth Politics, Leisure and Sexuality in Post-dictatorship Greece, 1974–1981* (New York-Oxford: Berghahn, 2015); Guya Accornero, *The Revolution before the Revolution. Late Authoritarianism and Student Protest in Portugal* (New York-Oxford: Berghahn, 2016).

7. As underlined by Olivier Fillieule: 'symbolic interactionism can be defined as a microsociological and process approach which systematically links the individual and the study of situations to broader contextual factors and social order rules and norms. In this perspective, not only are individuals and society interdependent but they also mutually construct each other' (Olivier Fillieule, 'Some elements of an interactionist approach to political disengagement', *Social Movements Studies* 9.1, 2010, 2). Kornetis appears to go in the same direction with a 'challenge the conventional antinomy between the study of social structures and that of emotional ones' (Kornetis, 2013, 328).

8. Michel Dobry, *Sociologie des crises politiques. La dynamique des mobilisations multisectorielle* (Paris: Presses de la Fondation nationale des sciences politiques, 1987).

9. D. Palacios Cerezales, *O Poder Caiu na rua. Crise de Estado e Acções Colectivas na Revolução Portuguesa, 1974–1975* (Lisbon: ICS, 2003).

INTRODUCTION
Kostis Kornetis, Eirini Kotsovili and Nikolaos Papadogiannis

In 1967 the popular comedy *O Spangorammenos* (*The Stingy*, 1967, dir. Kostas Karagiannis) was screened in Greece. Its protagonist was a wealthy married man, unrepentant womanizer and notorious for being thrifty. His business partner convinced him to change his attitude, prompting him to start buying expensive gifts for a woman he had met at an entertainment venue. To his dismay, she proved to be his wife's cousin. This turn of events and the subsequent revelation made him promise to end the affair, be a committed husband and, most importantly, offer his wife generous gifts. The film appeared in an era in which consumption was rapidly gaining ground (also) in Greece. The film reproduced various gender hierarchies, with the heterosexual man as breadwinner. His spending patterns were expected to change, however; the movie presented the male role model of a caring mate, no longer legitimized to impose an ascetic life on his wife, who demanded material comfort. The film, thus, captures the way in which central issues related to consumer culture and gender became intertwined within the Southern European context. It is precisely such interconnections that the present volume seeks to unravel by exploring practices dating back to the Long 1960s and dis/continuities in today's Spain, Greece and Portugal.

These three countries present an ideal testing ground for a comparative and transnational analysis of consumption and gender. Several contributors to this volume demonstrate flows of popular culture among them (see below, 'Irresistible Empire?'). While such transfers might not have been the driving force in the transformation of consumer patterns and gender roles from the Long 1960s onward, they formed, nevertheless, an integral piece of this puzzle. We have chosen to co-examine these three contexts mainly due to their potential for comparison, their political condition in this era having much in common. This fact is reinforced by the shared experience of short or long-lasting dictatorial rule: the so-called Second Francoist regime in Spain (late 1950s–1975), Marcelo Caetano's dictatorship in Portugal (1968–1974) that followed Salazar's death and marked the last phase of the authoritarian *Estado Novo* regime as well as the dictatorship in Greece (1967–74) that followed an era of 'disciplined democracy'.[1] Italy has thus been excluded despite some overlap with the other three countries.[2] The chapters authored by Kostis Kornetis, Richard Cleminson and Rosa Medina-Domenech take a directly comparative perspective, while the rest offer cues for such a comparison.

We refrain from portraying Southern Europe as a fixed geographical entity: until 1975 Portugal extended to Africa and Asia through colonies like Angola, Mozambique, Guinea Bissau and East Timor and as such was not a merely 'Southern European' society. To an extent this also applies to Spain which, albeit a fallen empire, still occupied African territories such as Spanish Sahara until 1975.

This book resonates with the goal set out by Victoria de Grazia, leading historian in the field of consumption, 'to capture the immense transformative powers of capitalist-driven consumption as it constantly refashions notions of authentic, essential woman- and mankind'.[3] Thus, consumption not only helps vindicate and refute specific gender roles, but simultaneously contributes to their reconfiguration. Concurrently, gender representations and practices also affect the shaping of spending patterns. The argument that emerges from the collaborating authors is that consumption helps construct gender and, to a lesser degree, the reverse, to paraphrase Joan Wallach Scott.[4] We believe that the reverse occurs to a lesser extent, since consumption is not necessarily differentiated along gender lines. In any case, this relationship is mediated by several factors, especially the political and financial condition of the countries in question.

The volume addresses consumer expectations and actual practices, scrutinizing spaces, materialities and performances bearing the imprint of consumption. Resonating with feminist cultural critic Angela McRobbie, it considers the material conditions that circumscribe these, examining gender roles and power relations in the 'production of consumption'.[5] Some chapters also address a domain between production and consumption, namely the craft and impact of advertising.[6] As the term 'consumption' (especially cultural consumption) is polysemic and often linked to 'reception' in general, we equate it with the purchase and use of commodities, including cultural products. Likewise, the volume analyzes the link between these aspects of consumption, as it changed, to gender representations and practices, including gender as a metaphor of social relations in general. It also addresses how consumer expectations and patterns help reshape understandings of 'public' and 'private'.

This book intends to bridge a gap in the scholarship of consumption in relation to gender: relevant research tends to focus on liberal democracies, state socialist regimes as well as Fascist Italy and Nazi Germany.[7] Significantly less has been written on the topic for (post-)authoritarian societies in Southern Europe. Especially in Greece and Portugal, relevant research has largely tended to adopt a sociological or geographical approach that puts emphasis on the reconfiguration of spending patterns and consumer expectations.[8] These otherwise illuminating works have neglected the agency of consumers and its relation to identity-making, including that of gender. Recent scholarship analysing cinema, tourism and youth culture has departed from this perspective and has engaged more directly with gender; this volume complements it and demonstrates that our case studies help refine a number of key concepts for the analysis of consumption and gender not only in the European South, but also in Northern Europe and North America. In particular, the key categories of the Long 1960s and 'cultural Americanization'[9] are scrutinized, tested and, often, complemented or even replaced by more accurate ones. The book investigates how the representations of the 'Model Mrs Consumer' appeared in Spain, Portugal and Greece, while challenging analyses that examine their transitions from dictatorship to democracy in the mid-1970s through a 'high politics' perspective. In contrast, it follows a novel view of the transitions through the exploration of changes in everyday life.

Introduction

Beyond consumerism?

The very term 'consumption' is polymorphous, posing obvious issues of definition, as de Grazia and Furlough have remarked.[10] Accordingly this book does not resonate with the Frankfurt School in approaching consumption as a means of manipulation and control. Herbert Marcuse, in particular, maintained that 'the so-called consumer economy and the politics of corporate capitalism have created a second nature of man which ties him libidinally and aggressively to the commodity form'.[11] These 'false needs', for Marcuse, imposed onto (wo)men by capitalism, prevent them from developing a relationship with things through creativity and play. On the contrary, the effort of the Birmingham School of Cultural Studies to decipher semiotically the meanings that consumers assigned to their spending patterns and purchases while shaping their style helps illuminate more facets of consumer-making.[12] The contributions to this volume that refer to the 2000s, especially that of Abigail Loxham, draw on analytical tools offered by cultural studies in order to show the links between television and the shaping of memory and lifestyle. However, the volume critically addresses the fact that, in general, conceptualizations of consumption stressing the 'active' character of the consumer tend to take the appearance of the latter as a 'given', to paraphrase historian Frank Trentmann's apt analysis.[13]

Understanding how consumers frame their consumer patterns poses an additional challenge, noted by scholars of material culture. Historian Leora Auslander, for instance, states that 'people use [things] differently from words to create meaning, to store memories (or enable forgetting), to communicate, to experience sensual pleasure (or pain) ... Even if they have words, those words may be less adequate to the meaning or feeling of the object than the object itself'.[14] While bridging this gap could pose an insurmountable challenge to scholars, it still makes sense to employ a 'vivid language' that may, to an extent, show how these consumers tasted, saw, touched, heard and smelled the goods they purchased or wished to purchase.[15] Thus, the volume approaches consumption as a multifarious experience that involves the entire human sensorium: as Kostas Yannakopoulos mentions in his chapter, gays in Greece in the mid-1980s used cosmetics to achieve 'sweatless' and 'artificial' bodies.

The volume draws on one more concern: we deem it necessary 'to contextualize the different forms and functions of consumption, and the affiliated social visions and political systems competing with each other at the same time', to quote Trentmann again.[16] A wide array of conflicting ways of understanding and practising consumption emerges. The lure of consumerism, namely 'of material goods for individuals',[17] appears to be just one of them, as shown in the chapters by Cleminson and Medina as well as that of Panagiotis Zestanakis. Elena Diaz Silva in her chapter sheds light on forms of collective consumption in this era and these contexts, especially the activity of women's groups that campaigned for the spread of utilities and protested the high prices of goods they expected housewives to purchase.[18] Kornetis' chapter highlights how new subcultures (and their representations) were rejecting and embracing consumption patterns simultaneously, as constitutive elements of their identity. Collective consumption was

3

not unique to (post-)authoritarian Southern Europe; it was manifest in Northern Europe as well.[19] In addressing consumption as both an individual and social practice, the chapters of Cleminson-Medina, Diaz Silva and Ines Brasao adopt perspectives top-down and bottom-up, stressing the preponderant role of the state in (post-)authoritarian Southern Europe defining lifestyle norms and allocating resources for them.[20]

Defining gender

Contrary to a deeply entrenched perception suggesting that consumption is specific to women,[21] this collection probes the links between consumption and gender in general. In illuminating consumption's transformative powers with regard to gender, the volume is premised on a series of developments in the analysis of femininities and masculinities, homosexual and heterosexual alike, as well as in-between queer identifications. It further deviates from an approach common among feminist historians in the 1970s and 1980s, based on 'separate spheres' and the discrete 'women's culture' argument.[22] Although this body of scholarship has produced important insights, it tends to revert to ahistorical and essentialized notions of gender; it has reproduced binary distinctions between 'men' and 'women', utilizing different categories and asking different questions for each. By contrast, this volume shows how consumption affected the forging of femininities in relation to masculinities. Thus, it is in agreement with the influential theses put together by sociologists Raewyn Connell and James Messerschmidt, who convincingly argued that the model of hegemonic (and complicit) masculinities is formulated in tandem with desirable or 'emphasized femininities', in opposition to subordinated masculinities.[23] In line with their analysis, this book illuminates what men regarded as the 'most honored way of being a man', regardless of whether they enacted this model. Thus, the volume does not approach 'hegemonic masculinity' in a 'statistical sense',[24] nor as a fixed notion, but rather as a malleable one, to which contribute, among other factors, the women's liberation movement, the emergence of models of 'managerial masculinity' and intergenerational conflicts in migrant communities. Moreover, we use Judith Butler's seminal work to illustrate how 'gender is produced through the stylization of [...] bodily gestures, movements, and styles of various kinds [that] constitute the illusion of an abiding gendered self. This formulation gets the conception of gender off the ground, from a substantial model of identity to one that requires a conception of gender as a constituted *social temporality*'.[25] With this guiding principle, we look at the strife in individuals' negotiation of difference, conformity and plurality regarding gender identities and sexualities in each cultural context. Assuming an interdisciplinary approach, we examine the recorded, longstanding and incipient views and practices regarding the sexualities of individuals in anticipation of the emergence of queer theory in the early 1990s by gender and cultural theorists.[26] This volume allows for the problematization of the hindrance or enabling of gender and sexual identities through specific cultural contexts, the social and gender norms relating to hetero- and homosexuality while performance is considered to be,[27] the acts of individuals as they propagate or challenge existing preconceptions (e.g. when consuming goods or interacting with 'foreigners'). The ensuing analysis is part of a broader intertext of initiatives that recognizes how key aspects of 'queer theory can be pushed in more sociological directions to deal with the materiality of sex, gender and sexuality and the role of institutional power in the construction of identities'.[28] It also sheds light on same-sex desire and sexuality[29] enriching our understanding of gay, lesbian and queer identities in Southern Europe. Finally, we also address the intersection of gender with social class and race/ethnicity.

The Long 1960s in (post-)authoritarian Southern Europe

In analysing the relationship between consumption and gender in Spain, Portugal and Greece from a comparative and transnational perspective, we do not regard these countries as totally isolated from the ways in which modernity and postmodernity unfolded in the 'West'. The analysis of social and cultural transformations in the 'West', including in the domains of consumption and gender, has employed the concept of the Long 1960s as introduced by Arthur Marwick's situating of the development of a 'cultural revolution' in the US, France, Italy and the UK from approximately 1958 to circa 1974. Marwick argues that, while the dominant political system in those countries was not under threat, they experienced fundamental changes, especially in the sphere of production and consumption, the outburst of individualism, the creation of a vast market for and by the youth and technological advances such as the spread of transistor radios and refrigerators. Moreover he maintains that sweeping changes occurred in the domains of culture and leisure, including an unprecedented international cultural exchange. These changes, in his view, were accompanied by a multifaceted and radical questioning of social mores, such as the formation of new subcultures, generally critical of one or more aspects of established society, upheavals in class, race and family relationships, the spread of multiculturalism and the advent of sexual liberation. These shifts were met with the 'measured judgement' of the authorities, Marwick concludes.[30]

The societies under investigation certainly did not remain unaffected by advances in technology and the concomitant spread of consumer goods.[31] From the 1960s to the 1980s, consumer patterns spread in Spain, Portugal and Greece, albeit unevenly: middle-class urban Greeks were the prime proponents of change within society, displaying a 'diminishing toleration of material deprivation', as sociologist Vassilis Karapostolis has noted.[32] Spain, on the other hand, witnessed a shift 'from autarky to technocracy' in the period from 1954 to 1964. While the Francoist regime had initially praised asceticism as a core component of its 'moral crusade', it changed gear from the late 1950s onwards, mostly due to the growing presence of Opus Dei technocrats in its cabinets: it aimed to integrate the country into the global market, reached agreements with the IMF, and encouraged imports, including those of consumer goods.[33] The Long 1960s were the years of the *apertura*: a Francoist machination for combining the regime's political oppression with liberalization to achieve longevity.[34] In the 1960s and early 1970s, 'the rate of growth (6.9% of GDP per annum in 1960–1975) was one of the highest in the world and even stronger in certain sectors of industry, as well as in services and tourism'.[35] As a result the landscape of consumption changed rapidly, as historians Jordi Gracia García and Miguel Ángel Ruiz Carnicer have demonstrated.[36] The spread of consumption did not proceed as swiftly in Portugal, but it certainly transpired there, too, as Brasao mentions in her chapter in this volume.[37]

Similarly, challenges to deeply entrenched sexual norms also appeared in Southern European societies: the rhetoric of chastity, which lambasted premarital sexual relationships for women, came under fire in Greece, where it was becoming legitimate for young women and men to flirt in public spaces from the late 1960s onward. In Spain, the *apertura* coincided with a more relaxed attitude regarding sexuality as well; *yé-yé* music for example progressively smoothed cultural rigidities, acting as a counterweight to both the strict Catholic mores of the time and the seriousness of left-wing ethics.[38] The spread of tourism in the Long 1960s affected sexual practices and norms as well as patterns of consumption in all three societies. Tourist resorts were increasingly visited by 'foreign' and domestic tourists. This development contributed to the financial growth that fueled consumption, and encouraged the emergence of novel commercial venues such as discotheques, which addressed tourists, as well as of films that referred to them, as shown in the chapters by Moritz Glaser and Michalis Nikolakakis.[39] In the case of Spain, representations of sexuality figured prominently in cinema. Sex with tourists, according to Hispanist Justin Crumbaugh, became 'a symbol of Spain's integration into consumer capitalism'.[40]

The impact of blossoming tourism on gender representations and practices was ambiguous, however. What had reigned supreme in the societies in question had been heteronormativity as well as a value system that regarded men's sexual drives as stronger than those of women.[41] In Spain during the 1960s, the so-called *comedias sexy celtibéricas*, which were spreading at that point, revealed a manifestation of gender polarization, since they commonly referred to the heterosexual archetype of the macho man chasing '*suecas*' (literally Swedish women).[42] While the dominant argument in relevant scholarship is that these films reinforced the pattern of 'macho' masculinity, film and literature expert Tatjana Pavlović has recently argued that these *comedias* actually ridicule and dismantle machismo.[43] Meanwhile, as Nikolakakis' chapter shows, popular magazines aimed to shape the consumer patterns of domestic tourists: they developed 'pedagogies of the sea', dictating how female (but not male) bodies should be exposed on the beach. Glaser's chapter deals with the impact of tourism on gender performance by analyzing the actual practices of Spanish tourists, and shows that tourism familiarized women living in tourist resorts such as those of the Costa Brava with less rigid sexual mores, without, however, questioning heteronormativity or the institution of marriage.[44]

In general, spreading consumption of material items or of commodified cultural products may have sometimes simultaneously subverted and upheld deeply entrenched gender norms: as Cleminson and Medina show in their chapter, a specific strand of advertising and consumption, that of medical drugs, aimed to regulate Portuguese and Spanish emotions about the diversification of gender roles in the Long 1960s. They catered, for instance, to the growing number of male managers from this era onward. In this sense, the consumption and advertisement of medical drugs accommodated and aimed to normalize such diversification, keeping it within the bounds of what the *Estado Novo* and the Francoist regime deemed acceptable.[45]

Some of these developments in the fields of consumption and gender were actually facilitated by factors specific to the very context of these Southern European societies. The migration from those countries to North America or Northern Europe contributed to the spread of consumption in several ways: migrants helped relatives who remained in their country of origin purchase more goods through the remittances they sent to them;[46] and they functioned as role models for those residing in their natal areas: Greek migrant workers in West Germany tried to visit Greece for a month each summer. As some saw their financial condition gradually improve, they bought and filled their own car with goods, such as television sets, which they brought back either as gifts or to equip a house for remigration.[47]

Still, the social and political condition of those societies was marked by a number of specificities that also restricted aspects of the Marwickian 'cultural revolution' from transpiring. The experience of Catalans and Basques/Euskadi, even in the late Francoist era, was a far cry from multiculturalism. All three regimes reacted to a greater or lesser extent in a harsh way towards their political opponents, far from 'measured judgement'. The dictatorial regimes ruling Spain and Portugal (as well as Greece between 1967 and 1974) did not totally dispense with their socially conservative language, either. They all reinforced gender hierarchies in collaboration with the Church. Quite tellingly, the contraceptive pill, a *sine qua non* of the so-called sexual revolution elsewhere,[48] did not become popular in Greece. Since contraception was considered to be incompatible with 'natural' coitus, abortion functioned as a means of dealing with an undesirable pregnancy.[49] Abortion, the contraceptive pill and divorce were all illegal in Francoist Spain. Throughout the existence of the *Estado Novo* in Portugal, abortion was a criminal offence, although not so rigidly enforced as in Spain.[50]

Moreover, changes to consumption and gender relations did not proceed at the same pace in Spain, Portugal and Greece – or even within these countries: a crucial difference, which Spanish historians Helen Graham and Alejandro Quiroga stress and which this volume also addresses, is the fact that Portugal remained a colonial empire, occupying vast swathes of land.[51] Interestingly, in contrast to the metropolis, male homosexuality and female homosexuality were tolerated in the Portuguese colonies from the 1960s and the 1970s, respectively, as Erica Faleiro Rodrigues' chapter demonstrates.[52] Changes to consumption and gender relations did not proceed at the same pace either: as Cleminson and Medina show in their chapter, new consumer lifestyles affected a greater proportion of the population in Spain than in Portugal where social class divisions, which shaped taste as well, were more immobile.

Therefore, Marwick's 'cultural revolution of the Long 1960s' is certainly not a one size fits all model, applicable to Spain, Portugal and Greece: no uniform 'Southwestern plus Greek' Long 1960s version of it appeared, despite these societies being to an extent linked to those transformations.[53] As the present volume demonstrates, it makes more sense as a point of departure to probe which of these developments appeared in each society in question, and how intensely.

Localizing the 'Model Mrs Consumer'

A development that showcases the complex relationship between consumption and gender in Western Europe in general and Spain, Portugal and Greece in particular is the spread of the representation of the 'Model Mrs Consumer' from the post-Second World War years onwards. The dichotomy between 'Mr Breadwinner' and 'Mrs Consumer' is a cultural construction, as Victoria de Grazia aptly remarks.[54] What appeared in the early Cold War era was a 'Model Mrs Consumer' model, requiring a household equipped with goods such as radio, television, refrigerator and indoor plumbing. Food would be stove-cooked; detergents would facilitate laundry. Women would continue to run the household but with novel skills: using technology and supplying the household with goods for a comfortable life for the husband and children. The conviction that these goods were indispensable transcended social class and regional boundaries. Particularly conducive to these changes were the improving purchasing power of workers, the fact that a growing number of women worked and could contribute to their acquisition and the increasing familiarization of consumers in Western Europe with credit. Those 'norms of comfort' and their gendered enactment were publicized by media, such as women's magazines, and served as a powerful Cold War weapon: a kitchen that was well-equipped with appliances was designated by policy-makers as a core component of a 'Western way of life', guaranteed by the hegemony of the US. Such representations of femininity brought a degree of reconfiguration to gender relations: men increasingly shopped at the supermarkets that spread in Europe from the late 1950s onwards, assisting the 'Model Mrs Consumer'. Still this was due to well-entrenched gender hierarchies, as those women did not feel comfortable venturing alone into the quarters where the supermarkets usually were.[55]

In elaborating on these developments, de Grazia focuses on Western European liberal democracies like France. What happened in Spain, Portugal and Greece during the Long 1960s, however, is not a replication but rather a localization of the 'Model Mrs Consumer' representation. Indeed, popular women's magazines such as *Pantheon* in Greece, *Ama* in Spain and *Flame* and *M&B* in Portugal advertised such equipment, as Brasao and Diaz Silva show in their chapters. These showcase not only how consumption (household spending on this occasion) shaped gender, but also the reverse. Gender representations in these magazines were hand in glove with the gender inequalities reinforced in the rhetoric and, to an extent, the practice of the authoritarian regimes: policy-makers favoured a comfortable life for the family supported by a 'Model Mrs Consumer' who would be, however, confined to the 'private sphere' as a homemaker and mother. While, at least in Spain, growing opportunities for women appeared in the job market from the Long 1960s onwards due to the expansion of the secondary and tertiary sectors of the economy, the version of femininity that those regimes advocated did not change: women in Franco's Spain were not allowed to work without their husband's permission. Thus, the emphasized 'Mrs Consumer' remained a quintessentially domestic figure, at least at the level of rhetoric of policy-makers and popular magazines: while, as Diaz Silva and Brasao demonstrate, *Ama* and *Flame* sometimes contained articles that deviated from this norm – like chronicles about the 'private' lives of famous actresses – they did not renounce the Francoist equation of femininity with motherhood and homemaking. Another element in this localization: the 'Model Mrs Consumer' served both as a Cold War weapon and a means of integration into the 'West'. She was used as a propagandistic tool that would testify that the regimes were aware of consumption tendencies in North America and Northern Europe (as juxtaposed to those in the Eastern Bloc) and were capable of providing a comfortable everyday life to their citizens. Nevertheless, in contrast to de Grazia's argument that the 'Model Mrs Consumer' representations transcended social class divisions, when Portuguese women's magazines in the Long 1960s promoted the 'Model Mrs Consumer', they targeted very specific women: middle-class, residing in the larger urban centres, as Brasao's chapter shows. Hence, this volume argues, the way in which technological advances and the spread of consumer patterns interacted with gender and social class relations across Europe was far from uniform.[56]

Revisiting transitology

Works that address consumption and gender in Europe tend to approach the early-to-mid-1970s as a rupture, be it as the end of the Long 1960s or as the realization of the 'Model Mrs Consumer'. In the case of (post-)authoritarian Southern Europe, this era was a watershed due to the very transition those countries experienced from dictatorship to democracy. Although these processes had profound effects on consumption patterns and gender relations in all three cases, transitological models that deal with these countries have largely neglected them. This is a serious lacuna that the present volume addresses directly.

Defining and periodizing the transition from dictatorship to democracy is complex. In the case of Portugal, several historians argue that the era of transition lasted from 25 April 1974 to the promulgation of the new constitution in 1976.[57] Political scientists embrace a different periodization and argue that the era of the transition lasted until the abolition of the Council of the Revolution in 1982.[58] The very moment of 25 April needs to be carefully defined as well: it was a coup-d'état, aiming to overthrow the *Estado Novo* and to bring the Portuguese Colonial War (or War of Liberation, depending on the perspective), which had started in 1961, to an end. Social mobilization and political radicalization transformed this initial coup into a revolution, pushing the various provisional governments to adopt more radical measures, such as purges of Salazarist elites and redistribution of land.[59] In the case of Greece, scholars use the term *Metapolitefsi* – 'regime change' – to refer both to the moment of the transition from dictatorship to democracy and to the post-authoritarian era, without necessarily agreeing on the duration of the latter: some political scientists claim that it lasted from 1974 to 1989, while some historians claim that it extended until the late 2000s.[60] In the case of Spain there is no consensus either: the transition could have begun in 1975 with the death of Franco, in 1976 with the law of political reform, in 1977 with the effective elections, or in 1978 with the constitution.[61] Its end, on the other hand, could be placed in 1981 with the abortive coup of Lieutenant Colonel Tejero or in 1982 with the electoral triumph of the Socialists.[62] The 'Third Wave of Democratization' in Southern Europe, according to Samuel Huntington's famous formulation,[63] was a set of relatively smooth transitions to democracy: all three countries made model transitions from authoritarianism to democracy. Spain's transition, in particular, was often hailed as a triumph of political moderation.[64] Greece's too is seen as swift, easy and successful.[65] Finally, Portugal, which went through a revolution, achieved an impressive record of democratic consolidation.[66] The focus of the analyses of these transitions has traditionally been on elites and their decisions and impact, including, crucially, the role of the army, the crown (in Spain) and the Church. International institutions such as the European Economic Community (EEC) and their effect on the transition to democracy in Southern European countries are also often stressed: a framework to consolidate and stabilize the democratization process.[67] The EEC supposedly helped by demanding that candidate members be consolidated democracies: Greece was admitted in 1981; Spain and Portugal in 1986.

In general, research on transitions from dictatorship to democracy in Southern Europe[68] has concentrated on what could be labeled 'high politics'.[69] Still, as Pamela Radcliff has aptly remarked, the juncture between 'economic development, political reform and social transformation' in Spain during this transition has so far been relatively underexplored.[70] The same is true of Greece and Portugal. This volume examines transitions both 'from above' and 'from below', illuminating interconnections between institutional and lifestyle change. The comprehensive analysis of this type of Southern European transition yields an intriguing outcome: their impact on consumption varied. In the case of Greece, it marked a further expansion of consumption. For instance, living standards improved between 1974 and 1987 despite the global recession of the 1970s, thus contributing to an expanding consumption. Testament to this improvement is the fact that in an era when right-wing governments in the UK and the US imposed austerity measures, the Socialist governments in Greece between 1981 and 1985 followed an expansionary fiscal policy to stimulate demand. The 'diminishing toleration to material deprivation' that had emerged already in the Long 1960s gained further traction.[71] Data published by the National Statistical Service of Greece indicate that the amount of money spent on leisure by different social strata tended to converge from 1974 to 1981.[72] Moreover consumption started spreading in the rural areas, especially from the 1980s onwards: the spread of electrification already during the years of the dictatorship, the return of graduates from the urban centres and the impact of tourism on some rural areas fundamentally transformed their residents' attitudes toward material goods. In Spain, the dawning of the *Transición* appears to be to a greater or lesser extent linked to spreading consumption: a number of scholars, such as Rafael Abella, go so far as to argue that the consumption patterns introduced during the *apertura*, especially in the domain of tourism, unleashed a cultural openness that allowed democratic ideas to flourish in

Spain, subverting the Francoist regime.⁷³ Nevertheless, during the *Transición*, some consumer patterns were affected by the global economic recession, as is manifest in the stagnation in foreign and domestic tourism in Spain between 1974 and 1981 and its impact on the local tourist industry.⁷⁴ Still, consumer expectations continued to be harboured, for instance through popular women's magazines, as Diaz Silva's chapter shows. Similarly, Portugal witnessed an interruption to the spread of consumption during the years of the Revolution, which may be attributed to both the global recession and the priorities of the revolutionaries. The sharp drop in the numbers of tourists visiting the country at that point and the concomitant contraction of the tourist industry is quite telling.⁷⁵ Still, consumer aspirations that segments of the population had been nurturing already during the Long 1960s did not cease: Giulia Bonali's chapter shows that the Portuguese fashion industry was influenced from the 1970s onward by the explosion of a new affluent urban middle class, tired of the colonial wars, dictatorial isolation and censorship. This was a 'Revolution' of sorts that occurred in parallel to the political Revolution that transpired post-25 April 1974. Referring to an era of Long 1980s that begins with the Revolution and lasts until the late 1980s, her chapter challenges periodizations of the Revolution and the transition in Portugal that focus on high politics.

The same transitions fundamentally affected gender relations in Spain, Portugal and Greece through protest movements and institutional change.⁷⁶ Quite tellingly, abortions were decriminalized, albeit not unconditionally, in all three countries in question in the 1980s. Changes to gender roles in post-authoritarian Southern Europe were also linked to consumption. The latter was conducive to the diversification of gender representations and practices that had appeared in the societies in question already in the Long 1960s and gained further momentum during the era of transition. Such diversification manifested itself in novel leisure spaces as well as through the reconfiguration of gender representations in popular culture. In the case of Greece, this was manifest in the diffusion of cafeterias in the rural areas in the 1980s.⁷⁷ In these venues, and in contrast to the old-style cafes, young village women could mingle with young men and develop courtship and pre-marital sexual relationships with no further prospects. Meanwhile, from the late 1970s onward, bars began to appear in the larger urban centres, attracting homosexual men, as Kostas Yannakopoulos describes in his chapter.⁷⁸ Yannakopoulos argues compellingly that consumer patterns contributed to the growing visibility of a distinct gay community that appeared in Greece from the 1980s onward. In Spain, the post-Franco years were a time for cultural radicalism or better yet – as scholars suggest – cultural transvestism, libidinal politics and embracement of consumer values.⁷⁹ This allowed for the *Movida*⁸⁰ movement to emerge. The lifestyle of the *Movida* protagonists, such as of filmmaker Pedro Almodóvar, was indelibly linked with particular consumer practices: not only did they patronize specific bars, restaurants and galleries, but also used many of their protagonists as actors and costume designers.⁸¹ Their work posed a challenge to heteronormativity that was unparalleled in comparison to the cinematic landscape of Greece and Portugal at that point.⁸² Moreover, in the *Transición*, as Diaz Silva demonstrates in her chapter, the consumer aspirations of Spanish heterosexual women expanded beyond the household, which was promoted by advertisements in popular magazines that showed them driving a car.[83] Vindicating Radcliff's argument, the *Transición* did not function solely as political change, but also had important repercussions for social and cultural norms. As women gained access to a far wider array of consumer activities, they abandoned the Model Mrs Consumer pattern, endorsed since the Long 1960s and focused on household activities. The link between femininity and the 'private' sphere, which had been endorsed by Francoism, was subverted also in the field of consumption. By contrast, in Portugal models of cultural consumption began to align with other capitalist societies after 1976. A significant turning point regarding this trend was the introduction of Brazilian soap operas, such as *Gabriela, garofano e canela*, to Portuguese television from the mid-to-late 1970s on. This marked the beginning of the long history of the Brazilian TV Globo investment, 'chang[ing] the course of television in Portugal and at the same time symboliz[ing] and anticipat[ing] the emergence of a new society and lifestyles centered on consumption and media'.[84]

However, growing consumption, including cultural, in post-authoritarian Southern Europe was not necessarily conducive to the challenging of gender norms. The diffusion of sexual explicitness in diverse soft- and hard-core pornographic films in Spain, Portugal and Greece in the moment of transition from dictatorship to democracy (in Greece already in the last years of the dictatorship, a trend that gained momentum after its collapse), as shown in Kornetis' and Faleiro Rodrigues' chapter, is telling in this respect. Such films sometimes reproduced heteronormativity; in the case of Portugal these films during the Revolution tended to cater to male heterosexual fantasies, as Faleiro Rodrigues points out. In Spain too, the *machista* culture that objectified women proved to be quite resistant in the face of transgression of gender roles promoted especially by the *Movida*. Such fantasies persisted in popular culture: Marisol, a protagonist in musicals addressing tourism and consumer pleasures under Franco, appeared topless on the cover page of a magazine shortly after Franco's death, causing a sensation.[85] The transition to democracy did not necessarily and automatically bring gender equality.

Similarly, the relationship between such transformations to gender representations and practices on the one hand, and the demands of the women's liberation movement that appeared in those countries on the other, is a rather complex one: the latter tended to be sceptical or even hostile to the ways in which femininities were represented and performed in popular culture, arguing that these were akin to the subordination of women to the male gaze. The approach of popular women's magazines, which continued to be a bastion of the promotion of consumption, to gender relations was complex: *Ama* in Spain neglected feminism and regarded politics as a masculine prerogative, while lambasting machismo and promoting a model of comradely masculinity. Meanwhile, *Pantheon* in Greece advocated a somewhat different perspective, including interviews of prominent feminists, such as Sheila Rowbotham.[86]

One way or another, consumption proved to be conducive to the redefinition of gender representations and concomitant practices in post-authoritarian Spain, Portugal and Greece in ways that pose questions for the application of Marwick's original framework: transition from authoritarianism to democracy produced mixed results for Long 1960s developments: the trajectory of consumption was not necessarily one of uninterrupted advent. Therefore, it would be erroneous to approach the moment of transition to democracy as the apogee of social/cultural developments that had appeared in authoritarian Southern Europe. Rather, it makes more sense to consider the diverse, ambiguous and non-linear ways in which these transformations unfolded from the mid-1970s on and conceptualize them as the partial continuation of those facets of the Long 1960s that manifested themselves in Spain, Portugal and Greece. In addition, at least in Portugal, the very moment of the transition was not merely part of a 'cultural revolution', but an effort that transformed radically, but briefly, the political landscape of the country. In this sense, the analysis this volume suggests seriously considers synergies between social-cultural norms and widespread protests.

A transition to postmodernity

In dealing with the time span of post-authoritarian times in Greece, most scholars, especially sociologists and political scientists, have delineated a process of transition from the latter to postmodernity in the mid-to-late 1980s, linking the latter with growing depoliticization, individualism and the spread of the consumption of so-called lavish goods.[87] They tend to construe the coming of post-/late modernity, often using those two terms interchangeably, as an indication of the ebb tide of mass mobilization. By contrast, scholars dealing with Spain argue that postmodernism there dawned already during the *Transición*. For instance, Jo Labanyi claims that 'the postmodernist sense of living after the "end of history" was expressed in the *desencanto* [disenchantment] years from 1979 to PSOE election victory in 1982 by the *pasotismo* [dropping out] that succeeded the immediate post-1975 political and sexual euphoria'.[88]

The comparative perspective that the present volume takes demonstrates that the transition era and postmodernity were entangled across post-authoritarian Southern Europe, including Greece. In contrast to the abovementioned analyses focusing on the Greek political landscape in the 1980s, the task to pinpoint a particular moment marking the emergence of postmodernity in the societies under study with regard to consumption and gender is far from uncomplicated. Actually, postmodernist tendencies gradually mark the shaping of consumption in relation to gender from the late 1970s or early 1980s onwards in Spain, Portugal and Greece. Videocassettes were quite indicative of this trend in Greece. As Ursula-Helen Kassaveti shows in her chapter, this was an alternative to the cinema and accommodated more flexible cultural consumption: viewers could choose not only what, but where, when and with whom to watch a film – often reproducing gender differentiations in terms of taste. Queer performance was not absent, as hardcore sex films also appeared, directed by the transvestite Aloma. Moreover, pastiche[89] also started spreading in popular culture of all these societies, often affecting gender representations. For instance, the performance art of the singer Maribel Quiñones, alias Martirio, in Spain was a pastiche that combined punk and folk music, functioning as antidote to 'fixed gender roles'.[90] In short, there is no obvious clear-cut entry to postmodernity in the consumption of goods linked to the making of gender in Spain,

Portugal and Greece. Rather, one witnesses the emergence of a growing variety of consumer activities, of pastiche style in commodified leisure as well as a flexibility of marketing strategies, addressing a public of increasingly diverse taste.[91]

Such diversity does not necessarily imply, however, fluidity in terms of the making of gender identities: the *poniroi* that Yannakopoulos describes in the case of Athens of the 1960s followed queer practices, in contrast to the clearly homosexual attitudes of the gay culture that appeared in that city in the 1970s.[92] Such a gradual and protracted dawning of postmodernity cannot be described in a normative fashion as either emancipatory or restrictive in terms of gender. It has actually brought a mixed bag of results. For instance, the refashioning of television in Portugal since the late 1970s was intimately linked to both opportunities and limits for heterosexual women: Luis Trindade's chapter focuses on the profound impact of television shows on the making of feminine identities in Portugal since the 1970s, when, in the context of postmodernism, the television started becoming an 'autonomous field', no longer serving political forces. As Trindade shows, continuity announcers/television presenters had to take care of their outer appearance, submitting to the objectifying male gaze; simultaneously, however, they broke free from the passivity that had hitherto been associated with femininity by developing managerial sophistication. Similarly, a pleasure-oriented masculinity spread among middle-class educated men residing in urban centres in Greece during the 1980s, which was tracked by the lifestyle magazines that appeared then. For those men, using cosmetics was no longer a preserve only of women. The enactment of such masculinity, however, was based on certain rules and norms: quite tellingly, these lifestyle magazines juxtaposed it to the behavioural patterns of politicized men.[93] The transformation of gender roles in the countries in question should not be equated with liberalization in gender roles and relations. The double-edginess of this sort of cultural practice, including both the presence of paradigmatically heteronormative gender behaviours and the capacity of potentially subverting them, are features that are particularly explored in the present volume.

An 'irresistible empire'?

The exploration of a conjoined analysis of consumption and gender since the 1930s has revolved around the issue of 'Americanization': has the US served as a role model that shaped consumer expectations and practices elsewhere in the world? And, if so, how have the latter influenced the making of gender identities? Several scholars have provided a positive reply to the first question. The US witnessed the first 'regime of consumption'; these norms and institutions later expanded to Europe.[94] Analysts who address specific facets of consumption, especially commodified leisure, have also stressed the trendsetting role that US society has played, not least through its film industry.[95]

The dissemination of North American cultural patterns has proven to be at the fulcrum of identity making in post-Second World War Europe. In post-fascist societies like West Germany and Italy, Hollywood films and rock 'n' roll music helped young people distance themselves from the recent past, by developing lifestyles distinct from those of their parents.[96] The same cultural products helped develop masculinities and femininities across Europe and elsewhere like Japan, which deviated from established gender norms. In the case of Britain, the reception of Hollywood films served as a means for the making of an 'American' feminine identity, which was 'exciting, sexual, pleasurable and in some ways transgressive'.[97] Scholars stressing the impact of such cultural patterns on youth lifestyles and gender identities have been increasingly reluctant to employ the term 'cultural Americanization', however. The latter may point to a top-down imposition of specific cultural politics, while what transpired, in their view, was a selective reception and resignification of American cultural products.[98]

The US figured prominently in the shaping of consumption and gender relations in Spain, Portugal and Greece as well. Standards of beauty that circulated in women's magazines and television shows in these societies rested upon American fashion icons. Moreover, here too the selective reception of American cultural patterns impacted youngsters throughout the Long 1960s, and often before, through film and song, as, for instance, Efi Avdela and Kostas Katsapis show for Greece.[99] Such transfers caused rancorous debates around whether and to what extent they jeopardized the dominant gender norms: a wide array of social and political subjects, both right and left, claimed that these flows made girls repudiate the 'advantages of purity' and rendered boys violent. The chapters by Glaser and Nikolakakis complement this body of literature, by showing that transfers from the US to Spain, Portugal and Greece through tourism further stirred discussions around gender. Accordingly, the influx of 'foreign' tourists to those countries, which was gaining momentum since the 1960s, also facilitated face-to-face interaction between locals and tourists from North America. In Portugal during the 1960s fashion and cultural consumption were influenced by American consumer patterns, as Brasao demonstrates in her chapter. Nevertheless, the term 'cultural Americanization' does not furnish a satisfactory explanation. This volume argues that syncretism and a selective reception of American cultural products led the way instead.

Meanwhile, a far more complex nexus of transnational flows has influenced consumption in relation to gender in the three societies under investigation since the 1960s. Glaser and Nikolakakis stress not only the contact with people from North America, but also the intra-European interaction through tourism in Spain and Greece, vindicating historian Sasha Pack's assertion that tourism was domestically viewed as 'Euro-Spanish rapprochement'.[100] Meanwhile, Amaia Lamikiz Jauregiondo shows in her chapter on Basque territories during the Long 1960s the entanglements between secularization and the circulation of commodified cultural patterns there mainly from France and Italy and secondarily from the US. Such transfers were selectively received by local youth, forming the basis for the reconfiguration of Basque national identity.[101] Transfers between Spain, Portugal and Greece were not rare, either: as Zestanakis mentions in his chapter, the (commercial) mediascape in post-authoritarian Greece was particularly influenced by norms that had appeared in Spain. However, it would again be erroneous to discern a process of 'Europeanization' of lifestyle patterns from below, at least in the sense of a common and indivisible European identity. Such movement of people and ideas often reinforced a North-South divide: it was not uncommon for tourists from Northern Europe to develop a 'reflexive Mediterranization', depicting everyday life activities in the locations they visited in Southern Europe as 'parochial'.[102]

A particularly intriguing set of transfers, especially to Portugal, stemmed from non-'Western' countries. Those flows in a sense reversed 'the traditional relation between a former colonizer with its former colony', as Trindade argues in his chapter. From this perspective, a conjoined analysis of consumption and gender shows the importance of 'parallel modernities', namely ones 'running parallel to the classical paradigm of the West', as formulated by anthropologist Brian Larkin.[103] One way or another, transnational cultural flows greatly influenced all three societies, especially from the Long 1960s onwards, to a great extent shaping the consumer patterns and gender relations of their citizens.

Entangled temporalities

That this volume extends to the present does not suggest that there is any linearity of sorts between the Long 1960s and now with regard to consumption and gender. The transition from dictatorship to democracy as well as the dawning of postmodernity in Spain, Portugal and Greece deserve a more complex periodization, mindful not only of continuities, but also ruptures. Hence, the volume takes into account the entanglement of temporalities, particularly in the context of the post-Cold War era, as well as the financial crisis that all three countries have been experiencing since the early 2010s. Post-1989 Spain witnessed a growing public reflection – especially from the early 2000s onwards – on the Civil War years and Francoist atrocities, which the dominant memory regimes of the *Transición* and the socialist governments that followed failed to address.[104] A reaction to such reflection was a 'retro-fashion', manifest especially in the popular television series, *Cuéntame cómo pasó*. The latter refers to the late Francoist era, placing particular emphasis on the gender relations and consumer cultures that appeared then. Scholars have not been unanimous in approaching this series: Kornetis depicts it as nothing less than 'trivialization' of the authoritarian character of the regime and short of catering to nostalgia for the late Francoist years.[105] In her chapter, Abigail Loxham approaches *Cuéntame* slightly differently, namely as an 'ambiguous political project' and stresses its diversity of 'voices'. Loxham claims that 'representational tensions [. . .] arise', addressing the shifting material conditions of families in Spain at that point and the 'challenges to the patriarchal structure that these bring about.' Moreover, the current financial crisis, as Zestanakis' chapter indicates, has prompted in Greece a revisiting of the hitherto dominant idea that the 1980s were an era of affluence; rather, this decade is increasingly treated as the onset of the egregious problems Greece would be called to face since 2010. Rethinking consumption has been indelibly linked with reflection on gender. A reshaping of gender roles due to the advent of 1980s consumption – especially the growing use of cosmetics by homosexual and heterosexual men – is increasingly lambasted in Greece as an undesirable 'feminization'. One way or another, debates around the present have been linked to memories of the past, addressing not only high politics, but also everyday life issues.[106] A recent 'memory performance' by Portuguese artist Joana Craveiro, for instance, focuses on the everyday life experience of grand scale events; in this case the Carnation Revolution and its aftermath; 'lost archives, small memory and individual agents of history', as she calls it, form the backbone of this deeply emotional show that helps redirect our attention to small-scale family histories and memories.[107] Therefore, the chronological scope has been chosen to include the present juncture since it not only inevitably affects the way we look at the past, but as standard narratives regarding the dictatorship and transitional years, in particular, are radically shifting. The turbulence caused by the economic and political crisis that hit the three countries almost simultaneously put in doubt the success narratives of the transitions and revived discourses, especially emanating from social movements such as the *indignados*, arguing for a certain continuity in repression between the dictatorial past and the disruptive present. One could not fail to recognize here that the shifting patterns of consumption in the three countries in times of crisis constitute a dramatic volte-face since the onset of the consumption trends fifty years ago.

Finally, the scope of this volume extends to the present also to address a major transformation in Spain, Portugal and Greece: while these societies exported migrants in the first post-Second World War decades, they have turned to importing migrants since the collapse of the state socialist regimes in Eastern Europe and the USSR in 1989, while they are both importing and exporting them in the context of the current crisis. This has had significant repercussions for consumer patterns in these countries. As Zestanakis convincingly argues in his chapter, the influx of migrants in Greece has been presented as a threat to the 'consumerist certainties' of the locals; migrants have served as 'scapegoats', especially in the context of the current crisis, a condition that is part and parcel of the rise of the extreme Right in that country. Beyond the perspective of the locals, however, we wish to encourage research on the very lifestyle practices of the immigrants. Quite revealing of changing times is the interesting fact that even in the small village of Pournari in central Greece, a woman of Bulgarian origin has recently transformed an old style cafe attracting solely local male customers into a cafe-restaurant that is frequented by people of all genders as well as both by locals and by migrants of Bulgarian origin.

Structure of the book

The volume is divided into three parts. The first is entitled 'Consumption and Gender in Dictatorship and Disciplined Democracy' and addresses the manifestations of the Long 1960s as well as of the 'Model Mrs Consumer' in Spain, Portugal and Greece from the late 1950s to the mid-1970s. It contains the chapters authored by Glaser, Cleminson and Medina, Lamikiz Jauregiondo, Brasao and Nikolakakis. The second part bears the title 'Consumption and Gender through the Moment of Transition'. It analyzes how consumer patterns and gender relations changed during (as well as shortly before and after) the transition to democracy, however this transition is defined in each country. In this vein, it describes the partial continuation of those developments of the Long 1960s that had transpired in Spain, Portugal and Greece. It includes chapters by Kornetis, Yannakopoulos, Faleiro Rodrigues and Diaz Silva. The final part deals with 'Consumption and Gender Between the Transition to Democracy and the Financial Crisis of the 2010s', and includes chapters by Trindade, Bonali, Kassaveti, Zestanakis and Loxham. It outlines the gradual dawning of postmodernity in those contexts, as well as its manifestations in gender and consumption. Further, it also analyzes the role that consumption and gender play in emerging memory regimes, as they are formulated in public debates in the context of the crisis of the 2010s.

Notes

1. Political scientists have described the 1949–67 period in Greece as such, since Greece was a parliamentary democracy, but a substantial segment of the population that supported the Left experienced persecution. See: Nikos Alivizatos, *Oi Politikoi Thesmoi se Krisi, 1922–1974. Opseis tis ellinikis empeirias* (Athens: Themelio, 1995).
2. A comparative analysis of consumption and gender between Spain, Portugal, Greece and Turkey lies beyond the scope of this volume, but it would be certainly intriguing to undertake. Turkey followed a different trajectory concerning its political condition, since it experienced a dictatorial regime in the early 1980s led by General Kenan Evren. Moreover, the potential impact of the Islamists' ascendancy to power in 2002 on consumption and gender also merits examination.
3. Victoria de Grazia, 'Introduction', in Victoria De Grazia and Ellen Furlough (eds), *The Sex of Things: Gender and Consumption in Historical Perspective* (Berkeley and Los Angeles: University of California Press, 1996), 8.
4. Scott has referred to the reciprocal relationship between gender and politics in her *Gender and the Politics of History* (New York: Columbia University Press 1999), 46; similarly, de Grazia and Fulrough have maintained that '. . . gender roles have inflected this dynamic of change and have been significantly inflected by it'; See De Grazia, 'Introduction', 4.
5. Angela McRobbie, *In the Culture Society: Art, Fashion and Popular Music* (London: Routledge, 1999), 31–45.
6. About the position of advertisements in between production and consumption, see particularly: Pamela Swett, S. Jonathan Wiesen and Jonathan R. Zatlin (eds), *Selling Modernity: Advertising in Twentieth-Century Germany* (Durham, NC: Duke University Press, 2007).
7. For instance, Erika Rappaport, *Shopping for Pleasure: Women in the Making of London's West End* (Princeton, NJ: Princeton University Press, 2000); Irene Guenther, *Nazi 'Chic'? Fashioning Women in the Third Reich* (Oxford: Berg, 2004); Emanuela Scarpellini, *Material Nation. A Consumer's History of Modern Italy* (Oxford: Oxford University Press, 2011); Rebecca Balmas Neary, 'Domestic Life and the Activist Wife in the 1930s Soviet Union' in Lewis Siegelbaum (ed.), *Borders of socialism. Private spheres of Soviet Russia* (Basingstoke & New York: Palgrave Macmillan, 2006), 107–22.
8. Concerning Greece, see: Vasilis Karapostolis, *I Katanalotiki Syberifora stin Elliniki Koinonia (1950-1975)* (Athens: EKKE, 1984). About Portugal: Antonio Barreto. *A situação social em Portugal, 1960–1995* (Lisboa: Universidade de Lisboa. Instituto de Ciências Sociais, 1996);

Norberto Santos, 'The consumer society in the communities of a semi-peripheral country: Portugal', in Fernanda Cravidão, Lúcio Cunha and Norberto Santos, *Regional and local responses in Portugal: in the context of marginalization and globalization* (Coimbra: Imprensa da Universidade, 2012), 99–114.

9. Whenever the term 'Americanization' appears in the introduction, it refers to cultural transfers from the USA Americanization.
10. De Grazia, 'Introduction', 3.
11. Herbert Marcuse, *An Essay on Liberation* (Boston, MA: Beacon Press, 1969).
12. For instance, see: Dick Hebdige, *Subculture: The Meaning of Style* (London: Routledge, 1979).
13. Frank Trentmann, 'Knowing consumers: histories, identities, practices: an introduction', in Frank Trentmann (ed.), *The Making of the Consumer. Knowledge, Power and Identity in the Modern World* (Oxford: Berg, 2005), 4. Instead, the volume analyzes the historical 'evolution of processes of identity and knowledge formation that crisscross the market or occur altogether outside its domain (including law, schools, the home and politics) . . .', as Trentmann notes. Ibid, 5.
14. 'AHR conversation: historians and the study of material culture', *American Historical Review* 114.5, 2009, 1356–7.
15. Ibid. See also the important work of Montserrat Miller, *Feeding Barcelona. Public Market Halls, Social Networks, and Consumer Culture* (Baton Rouge, LA: LSU Press, 2015).
16. Frank Trentmann, 'Beyond consumerism: new historical perspectives on consumption', *Journal of Contemporary History* 39.3, 2004, 373–401.
17. Ibid.
18. About the notion of collective consumption, see, for instance: Manuel Castells, *The City and the Grassroots* (Los Angeles, University of California Press, 1983).
19. For instance, about the attitude of the French Communist Party at that point, see: Jane Jenson, 'The French Communist Party and feminism', *The Socialist Register* 17 (1980), 124.
20. Anglo-American scholarly analyses of consumption tended to focus on its individual rather than social dimension until the mid-1990s and especially, until the publication of the pathbreaking *The Sex of Things*. For an in-depth analysis of the ways in which political and state structures have shaped consumption, see also Martin Daunton and Matthew Hilton (eds), *The Politics of Consumption: Material Culture and Citizenship in Europe and America* (Oxford: Berg, 2001).
21. De Grazia addresses and deconstructs this perception. See de Grazia, 'Introduction', 1.
22. An essay that rested upon this approach and was very influential among women's historians was: Carroll Smith-Rosenberg, 'The female world of love and ritual: relations between women in nineteenth century America', *Signs* 1.1 (1975), 1–18.
23. R.W. Connell, James W. Messerschmidt, 'Hegemonic Masculinity. Rethinking the concept', *Gender and Society* 19.6, 2005, 829–59.
24. Ibid.
25. Judith Butler, *Gender Trouble: Feminism and the Subversion of Identity* (London/New York: Routledge, 2002), 179.
26. Teresa de Lauretis, 'Queer theory: lesbian and gay sexualities', *Differences* 3.2, 1991, iv.
27. Butler, *Gender Trouble*.
28. Stephen Valocchi, 'Not yet queer enough: the lessons of queer theory for the sociology of gender and sexuality', *Gender and Society* 19.6, 2005, 751.

29. Leila J. Rupp, *Sapphistries: A Global History of Love between Women* (New York: New York University Press, 2009). See also Dimitris Papanikolaou, 'New Queer Greece?: Thinking Identity through Constantine Giannaris's *From the Edge of the City* and Ana Kokkinos's *Head On*', *New Cinemas*, 6.3, 2008, 183–96.
30. Arthur Marwick, *The Sixties. Cultural Revolution in Britain, France, Italy and the United States, c. 1958– c. 1974* (Oxford/New York: Oxford University Press, 1998).
31. Fantasies of material abundance had already appeared in Spain in the first Francoist years. In addition, women from a specific social background, namely the wealthy ones, used cosmetics throughout the 1930s and 1940s. See: Mary Vincent, '*Camisas Nuevas*: style and uniformity in the Falange Española 1933-43' in Wendy Parker (ed.), *Fashioning the Body Politic. Dress, Gender, Citizenship* (Oxford: Berg, 2002), 167–87.
32. Karapostolis, *I Katanalotiki*, 332.
33. Nigel Townson, 'Introduction', in Nigel Townson (ed.), *Spain Transformed: The Late Franco Dictatorship, 1959-1975* (Houndmills, Basingstoke: Palgrave Macmillan), 3.
34. Sally Faulkner, *A Cinema of Contradiction: Spanish Cinema in the 1960s* (Edinburgh: Edinburgh University Press, 2006), 3, 102–3, 129.
35. Tom Buchanan, 'How different was Spain?', in Townson (ed.), *Spain Transformed*, 86.
36. By 1974, 70 per cent of homes owned a TV, which, to quote historian Miguel Ángel Ruiz Carnicer, was the absolute 'star' of the 1960s in the country. Jordi Gracia García, Miguel Ángel Ruiz Carnicer, *La España de Franco (1939-1975): Cultura y vida cotidiana* (Madrid: Síntesis, 2002), 296. Spain also experienced a booming of supermarkets – the *autoservícios* – in the same period, radically reconfiguring the entire food distribution policies. See Alejandro Jose Gomez-del-Moral, 'Buying into change: consumer culture and the department store in the transformation(s) of Spain, 1939-1982', unpublished PhD Diss, Rutgers, The State University of New Jersey, 2014. Similarly, while in 1960 there was one car per fifty-five inhabitants, this changed to one car per nine in 1974. Borja de Riquer I Permanyer, 'Social and economic change in a climate of political immobilism', in Helen Graham and Jo Labanyi (eds), *Spanish Cultural Studies: An Introduction. The Struggle for Modernity* (Oxford: Oxford University Press, 1995), 265.
37. She mentions that one in every nine residents of Lisbon owned an automobile in 1966, while between 1958 and 1964, the sales of TV sets increased at the rate of 2,600 sets per month.
38. Kostis Kornetis, '"Let's get laid because it's the end of the world!": sexuality, gender and the Spanish Left in late Francoism and the Transición', *European Review of History-Revue européenne d'histoire* 22.1, 2014, 176–98.
39. Tourism to those countries was not only commercial, however. 'Alternative', anti-consumerist tourists from Northern Europe also visited those countries from the late 1960s. See, for instance: Anja Bertsch, 'Alternative (in) Bewegung. Distinktion und transnationale Vergemeinschaftung im alternativen Tourismus', in Sven Reichardt, Detlef Siegfried (eds), *Das Alternative Milieu. Antibürgerlicher Lebensstil und linke Politik in der Bundesrepublik Deutschland und Europa 1968-1983* (Göttingen: Wallstein, 2010), 115–30.
40. Justin Crumbaugh, *Destination Dictatorship: The Spectacle of Spain's Tourist Boom and the Reinvention of Difference* (New York: SUNY Press, 2009), 15–40.
41. Anthropologists John Campbell, Julian Pitt-Rivers and John Peristiany, who introduced the 'Mediterranean paradigm', argued that honour and shame were the core values in the entire 'Mediterranean society', both in rural and in urban settings. Both males and females were assigned honour, which, in the case of women, was linked with shame, since they had to conceal their sexuality or channel it to marriage and procration. See J.G. Peristiany (ed.), *Honour and Shame: The Values of Mediterranean Society* (London: Weidenfeld & Nicholson,

1965). However, this paradigm has been questioned on the grounds that it underestimates the capacity of women to resist or negotiate male power. American anthropologist Ernestine Friedl is well-known for putting forth the distinction of the nominal from the real power of men over women, stressing the important role that women played in the decision-making of families with regard to the nurturing of their children. See: E. Friedl, *Women and Men: An Anthropologist's View* (New York: Holt, Rinehart & Winston, 1975). Moreover, at least in the period under study no uniform 'Mediterranean paradigm' applies to the societies in question.

42. Sasha D. Pack, 'Tourism and political change in Franco's Spain', in Townson (ed.), *Spain Transformed*, 60.

43. About the dominant argument, see: Álvaro del Amo, Comedia *cinematográfica española* (Madrid: Cuadernos para el Diálogo, 1975), 383. For Pavlović's viewpoint, see her *Transgressive Bodies and Despotic Bodies: Spanish Culture from Francisco Franco to Jess Franco* (Albany: SUNY Press, 2003). Justin Crumbaugh largely agrees with Pavlović. See: Crumbaugh, *Destination Dictatorship*, 108–10.

44. Sasha D. Pack, *Tourism and Dictatorship. Europe's Peaceful Invasion of Franco's Spain* (Houndmills, Basingstoke: Palgrave Macmillan, 2006); Crumbaugh, *Destination Dictatorship*. Nevertheless, the consumption of commodified cultural products is linked to the consumption of material goods in complex ways. For instance, Greek popular films of the 1960s may have both promoted and lambasted the latter. About this complex relationship, for instance: Achilleas Hadjikyriacou, *Masculinity and Gender in Greek Cinema, 1949–1967* (London/New York: Bloomsbury Academic, 2013). About Greek popular films of the 1950s and 1960s in relation to the consumption of whisky, see: Tryfon Bampilis, *Greek Whisky: The Localization of a Global Commodity* (New York: Berghahn Books, 2013), 59–80. About the links between urbanization, consumption and popular culture in Greece in the 1960s, see Efi Avdela, *Dia Logous Timis. Via, synaisthimata kai axis sti metemfyliaki Ellada* (Athens: Nefeli, 2002), especially 235–44.

45. About the tensions that consumption brought to gender relations in Spain at that point, see also: Aurora Morcillo, 'Uno, don, tres, cuatro: modern women docile bodies', *Sport in Society: Cultures, Commerce, Media, Politics* 11.6, 2008, 673–84.

46. About Greek migrants in West Germany, see, for instance, Nikolaos Papadogiannis, 'Migrants on vacation. The travel patterns of young Greek migrants residing in West Germany in the 1960s–1970s', *Comparativ, Zeitschrift für Globalgeschichte und vergleichende Gesellschaftsforschung* 2, 2014, 67–87.

47. Ibid. The representation of the migrant as a trendsetter of consumption also manifested itself in popular cinema: slightly earlier, the movie *I theia ap' to Chicago* (*The Auntie from Chicago*, dir. Alekos Sakellarios, 1957) showed a relatively elderly aunt, living and working in Chicago and visiting her relatives in Athens, dictate how they would rearrange their household: they got rid of a piano, for instance – 'for goodness' sake', the auntie exclaimed, 'does it make any sense to have a piano nowadays?'. Instead, they purchased a record player, which allowed parties to start at this house.

48. About the impact of the contraceptive pill on 'sexual revolution' in Europe, see: Dagmar Herzog, *Sexuality in Europe. A Twentieth-Century History* (Cambridge: Cambridge University Press, 2011), 136–9.

49. Peter Loizos, Evthymios Papataxiarchis, 'Gender, sexuality, and the person in Greek culture', in Peter Loizos and Evthymios Papataxiarchis (eds), *Contested Identities: Gender and Kinship in Modern Greece* (Princeton, NJ: Princeton University Press, 1991), 224.

50. Ana Prata, 'The Portuguese women's movement struggle for bodily citizenship rights: the issues of abortion and prostitution', in Joyce Outshoorn (ed.), *European Women's Movements and Body Politics: The Struggle for Autonomy* (Houndmills, Basingstoke: Palgrave Macmillan, 2015).

51. Helen Graham, Alejandro Quiroga, 'After the fear was over? What came after dictatorships in Spain, Greece and Portugal', in: Dan Stone (ed.), *The Oxford Handbook of Postwar European History* (Oxford: Oxford University Press, 2012), 502–25.
52. Perhaps the first attempt for a comprehensive understanding of the topic was launched with the recent publication of Clara Sarmento (ed.), *Women in the Portuguese Colonial Empire: The Theatre of Shadows* (Newcastle upon Tyne: Cambridge Scholars Publishing, 2008).
53. Scholars such as Miguel Cardina and Guya Accornero have showed that the Portuguese youth, for instance, was quite in touch with the international protest currents and the countercultural stimuli coming from abroad. See: Miguel Cardina, *Margem de certa maneira. O maoísmo em Portugal, 1964–1974* (Lisbon: Tinta da China, 2011); Guya Accornero, *The Revolution before the Revolution. Late Authoritarianism and Student Protest in Portugal* (New York/Oxford: Berghahn, 2016).
54. De Grazia, 'Introduction', 3.
55. Victoria de Grazia, *Irresistible Empire: America's Advance through Twentieth-Century Europe* (Cambridge, MA: The Belknap Press of Harvard, 2005), 411, 416–57. About the relationship between gender and technology, see also Maria Rentetzi (ed.), *To fylo tis technologias kai I technologia tou fylou* (Athens: Ekkremes, 2012).
56. An issue that certainly awaits examination is how subjects who did not define themselves as heterosexual women received the 'Model Mrs Consumer' representations in Europe.
57. For example: Maria Inácia Rezola, *Os Militares na Revolução de Abril. O Conselho da Revolução e a transição para a democracia em Portugal* (Lisboa, Campo de Comunicações, 2006).
58. For instance, see: Juan J. Linz and Alfred Stepan, *Problems of Democratic Transition and Consolidation* (Baltimore, MD: Johns Hopkins University Press, 1996).
59. Raquel Varela, *Historia do Povo na Revoluçao Portuguesa 1974–75* (Lisbon: Bertrand Editora, 2014).
60. For 1989 as a rupture, see Yannis Voulgaris, *I Ellada apo ti Metapolitefsi stin Pagkosmiopoiisi* (Athens: Polis, 2008). For the crisis of the late 2000s as a watershed point, see Ioanna Laliotou, 'I evimeria kai I krisi os timoros', *To Vima*, 20 June 2010.
61. Nancy Bermeo, 'Redemocratization and transitions: a comparison of Spain and Portugal', *Comparative Politics* 19.2, 1987, 213–31.
62. José-Carlos Mainer, 'La cultura de la Transición o la Transición como cultura', in Carme Molinero (ed.), *Transición, treinta años después. De la dictadura a la instauración y consolidación de la democracia* (Barcelona: Peninsula, 2005), 153–71.
63. Samuel P. Huntigton, *The Third Wave: Democratization in Late Twentieth Century* (Norman, OK: University of Oklahoma Press, 2003). Huntigton probed why around 30 countries in Europe, Asia and Latin America witnessed transitions from authoritarian to democratic regimes between 1974 and 1990. Spain, Portugal and Greece as well as the former Eastern Bloc countries were among the case studies that he probed.
64. Linz, Stepan, *Problems of Democratic Transition*.
65. Tony Judt, *Postwar. A History of Europe since 1945* (London: Penguin, 2005).
66. Philippe C. Schmitter, *Portugal: do Autoritarismo à Democracia* (Lisbon: Imprensa de Ciências Sociais, 1999).
67. Richard Gunther, Nikoforos Diamandouros and Hans-Jürgen Puhle, *The Politics of Democratic Consolidation: Southern Europe in Comparative Perspective (Series on the New Southern Europe)* (Baltimore, MD: Johns Hopkins University, 1995).

Introduction

68. Relevant bibliography is extensive. A few relevant works are the following: Nicos Poulantzas, *La Crise des Dictatures* (Paris: Maspero, 1975); Yannis Voulgaris, *I Ellada tis Metapolitefsis, 1974–1990, Statheri Dimokratia Simademeni apo ti Metapolemiki Istoria* (Athens: Themelio, 2002); Paloma Aguilar, *Memory and Amnesia. The Role of the Spanish Civil War in the Transition to Democracy* (New York/Oxford: Berghahn, 2002); Kenneth Maxwell, *The Making of Portuguese Democracy* (Cambridge: Cambridge University Press, 1997); Carsten Humlebaek, *Spain. Inventing the Nation* (New York/London, Bloomsbury Academic, 2015), 77–115.

69. For some notable exceptions to the tendency of the research on the transition from dictatorship to democracy in Southern Europe in the 1970s to concentrate on 'high politics', see Pamela Beth Radcliff, *Making Democratic Citizens in Spain. Civil Society and the Popular Origins of the Transition, 1960–78* (Houndmills, Basingstoke: Palgrave Macmillan, 2011); Nigel Townson (ed.), *Spain Transformed*; Robert M. Fishman and Omar Lizardo, 'How macro-historical change shapes cultural taste: legacies of democratization in Spain and Portugal', *American Sociological Review*, 78.2, April 2013, 213–39; Pedro Ramos-Pinto, *Lisbon Rising: Urban Social Movements in the Portuguese Revolution, 1974–75* (Manchester: Manchester University Press, 2013); Nikolaos Papadogiannis, *Militant Around the Clock? Left-wing youth politics, leisure and sexuality in post-dictatorship Greece, 1974–1981* (New York/Oxford: Berghahn, 2015); 'Revisiting democratic transitions in times of crisis', *Historein* 15.1, 2015.

70. Pamela Radcliff, 'Associations and the social origins of the transition during the late Franco Regime', in Townson (ed.), *Spain Transformed*, 158.

71. This is evident in some figures indicating the percentages of families that possessed consumer goods: in the urban areas, 43 per cent owned a fridge in 1974 and 77 per cent in 1980 and 54 per cent owned a cooker in 1974, with this number rising to 87 per cent in 1980. Moreover, in 1976–7, 2.5 per cent of the residents of the urban centres owned a TV set, compared to 20.8 per cent in Italy and 11.8 per cent in Portugal in the same period. In the 1970s, these trends extended to leisure. See Karapostolis, *Katanalotiki*, 332.

72. Nikos Souliotis, 'Dievrynsi tou koinou, ekleptynsi ton diakriseon: koinoniki kataskeyi tis zitisis stin athinaiki symvoliki oikonomia apo ta mesa tis dekaetias tou '70 os simera', in Dimitris Emmanouil, Ersi Zakopoulou, Thomas Maloutas, Roxani Kaytantzoglou and Andromachi Hadjiyanni (eds), *Koinonikoi kai chorikoi metaschimatismoi stin Athina tou 21ou aiona* (Athens: EKKE, 2009), 279–320.

73. Rafael Abella, *La vida cotidiana bajo el franquismo* (Madrid: Temas de hoy, 1996), 181. Crumbaugh, by contrast, regards this argument as 'rather optimistic'. Crumbaugh, *Destination Dictatorship*, 34.

74. Pack, *Tourism and Dictatorship*, 188.

75. Maria Remedios Brito, *Notas sobre a Evolução do Viajar e a Formação do Turismo*, vol. 2 (Lisbon: Media Livros, 2003), 829–30.

76. About the feminist and the homosexual liberation movement as well as state policies toward gender relations in post-authoritarian Spain, Portugal and Greece see the second part of this volume. See also, for instance: Papadogiannis, *Militant*, 252–75; Rosa Montero, 'The silent revolution: the social and cultural advances of women in democratic Spain' and Chris Perriam, 'Gay and lesbian culture', in Graham and Labanyi (eds), *Spanish Cultural Studies*, 381–5, 393–5; Javier Ugarte Pérez (ed.), *Una discriminación universal: la homosexualidad bajo el franquismo y la transición* (Barcelona/Madrid, Egales S.L., 2008); Prata, 'The Portuguese'; Ana Cristina Santos, *Social Movements and Sexual Citizenship in Southern Europe* (Houndmills, Basingstoke: Palgrave Macmillan, 2012).

77. For instance: Jane K. Cowan, 'Going out for coffee? Contesting the grounds of gendered pleasures in everyday sociability', in: Loizos, Evthymios and Papataxiarchis (eds), *Contested Identities*, 180–202.

78. Some of the bars that have appeared in Greece since the 1970s have been key to non-heterosexual identities. For instance, anthropologist Elisabeth Kirtsoglou stresses the importance of a bar in a provincial town near Athens in the 1990s and early 2000s for the enactment of desire of a group of non-heterosexual women that did not describe themselves as lesbian. See Elisabeth Kirtsoglou, *For the Love of Women. Gender, Identity and Same-Sex Relations in a Greek Provincial Town* (London/New York: Routledge, 2004).

79. Barry Jordan and Rikki Morgan-Tamosunas, *Contemporary Spanish Cinema* (Manchester: Manchester University Press, 2001), 114.

80. This was a countercultural movement that appeared mainly in Madrid from the late 1970s to the mid-1980s and left its imprint on art.

81. Emma Dent Coad, 'Designer culture in the 1980s: the price of success', in Graham and Labanyi (eds), *Spanish Cultural Studies*, 376–77.

82. Jo Labanyi, 'Conclusion: postmodernism and the problem of cultural identity' in Graham and Labanyi (eds), *Spanish Cultural Studies*, 396.

83. Meanwhile, a growing number of women in Athens became willing to drive a car from 1980 onward. See Panagiotis Zestanakis, '"Dexia lorida": epiloges metakinisis kai (ana)simasiodotiseis tis thilykotitas stin Athina tis dekaetias tou '80', in Dimitra Vasileiadou, Panagiotis Zestanakis, Maria Kefala and Maria Preka (eds), *(Anti)milontas stis vevaiotites. Fyla, anaparastaseis, ypokeimenikotites* (Athens: OMIK, 2013), 173–96.

84. Isabel Ferin Cunha, 'A revolução da Gabriela: o ano de 1977 em Portugal', *Cadernos Pagu* 21, 2003, 4.

85. Crumbaugh, *Destination Dictatorship*, 111–12.

86. Papadogiannis, *Militant*, 261.

87. For instance: Nicolas Sevastakis, *Koinotopi Chora. Opseis tou Dimosiou Chorou kai Antinomies Axion sti simerini Ellada* (Athens: Savvalas, 2004); Voulgaris, *I Ellada apo ti Metapolitefsi stin Pagkosmiopoiisi*.

88. Jo Labanyi, Helen Graham and Antonio Sanchez, 'Conclusion: modernity and cultural pluralism', in Graham, Labanyi, *Spanish Cultural Studies*, 396.

89. Fredric Jameson describes postmodernism as the 'cultural logic of late capitalism', adding that this era is characterized by pastiche: a 'play of random stylistic allusion' which does not reflect an 'external' reality. See Fredric Jameson, *Postmodernism, or, the Cultural Logic of Late Capitalism* (Durham, NC: Duke University Press, 1991), 18.

90. Jo Labanyi, 'Conclusion: postmodernism', 405.

91. Our argument largely overlaps with that of Panagiotopoulos and Vamvakas, according to whom the 1980s witnessed a cultural pluralism in Greece, a core component of which was the spread of devices, such as home video-game consoles and satellite television. These devices led to the diversification of consumption, rendering it an issue of individual choice. See: Vassilis Vamvakas and Panayis Panagiotopoulos, 'I Ellada sti dekaetia tou '80. Koinonikos eksynchronismos, politicos archaismos, politismikos plouralismos', in Vassilis Vamvakas and Panayis Panagiotopoulos (eds), *I Ellada sti dekaetia tou '80. Koinoniko, politiko kai politismiko lexiko* (Athens: To Perasma, 2010), LX–XI.

92. In general, fluid gender roles in the 'West' were not necessarily the outcome of such fragmentation/multiplication of consumer patterns in postmodern times: as Matt Houlbrook

argues, queer identities and performance were widespread in London already in the interwar years. See Matt Houlbrook, *Queer London: Perils and Pleasures in the Sexual Metropolis, 1918–1957* (Chicago: University of Chicago Press, 2006).

93. Panagiotis Zestanakis, 'Ekdoches tou andrismou sta ellinika lifestyle entypa tis dekaetias tou '80: *Playboy, Status, Click* (1985–1990)', unpublished MA dissertation, University of Crete, Rethymno 2008.

94. De Grazia maintains that a 'Market Empire' manifested itself first in the US and spilled over into Europe in the second half of the twentieth century, being 'irresistible'. See: De Grazia, *Irresistible Empire*.

95. Peter Stearns, *Consumerism and World History. The global transformation of desire* (New York/London: Routledge, 2001), 148.

96. About West and East Germany, see Uta Poiger, *Jazz, Rock and Rebels, Cold War and American Culture in a divided Germany* (Los Angeles: University of California Press, 2000).

97. Jackie Stacey, *Star Gazing, Hollywood Cinema and Female Spectatorship* (London: Routledge 1994), 204.

98. Some scholars, such as anthropologist Kaspar Maase, no longer employ it, referring to 'cultural democratization' instead. See Kaspar Maase, 'Establishing cultural democracy', in Hanna Schissler (ed.), *The Miracle Years: A Cultural History of West Germany, 1949–68* (Princeton, NJ: Princeton University Press, 2001), 428–50.

99. Historians Efi Avdela and Kostas Katsapis have analyzed in depth these developments in Greece. See: Efi Avdela, '"Corrupting and Uncontrollable Activities": Moral Panic about Youth in Post-Civil-War Greece', *Journal of Contemporary History*, 43.1, 2008, 25–44; Kostas Katsapis, *Ichoi kai apoichoi. Koinoniki istoria tou rock 'n' roll phenomenou stin Ellada, 1956–1967* (Athens: IAEN, 2007). For the spread of comics from the US in Spain, see Louie Dean Valencia-García, 'Truth, justice, and the American way in Franco's Spain', in Joseph J. Darowski (ed.), *The Ages of Superman: Essays on the Man of Steel in Changing Times* (Jefferson, NC: McFarland & Company, 2012), 45–7.

100. Sasha Pack, *Tourism and Dictatorship*, 62.

101. The blossoming of local nationalisms in (post-)authoritarian Spain is unique in comparison to Greece and Spain. However, local divergence in terms of gender and consumption in Spain should not always be attributed to local nationalisms. The issue whether the latter cause the former needs to be probed rather than taken for granted. For instance, Diaz Silva refers in her chapter to the *Castellanas* housewives, who did not subscribe to a local nationalism.

102. About the term 'reflexive Mediterranization', see Regina Römhild, 'Reflexive Europäisierung. Tourismus, Migration und die Mediterranisierung Europas' in Gisela Welz and Annina Lottermann (eds), *Projekte der Europäisierung. Kulturanthropologische Forschungsperspektiven* (Frankfurt a.M.: Institut für Kulturanthropologie und Europäische Ethnologie der Johann Wolfgang Goethe-Universität Frankfurt am Main, 2008), 261–76.

103. In his work on Indian films in Nigeria, Larkin has discerned the 'parallel modernities' concept – whereby the cultural flows from the 'West' to other regions tend to be erroneously overrepresented in scholarship. Brian Larkin, 'Indian films and Nigerian Lovers: media and the creation of parallel modernities", *Journal of the International African Institute* 67.3, 1997, 406–40.

104. Graham, Quiroga, 'After the fear'.

105. Kostis Kornetis, '"Is there a future in this past?": Analyzing 15M's Intricate Relation to the Transición', *Journal of Spanish Cultural Studies* 15.1–2, 2014, 83–98.

106. An obvious concomitant question is whether the utopia of a welfare society and widespread access to consumer goods has been shattered due to the current crisis, as historian Antonis

Liakos remarks. See Antonis Liakos, *Apokalypsi, Outopia kai Istoria. Oi metamorfoseis tis istorikis syneidisis* (Athens: Polis, 2011). Does the ongoing downward social mobility, which reversed the optimism that, at least in the case of Greece, the era of the *Metapolitefsi* had unleashed, fundamentally alter the consumer aspirations of the Greeks? This issue deserves further examination. About the remaking of narratives on consumption and consumer expectations in Spain in the context of the crisis of the 2010s, see Luis E. Alonso, Carlos Jesús Fernández Rodríguez and Rafael Ibáñez Rojo, 'From consumerism to guilt: economic crisis and discourses about consumption in Spain', *Journal of Consumer Culture* 15, 2015, 66–85.

107. Joana Craveiro, 'When was the revolution over? Memories of the transition process after the April Revolution', *CES-Coimbra*, 8 October 2013.

PART I
CONSUMPTION AND GENDER IN DICTATORSHIP AND DISCIPLINED DEMOCRACY

CHAPTER 1
GENDERING TOURISTIC SPAIN, 1950s–70s
Moritz Glaser

'Spain lived until recently still completely in the Middle Ages. By experiencing Spain we can see a piece of our own past still today as reality [...].'[1].

This quote from a German travel magazine shows how German tourism entrepreneurs tried to convert Spain into an attractive tourist destination. For that purpose, they aimed to describe Spain as a land that was different from Germany and other countries of Northwestern Europe. In Spain, tourists would be able to experience their own society's past based on the assumption that Spain was still a country marked by backwardness and tradition. Overall, there was one aspect of Spanish society that was frequently used to describe supposed Spanish otherness: gender roles and their representations. The importance of marriage, the specific behaviour of men and women in everyday life, especially in the different spheres of work and the household, were specific expressions of gender roles that were used in travel magazines, catalogues and travel guides to mark Spanishness.

The attractiveness of Spain as a country that was not only exotic and archaic but also at the same time very cheap led to a major increase in foreign tourism, particularly as shifts in the policies pursued by the Spanish regime in the late 1950s opened the country's borders. With the stabilization plan of 1959, the regime no longer opted for autarky in financial terms, and tourism was now to be an instrument to bring foreign currency to Spain in order to foster economic development.[2] Figures show that the number of tourists rose from 4,194,686 in 1959 to 14,102,888 in 1964 and 30,342,871 in 1974.[3]

While the political exploitation of tourism[4] and its representation in movies and television series[5] are already well known, very little research has been conducted on the concrete impact of tourism on Spanish society in the affected regions. Also missing until now is a clearer connection to studies of European history and the question of convergences and divergences through transnational interaction within Europe.[6] The examination of tourism as a transnational flow that affected primarily the communities on the Mediterranean coast can therefore provide new insights regarding relations between Southern and Northwestern Europe in the 1960s and 1970s. Using the example of gender roles, this chapter provides an analysis of the repercussions of tourism in Spain as well as the possible convergences and divergences between Spain and countries like Great Britain, France and West Germany from where the tourists came. The chapter will first focus on the consequences of tourism with respect to gender roles in the tourist regions of Costa Brava, Costa del Sol and Mallorca. Specifically, it will deal with changing images of masculinity, the position of women in the workplace and gender specific attitudes towards sexuality and morality. The chapter will argue that tourism challenged existing concepts of gender norms but imposed at the same time new constraints on women who tried to overcome these norms. Secondly, the analysis will focus on the broader context of European perceptions of Spain in relation to tourism. I wish to argue that tourism as a form of transnational communication from below[7] did not bring a change of represented gender norms in the touristic media. In fact, tourism led not to a reduction in stereotypes and othering but to an accentuation of strangeness and difference engraved in the 'tourist gaze'.[8] The first part of the chapter is based on archival files, newspaper articles, contemporary surveys and ethnological observations. The second part deals mostly with touristic media promoting package tourism,[9] such as guide books, travel brochures, catalogues and magazines from Germany, Great Britain and France, the countries where the majority of the foreign tourists came from.[10]

Touristificated contact zones and gender roles

The massive presence of foreign tourists in many places along the Spanish Mediterranean coast resulted in fundamental changes in existing structures. Small fishing or farming villages became major touristic resorts as new settlements developed especially for tourists. Necessities of tourists became the highest priority in spaces that were created exclusively for them. A touristic regime of space therefore determined the development of whole landscapes.

Tourism, employment and emancipation

For the tourists, these spaces had mainly 'heterotopic'[11] characteristics, whereas for the locals they were essentially spaces of labour. On the 'backstage'[12] of the touristic regions, fundamental processes of social change were taking place that also affected gender roles. Franco's regime had a clear idea of gender norms. While men would provide the family's income and represent the family, women would stay at home, cook and be a mother. The regime tried to maintain the existing gender roles in society and foster the Francoist view through laws and extensive propaganda. The women's section of the National movement, the *sección femenina*, and the Church played crucial roles in this process. The *sección femenina* provided education, especially for girls, to prepare them for their duties as women and mothers caring for their families.[13] However, these gender norms clashed with the new realities yielded by tourism in regions with a massive influx of foreign tourists.

On that score, tourism also contested existing notions of masculinity. The phenomenon of Spanish men chasing women from North Western Europe during the summer season led to its appearance in movies and TV series. Indeed, the representation of 'male prostitutes' who lived at the expense of the proverbial '*suecas*' – Swedish women – attracted national attention and introduced a new perspective on the possible roles for a man: one that was financially dependent on a foreign woman. Yet, since these movies always ended with the re-establishment of the traditional image of the Spanish male in the sense that the '*macho ibérico*' himself became once again financially independent, they perpetuated the traditional image of masculinity.[14] Thus, movies like *El Turismo es un gran invento* (1968), *Tres suecas para tres Rodríguez* (1975) or *Los días de Cabirio* (1971) showed a new field of possible gender roles in which men, at least occasionally, adopted a role that was hitherto connoted feminine.

Tourism also challenged the employment patterns of women, affecting gender norms by raising the question of whether women should work and contribute to the family income or stay at home as the regime's propaganda favoured. Additionally, tourism provided new possibilities of employment for women. In touristic towns like Lloret de Mar on the Costa Brava in North-Eastern Spain, the percentage of employed women was significantly higher than in the surrounding areas, where mostly agrarian villages were located, and also higher compared to the national average. Statistical data on the proportion of women integrated into the employment market show that in Lloret de Mar during the 1968 summer season, 36.7 per cent of all women had employment.[15] The national average of this time was 23.8 percent.[16] This did not necessarily mean that more women worked on the coast than in the country's interior. Yet in touristic centres, employees were paid regularly, whereas in the countryside, many women helped in agrarian family businesses, were not correctly listed as workers and did not receive a salary. For example, in the small village Palau Sator in the hinterland of the Costa Brava, the employment rate of women was only 12.2 per cent.[17] Touristic spaces offered women the possibility to earn money on their own and to contribute to the family income or to possibly sustain it entirely. This was accompanied by a new self-assurance that made women more independent from the male head of the family and countered the traditional gender roles propagated by the Spanish government. Those saw the man as the breadwinner of the family and the woman as responsible for the household and the children.[18] However, not all of these working women were locals. Touristic towns like Lloret de Mar or Paguera in Majorca attracted large numbers of internal migrants, with many from poorer regions like Andalusia and Murcia. In the touristic centers, women had the opportunity to earn money during the summer season and move back to their hometowns in winter. This process was reflected in the employment rate. In winter, the employment rate of women in Lloret de Mar decreased from 36.7 to 22.9 per cent, which was still close to the national average.[19] Lloret was primarily attractive as a job location for internal migrants. The winter months saw the return of the migrants and a drop in female employment levels due to the absence of tourists. Many of these internal migrants were young single women. Tourism offered them the possibility of escaping the constraints of their families, at least temporarily, and attaining new liberties, even after they returned to their homes. An ethnographical study, conducted in 1979 and 1980, reveals that internal female migrants were much more respected by men when they stayed with their families because they contributed to the family income, they were able to decide for themselves about their daily routine and could define when and for how long they went out.[20]

Notwithstanding, precarious labour conditions relativized their possibilities for emancipation. Women worked, for example, in hotels predominantly as chambermaids, kitchen helpers or waitresses, in low-salaried positions. On the other hand, men worked as cooks or head waiters and earned more. The higher paid jobs for women in reception or the office were mainly filled by female foreigners.[21] Even the new roles available to women in the entertainment industry – newly created for tourists – have to be considered critically. One possibility for women to become more independent and earn a living of their own was to work as 'go-go-dancers' in nightclubs, where they were supposed to entertain the clubs' visitors and to encourage them to dance. According to the women's own statements, they turned their hobby into a profession and gained new liberties as a consequence.[22] Often internal migrants from other regions of Spain, as was the case in this example from Majorca and far from home, it was possible for them to work in such locations without the fear of repercussions from their families. In fact, the press in Majorca published an extensive report about these women but did not condemn their behaviour and remained neutral and objective.[23] This leads to the conclusion that at least since the late 1960s, even rural societies accepted independent work for women. And dancing in a club for foreigners was thus not perceived as a loss of honour or as a symbol of shame. Contemporary ethnographers like Jean G. Peristiany[24] and Julian Pitt-Rivers[25] tended to describe the Mediterranean from the perspective of the supposedly pivotal values of honour and shame. Yet, the findings here make clear that rural Mediterranean societies were much more dynamic than most Western anthropologists assumed. However, in their everyday work routine, these women were confined to traditional roles as objects of men's desire, and notions of emancipation were therefore limited.

Nevertheless, touristic spaces had the potential to change gender roles at least partially or temporarily. First and foremost, it has to be emphasized, they fulfilled this function mainly in the rural periphery. Here, touristic areas provided new possibilities for social change, as the example of the internal migrants shows, beyond their territorial limits. The established lines between the spheres of men and women were actually blurred – whether as a woman who contributed to the family income or a man who was financially dependent on foreign female tourists during the summer.

Tourism, morality and hegemonic masculinity

Furthermore, tourism led to a new definition of sexual and moral behaviour. As a survey conducted by sociologists on behalf of the Catholic Church on the Costa Brava in 1964 shows, 39 per cent of respondents answered the question whether tourism had led to a decline in morality with the statement that morals had become freer. Ten per cent claimed that morals had declined since the arrival of the first foreign tourists on the Costa Brava in the 1950s. Almost 50 per cent of the population – assuming that the survey was representative – connected tourism to a less rigid code of morality and a decline in the regulation of the relations between men and women. If morality means primarily the rules that existed for women and therefore the image of gender roles propagated by the regime, then tourism signified for half of the population a kind of liberation. More interesting, however, is what was not said in the survey; that 34 per cent of respondents, most frequently married men, refused to answer the question.[26] We may assume that a great number of the men did not want to talk about liberation or a decline in morality triggered by tourism because they did not want to describe themselves as less moral than they were before. Additionally, they may not have wanted to be associated with the image of the '*picadores*', the Spanish men who were chasing foreign women. This could be interpreted as a strategy the men employed in order to sustain a certain 'hegemonic masculinity'.[27] Obviously, some of the men perceived a growing instability in terms of the relations between men and women, but as they did not want to be identified with the '*picadores*', they tried to stabilize their dominance both over women and the differing concepts of masculinity.

In opposition to this specific male vision of gender notions and morality, the majority of women responded that morality had become freer than in earlier times,[28] and fewer confirmed a negative effect of tourism on morality (54 per cent of men versus only 33 per cent of women).[29] So tourism did indeed have an influence on the concepts of gender and morality in touristic regions, and these changes were for a great percentage of the population more positive than negative. Women, in particular, appreciated the less rigid notions of morality and their impact on gender roles.

Broader concepts of gender roles like marriage and heteronormativity, however, were not changed under the influence of foreign tourists. Statistics on marriage in the touristic regions show no substantial difference from the national average. Marriage rates were not lower and sometimes even higher[30] than in other rural areas where tourism was only a marginal phenomenon. For example, the marriage rate in the province of Gerona (Costa Brava) in 1964, as measured by the figure of marriages per 1,000 persons, was 6.5 while the national average was 7.4. By 1974 the picture had not changed a lot. The figure for Gerona was 7.8, while the national average was 7.6.[31] Heteronormativity was also not contested in these regions. Although it was obviously practised in public in touristic spaces by the late 1950s, there are very few sources available referring to homosexuality and even those do so in a pejorative manner. A group of residents of the touristic quarter El Terreno complained in a letter to the civil governor of the province of the Balearic Islands in 1958 that 'homosexual couples are fondling each other for all the world to see. [T]hese degenerate subjects meet in shabby bars in the street Calvo Sotelo'.[32]

Touristic spaces created an atmosphere where homosexuality was possible, but residents denounced it as a scandal and something that would subvert the standards of morality. This attitude was still apparent in 1966 when a French homosexual and transvestite was arrested and expelled from the country.[33] Archival files talk of an incident in the town of San Feliu de Guíxols on the Costa Brava. The Guardia Civil seized a young Frenchman, described as looking like a woman and apparently molesting other men. Apparently, the Guardia Civil was called by residents in order to remove the man from the street. After detention, the Frenchman was expelled to France.[34] Certainly, generalizations from individual cases are difficult. However, they make it clear that there was no broader acceptance of homosexuality or transvestism in touristic spaces in Spain until at least 1966. Heteronormativity was therefore not contested as a result of foreign tourism.

Nevertheless, gender relations and social mores were definitely changed due to the influence of tourism. Furthermore, the communities on the Spanish Mediterranean coast affected by tourism were not the static social complexes ruled by the structural variables 'honour and shame' that many contemporary ethnographers conceived them to be, as mentioned above. Instead, they were intricate social spaces where tourism triggered new conflicts about morality and gender roles even if these conflicts did not necessarily lead to radical changes.

European perceptions of Spanish gender roles between 'Hispanization' and 'Mediterranization'

If tourism had a certain influence on gender roles, even if restricted, it is also interesting to ask whether it modified the tourists' perception of Spanish gender roles. In other words, did tourism lead to some sort of transnational communication from below that resulted in a reduction of otherness and stereotypes? Or did tourism instead result in an accentuation of strangeness and difference in terms of gender roles in Spain when compared to gender roles in Northwestern European countries?[35]

Representing Spanish otherness

When foreign package tourism started in Spain in the late 1950s, European tourists learned from travel magazines, guide books and catalogues that archaic gender roles were deeply rooted in the Spanish mentality and that Spain would differ substantially in terms of the modern gender roles that were supposed to exist in the countries from which the tourists came.

Not only the earlier mentioned ethnographers at universities in Northwestern Europe had begun in the 1950s to conceptualize Mediterranean society mainly through the lens of the two supposedly most important social values, honour and shame, that shaped everyday life from Spain to Greece, Italy to Tunisia.[36] Also, in the 'tourist gaze' between the 1950s and 1970s, gender roles were crucial. Images of Spanish men and women in the touristic media were used to denote the striking differences between Spanish and Northwestern societies. The Spanish male was supposed to be hot-blooded[37] and anxious not to lose his honour and pride.[38] A British travel guide from 1954 highlighted this obsession: 'Politics, love and business are all things to be taken with a grain of salt – unless pride and honour happen to be involved. In this case the Spaniard will go to any length to keep his word of honour or to save his pride'.[39] Additionally, Spanish men were described as spending the whole day in cafes, drinking coffee and chatting about the same topics.[40] In addition, the phenomenon of the *piropos*, compliments made by men to women in the street, was depicted in travel guides as a behaviour specific to Spanish men.[41] But not only British, French or German travel guides and magazines drew such a picture. Also official publications of the Spanish Ministry of Tourism presented Spanish men as proud, anxious for their honour and gallant.[42]

In contrast, women were described as passive and passively accepting the compliments made to them by Spanish men. Spanish women were supposed to be mothers and do only housework instead of hired labour. This, after all, was the aim of Franco's gender politics, and a German book on Spain for tourists states the following:

> As head of the family, the woman is concerned the whole day with her family. She will hardly be seen outside of the house. [...] You rarely see a woman alone in the street, and never in the evening. Although Spanish women have gained more public visibility in recent years, especially in philanthropic and social facilities, she has nowhere near the independent, autonomous position of other European women.[43]

At the same time, Spanish women were objects of desire for men, were good looking and attractive. This was suggested in German travel guides during and after the Francoist era. For instance, a German travel guide in 1985 suggested: 'The young Andalusian women are not only beautiful but also have the reputation to be the most "graceful" of all Spanish women. They know how to emphasize this with their flamenco dresses.'[44] Indeed, the haughty flamenco dancer came to symbolize Spanish womanhood in the touristic media. The stereotypical descriptions of Spanish women were primarily associated with Andalusia and the Spanish South in general.[45] Spain was 'most Spanish' in Andalusia, which at the same time was revisioned near Africa and the Orient. Drawing on pseudo-historical explanations, authors of guidebooks emphasized how heavily Andalusia had been affected by the presence of Arab culture and how this influence was still in evidence. Thus, Andalusia was seen as a Spanish extension of the Orient, which was supposed to exude a special fascination.[46] In order to explain typical traits of Southern Spain, the authors seized on the 'Moorish element':

> The Andalusian and inhabitant of Southern Spain are racially, linguistically, and culturally heavily influenced by the more than seven centuries rule and settlement of this country by the Arabs. The 'typical' Andalusian is located – generally speaking – with regard to his mentality, temper and looks in a middle position between the serious and measured Castilian and the reckless and fatalistic Arab of Northern Africa. The Andalusian is overall more cheerful and happy, more imaginative, funnier, more nimble-witted but also less eager to work than Spaniards in other regions.[47]

Not only in travel guides were the stereotypes of Spanish gender roles associated with Southern Spain and Andalusia, which linked the Spaniards to 'oriental' habits and, therefore, established otherness. In travel catalogues, gender roles were also used, albeit more subtly, as a topic to describe Spain as an exotic holiday destination. Here Spanish women were almost exclusively flamenco dancers, and Spanish men were bullfighters.[48] Such images were only strengthened when the tourists came to Spain and witnessed one of the frequent folkloristic spectacles held especially for them. Whether it was a flamenco performance[49] in one of the countless nightclubs or a bullfight in one of the arenas built especially for tourists, as was the case in Lloret de Mar,[50] tourists met Spaniards everywhere with an apparently non-ambiguous traditional concept of gender. The differences between the supposed social values in Spain regarding gender relations and those of the tourists were also stressed in specially organized events. The propagandistic anniversary 'Year of Peace' in 1964,[51] for example, to commemorate twenty-five years since the end of the Civil War, aligned itself with the new 'Day of the Tourist' (*Día del Turista*). The ceremonies in honour of the end of the war aimed to promote the image of the regime in the interior of the country. At the same moment, the Ministry of Tourism was trying to show tourists a country that was simultaneously traditional, folkloristic and open to modernity. In the following years, the 'Day of the Tourist' became an occasion for self-representation that offered tourists on-site possibilities for the symbolic consumption of otherness. The government urged towns and villages to provide something special for tourists, such as events at which local traditions and folkloric dancers were presented.[52] Next to the representation of dances that were conducted by the *sección femenina* of the National Movement and local associations, many places arranged beauty contests. The regional press pictured young women from Northwestern Europe, freshly elected as 'Miss Tourist' and almost exclusively blonde, next to young, but usually dark-haired Spanish women in traditional dress.[53] This contrast between the German, Danish or Swedish women and the folkloristically dressed Spanish women encapsulated the presumed difference between Spaniards and other Europeans. The photos of locals and tourists, together on stage, created the impression that the Spaniards were rooted in tradition whereas the tourists represented a modern Americanized ideal of beauty. These images confirmed the tourists' sense of their own modernity and depicted Spain as a country with a deep sense of tradition, which was precisely what made it so fascinating. The immediate experience of this staged contrast between the presumed modern Northwestern Europe and traditional Southern Europe during the 'Day of the Tourist' celebrations was therefore an intentional play with stereotypes, identities and the fascination of the Other that was supposed to strengthen the image of Spain as an exotic and attractive holiday destination.

Reflexive Mediterranization

After this discussion of the tourist gaze and Spanish gender roles, it is reasonable to ask why such traditional and archaic images were so widespread in publications addressing foreign tourists. The answer lies in a common strategy that was pursued by the writers of travel books and magazines, by the designers of travel catalogues, and by the public authorities concerned with attracting tourists to Spain. Apart from the attempts of the Franco regime to present Spain as a modern, tolerant country open to tourists, the regime was also keen on maintaining a picture of the country that differentiated it from Northwestern Europe. This was done by promoting the image of a deeply traditional and folkloristic society in which the influences of the modern world had not corroded its uniqueness.[54] The motivation for the writers of travel guides and designers of catalogues was therefore quite similar. They wanted to show that Spain was a country in which tourists could find the amenities they expected and the catalogues were therefore dominated by images of hotels with sumptuous buffets and pools that had little to do with Spain itself. On the other hand, to make Spain attractive as a destination differentiated both from the tourists' home countries and competing touristic destinations like Italy or Greece, the country's traditional gender roles were considered a selling point. The aim of the Spanish public authorities and touristic marketing experts was therefore to produce such a distinctive otherness. From touristic advertising therefore emerged a representational regime[55] that enforced Spain's otherness in order to make it, and keep it, an attractive tourist destination. The description of gender roles and images of the 'typical' Spanish woman or man were useful constructs to highlight differences and promote Spain's supposedly unique position vis-à-vis other European countries.

German anthropologist Regina Römhild describes a similar contemporary process when referring to 'reflexive Mediterranization',[56] a strategy that people involved in tourism draw on to give holiday destinations the appearance of traditionality and elementariness because that is supposed to be exactly what tourists are looking for when they go on holiday. Since Northwestern Europeans had long associated the Mediterranean with backwardness, 'Mediterranization' signifies the process by which holiday destinations in the Mediterranean are explicitly associated with features that displayed such backwardness as a sort of exotic countermodernity. This has exactly the same function as the described traditional gender roles in government publications, travel guides, brochures, catalogues and magazines, all of which were trying to promote tourism to Spain. Tourists should find in Spain what modernity had destroyed within the societies of Northwestern Europe.

As the exploitation of gender roles in Spain would be equally possible in other Mediterranean societies, especially Southern Italy or Greece, the term 'reflexive Mediterranization' may need further analysis. Italy and Greece could also be advertised based on a strategy of 'Mediterranization', and so for the individual destination it became important to establish further differentiations.[57] While Greece and Italy were always associated with their respective antiquities, Spain was obviously without such a defining feature and therefore even more dependent on the notion of a contemporary society still shaped by traditional values and gender roles. This is why it may be best to articulate not only a strategy of 'reflexive Mediterranization' but also as one of 'reflexive Hispanization' with the aim to associate Spain with a specific set of unique features that would establish difference and otherness. The female flamenco dancer and the bullfighter became national symbols because they not only differentiated Spain both from Northwestern Europe and the other Mediterranean countries but were additionally a sign of traditionality and singularity.

Conclusion

The discussion of gender roles in Spanish touristic regions shows that tourism did not lead to a simple convergence between the tourists' home societies and Spain's touristic regions. It did not result in a simple cultural transfer of emancipatory ideas from a more modern Northwestern Europe into the backward South. Changes in gender roles were, in fact, the result of the changing socioeconomic structures affected by tourism. Instead of a direct impact, tourism had mediated repercussions. Conceptions of gender roles and social norms different from those advocated by the Franco regime emanated through new employment possibilities. However, actual changes were limited, and tourism also brought new constraints.

Tourism, seen as a sort of transnational communication from below, bringing millions of Germans, Britons, French and Spaniards in close contact, led neither to a shift in perceptions nor a reduction in stereotypes. On the contrary, stereotypes were commercialized and exploited in the context of a reflexive Mediterranization and Hispanization in order to increase the distinctiveness of Spain as a tourist destination. Reflexive Mediterranization and Hispanization were contemporary strategies, promoted by tourism experts, and therefore a reflection on the relationship between tradition and modernity in order to stimulate tourism.[58] Reflexive Mediterranization is therefore not a recent phenomenon and has a history that dates back at least to the second half of the twentieth century.

After the analyses of the consequences of tourism on gender roles and tourists' perceptions of them, it may be more than appropriate to ask what impact their holidays in foreign countries had on the tourists themselves. What did tourists bring with them concerning their own notions of gender and their own comprehension of the relationship between men and women in their own countries? Did tourism have repercussions on the reformulation of gender concepts when they returned home? To answer these questions, further research is needed, but it will be important and necessary to examine different patterns of travel. Whereas package tourism is based on accommodation in massive hotel complexes, an examination of alternative, individual forms of tourism and youth travel may generate very different answers.[59]

Notes

1. Hubert Tigges, 'Fern im Süd das schöne Spanien', *Die Fahrt. Unsere Reiseschrift* 1, 1955, 1–8, here 4. Translated by the author.
2. Sasha D. Pack, *Tourism and Dictatorship. Europe's peaceful invasion of Franco's Spain* (New York: Palgrave Macmillan, 2006), 90.
3. Ana Moreno Garrido, *Historia del turismo en España en el siglo XX* (Madrid: Síntesis, 2007), 240.
4. Pack, *Tourism and Dictatorship*.
5. Justin Crumbaugh, *Destination Dictatorship. The spectacle of Spain's tourist boom and the reinvention of difference* (Albany: State University of New York Press, 2009).
6. Hartmut Kaelble, *Sozialgeschichte Europas. 1945 bis zur Gegenwart* (München: C.H. Beck, 2007). Hartmut Kaelble, *Kalter Krieg und Wohlfahrtsstaat. Europa 1945–1989* (München: C.H. Beck, 2011). Hartmut Kaelble, 'Konvergenzen und Divergenzen in der Gesellschaft Europas seit 1945', in Lutz Raphael (ed.), *Theorien und Experimente der Moderne. Europas Gesellschaften im 20. Jahrhundert* (Köln, Weimar, Wien: Böhlau 2012), 21–36. Thomas Mergel, 'Die Sehnsucht nach Ähnlichkeit und die Erfahrung der Verschiedenheit', *Archiv für Sozialgeschichte* 49, 2009, 417–34.

7. Konrad H. Jarausch and Thomas Lindenberger (eds), *Conflicted Memories. Europeanizing Contemporary Histories* (New York, Oxford: Berghahn Books, 2007), 133–153. Thomas Mergel, 'Transnationale Kommunikation von unten. Tourismus in Europa nach 1945', in Martin Sabrow (ed.), *Potsdamer Almanach des Zentrums für Zeithistorische Forschung 2008* (Göttingen 2009), 115–126.
8. John Urry, *The Tourist Gaze. Leisure and travel in contemporary societies* (London: Sage, 1990). Following Urry the 'tourist gaze' is a collective mode of perception that tourists develop tourist. The 'tourist gaze' is shaped by touristic media like travel books, travel guides, catalogues and so on. Very important for the emergence of the 'tourist gaze' are pictorial representations.
9. Christopher Kopper, 'Eine komparative Geschichte des Massentourismus im Europa der 1930er bis 1980er Jahre. Deutschland, Frankreich und Großbritannien im Vergleich', *Archiv für Sozialgeschichte* 44, 2004, 665–77. Christopher Kopper, 'Die Reise als Ware. Die Bedeutung der Pauschalreise für den westdeutschen Massentourismus nach 1945', *Zeithistorische Forschungen/Studies in Contemporary History* 4, 2007, 61–83.
10. See Instituto Nacional de Estadística, Anuario Estadístico 1965, Cap. XII Turismo, 1.1.2. Principales características, 356. <http://www.ine.es/inebaseweb/pdfDispacher.do?td=177427&ext=.pdf> [accessed 23 January 2015].
11. Michel Foucault, 'Andere Räume', in Karlheinz Barck (ed.), *Aisthesis. Wahrnehmung heute oder Perspektiven einer anderen Ästhetik* (Leipzig: Reclam, 1992), 34–46. Foucault's heterotopia denotes a space which is characterized by the opposition to everyday experiences.
12. See Dean MacCannell, 'Staged authenticity. Arrangements of social space in tourist settings', *American Journal of Sociology* 79, 1973, 589–603, here 598. MacCannell conceptualized touristic spaces as divided in front and back regions that could be decorated as a backstage. By decorating a backstage with authentic features locals satisfy the tourists' desire to experience a different and authentic culture.
13. Pilar Folguera Crespo, '*La mujer*', in Juan Pablo Fusi Aizpurúa (ed.), *Historia de España Menéndez Pidal, La Época de Franco (1939-1975)*, 41.2 Sociedad, Vida, Cultura (Madrid: Espasa-Calpe, 2001), 298–339.
14. Crumbaugh, *Destination dictatorship*, 101f.
15. Instituto Nacional de Estadística, *Encuesta Población Activa*, 1968, Arxiu Històric de Girona, (AHG), 3 Instituto de Estadística 1239, Ficha Lloret de Mar.
16. Nicolau Roser, 'Población, salud y actividad', in Albert Carreras and Xavier Tafunell (eds), *Estadísticas históricas de España*, vol. 1 (Bilbao: Fundación BBVA, 2005), 77–154, here 148. Rafael Domínguez Martín and Nuria Sánchez-Sánchez, 'Los diferenciales salariales por género en España durante el desarrollismo franquista', *Revista española de investigaciones sociológicas* 117, 2007, 143–60, here 149.
17. Instituto Nacional de Estadística, *Encuesta Población Activa,* 1968, AHG 3 Instituto de Estadística 1239, Ficha Palau Sator.
18. Amparo Moreno Sardá, 'Mujeres en el franquismo', in Isabel Tejeda and Oliva María Rubio (eds), *100 años en femenino. Una historia de las mujeres en España* (Madrid: Acción Cultural Española, 2012), 79–97, here 86.
19. Instituto Nacional de Estadística, *Encuesta Población Activa*, 1968, AHG 3 Instituto de Estadística 1239, Ficha Lloret de Mar.
20. Alison Lever, 'Spanish tourism migrants. The case of Lloret de Mar', *Annals of Tourism Research* 14, 1987, 449–470, here 455.

21. See for example the situation in a classical mid-range hotel in Lloret de Mar in 1967. Hotel Eugenia, *Balance de comprobación octubre 1967*, 1967, Arxiu Comarcal de la Selva (ACSE) 27 Hotel Eugenia, Expediente, 5.1 Balanços inventari 1965–85.

22. Ismael Fuente Lafuente, 'El mundo de las Go-Gó's Girls I. Bailar sobre una tarima', *Baleares*, 24 July 1970, 9. Ismael Fuente Lafuente, 'El mundo de las Go-Gó's Girls II. Silvia: 'Se puede vivir trabajando como Go-Gó', *Baleares*, 25 July 1970, 9. Ismael Fuente Lafuente, 'El Mundo de los Go-Gó's Girls. ¿Se acaban las Go-Go? Una Go-Go por dentro', *Baleares*, 26 July 1970, 13.

23. Ismael Fuente Lafuente, 'El mundo de las Go-Gó's Girls I. Bailar sobre una tarima', *Baleares*, 24 July 1970, 9. Ismael Fuente Lafuente, 'El mundo de las Go-Gó's Girls II. Silvia: 'Se puede vivir trabajando como Go-Gó', *Baleares*, 25 July 1970, 9. Ismael Fuente Lafuente, 'El Mundo de los Go-Gó's Girls. ¿Se acaban las Go-Go? Una Go-Go por dentro', *Baleares*, 26 July 1970, 13.

24. See John G. Peristiany (ed.), *Honour and Shame. The Values of Mediterranean Society* (London: Weidenfeld & Nicolson, 1965).

25. Julian A. Pitt Rivers, *The People of the Sierra* (Chicago: University of Chicago Press, 1954).

26. Jesús María Vázquez (ed.), *Estudio socio-religioso de la Costa Brava en relación con el turismo* (Gerona, 1964), 219.

27. R.W. Connel and James W. Messerschmidt, 'Hegemonic masculinity. Rethinking the concept', *Gender & Society* 19, 2005, 829–59, here 832. R.W. Connell, 'The study of masculinities', *Qualitative Research Journal* 14, 2014, 5–15, here 8.

28. Vázquez, *Estudio socio-religioso*, 219f.

29. Ibid., 240.

30. This could possibly be explained by the rise in economic wealth through tourism that made it possible for more couples to start a family while marriage as the hegemonic concept in gender relations was not questioned. The increase of the figure in the province of Gerona between 1964 and 1974 could also be attributed to the rising numbers of internal migrants that settled in the province due to employment possibilities in the tourism industry.

31. Calculated from the figures of National Statistical Institute of Spain (INE): INE, *Movimiento Natural de la Población: Matrimonios*, 1964, <http://www.ine.es/jaxiT3/Datos.htm?t=6539> [accessed 26 January 2015]. INE, *Anuario Estadístico 1965*, *Población calculada para 1° de julio de cada año*, 472, <http://www.ine.es/inebaseweb/pdfDispacher.do?td=176882&ext=.pdf> [accessed 26 January 2015]. INE, *Movimiento Natural de la Población: Matrimonios*, 1974, <http://www.ine.es/jaxiT3/Datos.htm?t=6530> [accessed 26 January 2015]. INE, *Anuario Estadístico 1975*, *Población calculada para 1° de julio de cada año*, 455, <http://www.ine.es/inebaseweb/pdfDispacher.do?td=32391&ext=.pdf> [accessed 26 January 2015].

32. Vecindario de El Terreno (Palma de Mallorca) to Gobernador Civil de Baleares, *Denuncia referente a la inmoralidad pública* 1958, Arxiu del Regne de Mallorca, Govern Civil 890.

33. Gobierno Civil de Gerona to Comisario del Cuerpo de Policía, San Feliu de Guíxols, *Multa y expulsión del territorio Nacional de dos súbditos franceses*, 23 August 1966, AHG 3 Govern Civil 1109.

34. Ibid.

35. Hans Henning Hahn and Eva Hahn, 'Nationale Stereotypen. Plädoyer für eine historische Stereotypenforschung', in Hans Henning Hahn (ed.), *Stereotyp, Identität und Geschichte. Die Funktion von Stereotypen in gesellschaftlichen Diskursen* (Frankfurt a. M.: Lang, 2002), 17–56, here 22.

36. See Peristiany (ed.), *Honour and Shame*. Pitt Rivers, *The People of the Sierra*. Peregrine Horden and Nicholas Purcell, *The Corrupting Sea. A Study of Mediterranean History* (Oxford: Blackwell, 2000), 463–523.
37. Kripal Singh Sodhi and Rudolf Bergius, *Nationale Vorurteile. Eine sozialpsychologische Untersuchung an 881 Personen* (Berlin: Duncker & Humblot, 1953), 42f. See also F.W. Buri, 'Spanische Meditationen', *Merkur* 12, 1958, 721–37.
38. R. Rotraut Hinterlohr, *Umgang mit Spaniern* (Nürnberg: Luken & Luken, 1954), 20.
39. *Fodors Spain and Portugal* (The Hague: Fodor's Modern Guides, 1954), 40.
40. Ibid.
41. *Michelin Espagne* (Clermont-Ferrand: Michelin 1973), 26.
42. Subsecretaría del Turismo (ed.), *Spanien für Sie* (Madrid: Subsecretaría del Turismo, 1964), 67–70.
43. Hinterlohr, *Umgang mit Spaniern*, 11.
44. Hans Lajta, *Polyglott Reiseführer Costa del Sol* (Granada, München: Polyglott-Verl., 8th ed., 1985), 6.
45. Horst J. Becker, *Polyglott Reiseführer Südspanien* (Köln, München: Polyglott-Verl., 3rd ed., 1967), 12.
46. Paul H. Ewerlöf et al., *Polyglott Reiseführer Spanien* (München: Polyglott-Verl. 16th ed., 1978), 3. Similar already in the Baedeker: *Baedekers Autoreiseführer Spanien und Portugal* (Stuttgart: Baedekers Autoführer-Verl., 4th ed., 1963), 8. Likewise: *Baedekers Allianz Reiseführer Spanien. Ferien – Städte – Landschaften. Der große illustrierte Reiseführer* (Stuttgart, Freiburg: Baedeker-Verl., 2nd ed, 1985), 15–16.
47. Lajta, *Polyglott Costa del Sol*, 6.
48. See the collection of travel catalogues of the Historical Archive on Tourism (HAT) Berlin. Touropa, Ferienführer 1962, 1962, HAT * D 06 / 45–80 Touropa. Reisekatalog, 105, 161, 171, 185. Touropa, Ferienführer 1963, 1963 HAT * D 06 / 45–80 Touropa. Reisekatalog, 111. Scharnow-Reisen, Flugreisen Sommer 1965, 1964 HAT D * 06 / ca. 45–70 Scharnow 4, 42. Scharnow-Reisen, Flugurlaub Winter 1965/1966, 1965, HAT D * 06 / ca. 45–70 Scharnow 4, 12. Scharnow-Reisen, Handex '66, 1965, HAT D * 06 /ca. 45–70 Scharnow 1, 17. Touropa, Touropa 1988, 1988 HAT, * D 06 / 45–80 Touropa Reisekatalog, 212. NUR. Neckermann, Der Urlaub für uns alle, 1974/1975, HAT * D 06 / 74–90 NUR, 74f.
49. See the collection of advertisement flyers, tickets and other sources that illustrate the nightlife in Lloret de Mar: Arxiu Históric Lloret de Mar (AHL), 66.166.3; 66.2231.2; 66.231.5; 66.231.6.
50. Expediente Plaza de Toros, AHL 70.47.197.62
51. Walter L. Bernecker and Sören Brinkmann, *Kampf der Erinnerungen: Der Spanische Bürgerkrieg in Politik und Gesellschaft 1936–2010* (Nettersheim: Graswurzelrevolution, 5th ed., 2011), 127f.
52. Ministerio de Información y Turismo, Dirección General de Promoción del Turismo an Delegado Provincial de Gerona, *Día del Turista*, 10 December 1963, AHG 3 Informació i Turisme 164. Delegación Provincial del Ministerio de Información y Turismo, *Photos Día del Turista 1967*, 1967, Archivo Histórico Provincial de Málaga (AHPM), Información y Turismo 433, Carpeta 6, Día del Turista 1967. 'La Sueca Ulla Kristina Fernberg, Miss Turista Provincial', La Tarde, 11 May 1970.
53. Delegación Provincial del Ministerio de Información y Turismo, *Día del Turista 1967*, 1967, AHPM, Información y Turismo 433, Carpeta 6, Día del Turista 1967.

54. Subsecretaría del Turismo (ed.), *Spanien für Sie* (Madrid: Subsecretaría del Turismo, 1964), 70.
55. Stuart Hall, 'The spectacle of the "Other"', in Stuart Hall (ed.), *Representation. Cultural Representations and Signifying Practices* (London: Sage, 1997), 223–290, here 236.
56. Regina Römhild, 'Reflexive Europäisierung. Tourismus, Migration und die Mediterranisierung Europas' in Gisela Welz et al. (eds), *Projekte der Europäisierung. Kulturanthropologische Forschungsperspektiven* (Frankfurt a.M.: Institut für Kulturanthropologie und Europäische Ethnologie der Johann Wolfgang Goethe-Universität Frankfurt am Main, 2008), 261–76, here 271f.
57. See Hasso Spode, 'Homogenisierung und Differenzierung. Zur Ambivalenz touristischer Chronotopie-Konstruktion', in Burkhard Schnepel, Felix Girke and Eva-Maria Knoll, *Kultur all inclusive. Identität, Tradition und Kulturerbe im Zeitalter des Massentourismus* (Bielefeld: transcript, 2012), 93–115, here 100.
58. See Römhild, 'Reflexive Europäisierung', 274. Römhild delineates 'reflexive Mediterranization' as a form of 'reflexive modernization' following Ulrich Beck to describe the fact that people use supposed traditional elements in order to foster tourism. So, 'reflexive Mediterranization' is a reflection about the characteristics of modernity in itself.
59. See, for example, Nikolaos Papadogiannis, 'Travel and Greek migrant youth residing in West Germany in the 1960s-1970s', *Comparativ. Zeitschrift für Globalgeschichte und Vergleichende Gesellschaftsforschung* 24, 2014, 2, 67–87. Axel Schildt, 'Across the border. West German youth travel to Western Europe', in Axel Schildt and Detlef Siegfried (eds), *Between Marx and Coca Cola. Youth Cultures in Changing European Societies, 1960–1980* (New York: Berghahn Books, 2006), 149–60.

CHAPTER 2
BASQUE NATIONAL IDENTITIES, YOUTH CULTURE AND GENDER IN THE 1960s: BEYOND THE FARMHOUSE AND THE *YE-YÉ*

Amaia Lamikiz Jauregiondo

Introduction

The following pages shed light on the social life of Basque youth groups during the last decades of the Franco dictatorship. I examine the extent to which the process of modernization of society and the new trends coming from other countries had an effect on youth during that period. The 1950s to the 1960s period coincided with important transformations in Spain's economy and society: the country left behind the postwar autarchy and isolation and began a period of progressive economic liberalization. Spain began to open up to the rest of the Western European countries as a generation of young people was emerging with a renewed interest in the social and political situation of their country.

In the Basque provinces, this renewed interest included a revised view of local culture and an awareness of changing times. Younger generations of Basque nationalists listened to modern music and followed habits and fashions from France or Britain. In addition, they reacted against the traditional understanding of Basque culture as a relic of the past promoted by the Franco authorities, as it no longer corresponded to the one they were experiencing. Consequently, by the 1960s, a Basque cultural revival movement emerged as a kind of re-elaboration of the main features of the existing Basque culture.

A close look at the social activity and cultural practices of young people will help us understand the ways they perceived and faced the transformations that preceded the process of transition to democracy. As consumers of culture, they were active participants and contributors to the distinctive 'Basque culture', while experiencing the transformations in their society.[1]

This approach implies drawing our attention to how things are appropriated and transformed by use in everyday life as well as the context of consumption. The value of oral sources should be underlined here: I rely mainly on information gathered from interviews carried out with young members of associations in Gipuzkoa, combined with information contained in newspapers and memoirs.

Furthermore, the following pages examine issues relating to gender: to what extent did women start to gain prominence in this new context, did they increase their participation and how did they react to the changes taking place in their environment? What was expected of them and what did they want for themselves? How did their experiences influence their attitude towards the changes occurring in the last years of the Franco dictatorship?

Being a young girl in the 1950s

For women living in the late 1950s and early 1960s under Franco's dictatorship, there was a phase in their life that started when they left their childhood for good and finished when they created a family: it was considered to be their youth, which comprised the years between leaving school and getting married – becoming housewives and mothers. During that period, young girls started to work and participate more actively in the associative networks of their towns.

The Franco regime – through education, the Catholic Church and *Sección Femenina* (women's section of *Falange*) – promoted the ideal woman whose main role was to be a mother taking care of the family. Girls had to be educated in service, obedience and discipline in order to become the care provider for the family. Any attempt to gain autonomy by young girls was accompanied by political and social indoctrination: to get a job in the administration, a driving licence or a passport, they had to first complete what was called the *servicio social*. This meant that they had to learn the principles of the *Movimiento* – Spanish only party – to carry out domestic tasks and the main rules of urbanity. Some of the women I have interviewed remember how they had to travel from their towns to the capital city of the province to deliver a baby layette that they had prepared themselves, and that they were obliged to learn the main principles of the *Movimiento*. Their memories, however, suggest that this indoctrination was not really successful in achieving consensus and acceptance of the role they were ascribed.[2]

With regard to education, the fast economic development within the province and the consolidation of industrial towns created new needs in the field of learning. As a result, industry owners and members of industrial cooperatives collaborated with local institutions, parents' associations and town councils in order to provide education for young people and ensure the availability of specialized workers. These efforts were often accompanied by complaints about insufficient support from official institutions. Private initiatives were forced to compensate for the shortcomings of state initiatives over a period of many years.[3]

In the case of girls, the lack of educational institutions was even more visible. Schools distinguished very clearly the roles of men and women. Women's education was seen as training for marriage and becoming housewives. The association Lartaun, which aimed at providing young town people with an adequate education, tried to promote a polytechnic for young boys and a 'domestic science school' for young girls.[4] According to my interviewees, the education of young girls included domestic studies and sewing, as well as accounting and typing for those who would later seek work as a secretary or an assistant.[5]

Many girls worked in factories or small shops. It was a period of economic development and growth in Spain, which created enough opportunities for these young girls to find jobs in the factories and businesses of their towns. My interviewees remember that employers went to the religious schools to offer jobs to the girls finishing their schooling. These jobs were usually not very specialized, at least in the beginning, and some girls combined their jobs with further studies in order to complete the higher levels of education. Few girls had the opportunity to get more specialized training, usually in the fields of child education and health, both closely connected to the traditional role of women as carers. These were the only ones that usually did not leave their jobs once they got married. In families with lower incomes, housewives had the possibility of working at home as dressmakers and knitters.

With the beginning of the development plans launched by the Spanish government in the early 1960s and the consequent economic development, things started to change for women in the labour market: an increasing need for labour and new laws allowed women to participate in economic activities outside the home. Although they still needed permission from their husbands, married women were allowed to participate in the labour force from 1962 onwards.

But the presence of women in the labour market did not change much in the next decades. According to a report reflecting on Basque women during the late 1970s, women's active participation in society was quite limited.[6] Marriage determined their social and economic activity to a large extent: family and domestic work were their designated domains. Attendance of women at educational institutions diminished visibly from secondary education and professional training onwards; only a few women registered for university studies.

The male breadwinner family model predominated during these decades of economic growth. The State, together with advertising in the new consumer society, promoted this model and women themselves ended up accepting it as the ideal. The Franco regime reinforced and promoted the aforementioned model using labour and family legislation, educational and demographic policies.[7] This situation mirrored women's dependence on males and subsidiary role in society.

In this context, we find a group of young girls aged between fourteen and twenty-four that had started to work and, according to what many of them explained, had more money and time at their disposal.[8] It is not surprising, then, that the Catholic Church showed special interest in these young girls' leisure and socialization. By developing a moralizing discourse regarding the appropriate recreation and fashion for young girls, the Catholic Church organized their leisure and associative life, and published journals with sections devoted to them to promote the same image of honest women, future wives and mothers that the regime was trying to impose.

Along these lines, the weekly newspaper *Zeruko Argia* included – in the early 1960s – a section dedicated to young girls so as to educate or give some guidelines on their habits and tastes. This section reiterated the moralizing discourse of the Catholic Church regarding youth. Articles about beauty and fashion included many comments on appearance and being 'proper', for example, wearing the right length of skirts. There were articles warning about wearing trousers when it became an option to do so. My interviewees recall French journals showing girls wearing trousers by the mid-1950s, although they recognized that it was quite uncommon to wear them then. Some wore their first jeans at the age of fourteen, in the early 1960s; shorts were only for more daring girls. Most girls still went to dressmakers for their clothes, since there were not many shops in their towns, and fabrics and other products were often brought from France.[9]

As for their social life, young girls participated in associations that were created as a response to a widespread preoccupation with the need for proper leisure time activities.[10] Behind these initiatives there was an increasing awareness of the presence of young people as a distinct group in society and the need to guide their activity. The Church offered spaces and infrastructure to create associations, and young girls participated in girls' parish groups such as *Mariaren Alabak*.

During the 1950s and early 1960s the Catholic Church tried to organize the leisure of youth through a wide associative network, which included both boys and girls from different backgrounds. At that time, OARGUI was founded with the main aim of organizing hiking excursions and leisure activities for the youth of the province. The first OARGUI centres emerged in some parishes in the city of Donostia in 1950, but it was mainly after 1957 that this organization expanded its activity to other areas of the province. In the following years, most centres were established as a fusion of previous male and female parish youth groups and were devoted to religious activities – *Luistarrak* and *Mariaren Alabak*.[11] The youth group *Baserri Gaztedia* (created circa 1959) carried out its activity in rural areas, while JOC focused on youth living in industrialized environments. By 1961, *Baserri Gaztedia* was active in at least thirty villages of the province.[12] In these first years there was a growing interest in organizational matters in order to consolidate the different groups and a clear preoccupation with the role of youth groups in society as a whole.

'Modern girls do not want to speak Basque . . .'

The sections above reveal a society in which women maintained a traditional role and that was rapidly evolving, with urban ways of life quickly prevailing. People were aware of these changes; proof of this awareness was the so called 'farmer complex'. One of the associations' participants that I interviewed noted that farmers were considered to be backward and associated with negative qualities while *kaletar* – people living in urban environments – were considered to be modern and therefore connected to positive ones.[13] He also connected these distinctions to the attitude towards the Basque language: people had internalized this difference, therefore farmers did little to defend their language and culture.[14]

Women seem to have been more sensitive to this stereotype: most interviewees explained that young women spoke more Spanish because they did not want to be identified with the farmhouse whereas young men spoke mostly Basque.[15] According to different sources, the Basque language was not only connected to the farmhouse, but also to the kitchen and the family, while Spanish was related to urban environments and modern ways of life. Young girls tended to avoid speaking Basque in public spaces as a way of rejecting the role that had been ascribed to them. Another woman I interviewed made similar comments regarding the tendency of women to speak Spanish:

> Basque language was mainly confined to the sphere of the family. On the streets, men and young boys have spoken more Basque than women. [...] Young boys used to speak Basque in their peer groups, while girls used to speak Spanish. I would say that it was a question of prestige. And speaking with other women, I think we were all of the same opinion: the rural world had certain negative connotations, and women felt that very deeply and when they went out on the streets they tried to speak Spanish.[16]

Articles of the time included similar comments. An example would be one on Lartaun in December 1967, which described the change of atmosphere in the town and criticized those who did not use the language and spoke only Spanish. Again, the message was directed at women, some of them being young mothers who sent their children to Basque schools to learn Basque and then spoke Spanish themselves: 'Young women of Lartaun! Try to spread a Basque atmosphere everywhere you can, at home, in the factory, in the playground, in all your activities. Try to impose the "fashion" of Basque. [...] it is so sad to see all those young mothers speaking in Spanish!'[17]

Women of the association Bordaxuri confirmed this view. Coming from a small town, they remember that on Sunday afternoons the girls used to go to the cinema in the neighbouring town of Beasain. On such occasions they tried hard to speak Spanish: they thought that only people from little villages spoke Basque; Spanish was 'the language of culture'.[18] The centre of the problem seemed to be the lack of social prestige of the rural world in the context of industrialization and urbanization in the country. As a consequence, women were made responsible both for the language and the farmhouse, which Basques considered to be the core of their identity. It is obvious that women were not responsible for the deep transformations taking place in those years; this argument was another attempt to keep them within the limits of their traditional role as care providers and guardians of tradition.

But the interesting point here is the reaction of younger generations of girls towards the role ascribed to them. If they did not want to be identified with traditional ways of life, what was their ideal?

The 1960s and the arrival of a new generation[19]

The fast economic development that took place in some parts of Spain in the second half of the twentieth century put the province of Gipuzkoa at the forefront of economic development within the country. In this rapidly evolving social and economic setting, a group of young people who were about to start working in industry and the service sector of employment within the region emerged.

These young people had more leisure time, but there were not that many activities for them apart from those organized by religious groups. Girls did not have as much leisure time in previous decades. They'd usually spend their free time strolling around the streets of their towns and cities with their friends and then dancing on Sundays in the main square of the town, where there was live music. They did not engage in any sports except for hiking activities in the nearby mountains. Girls did not go to bars unless accompanied by a male of their family or formal boyfriend. They also didn't drink alcohol.

In 1962 the journal *OARSO* from Errenteria published an article on the lack of proper leisure time activities for the youth of the town at weekends.[20] The only activities available were going to cinemas, bars and dances. Since youth could not spend every Sunday afternoon in the cinema, there were only the bars and dances left as an alternative to the streets. Bars were not considered suitable entertainment, so the article expressed the urgent need for a gathering place, where young people would be able to meet in a secure and comfortable environment.

Comments on the lack of adequate recreational activities were quite common. Some of my interviewees explained that they joined the association in order to organize activities for the young people of the town, as an alternative to religious groups.[21] In fact, in the mid-1960s there was a decline of interest in Catholic youth groups as other, non-confessional groups were taking over as the promoters of the associative network in the province.

My interviewees also mentioned that strolling around with their friends in the early 1960s was one of their favourite activities together with going to the cinema and dancing.[22] They attended the weekly open-air dance in the main square of their town; an excellent opportunity to meet the boys. As a member of a youth group in Beasain recalled:

> We used to dance in the main square of our town on Sundays. We usually went to the cinema at five and afterwards we went dancing. During the pause we went strolling around the streets of the town, we greeted each other and talked to the people we met. It was not considered appropriate to dance with boys before we were 14, if the nuns knew we had danced with them, we would be punished. So we usually danced with our girlfriends.[23]

Going to the cinema was thus one of the favourite activities of younger generations. As a response to this trend, Church organizations began to consider organizing film clubs as an attempt to educate audiences. Some of my interviewees remembered the film forum activities they carried out within their association, where they'd start discussing films and end up immersing themselves in profound discussions about life and politics. Several journal articles insisted on the importance of cinema and the need to train critical audiences through film forum activities.[24] The aim of film forums was to watch films and discuss them, and become aware of the influence that cinema may exert on audiences. According to a journal article published in the youth section of *Zeruko Argia*, those who went to the movies became slaves of cinema; children in particular were regarded as susceptible to the influence of cinema, which in turn was considered a means of propaganda. Interviewees remember that they used to watch Spanish and American films. They learnt a lot about America in those films, they recall now, but not without a certain irony.[25]

Movies, journals and advertising offered different portrayals and ways of living. Research done in the field of advertising, however, warns us about the introduction of foreign models: the North American domestic iconography introduced in Spanish homes via advertising during the 1950s and 1960s did not correspond to the reality of those years.[26] They provided depictions of future possibilities that allowed people hope for those goods and for progress. Along these lines, I suggest that what young boys and girls of the 1950s and 1960s received through cinema, TV, journals and music should be seen as a source of inspiration that played an important role in creating new attitudes and habits. Many people identified those images with progress and a freedom they lacked in the context of the Franco regime. Music in particular was one of the fields where new influences were most visible. My interviewees started playing modern music in the early 1960s and dancing the twist; a dance similar to rock and roll for which couples did not need to touch each other, as in more traditional dances. Young people would gather at the associations that had record players to listen to foreign music and dance; they listened to groups such as The Beatles and French and Italian singers. Gradually, modern songs were translated into Basque, while groups singing in Basque thrived. There were many song contests that made some of the participating groups quite popular at that time as they made music records and performed their songs in the festivals of the different towns of the province. This is supported by the youth section of the weekly publication *Zeruko Argia* which, in the late 1960s, reported on the numerous concerts given by these new modern music groups and praised their new records.

Reflecting on the above, many of my interviewees have connected modern music to the *ye-yé* movement. They used the term '*ye-yé* youth' to refer to young people that were seen as modern, sometimes even transgressive, who followed new trends and new attitudes or habits (e.g. boys with longer hair, imitating The Beatles, and girls wearing trousers or mini-skirts, were described as *ye-yé*). They represented a change in the looks of young people, who were following trends coming from foreign countries such as France. *Ye-yé* were also characterized by the type of music they listened to: French and Italian singers (e.g. Adamo, Rita Pavone, Johnny Hallyday or Sylvie Vartan). They bought their records and listened to them in the premises of their youth groups; some of their songs were translated into Spanish or Basque. They would even buy a journal called *Salut les copains* that was considered a point of reference for the *ye-yé* youth in France. As the above suggests, this movement was quite successful among young people in the mid-1960s.

This is precisely the time when Basque society witnessed the emergence of a group of people who started to talk of 'youth' as 'us', thus consciously distancing themselves from adults and referring to themselves as a new generation who wanted to take a more active role regarding the problems of their society. The journal *Zeruko Argia* began to include a section with the title *Gazte naiz* (I am young) in the mid-1960s, in which young authors expressed the concerns and opinions of their peers, mirroring the shift of focus onto young people talking about their own problems and trying to differentiate themselves from the older generation, often criticizing the latter's intolerance and lack of initiative. A group of young men who would become well known Basque writers and intellectuals used to write in that section every week.

Among those contributing to the youth section of *Zeruko Argia* was a young woman called M. Carmen Garmendia,[27] who used this opportunity to write many articles about women. It was her aim to give prominence to them while reacting against the stereotype of Basques as backward-looking farmers in order to demonstrate that it was possible to be both Basque and modern. As she recognized later on, French intellectuals and the events of May 1968 were the main influences for her and her peers.[28] After all, most of them spoke French and could easily travel to France if living in Gipuzkoa.

By the late 1960s Paris had become the centre of attraction for many young intellectuals as the number of Basque students in the universities of Paris, Brussels and Leuven was increasing.[29] Many of them would become university professors, leading intellectuals and politicians in the next decades. In her memoirs about her first student year in Paris (between 1968 and 1969) Mariasun Landa, author of children's literature, recalls watching the May 1968 demonstrations on television just before travelling to Paris. She also reflects on her experiences as a young Basque student coming from a rather conservative environment that was not used to the open-minded attitude of her house-mate and colleagues in Paris.[30]

Another interesting example from the press is an article written in 1966 by Rikardo Arregi; it reflects on a new attitude, on young people being a force within associations and in society in general. The article refers to the young people from the town of Andoain, but describes a change which could have been observed in many other towns of Gipuzkoa at that time:

> We can say that the youth of Andoain has awakened [...] In fact, those who know Andoain and its evolution in the last year have affirmed that the spirit of the town has changed much, and that young people have played an important role in these changes. Following the trend of the Basque Country as a whole, also here, probably even more than in other places, we can notice that a new generation has arrived, and that they are claiming their own place within society.[31]

In fact 1966 became a tense year as the attendance of younger people at festivals increased considerably. Youth claimed their place in society by making themselves visible in these celebrations. Furthermore, at this point it was no longer older people who reported about youth activity, but 'youth' as a subject talking about their own experiences and projects. In turn, leading authorities reacted by suspending and prohibiting many of these celebrations.

However Arregi, and it is likely that this was also the feeling of many other young people at that time, was not satisfied: in spite of all the work that these young people were doing, they still could not find a place in their society and their needs went largely unrecognized. Apart from bars, there was no place to go to in the towns. As a consequence, most young people left their home towns on Sundays and holidays in search of leisure activities. According to Arregi, instead of waiting for someone else to intervene, it was preferable that young people take the initiative to solve this problem and control their own activities.

In my opinion, Arregi's words are an extremely accurate description of the problems youth culture had and the changes in youth mobilization in most towns of the province. His argument brings into focus the thoughts and problems of many of my interviewees – young people in the 1960s – thus constructing a kind of 'counter discourse' to the interventionism of institutions such as the Catholic Church. The discourse elaborated by Arregi and many other young people who participated in associations provided a base upon which peers could add their own input.

In the previous decade associations may have been created by adults worried about the educational and cultural needs of youth, but young people now began to take charge of associations; this opened the way for numerous transformations. Young people acquired the capacity to determine the kind of activities that could be pursued. Associations such as Kresala (Donostia, 1964), Alkar (Aretxabaleta, 1964) and Ozkarbi (Elgeta, 1965) were created with the aim of integrating both male and female youth groups of the parish, thus offering an opportunity for girls to participate more actively.[32]

As in the case of the labour market, women's participation in associative life was determined by the appropriate life cycle phases: young girls started to participate in associations at the age of twelve to fourteen, and left them when they were getting married. Afterwards, family responsibilities and lack of time would be the cause for abandoning their activity within the association. There were only some exceptional cases, for example single women, who maintained a presence in associations for longer periods.[33] Few women were members of the governing bodies of associations, but they were not responsible for sections within the associations. If there was something to discuss with local authorities, it was men who would attend the meetings. Those were usually understood as male responsibilities. The role of girls continued to be subordinate to that of boys.

But it is possible to observe an increasing presence of women in the associations' activities. Apart from the traditional Christmas celebrations, these groups helped in the organization of festivals, music concerts, theatre groups, choirs and dance groups. In some cases, this participation of girls brought about significant changes: events that had previously been celebrated exclusively by men started to include women as well. Around 1963 the folklore section of the association Lartaun lamented the fact that there was no group to walk around the town's streets and sing the traditional songs of the Sta. Agueda Evening; however, a group of women dressed in traditional costume circled the streets of the town performing the traditional songs in a celebration with deep roots in the country.[34] Tradition was thus rediscovered but also altered according to widespread changes in society.

But the process of integrating women in activities traditionally carried out by men was not as quick as it may seem. Although the association Kresala had participated in the drummers' parade called *tamborrada* of Donostia on the day of the Patron Saint since 1972, women were not allowed to serve as drummers in the parade until 1980. It was the first association to include women in such parades.

The importance of singing modern songs in the Basque language

As we have seen, by the mid-1960s a generation of younger people strongly reacted against the old stereotypes of Basques (e.g. as backward-looking farmers). In fact, young people coming from rural areas were starting to participate more actively in the life of towns and the differences between their way of life and those living in town were diminishing. By the late 1960s young people were more used to participating in the social life of the town than the older generations and the difference in social consideration of the farmer compared to the *kaletar* was fading.[35] At the same time, the use of the Basque language acquired increasing prestige both in rural and urban environments. As interviewees explained, they slowly became aware of the situation and started to organize activities to protect what they considered to be at the core of their culture.

This new awareness of the need to protect the Basque language and culture seemed to come from those people living in towns, often politically linked to Basque nationalism. They had witnessed discrimination towards the Basque language and were not willing to accept the old stereotypes, so they started to promote activities to defend the language; to fight for what they considered to be one of the main characteristics of their identity as modern Basques.[36]

By the mid-1960s, younger generations defended the need to keep track of time but also to adapt to changes brought about in the Basque Country by the new industrial society. Instead of looking backwards in an attempt to recover the old traditions of the farmhouse, people had to become aware that they lived in an industrial, modern society and therefore should try to be modern Basques. Rikardo Arregi criticized the view of youth as simply going through a phase of disorientation, apathy and indifference.[37] On the contrary, he argued, young people had proven their commitment: many of them worked during the day and studied in the evenings in order to educate themselves; some invested great efforts to promote the Basque language and culture, others actively worked for their towns, and most of them proved their dedication to Basque nationalism with their choice to speak Basque to each other. Arregi stressed the fact that this attitude was not visible previously, hence indicating that a significant change had occurred in recent years. The mobilization of the mid-1960s was proof of this commitment.

A product of this new atmosphere was the music group *Ez Dok Amairu*, the symbol of the emerging Basque cultural movement.[38] Some Basque musicians and singers had decided to innovate in the field of Basque music, aware of the success that modern music had among younger people. One of the most prominent members of this group – and the only female – was Lourdes Iriondo. Born in Donostia in 1937, she became very popular in the second half of the 1960s and produced several records by the end of the decade. She used to sing both traditional Basque songs and modern rhythms in Basque, often assuming a clear form of protest. Furthermore, her appearance reminded one of Joan Baez whose songs were quite popular among young people at that time. One of Iriondo's most popular songs, *Ez gaude konforme*[39] – published in 1968 – gave its name to the youth section *Gazte gera gazte* of *Zeruko Argia* in that same year.[40]

Members of *Ez Dok Amairu* had realized that Basque people did not sing in Basque any more, because the modern rhythms they sang had been produced in other languages. If they wanted young people to continue singing in Basque, they would have to make the kind of music young people wanted to hear.[41] Furthermore, it was not only a problem of language, but also of the themes these songs dealt with: young singers did not want to sing old songs, when society around them was undergoing deep transformations and new preoccupations were emerging. They could not continue singing the old song of the white dove 'when the white dove had long ago become black due to the smoke of the factories'.[42] They recognized the great influence that music had on younger people, making them aware of many issues, and therefore they decided to incorporate the kind of themes that characterized the modern society in which they lived.

In January of 1965, the decision by a group of young people to organize a Basque song festival added fuel to the flames. The theatre group *Jarrai* organized a music festival in Donostia, *Euskal Abesti Berri Jaialdia*, where members of *Ez Dok Amairu* participated. They sang new songs and rhythms in the Basque language. This celebration provoked a strong reaction from some sectors of Basque society, since many defenders of Basque folklore saw it as a threat to what they perceived to be true Basque culture. Sectors that were more progressive supported the initiative since they believed that Basque culture needed to adapt to the times if it were to survive. The future Basque culture would also have to be produced in the Basque language to ensure that they continued as a living language and a living culture. The debate was part of a broader discussion on how Basque society should face the deep transformations that were occurring in those years. As Rikardo Arregi suggested, the evolution of Basque culture since 1960 was not independent from the deep social and economic transformations that Basque society was undergoing.[43]

These attitudes suggest the appearance of a new 'Basqueness' that was not necessarily connected to the traditional farmhouse, and the acceptance of an existing modern culture which one did not need to feel ashamed of. Young people at that time spoke of 'acquisition of awareness' and of 'efforts to change things': that is, they succeeded in turning the opposition between backwardness and modernity to their own advantage. Speaking Basque would no longer be considered backward-looking; it was at the very core of modern Basque culture.

In the process of conferring new components and values on the Basque language, the work of associations played an important role: they offered an opportunity to live in a more Basque atmosphere and to work for the Basque language.[44] Their interest in the promotion of Basque culture led members of these associations to promote an increasing number of activities in the late 1960s (e.g. collaboration in the organization of culture weeks, music and book fairs, promotion of Basque schools and Basque language courses for adults).

In this new context, women recovered their prominence in Basque language teaching with the emergence of *Ikastola* or Basque schools. Several interviewees underlined the role of women in the promotion of language given that they were the leading teachers in Basque schools, because they spoke very good Basque, and they loved their fatherland.[45] They emphasized that Basque schools made an essential contribution towards restoring the Basque language's prior status. Even if it had been a movement 'from below', the people who led it were educated and were important in the process of reinstating the appropriate relevance to the Basque language. *Ikastola* at the same time broke with old patterns of education and reintroduced the language to the public, leaving behind the domestic sphere while making way for a cultured language.

Conclusions

The images young people saw in cinemas and advertising, or the music they listened to, hinted at new models for young people, which did not match with the traditional stereotyped image of Basques. As we have seen, these differences led many young Basques – especially young girls – to reject their language and try to identify with those new ways of life. My interviewees have noted mainly French influences in fashion, music and youth culture, suggesting that foreign influences arrived mainly via the neighbouring country. Furthermore, many people identified those images and examples with progress and freedom that they did not find under the Franco regime.

But slowly new generations emerged, trying to promote an updated image of youth culture. Youth such as the so-called *ye-yé* beheld movements developed abroad and danced foreign rhythms that were not considered Basque enough by young Basque nationalists. In their opinion, young Basques had to adapt to new times and create their own model of modern Basque youth.

This is also when the associative movement started becoming independent from previous Church control and young boys and girls created their own groups where they could participate together in the organization of festivals, theatre groups, dance groups and hiking excursions. They managed to establish their own meeting places, where they could discuss and listen to the music they liked.

The promotion of Basque book and music fairs, Basque language lessons and Basque music groups should also be understood in this context. The *Kanta Berri* initiative and the group *Ez Dok Amairu* were created to demonstrate that there could be a modern Basque youth singing modern rhythms and themes in Basque. This transformed views about 'Basqueness' and should be viewed both as a response to changing times and an alternative to the official culture of the Franco regime.

Through their cultural practice, Basque youth not only expanded on traditional views about their culture, but also appropriated new trends and fashions in a creative way, adapting them to their own context. That is, they went beyond the farmhouse and the *ye-yé* to create a modern Basque culture. Given that the aforementioned implied a considerable influence of foreign trends and a strengthened role of youth culture, this process can be considered to be another example of the cultural revolution of the Long 1960s.[46] Furthermore, the young people participating in this Basque cultural revival movement would do so once again in the intellectual and political life of the Basque Country in the decades to follow.

Notes

1. On the active role of consumers and the notion of cultural appropriation see the introduction of Hugh Mackay (ed.), *Consumption and Everyday Life* (London: Sage, 1997). Studying the cultural activity of associations as cultural practices, and taking into account that different people may appropriate cultural expressions in different ways, have both been fruitful ideas when carrying out this research. The notion of appropriation as used by Chartier should be mentioned here, since it brings to mind the importance not only of meanings and symbols, but also the role of the people who interpret and use them. See Roger Chartier, 'De la historia social de la cultura a la historia cultural de lo social', *Historia Social* 17, autumn 1993, 97–103.
2. M.R.J. OARGUI Beasain. See also C. Calvo, *Poder y consenso en Guipúzcoa durante el Franquismo. 1936–1951* (Salamanca: Universidad de Salamanca, 1994), 481–2.
3. Siadeco, *De una economía rural a una economía industrial: estudio socio-económico de una comarca del Goiherri*, 1974, 273.
4. See Journal *Lartaun*, 1, 1960, 25.
5. M.R.J., member of OARGUI Beasain and members of the association Bordaxuri, Lazkao.
6. Araldi Azterketa Elkartea, *Emakumearen egoera Euskadin. Situación de la mujer en Euskadi*, 1982.
7. P. Perez Fuentes, '*Ganadores de pan' y 'amas de casa': otra mirada sobre la industrialisación vasca* (Bilbao: Universidad del País Vasco, 2004), 205–55. Although Perez Fuentes insists on the idea that this was rather a model than reality, since most working-class families needed the work of women to supplement the family income.
8. M.R.J. OARGUI Beasain and B.M. Alkar Aretxabaleta. The journal *Zeruko Argia* included an article in 1968 about young girls working in the newly founded cooperatives in Gipuzkoa, and commented that since girls had more money at their disposal, they should learn to make good use of it. *Zeruko Argia*, 1968-07-04, 7.
9. M.R.J. OARGUI Beasain. See also M. Landa, *La fiesta en la habitación de al lado* (Donostia: Erein, 2007), 86. Landa describes how she used to cross the border, hiding in her clothes products she had acquired in France, such as wool, nylon and other fabrics to make dresses, skirts or jackets that were fashionable in France but had not yet arrived to Spain . . . everything seemed to be better in France, she comments.
10. Amaia Lamikiz, 'El problema del ocio: la organización del tiempo libre de la juventud trabajadora en Guipúzcoa en la década de 1960', *Vasconia* 30, 2000, 283–93.
11. Basque names of the Catholic Congregation of St Louis Gonzaga and the Daughters of Mary.
12. See '*Baserri Gaztedia zer da?*', in *Gazte*, 1961.
13. J.F.S. advisor priest in Lazkao.
14. Farmers were most reluctant to send their children to Basque schools. See M. Etxezarreta, *Euskal baserriaren oraina eta geroa* (Oñati: Jakin, 1977), 109–10.

15. M.A.A. Ozkarbi, J.F.S. advisor priest in Lazkao, women of Bordaxuri, B.M. female Basque school teacher, I.S. OARGUI Lazkao.
16. B.M. female Basque school teacher in Lazkao.
17. Journal *Lartaun*, 21, 1967.
18. I.S. OARGUI Lazkao and members of Bordaxuri.
19. Regarding the use of the term 'generation' here, the protagonists labelled themselves as 'generation' and mobilized such generational rhetoric in order to mark their distance from adults. Furthermore, it was a way of expressing their feeling of belonging to an imagined group that shared common experiences and expectations. But Anna von der Goltz warns us of the problems posed by the inflationary use of this term and reminds us of the need for a more refined approach. In our case, we should refer to young Basque nationalists from rural and urban backgrounds as a 'generation-unit', in order to underline the diversity that can be found even among the apparently homogeneous group of Basque youth. About the generations see Anna von der Goltz, 'A polarised generation? Conservative students and West Germany's "1968"', in Anna von der Goltz (ed.), *'Talkin' 'bout my generation'. Conflicts of generation building and Europe's '1968'* (Göttingen: Wallstein Verlag, 2013), 195–215.
20. See 'Un problema que exige solución', in *OARSO*, 1962, 31. See also Journal *Lartaun*, 1, 1960, 12.
21. I.S. OARGUI Lazkao, J.M.B of JOC and A.S. OARGUI Beasain.
22. An article about youth and their free time published in *Zeruko Argia* confirms this view: in winter time, going to the cinema and dancing seemed to be the most popular activities of youth, while in summer time hiking excursions to the nearby mountains and strolling around were the most popular together with dancing. See *Zeruko Argia*, 'Zer egiten dute gazteak jai arratsaldeetan', 14 January 1960, 4.
23. M.R.J. OARGUI Beasain
24. In 1960 there was a section in *Zeruko Argia* called *Aupa gazte . . . mutil eta neska!*, devoted to young boys and girls. This section included several articles about film forums warning about the dangers of cinema.
25. J.M.I. OARGUI Beasain.
26. C. Rodríguez, 'Mr. Marshall viene a casa. La escenografía de la modernidad americana en el tiempo del desarrollismo español', in *Congreso Internacional de Historia de la arquitectura moderna español* (Pamplona: Escuela Técnica Superior de Arquitectura de la Universidad de Navarra, 2006), 205–16.
27. Born in the late 1940s in the small town of Gipuzkoa, around 1962 she joined the Catholic group *Baserri Gaztedia* and later on she participated in the creation of the youth section *Gazte naiz* in *Zeruko Argia*. After a period working as teacher, she participated in Basque politics and became a member of the Basque government in the late 1980s.
28. See 'Iragana eta Etrokizuna uztartzeko ahalegina', interview with M.C. Garmendia published in *Emakunde*, July 1990, 36–9. The reference to the events of May 1968 shows to what extent these had become a kind of *lieu de mémoire* for young people during the 1960s. Even if the new attitudes were visible some years earlier, most of my interviewees coincide with Garmendia when in hindsight they connect their acquisition of awareness with May 1968.
29. Articles in *Zeruko Argia* report the activity of Basque students abroad, especially during the spring and summer of 1968, and the celebration of a Basque festival at the University of Leuven in spring 1969. See for example: 'Ikustalde bat Bruselako unibertsitatean', in *Zeruko Argia*, 8 September 1968, 7 and 'Euskal Jaia Lobaina'n', 13 May 1969, 7.

30. M. Landa, *La fiesta en la habitación de al lado* (Donostia: Erein, 2007). Apart from references to Sartre, Fanon or Simone de Beauvoir, in these memoirs Landa recalls having attended a meeting of Pasionaria and having carried political propaganda from France hidden in her clothes on the occasion of one of her visits to see her family in Spain. She also mentions conversations with her girlfriends in Paris about free love and sex, contraception and the right of women to decide on their own, issues that were taboo in Spain at that time. She describes the encounter with a new world that was very different from the experiences of those who had remained at home.

31. Ricardo Arregi, 'Andoaingo gazteria', *Zeruko Argia*, 1966-01-30. Rikardo Arregi was a young intellectual who did a great deal to promote the standardization of Basque language in the 1960s.

32. Amaia Lamikiz *Sociability, culture and identity: associations for the promotion of an alternative culture under the Franco Regime* (Florence: European University Institute, 2005).

33. B.M. Alkar Aretxabaleta.

34. Journal *Lartaun*, 12, 1963, 270.

35. Etxezarreta, *Euskal*, 110–11.

36. I.S. OARGUI Beasain and women of Bordaxuri Lazkao.

37. Ricardo Arregi, 'Andoaingo gazteria', *Zeruko Argia*, 30 January 1966.

38. *Ez Dok Amairu* was a group created by several young Basque singers and musicians who tried to create a new kind of Basque song, which moved away from the folklore that predominated in the previous years and was committed to the contemporary social and political situation of the Basque Country in the second half of the 1960s under the Franco regime. As a consequence of this commitment, their work was criticized by the most conservative sectors of Basque nationalism and was prohibited by the Franco authorities at the beginning of the 1970s. The group was dissolved in 1972.

39. The complete title of the song was *Gazte gera gazte eta ez gaude konforme*, which in English means: 'Young, we are young, and we are not satisfied'. This song became a symbol for many young people at that time.

40. It is probably no coincidence that this section started in summer 1968, right after the events of May 1968 in Paris. In the preceding weeks there were various articles about the 'revolutionary events' of May 1968 written by Larresoro, pseudonym of J.L. Alvarez Enparantza, *Txillardegi*, who would become a leading Basque intellectual in the next decades.

41. Lourdes Iriondo was interviewed by *Zeruko Argia* in December 1966 and described this group as an attempt to revive Basque music. Members of this group had realized that young people did not identify with old Basque songs and they preferred to sing modern songs they heard on the radio. This is why young Basque singers came together to form the group *Ez Dok Amairu*. The group sang modern songs translated from other languages, or they created new songs, often protest songs, as is the case of Xabier Lete, Lourdes Iriondo and Julian Lekuona. See 'Mª Lourdes Iriondori elkarrizketa', in *Zeruko Argia*, 11 December 1966, 12.

42. Julian Lekuona: 'Euskal musika berri', *Zeruko Argia*, 12 May 1966, 12

43. 'Euskal kultura gure gaurko gizartean' in *Zeruko Argia*, 25 December 1966, 5.

44. J.T. OARGUI Beasain, G.Z. Alkar Aretxabaleta, M.A.A. of Ozkarbi and I.S. of OARGUI Lazkao.

45. B.M. from Lazkao.

46. Arthur Marwick, *The Sixties: Cultural Revolution in Britain, France, Italy and the United States, 1958–1974* (Oxford: Oxford University Press, 1998).

CHAPTER 3
CONSUMERISM, GENDER DIVERSITY AND MORALIZATION OF SEXUALITY IN THE IBERIAN 1960s

Rosa Maria Medina-Domenech and Richard Cleminson

Introduction

During the 1960s, despite their long-standing dictatorships, Portugal and Spain became immersed in profound political and cultural transformations that shook both countries and confronted existing traditional gender models with new portrayals of identity. These gender models and performances were further diversified by changing representations of men and women in the media and by major population movements such as tourism, particularly in the case of Spain, the colonial wars in the Portuguese case, and emigration primarily to other European countries from both countries.

In the same decade, the French philosopher Jean Baudrillard argued that consumer society had taken the drama out of identity, transforming (gender) identity into a game whereby it was chosen among a range of different models.[1] In the Spanish and Portuguese cases, however, we find a more nuanced resonance for Baudrillard's arguments, whereby in the 1960s more diversified models of masculinity and femininity were available and could be acquired, contested and repressed in the context of dictatorial regimes.

In order to examine the contours of gendered change in Iberia in the 1960s our historical account will scrutinize the ambivalences generated by incipient consumerism in both countries in which traditionalist and religious cultures were undergoing a transformation. In particular we will examine the ambivalences generated by new consumer models by means of an analysis of gender-inflected advertisements for new psycho-pharmaceutical drugs in Spanish and Portuguese medical journals in the 1960s. Such drugs increased hugely in availability within European societies and the Iberian countries were no exception to this trend; these countries also experienced an accompanying rise in consumer culture, much of which was infused with North American flavours. This analysis enables us to evince how new gendered identities of consumption, new categories of gendered subjectivities and the consumption of equally new forms of medication became mutually reinforcing with profound social effects. Advertisements, a domain in between consumption and production, offer a suggestive set of insights for a reinterpretation of the hegemony of the regimes studied and the tensions that emerged within them in the 1950s. To date, scholars have generally treated Spain and Portugal as separate entities in spite of their intimate proximity and the current balance of historiographical work is significantly skewed in Spain's favour, a limitation reflected in our chapter.[2] Despite this, we believe that comparison between the Iberian nations offers a fruitful insight that prompts new research agendas for both countries, thus hopefully generating a more diverse vision of consumerism and the Iberian dictatorships themselves than prevailing models appear to offer.

'Miniature consumer societies'? Economic and gender transformations in Iberia

The Salazar and Franco regimes shared certain political outlooks and characteristics but also had their differences. Both emerged out of military interventions, the first after a military coup on 28 May 1926 and the second after a three-year civil war resulting from a failed military rising in July 1936. Both regimes flirted with fascist and Nazi models, both were fiercely authoritarian and repressive, traditionalist and Catholic, although the underlying ideology and modus operandi of each differed considerably.[3] Franco was far more aggressively repressive and exterminatory of his enemies and established closer relations with the Axis powers. Salazar's regime, institutionalizing an optimum of terror rather than a sheer maximum under the auspices of the secret police (the PVDE from 1933 up to 1945 and the PIDE from 1945 up to 1969), was effective in its repressiveness in different ways.[4]

The Portuguese *Estado Novo* or New State, established by the Constitution of 1933, retained the republican regime (the Spanish rebels' victory eliminated the Republic) and was headed by a 'shy, misanthropic economics professor' of Coimbra University who laboured 'to preserve traditional values, the Catholic faith, and the established social hierarchy against the threats of Communism, Freemasonry, and modernism'.[5] Dr António Oliveira de Salazar, appointed Minister of Finance in 1928 and Prime Minister in 1932, presided over a regime which slowly faded into a 'weak, semi-peripheral fascism, appropriate to the position of a weak, semi-peripheral country',[6] a kind of 'governmental dictatorship' modelled on nationalism, colonialism and corporatism that lasted until 1974.

The goal of a unitary and cohesive national community was to be accomplished by 'the institutionalization of Portugueseness' which in turn aimed at 'promoting an essentialist, transhistorical and seemingly unmoving ordering of national identities and spaces'.[7] Even though there was no institutionalization of 'National Catholicism' along the lines of what eventually presided in Spain,[8] the Church exercised strict control over many aspects of people's everyday lives.[9] Contraceptives were outlawed, nudism was prohibited[10] and women were consigned primarily to the domestic sphere in accordance with a strict division of labour in society.[11] Women, in Salazar's words, would play a special role and would form 'an indispensable foundation in any work of moral reconstruction', and would be 'cherished, loved, and respected' for their ability to bear children.[12] God, Family and Homeland (*pátria*) became the watchwords of the regime.[13] Women's organizations such as the OMEN (Organização das Mulheres para a Educação Nacional, Organization of Women for National Education), formed in 1936, and the

MPF (Mocidade Portuguesa Feminina, Portuguese Female Youth Movement), established in 1937, which compulsorily enrolled girls from the age of seven to fourteen and voluntarily up to the age of twenty-five in the case of students, confirmed women's roles.[14] The MPF became a channel for regime values through a programme of 'moral, civic, physical, and social education'.[15] These organizations followed a similar path to those taken by women's organizations in other authoritarian or fascist regimes of the period, including pro-natalism and basic child hygienics.[16]

The pro-family measures implemented by the New State, limited though they were, must be understood not only as part of the roles envisaged for women; they also fell within the legal framework that ushered in a kind of 'welfare state' constructed by the regime within the sociopolitical framework of corporatist Catholic nationalism.[17] Important though this gendered structure of the regime was, it does not sum up women's roles under the regime or account for them entirely. As in Spain, ambivalences existed as to women's visibility and status; women with university degrees were given the right to vote in 1931, legal equality was enshrined in the 1933 Constitution, but any rights were to be bestowed in accordance with women's 'natural differences'. But cracks and fissures were present in the regime from the start and these began to widen in the 1950s. One of the results of this restrictive state of affairs was, apparently paradoxically, the possibility of a body of narrative and literary work centred on women's realities as a locus of resistance.[18] The 'nationalist pragmatics of femininity' was not necessarily all-encompassing or ever-lasting.[19] Further cracks in the Salazarist model of containment and aversion to modernity began to appear in the 1960s as the relationship between authoritarianism, modernization, new subjectivities and greater access to consumer products, including medicines, became pulled in new directions.

From the mid-1940s, the emphasis on political and economic autarky came to an end as the regime entered what one historian, Braga da Cruz, has termed its 'diversification phase'.[20] Although this was by no means an abrupt sea-change as old attitudes, infrastructures and economic models continued to prevail, alterations in the course of the regime were coming. Salazar had refused participation in the European Recovery Programme (Marshall Plan) in 1947, but accepted two years later the offer of US\$54 million between 1949 and 1951, a *volte face* 'explained by the deteriorating economic situation with rising imports and falling exports'.[21] Despite this, low investment and a dependence on trade with the colonies meant that at the start of the decade, 50 per cent of employment was based in the agrarian sector, which produced 25 per cent of national income.[22]

The Development Plans of 1952 and 1958 consolidated this incipient diversification, although, increasingly, resources were diverted to military spending to fight the colonial wars. Portugal's integration into the EFTA in 1959 provided a fillip to the country's internationalization and developing consumer model.[23] The development plans of the mid- to late 1960s placed more emphasis on social investment, thus contributing to greater private consumption.

High levels of emigration constituted a further factor influencing rising consumption; during the 1960s remittances became a vital element of Portugal's income.[24] This may well have sparked an increase in consumer demand but this was fragmented and confined to particular groups and social classes. Indeed, consumption was primarily an urban phenomenon, rural areas only experiencing this change in the 1970s.

Finally, to this unequal mix must be added the increase in the tourist trade. Although slowly consolidated in Portugal in comparison to Spain, 200,000 foreign visitors and tourists came to Portugal in 1956; in 1960 this stood at 400,000 and in 1964 it had increased to 1 million.[25] This was confined to the southern coastal parts of the Algarve and the Lisbon area and, overall, the Portuguese government 'displayed remarkably little interest in sun and beach tourism [...] favoring instead a more elitist approach that would not involve significant social changes [...]'.[26] It was only in the years 1964–7 that revenues from tourism exceeded those derived from remittances from emigrants abroad.[27]

During the 1960s the workforce experienced an increasing process of 'feminization'. The pro-independence conflicts in the Portuguese colonies of Africa meant that more men left the country to fight and this brought more women into the workplace, especially in the textile industry. Such greater economic and social independence had its effects in terms of identity, personal strain and health.[28] New foreign investment coupled to a new set of Portuguese entrepreneurs progressively invigorated business and a wide range of industries, including textiles, electronics and domestic goods and 'created a miniature consumer society impatient with the old social constraints'.[29]

Like Portugal, Spain began to move beyond its period of autarky in the 1960s. The cabinet installed in 1957 reflected the technocratic and modernizing leanings of three key Opus Dei ministers.[30] These changes should not be confused with democratization; the regime maintained its dictatorial stance and regulated politics and morality tightly within what today is commonly known as 'sociological Francoism' or a 'mood of acceptance' of the regime's status quo.[31]

The regime's repressive style neatly cohabited with population displacements from rural to urban areas, immigration to other countries and economic transformations under the impulse of capitalism and economic growth in Europe in what can be termed, as Pavlović suggested, an 'uneven [social] mobility'. The arrival of an immense number of foreign tourists to the *costas* challenged sexual conservatism and brought more diverse gender roles as was shown in some cultural products at the time.[32] The regime sought to exploit this 'opening' propagandistically in order to appropriate its modernizing effects.[33] The accelerated economic expansion ('*desarrollismo*') that took place in some regions during the 1960s, termed the 'economic miracle' by the regime, had in fact less to do with the regime than with a broader European process of social and economic change.[34] Nevertheless, the limited state budget in the absence of tax reforms constrained social change, propitiating a period of 'restricted tolerance', as minister Manuel Fraga termed it in 1980, or one of 'portable morality', as Marxist writer Vázquez Montalbán defined it.[35]

In countries such as the USA, the consumerism boom fostered unattainable expectations for the middle classes, generating more frustration than success for both men and women, trapped by the routine of everyday life and the gendered emotional order. Betty Friedan in *The Feminine Mystique* (1963) critiqued the so-called 'condition that has no name' felt by women who had, after the Second World War, been consigned to large houses in the periphery of American cities and whose life project was limited to satisfying their husbands' demands.[36] Though consumerism had liberating effects, it also confined women to the home as authentic technologists in charge of all the new artefacts offered by the consumerist society.[37]

In Spain, consumerism increased, especially in certain regions such as the Madrid area, Navarre and Catalonia and the percentage of GDP spent on foodstuffs diminished from 35.25 per cent in 1954 to 24.14 per cent in 1975. Between 1960 and 1966 the number of televisions increased from 1 to 32 per cent, reaching 60 per cent in 1970 in municipalities of over 50,000 inhabitants.[38] The number of washing machines increased from 19 per cent in households to 36 per cent, ownership of family cars increased from 4 per cent (1960) to 35 per cent (1971). However, this increase in belongings was not matched by improvements in education or newspaper reading, which actually fell during this period just as those leaving school without completing formal education stood at 25 per cent.[39] The availability of housing was differentiated according to class, just as a popular film from the period, *El Pisito* (1959, Marco Ferreri), shows.[40]

Perceptions on consumerism and femininity also changed throughout the decade. Early novels, such as María Mercedes Ortoll Vintró's *Todos se han ido* blamed the female consumer for disrupting family and social harmony. The novel contrasted Martina, the 'mean' wife and 'bad' mother who loved going shopping with the austere Cecilia, the nurse who diligently worked with the male protagonist and became the ideal wife.[41] However, other 1960s novels such as *La ciudad de los muertos* by Consuelo Álvarez Sierra showed a more nuanced picture.[42] Consumerism was portrayed as an intense desiring stimulus, just as Stearns noted.[43] Its greedy appetite could never be satisfied: living, one character stated, 'had a more gluttonous aspect'.[44]

Tensions were also reflected in films. Responding to some changes in legislation, including the right to work,[45] one film, *Amor a todo gas* directed in 1969 by Ramón Torrado portrays different female workers' roles, such as a petrol station attendant and two women entrepreneurs. Patro, who owns the taxi company where the male protagonist Peret works, and Laura are both successful women. Laura and Peret are both singers. At the end of the movie, Laura seems happy to quit her career affirming 'Oh, Peret, how happy I am! All my problems are gone.' However, Laura's manager is planning to promote them as a duo and make a profit out of them. The double finale (Laura quitting her career and the manager planning the duo's career) probably satisfied the contradictory expectations from increasingly diverse audiences.

Paralleling the ambiguities portrayed in fiction, recent studies on the effects of consumerism in Spanish women have shown a divided vision of its ambivalent workings. Aurora Morcillo in *The Seduction of Modern Spain* argues that the historical move from the 'mother' in early Francoism to the 'consumerist' woman in the 1960s was not a liberatory process but one that in fact constituted another form of submissiveness.[46] In contrast, Pavlović seems to claim a more optimistic outcome of consumerism. She argues that the introduction of television in Spain had liberating effects as 'it becomes harder to sustain the traditional discourse on womanhood by the existing ideological apparatus'.[47] Jorge Pérez agrees with both authors on the contradictions of modernity stimulated by consumerism, analysing the movies of the young and popular Rocío Dúrcal.[48] These movies usually reflected the 'ennoblecimiento de la España del franquismo' (ennoblement of Francoist Spain) through Cinderella stories of social mobility. For this author the popular star Rocío Durcal 'condensa las tensiones del cine del desarrollismo' (condenses the tensions of *desarrollista* cinema), combining apparent social change with a reinforcement of traditional gender roles.

As we will see in the next section, these ambiguities were also embedded in gender representations portrayed in drug advertisements.

Consuming psychotropic drugs to mould subjectivity

Advertisements for psychotropic drugs were the result of the mass production of medication launched in the West and egged on by the 'discovery' of new psychological problems brought about precisely by new materialism. Their analysis enables us to see how complicated lifestyles, changing gender patterns, stressful work practices and consumer demands were intertwined. Medical advertisements also allow us to explore how the content of publicity was inflected according to gendered expectations, sometimes breaking with established norms and at other times reinforcing them.[49]

The expansion of psychotropics in Western societies shows how the pharmaceutical industry exploited the effects of a changing work and social environment in order to find a market for its products. The contradiction between desire, both acquisitive and sexual, and the reality, governed by class, gender and economic status, generated contradictions and imbalances that the new drugs promised to alleviate.

During the 1960s, two psychiatric journals were published in Spain. The *Actas Luso-Españolas de Neurología y Psiquiatría*, re-established in 1947, was co-edited by the pro-regime Spanish psychiatrist José López Ibor and the less pro-Salazar Portuguese psychiatrist Barahona Fernandes. The *Actas* often published popular psychological and religious content that, during the 1960s, evolved into more biological accounts of mental disorders. Another journal, the *Archivos de Neurobiología* published more 'scientific' content. This journal was founded in 1919 by the Nobel laureate José Ortega y Gasset, Gonzalo Rodríguez Lafora and J.M. Sacristán, none of them particularly akin to the ideological premises of the regime.

Eighteen different psycho-drugs were advertised in these two journals. Most of them suggested a gendered psychological profile of their potential consumers. Though some drugs (Miltown and Distovagal) were advertised both for women and men, only four advertisements included female patients. Eight of the drugs were produced in Spanish laboratories, six in the USA, two in France and one in Italy.

Advertising in Spain expanded in this decade. By the mid-1960s, the main agencies from the US and Britain were already established in Spain. However, Cuban publicity creatives arrived earlier to Spain after the communist revolution and they imported the

American style of marketing.⁵⁰ In the 1960s Ernest Dichter visited Madrid. Dichter was a motivational and marketing psychologist who wrote *The Strategy of Desire* (1960) where he argued for the emotional and subconscious drive involving marketplace decisions. In a talk, on how motivational research could help 'underdeveloped countries', he asserted that there was a lack of desire in countries, such as Spain, and that publicity had a huge role in stimulating desires. Psychoanalytical interpretations were criticized in Spain as well as by contemporary theoreticians such as Jean Baudrillard. He claimed that in the eroticized festival of consumerism there was no involvement of the individual unconscious drive, but a common place generated from culture, whereby sexuality is emptied of its substance and becomes 'material for consumption'. He argued that it is here that consumption takes place and this is of 'quite a different order of seriousness from naïve exhibitionism, fairground phallicism and knock-about Freudianism'.⁵¹ Baudrillard emphasized, therefore, the social engineering of consumerism rather than understanding desire as a mere personal drive. The psycho-drug industries were also well aware of the importance of triggering desire to consume, as the campaigns testified. The globalization of theories on marketing and the historical evidences we have compiled suggest that the advertising techniques used in Iberia were quite similar to the ones used in American journals, particularly for drugs produced in the US.

Consumerism also incorporated scientific rationality as a persuasive selling strategy, particularly in the pharmacological arena. Some drugs such as Deplix, a cocktail of Miltown and the antidepressant Benacticina, claimed 'confirmed efficiency' and 'tested security'. In spite of their unknown mechanism, some companies persuasively used anatomical models in their ads, emphasizing and simulating a straightforward mechanism of action, and they showed how the drugs reached specific neurological locations to deliver their chemical effects with precision. The flyer for Deplix displayed how it acted at three specific levels in the nervous system (hypothalamus, thalamus and the spinal cord). In tune with consumerist culture, the publicity for Deplix and Miltown, a 'blockbuster' produced in the USA,⁵² insisted on the drugs' scientific soundness, their efficiency and the novelty of their compounds. For twenty-first century readers it does not seem strange that drugs publicity for doctors included the rhetorical resource of proclaiming their scientific reliability. However, the re-balancing of the psyche through chemical means did not need to pass any medical trials until the 1970s and, as Fernando Álvarez Ude explained in 1960, ignorance prevailed amongst psychiatrists as to the mechanism of the drugs supplied.⁵³

Moulding the psyche of the 'sexy and domestic' secretary: the meaning of female emotional discontent

Many commercial drugs dealt with ambiguous and contradictory situations both in women's lives and their physical symptoms. Deplix, for example, was employed for depression and anxiety and it was claimed to be useful for both psychic and physical symptoms (muscular relaxation). In dealing with these ambivalences, the advertising strategy used by Distovagal, made in Spain by Aben Laboratories, is particularly interesting. Its publicity included both male and female workers. Women workers were specifically represented by 'the secretary', also a potential consumer in Spain. Franco's law of 26 July 1961 allowing women to work meant that female workers under contract increased from 12 per cent (1940) to 25 per cent of the active population (1970).[54] The ad suggested that hypnotic-barbiturates could help to reach the paradoxical mood of feeling 'without nervousness but [feeling] alert', the expected mental setting necessary for working in a gendered context. The 'secretary' glanced submissively up at the camera and the accompanying text used women's hyper-excitability, an old platitude that naturalized sex differences. Specially prescribed for 'hyper' states of blood pressure, thyroid function, menopause and the so-called 'visceral neuroses', the drug supposedly worked as a 'stabilizer of [. . .] emotional equilibrium'.

Female representations in adverts for calming drugs were consistent with the modernized 'regime of docility' advocated by the regime to allow women's controlled participation in the public arena. The Sección Femenina modernized its tactics to induce docility as part of female behaviour. The 'Sportsman's Rules of Conduct' published in 1973 still taught women to be docile: 'If you win do not be petulant'; 'If you lose do not be defiant'. These norms were easily applied in the workplace, though barbiturates could be an excellent help.[55]

The pursuit of emotional and behavioural 'balance' was also part of the new modelling of the mind and the advertising motto for Miltown, a successful tranquilizer in the US before Valium, commercialized in 1955 by Wallace Laboratories (New Jersey). The drug was a resounding success, and it was prescribed over 36 million times in its first two years.[56] A decade later, in 1965, it was confirmed that it acted as a sedative and was then placed on the abuse control list under the Food, Drug and Cosmetic Act. Prescriptions became more limited from December 1967. In 1970 it was proven that it entailed not only psychological but also physical dependency. In spite of its regulation in the US in 1967, it was advertised in Spain in 1966 as 'the first and most accredited meprobamates', 'also used in hundreds of clinical studies'. Miltown was finally suspended in Spain in 2008.[57]

When advertised for women, it was aimed at stopping anxiety and normalizing their behaviour in order to entail happiness and lightheartedness in the absence of any 'complexes'. Psychological theories of the inferiority complex became popular during the Spanish 1950s in both cultural and medical discourses. These theories contributed to shape a gendered psyche. Being a 'person with a complex' was considered an attractive trait for men, but a handicap for women for whom easygoingness was a core trait in idealized femininity.[58]

The five drugs that included women in their publicity described different situations that ranged from obtaining docile efficiency at work to coping with deep mental suffering. For women, it seems that it was marketing that coined the term 'emotional crisis'. Valium seemed helpful in this acute situation of desperation expressed in ads by young women with deep sadness and severe discomfort. However, the most extreme problems of mental suffering were depression and psychosis.

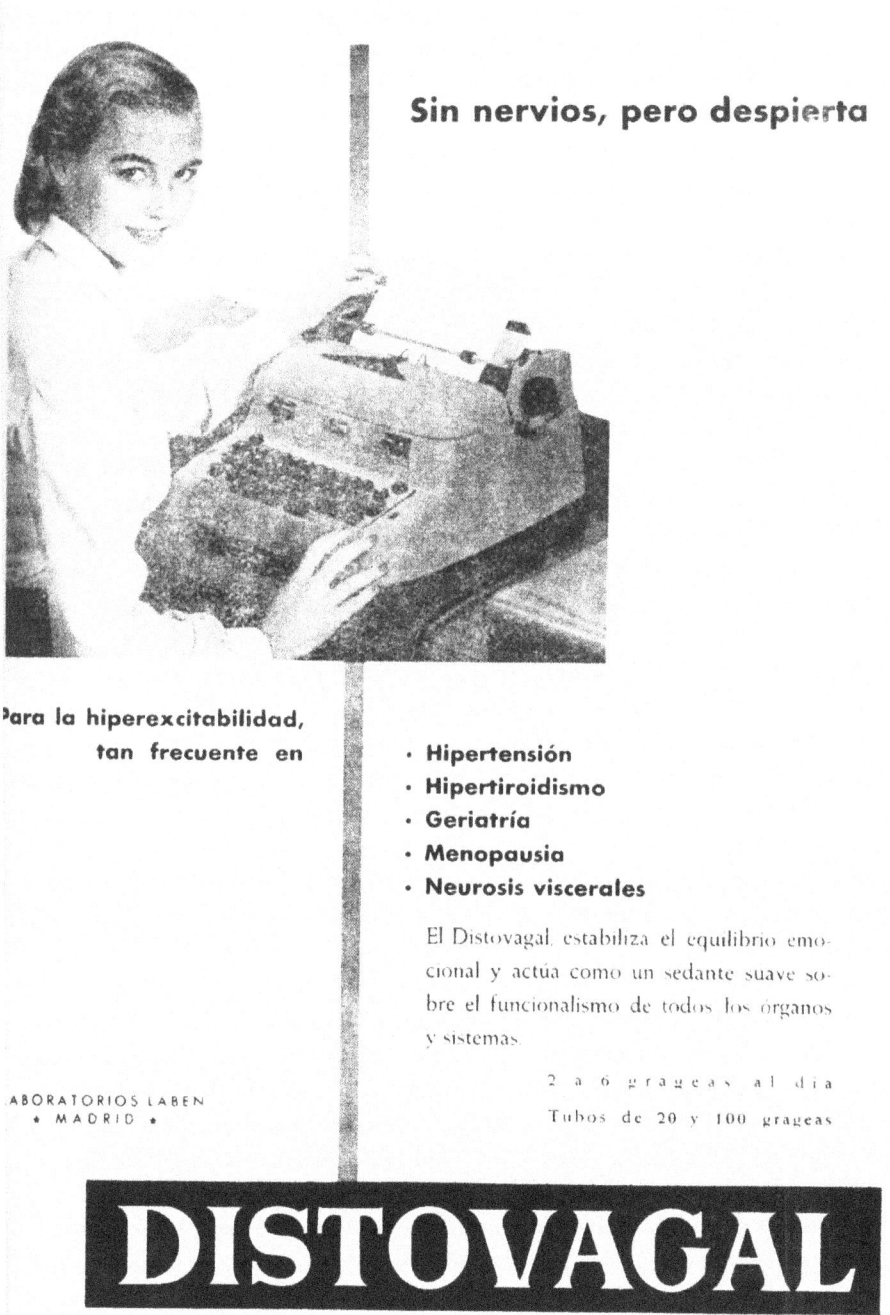

Figure 3.1 Distovagal (The secretary), *Archivos de Neurobiología* 29.1, 1966.

Surmontil, produced by the Swiss laboratory Rhone-Poulenc, presented depression as the 'most frequent problem in the clinic'. A drawing of a long-haired young woman imitating the languid faces of the avant-garde paintings by Picasso or Modigliani linked the challenges of modern life to the personal failures caused by depression. Her face expressed sadness, lack of enthusiasm and a disconcerted look, precisely the opposite to attitudes required for the active consumption of commodities and for the aspirational secretary.

However, enthusiasm was not only a desirable mood for practising consumerism in the 1960s, it was also part of the 'emotional regime'[59] propitiated by the dictatorship, in which happiness was a core emotion. The ideal of unquestioning enthusiasm was part of the regime's techniques to delete the traumatic memory of the civil war and to instil a naïve and uncritical attitude towards the family as the basic social institution in the regime's population biopolitics.[60]

Apacergil was offered as useful for hallucinatory processes as well as alcoholism, drug addiction or even pain and vomiting and was advertised in a highly commercial style. The ad showed a woman in what looked like a Hollywood horror-movie setting, with a spectral light illumining her terrified face behind bars. In contrast to the terrifying face in the picture, the drug promised to create a smoother mood and docile collaboration for treatment.

The psychological and pharmacological medicalization of women was sharply critiqued by North American feminist Betty Friedan in *The Feminine Mystique* (1963). Friedan denounced the mental health effects of postwar social changes on women's subjectivities, rather than accusing women of having inherent psychological 'complexes'. Surprisingly, her work was quickly translated into Spanish (1965), probably thanks to the influence of the Catholic feminist and tennis laureate, Lilí Álvarez, who was deft at navigating the prohibitions of the regime. In the prologue to the Spanish edition, Álvarez endorsed the author's arguments against the excessive sexualization of women in Freudian theories and defined Friedan as a supporter of family values.[61]

Álvarez highlighted Friedan's words regarding the 'sexual sell' strategy used in consumerist society. This strategy made women, who were responsible for some 75 per cent of all purchases, simultaneously 'sexy and domestic' having attained happiness through the acquisition of commodities. After advances in women's liberation in previous decades, 'the feminine mystique' that confined women to their homes in the 1950s and 1960s undermined self-satisfaction to the point of despair, questioning their own role. The Spanish feminist argued that the problem was not exclusive to North American society. In fact, she believed that the normalization of women's lives, lived 'in thrall to male protectiveness', was, in reality, a form of alienation caused by submissiveness.

'Pathologies of lifestyle' and the balanced man

Spanish advertisements for psychotropic drugs often portrayed middle-aged male figures expressing anger or tension, sometimes in confrontational attitudes related to work situations. The diffusion of psychotropic drugs took place in a changing work space within the new expanding corporate culture. It is helpful to recall the portrayal of vulnerable and solitary masculinities, ill-adapted to Taylorism, anonymity, boredom and lack of success in North American movies of the time such as *The Apartment* (Billy Wilder, 1960). In contrast to personalized human relationships in family businesses, the new, cold and often cruel environment of the big managerial businesses was the perfect target for the new drugs to combat stress, apathy and depression. In Spain, between 1960 and 1975, jobs in the primary sector decreased considerably in contrast to the service sector, which increased by 114.7 per cent. Industrial automatization was introduced by multinationals, prompting a new work culture in the cities.[62] Historians Carr and Fusi explain this shift: 'the new slogans of the 1960s were rationality, efficiency, the maxims of the world of the impersonal, competitive business corporation rather than of the comfortable world of family connection and personal favour'.[63] It is not adventurous to suggest that these changes also started to challenge traditional male roles in Spain as represented in advertisements.

Some drugs prescribed to men dealt with the pathologies of 'lifestyle', usually represented as *surmenage* or 'burnout'. Therefore, anxiety was advertised as the most frequent disease of 'civilized man'. Distovagal, a drug produced in Spain, used a simple story in which a perfectly tidy and composed man (shaved, dressed and clean and portrayed only from the neck up) seemed in need of self-confidence and a more relaxed temperament. Interestingly, the drug was also prescribed for increasing trust in doctors during the clinical relationship. The targeted symptoms implicitly pointed to an idealized masculinity that was composed of unstoppable activity while, at the same time demanding tranquility, clarity of mind and the ability to 'enjoy life' at every moment. Although advertised as a drug to increase stamina, Distovagal was a hypnotic-barbiturate with sedative and addictive effects. It was sold in Spain until 1998. Amphetamines, such as Simpatinas were probably used by upper-class young people, as shown in the film *Brillante porvenir* (Vicente Aranda, 1965), to enhance stamina during parties. Witnesses of those years also remark that 'Centraminas' were advertised at the hall of the School of Medicine in Barcelona addressing medical students. The package leaflet recommended that they were used in jobs that required being awake for long hours, such as those undertaken by soldiers, policemen and truck drivers.[64]

Paliatín, another Spanish drug, also seemed to help in accomplishing (or making bearable) an active and entrepreneurial lifestyle. Apparently, it would help in dealing with the contradictory requirements detailed above. Its publicity transmitted an ideal of 'strong' masculinity which associated physical with psychological strength.[65] Paliatín promised to suppress anxieties and to empower the 'classical' man to overcome gracefully his challenges and dilemmas. The opposite side of this idealized masculinity, the 'undesirable' man, anxious, hesitant and full of dilemmas, would disappear under the effects of the pills. In the ad, a male torso appears tied up with rope to emphasize how any strong man could be gripped by modern social tensions and suffer pain and affliction. 'Paliatín estimulante', another presentation of the same product, included a stimulant component in its formula. In this case, a clean-shaven, formally dressed man seems to be suffering from a severe weariness that he was probably alleviating by stopping at a bar on his way back home from work. The publicity message suggested that new drugs worked better than alcohol.

It is not strange that the energetic requirements of the active modern man exacerbated the need for proper sleep.[66] Amytal (Amobarbital), a barbiturate, commonly known as the 'truth serum', and used to treat shell-shock, was advertised as 'the secret to a peaceful sleep'. The ads portrayed a modern city in rush hour, inhabited only by men with active and purposeful lives. The advertising strategy opened the drug to a wide range of masculinities. Therefore, the potential consumer also seems to be the common middle-aged white-collar worker, instead of the elegant, good looking and successful businessman. Every man was in need of reparative sleep to recover stamina and avoid *surmenage*. Though these representations of urban life contrast with the idiosyncratic laziness and *siestas* often attributed to Spaniards supposedly living in a slow anti-modern society, they suggest changes in sleeping patterns that would deserve further research.

Other companies sold their products by promising a recovery of personal balance and energy. Meratran (Pipradol), a drug made by Merrell and commercialized in Spain by Industrial Ibérica Químico Farmacéutica, advertised the idea that 'normal' masculinity required balance. In its ad, a man dressed in black, with a derby hat and cane, walks above a graphic representing his mood. The drug treated emotional lability and euphoria.

Betavida (vitamin B12 produced in an Italian laboratory) and Clomiazol used classical images of masculinity (medieval and biblical) to convey their persuasive messages. Betavida represented the emotional regime of the time with a medieval knight in a buoyant mood and ready to fight. This light-hearted representation of struggle and protection in modern life also suggested the need for vitamins to enhance the body's defenses. Less joyously defensive, though equally classical, was the persuasive strategy of Clomiazol, an antihistamine produced in Spanish laboratories (J. Navarro). A biblical masculine figure riding a winged horse handling a stick with a coiled serpent (the symbol of pharmacy), appeared to deal with and tame a complex nervous system, pictured more as an intricate enemy than as an essential part of our human bodies.

Representations of anxiety or anger were not always kindly symbolic. Explicit scenes of male confrontation were used to advertise Miltown. Instead of a fearful and depressed face, the scene describes a furious dispute between two men dressed in suits. Their angry faces tinted with rage were tagged with the terms 'tension and anxiety'.

Even in the era of consumerism, this confrontational model of masculinity was probably less censured in Spain than in the US, where the use of mood stabilizers expanded along with the growing culture of 'coolness' which became almost idiosyncratic for the middle classes during the 1960s.[67] Stearns has shown how the expression of jealousy was progressively considered childish for a more generally permissive sexual culture. This probably reduced confrontations between men. He also argues that the regulation of managers' bad-tempered behaviour was essential for the new work culture. For Spain, further research seems necessary to ascertain how far the contention of rivalries was also taking place, two decades after the civil war, when cruel repression was

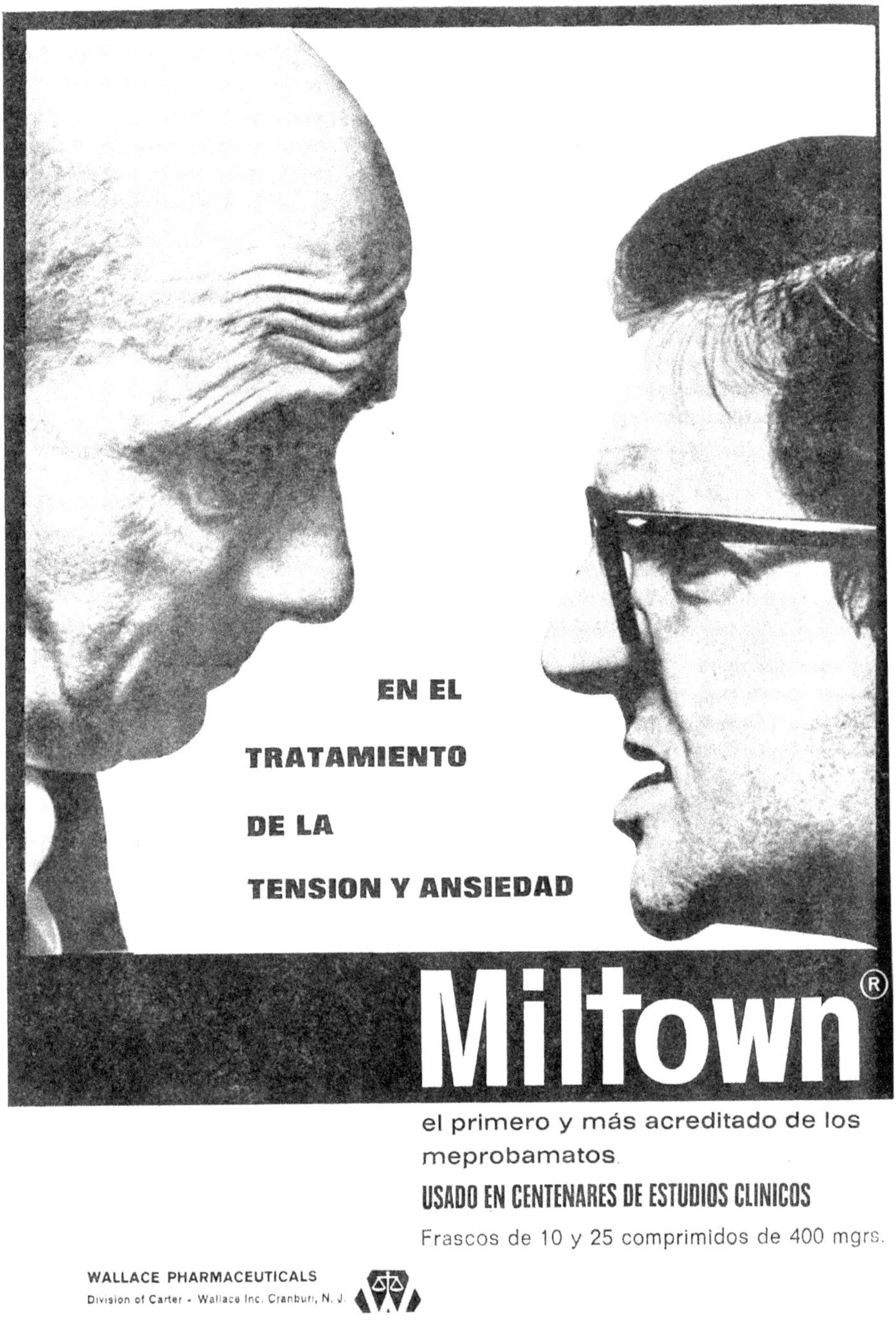

Consumerism, Gender Diversity and Moralization of Sexuality in the Iberian 1960s

Figure 3.2 Miltown, *Archivos de Neurobiología* 34.2, 1971.

still a common political feature. Some fictional pieces, such as *Tormenta de verano*, written by Juan García Hortelano in 1962, reveal how attitudes towards the management of jealousy were already experienced by the upper-middle classes.[68]

As Perich's vignette from *La Vanguardia* (22 September 1971) shows, money – and its meaning, the expectations of consuming and the stimulation of desire – seem to share with psychoactive drugs the capacity to temper irritating feelings, including political discontent. But, in contrast to the emphasis of publicity on the effects of modern life in mental health, Spanish doctors emphasized neuroticism as a genetic and moral, rather than social, problem. In a talk at the Regional Branch of the Royal Academy of Medicine, Francisco Alonso Fernández, Chief of the Department of Psychiatry in La Coruña, defined psychiatry as a 'science of moral responsibility'.[69] On one hand, he looked at the 'neurotic' with suspicion, as a hypocrite and pretentious liar; consequently it did not make sense to talk of the patient as 'suffering from neurosis', but to blame him for being a 'neurotic man'. On the other hand, he recognized that 'the man of atomic time' was negatively affected by 'social instability', an 'over-abundance of psychological stimuli' and a narcissism resulting from modernity. When coping with social experiences of vulnerability and isolation, this man will either become despotic and antisocial or docile. As for the treatment, Alonso was contradictory and opposed to 'getting rid of' the neurotic with a prescription of pills. He also defended a religious approach to psychotherapy by increasing personal contact between doctor and patient.

As we have shown, minor tranquilizers and stimulants used gender figures in their publicity, more often than anti-hallucinatory drugs which often used a queer representation of gender. Clorpromacin, produced in Barcelona by laboratories Bama, was prescribed for severe melancholic and manic schizophrenia and also for minor psychosomatic diseases. Its 'spectrum' covered a wide range of psychological situations for both sexes. Paralleling its wide spectrum, the ad represented an abstract drawing evoking the Rorschach test. Closerpil, similar but with added Reserpin, used a striking, almost psychedelic image of a head with an ambiguous gender assignment. This bizarre drawing recalls the hallucinating mind, with long and curly hair representing plants or waves, and filled with images of animals, houses and objects.

But ambiguity about gender and sex seemed to be more than mere advertisement technique. Anxieties about changing gender roles and sexual orientations were also present in the clinic. The psychiatric treatments for these ambiguities included unproven brain surgery. The surgeon S. Obrador and his colleagues (1967) reported on a patient with hallucinatory ideas who apparently hated his 'effeminate face'. He believed it was caused by a 'genital weakness', despite the fact that his doctors considered his face 'completely masculine'. The therapeutic process was terrifying. The patient was very conscious of his medical process and rejected treatment with neuroleptics as ineffective. He was therefore treated over the decade with insulin-induced coma, electroshock, anterior cyngulectomy (1961) and bilateral lobotomy (1962). Finally, the patient accepted the surgical stimulation of his hypophysis as advised by his local doctor,[70] but later threatened his doctor because the surgery 'had not resolved the abnormality of his

Figure 3.3 $, Perich, *La Vanguardia* from 22 September 1971.

face'.[71] Though the patient could nowadays be identified as a sexually diverse, possibly transgender person, at the time the clinical tag 'schizophrenia' helped doctors to avoid any sexual implications and to interpret the patient's suffering as a hallucinatory state. At the time of this surgical intervention, the regime was examining ways of controlling and eliminating those marked as 'socially dangerous' for society's delicate equilibrium. Homosexuality, in particular, was targeted as potentially disruptive and was included as a socially dangerous category within legislation that would come on stream in 1970, the Law of Dangerousness and Social Rehabilitation.[72]

Consumption and Gender in Dictatorship and Disciplined Democracy

Modernizing gender advertising in Portugal

In this section we chart the representation of new medicines related to psychiatric conditions as advertised in three Portuguese medical journals. These examples are considered from two principal standpoints; first, the modernity or otherwise of the representation of the drug; second, the gendered aspects of the representation. The three journals surveyed, while all dedicated to medicine, had different histories and different ways of engaging with the profession. The journal *Acção Médica*, published in Lisbon, was the journal of the Catholic Doctors' Association and constituted a generally conservative voice of medicine. *Coimbra Médica, Revista Mensal de Medicina e Cirurgia* hailed from the country's historic university city and was conservative but not overtly Catholic in its stance. The third journal studied, *Jornal do Médico*, based in Oporto, was an outstandingly modern publication, less traditional in its graphics, more adventurous in its contents and with a strong 'social medicine' bent, without necessarily professing Catholic interpretations.

The number of advertisements for drugs within *Acção Médica* (surveyed from 1960 to 1965) was far fewer than in the more practitioner-oriented and modern journals *Coimbra Médica* and *Jornal do Médico*. In the first case, the approach was basic, unartistic and generally informative rather than evocative or displaying a 'hard-sell'. There were reviews of vaccines, such as the quadruple vaccine for diphtheria, tetanus, whooping cough and polio, drawn from news in foreign journals, for example, *The Lancet*. The advertisement for the tranquilizer 'Meprofene', guaranteed to bring about a 'good sleep', was textual and detailed the composition and therapeutic qualities of the drug. The advertisement for an antibiotic, Omnacilina, made by the Portuguese Azevedos, was again textual, although enhanced by a small image – a cluster of rhomboids of various orange-red colours. Adverts were primarily scientific, cool in their tone and less emotive than in other journals.

In *Coimbra Médica* (surveyed from 1965 to 1969) and the *Jornal do Médico* (analysed from 1961 to 1966), the style and contents were markedly different. In the first of these, advertisements for sedatives, irritability, psychosomatic disorders, digestion problems, tranquilizers and headache pills, as well as for the contraceptive pill dominated. In the second journal, the categories were broader, including protein drinks, antidepressants, solutions for lethargy, depression, insomnia, stress and tension and pain relief. At first sight, we can deduce that, given the fact that our attention has been focused on similar periods for these two journals, there was a difference between them in respect of the kinds of illnesses or complaints addressed. Such a difference, in turn, shows what was effectively a distinct editorial ethos, with the *Jornal* clearly a more 'modern' journal, attending to 'lifestyle' issues such as emotional disturbances, sexual performance, different mental states and tension. In addition, these different maladies were also inflected along gendered lines, especially in the case of the *Jornal*, more open to the use of images.

A further difference in advertisement style can be seen between national and foreign or international journals. In *Coimbra Médica* publicity for the Portuguese-produced sedative Nersan by Laboratórios Fidelis was textual and organized horizontally and vertically. The advertisement for the Roche product, Valium, by contrast, was more evocative, used text that went beyond the contents or qualities of the drug ('a new way of obtaining psychosomatic relaxation and calm'), and was artistically more daring. Similarly, Sandoz's Melleril was presented as a solution for psychosomatic disorders of a cardiovascular nature with the image of a middle-aged man tugging at his shirt in discomfort while a female figure looks on with concern. A further advert for Valium employed an image of what appears to be a female body, internal organs being affected by waves of 'stress' coming from the modern, built-up world, with text alongside stating that the human being is immersed in emotional irritants that can only be solved by taking Valium. Portuguese-based companies did not only employ strict textual advertisements, however. The publicity for Atarax, to be employed against irritability, depicted an androgynous form alive with what appear to be electrical pin-pricks denoting nervousness against a red background.

While adverts in the Spanish medical press over this period were more clearly gender-inflected, similar implications were present in much pharmaceutical publicity in the Portuguese case. One advert suggested the purchase of Wyeth's Serenal for nervous dispositions for both men and women; others were more clearly directed towards one sex. An advert for the contraceptive pill was evidently addressed to women, showing not only the modernity of the journal but also a break with standard Catholic teachings on fecundity and reproduction.[73] Sandoz displayed how taking its own Calcibronat allowed for calm, collected control and depicted a woman coolly threading a needle superimposed on the image of her face.

Finally, headache pills made by the German Arznei-Mittel could be called upon as a remedy for the stresses of everyday life for both sexes. In accordance with Erving Goffman's analysis of gender in advertisements, women were generally in the background and, when advertisements were directed towards men's conditions, in a subordinate position to them. If women were in the foreground, they were, like the needle-threading woman, engaged in 'typical' feminine pursuits.[74] The behavior displayed in the advertisements captured daily interactions and, in turn these representations structured gender relationships.[75] In the Portuguese case, those gendered differences were marked in respect of the 'neurochemical selves' that were being forged in the 1960s in a traditional society which was undergoing a number of what Fernando Rosas has termed 'invisible changes'.[76]

As stated above, the contents of the *Jornal* were decidedly more modern and more diverse in respect of the maladies alluded to. Although some adverts were mainly textual, such as one for Proticeril, a vitamin supplement, they were often in colour and shaded with different boxes, many at an oblique angle. Others, for antidepressants, such as the Geigy advert, employed a different font and imagery not far from an abstract painting with different shades of grey. A large proportion of advertisements in the *Jornal* were for antidepressants, sedatives and tranquilizers or treatments for insomnia; all diseases of the modern, Westernized human psyche. This type of advert also had its gender dimension. Even though some advertisements were directed at men, such as the sedative

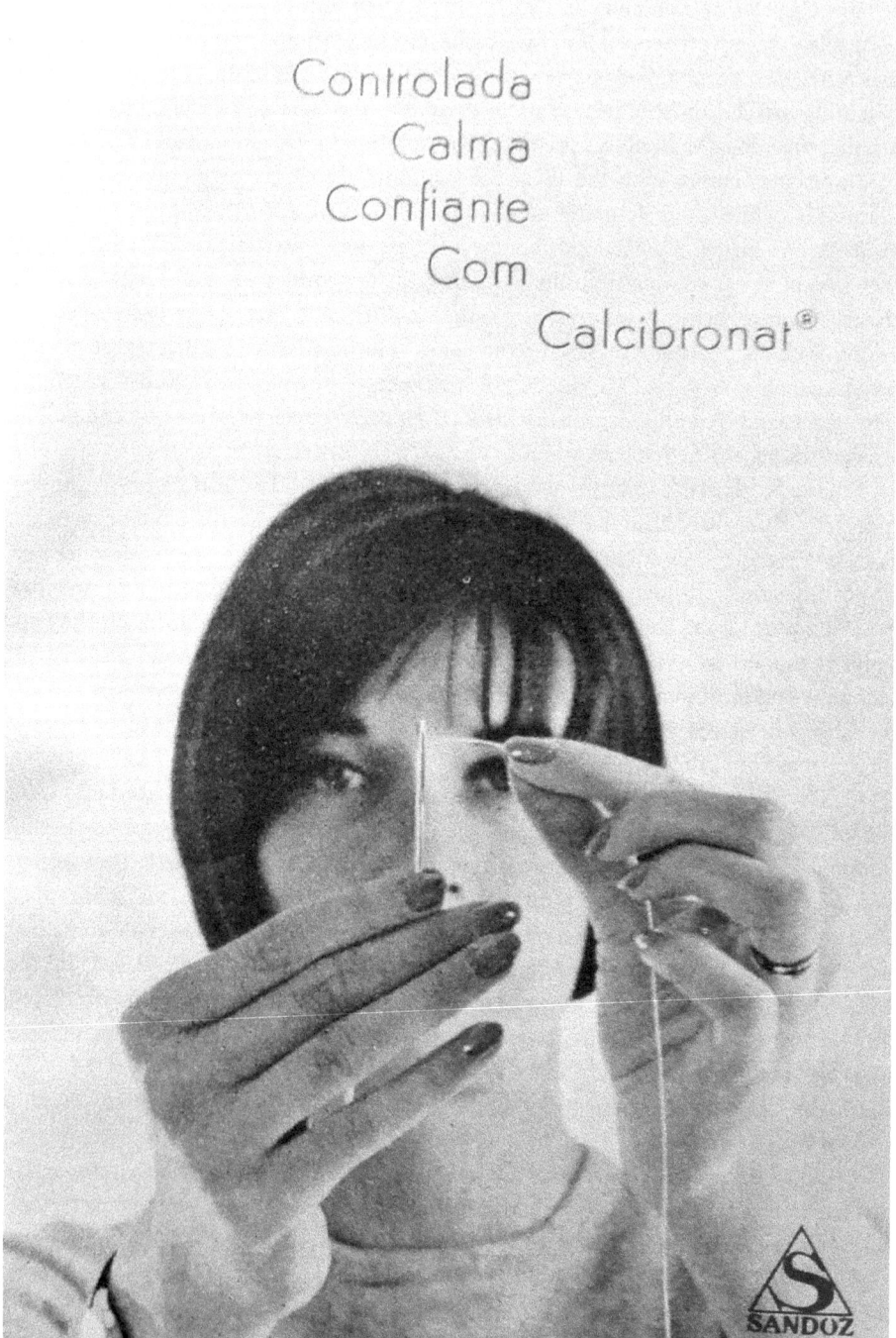

Figure 3.4 *Coimbra Médica*, XV, June 1968.

Hemicral produced by the Portuguese Fidelis (a man dressed in typical Portuguese attire lounges on a vessel 'all at sea'), in the case of the *licor* to remedy sexual dysfunction and neurasthenia, or in the case of a hormonal treatment of testicular extracts (with the image of a cockerel dominating the advert), most of the advertisements for depression were directed towards women. Multiple national and foreign advertisements underscored this association throughout the 1960s. With such a proliferation of illnesses and their gendered dimensions, Portugal confirmed its entry into the materialist, consumerist Westernized model of both medicine and society.

The scientific morality of sexuality in Portugal

It was perhaps in Portugal that the control of sexuality by a particularly conservative medical class was most evident. At the same time, this class also portrayed certain modernizing tendencies, particularly those emerging within Catholicism itself. In many cases, the Catholic medical position on gender and sexuality was not simply obscurantist but instead 'scientific', although highly influenced by moral and religious constraints. Bearing in mind the uneasy and uneven process of modernization in Portugal, we need to ask, how did such official traditionalism affect consumerism and, in particular, the reception of new medical treatments and medications? What was the relation between anti-modernity, consumerism and medicine?

Medicine, like other highly trained areas such as the legal profession and the university world, was a deeply conservative field in Portugal in the 1940s and 1950s. 'Although different journals placed different emphases on the scientific and the social realms, and despite a strong positivist leaning dating from the late nineteenth century, the political circumstances of the time meant that radical medical solutions to societal problems were not often entertained and, if they were, were barely implemented by the regime.' The stance taken by our first source, *Acção Médica*, is indicative of this social conservatism, albeit from a particularly strong Catholic perspective.

A number of articles from the 1960s represent this position. Writing about medicine and morality, Abel Sampaio Tavares of the Oporto Faculty of Medicine squarely asserted the moral authority of Catholicism.[77] The fundamental linkage between medicine and human activity was made by Sampaio Tavares in respect of 'behaviour and social and family equilibrium' and it was the recent developments in medical techniques that were acknowledged to place such a relation in jeopardy because 'Man is not morally prepared to receive the benefits of material civilization that can be enjoyed today'.[78] This lack of moral ability was confirmed by the existence of war, crime and the rise of an unspecified set of 'perversions'. The border between good and bad had been, in the words of Alex Carrel cited by Sampaio Tavares, lost among the 'fog of ideologies'. However, even among non-Catholic medics, the distance between technique and morality was not generally extensive. Catholicism's role in shoring up this threatening divide was clear: Christ had reaffirmed ancient medico-moral codes and, more recently, Popes Pius XI and Pius XII, the latter by means of *Casti Conubii*, had secured this relationship.[79]

However conservative in sexual matters, Sampaio Tavares took what could be qualified as a progressive Catholic stance on new technical advances: these should not be despised but the art of medicine should not be depersonalized and should always be based on human solidarity. Doctors, especially Catholic ones, should be guided by the alleviation of suffering and medics should be careful not to be 'dazzled' by technical advance. Further, many physical and psychosomatic illnesses arose because of the transgression of biological laws and those governing natural morality.[80] In this way, Sampaio Tavares made it clear that doctors should not be opposed to medical advances, but should be aware that technique could do little against personal and social moral decay.

The desire to reassert the intimate relationship between medicine and morality was evident in the brief highlighting within the journal of the commemoration of twenty-five years of labour 'in a field that, because of its focus on the body alone, is often tempted to forget the spirit'.[81] As had been the case earlier in the twentieth century in enlightened or progressive Catholic circles, the issue of human sexual relations was a significant area of Portuguese Catholic medical attention and it is here that differentiated and carefully choreographed gendered relations came clearly to the fore. A summary of the Oporto Faculty of Medicine dissertation by Ana Rosa Almeida on moral problems in the field of gynecology considered the issue from eight angles including sex education, the pre-nuptial certificate, neo-Malthusianism, artificial insemination and prostitution.[82] Other articles focused on whether chastity was harmful or not.[83] By arguing that there were differences between humans and animals in respect of the bodily functions, it was stated that human chastity was neither impossible nor harmful. Indeed, sexual intercourse among humans only gained social significance within the bounds of matrimony.[84] Any dangers presented by chastity, such as the descent into sodomy, had more to do with a fixation of the instinct at infantile level or were as a result of certain pathologies, rather than as a result of abstinence. Essential in order to guide society through such a conundrum was an alliance of expert voices involving doctors, educators and priests.

Although sexual relations within matrimony was one area of Catholic doctors' competence, it was particularly with respect to youth that their mission was clearly stated. A battleground both in Portugal and Spain between secular advocates and Catholic teachers, the debate on youthful sexuality often presented international dimensions.[85] Such was the case in *Acção Médica*. An original document written in German, translated into French and then subsequently into Portuguese, drawn up by the German Episcopate, is indicative of this transnational flow of ideas. The 'sexual problem of youth', the document noted, was to be resolved by the acknowledgement that human beings had been created by God as two distinct sexes with different personalities.[86] It was up to each young person to take on board the different characteristics of his or her own sex and make them reality. Sex needed to be viewed as a gift from God and, by means of correct sex education, should be practised properly within matrimony. Any contact between girls and boys needed to be overseen with care in order to enable 'healthy encounters between the two sexes'.

Conclusions

Although analysing and writing about contradictions is always a difficult task, especially with lack of historical knowledge, it is necessary to examine their suggestive historical effects. The institutions and gender ideologies of both dictatorial regimes were evidently still at work in Iberian societies during the 1960s and attempted to attenuate the effects of modernity. However, as we have explored in this chapter, the advent of 'miniature consumerism' facilitated a diversification of gender roles in these societies, affecting both women and men, and a set of challenges to the regimes, some of which were absorbed more easily than others. The flourishing of contradictions, many of which were incipient and, particularly in the case of Portugal, quite modest, did allow for all-important ongoing historical change in social, political and gender terms.

The marketing of 'neurochemical selves' in psychiatric journals used everyday work and domestic situations to normalize drug consumption, while playing down or ignoring the risks of regular medication. Medical discourse in both countries attempted to regulate and 'scientifically' moralize the new ambiguities and challenges in sexuality that gender diversification provoked. More than this, both the advertisement and the production of new medicines were contingent upon the new consumer lifestyles – with all their contradictions and stresses – that the 1960s brought about. This was particularly the case for Spain, where these changes were more widespread and affected a greater swathe of the population. In Portugal, divisions between the socioeconomic classes were greater and more immobile; in Spain, tourism and the influx of other countries' mores produced tensions in the regime that would eventually become difficult to contain.

The gender roles promoted by the managerial work culture introduced new anxieties in the modern gendered subjectivity that had to adapt to dictatorial as well as new emotional regimes arising in Europe and further afield, particularly in the US. Advertisements typified these gender roles and, notably in Spanish medical advertisements, responded to American marketing strategies, while in Portugal a national pharmaceutical industry was still very strong. As Baudrillard claimed in 1970, the dichotomy between the sexes crystalized in two advertising models that were also reproduced in psychoactive drugs: the feminine model of 'being pleasing' and the masculine model of 'being demanding'. For women, as part of this *complaisance*, the options ranged from submissiveness at work to the docile assumption of overwhelming domestic work and a focus on antidepressants, particularly in Portugal, became customary. For men, the prescription was a combination of balance and aggressive ambition. Although stress may have been regarded as a male problem, depression and insomnia, for Portugal in particular, largely, but not exclusively, were seen as female maladies.[87] Either way, the message for both men and women was that drugs, as much as money, were able to 'vaccinate' against the emotional reactivity caused by the contradictions of modernity in changing traditional, religious but still dictatorial regimes.

Historiography has universalized a temporality of contemporary history but this is not necessarily applicable to all societies. This is particularly true for the so called 'sixties'. In this chapter we attempted to problematize this temporization, deepening the historical knowledge of a period to show the contradictions of modernity inside Iberian societies during a decade that deserves further attention.

Notes

1. J. Baudrillard, *The Consumer Society: Myths and Structures* (Los Angeles/London: Sage, 1998 [1970]).
2. A recent exception is A. Ribeiro de Menezes and C. O'Leary (eds), *Legacies of War and Dictatorship in Contemporary Portugal and Spain* (Bern/Oxford: Peter Lang, 2011).
3. See I. Saz, 'Mucho más que crisis políticas: el agotamiento de dos proyectos enfrentados', *Ayer* 4, 2007, 137–63, where the anti-liberalism of Spanish fascism, the product of an interpretation of nineteenth- and twentieth-century history, is contrasted to the position of (Catholic) reactionary nationalism that rejected everything that 'European modernity' had brought from the sixteenth century onwards (p. 142). Both tendencies fought for hegemony under the Franco regime; eventually, the fascist model lost out. On the Portuguese regime, see A. Costa Pinto, *Salazar's Dictatorship and European Fascism: Problems of Interpretation* (Boulder, CO: Social Science Monographs, 1995), and M. Loff, 'Dios, Patria, Autoridad: la iglesia católica y la fascistisación de los regímenes ibéricos, 1933–1945', *Historia Contemporánea* 25, 2013, 49–66.
4. T. Gallagher, *Portugal: A Twentieth-Century Interpretation* (Manchester: Manchester University Press, 1983), 117–20. For the Franco regime, see A. Cenarro, 'Violence, surveillance, and denunciation: social cleavage in the Spanish Civil War and Francoism', in P. Spierenburg, C. Emsley and E. Jonson (eds), *Social Control in Europe, Volume Two, 1800–2000* (Columbus, OH: Ohio State University Press, 2004).
5. D.L. Raby, *Fascism and Resistance in Portugal: Communists, liberals and military dissidents in the opposition to Salazar, 1941–74* (Manchester/New York: Manchester University Press, 1988), 2.
6. Ibid., 5.
7. A.P. Ferreira, 'Home bound: the construct of femininity in the Estado Novo', *Portuguese Studies* 12, 1996, 133–44 (here 133). The reference to 'Portugueseness' is taken by Ferreira from Ramos de Ó, J., 'Salazarismo e Cultura', in F. Rosas (ed), *Portugal e o Estado Novo (1930–1960)* (Lisbon: Editorial Presença, 1992), 394.
8. D. Birmingham, *A Concise History of Portugal* (Cambridge: Cambridge University Press, 2nd ed., 2003), 166; T.C. Bruneau, 'Church and State in Portugal: crises of cross and sword', *Journal of Church and State* 3, 1976, 471–72.
9. M. Braga da Cruz, 'As elites católicas nos primórdios do salazarismo', *Análise Social* 116–17, 1992, 547–74 (here 549–52).
10. I. Freire, *Amor e sexo no tempo de Salazar* (Lisbon: A Esfera dos Livros, 2010), 76–8.
11. On the broader European picture, see G. Bock and P. Thane (eds), *Maternity and Gender Policies: Women and the rise of the European welfare states, 1880s–1950s* (London: Routledge, 1991).
12. A. Ferro, *Salazar. Portugal and her leader*, trans. H. De Barros Gomes and J. Gibbons (London: Faber & Faber, 1939), 235.
13. For further analysis, see A. Adão and M.J. Remédios, 'A narratividade educativa na 1ª fase da governação de Oliveira Salazar. A voz das mulheres na Assembleia Nacional portuguesa

(1935–1945)', *Revista Lusófona de Educação* 5, 2005, 85–109. More generally, see A. Cova and A. Costa Pinto, 'Women under Salazar's dictatorship', *Portuguese Journal of Social Science* 2, 2002, 129–46.

14. I. Pimentel, 'Women's organisations and imperial ideology under the *Estado Novo*', *Portuguese Studies* 18, 2002, 121–31; I. Alves Ferreira, 'Mocidade Portuguesa Feminina. Um ideal educativo', *Revista de História das Ideias* 16, 1994, 193–233.

15. Pimentel, 'Women's organisations', 123, citing Decree 28,262 on the establishment of the MPF.

16. A. Taylor Allen notes that authoritarian regimes mobilized women 'by politicizing the home and its domestic and reproductive activities'. *Women in Twentieth-Century Europe* (Houndmills/New York: Palgrave Macmillan, 2008), 48. See also V. De Grazia, *How Fascism Ruled Women: Italy, 1922–1945* (Berkeley, CA/Oxford: University of California Press, 1992) and M. Nash 'Pronatalism and motherhood in Franco's Spain', in Bock and Thane (eds), *Maternity and Gender Policies*. For a comparative perspective, see M.S. Quine, *Population Politics in Twentieth-Century Europe: Fascist dictatorships and liberal democracies* (London/New York: Routledge, 1996).

17. Decree 18,565, 15 July 1930 (http://dre.pt/pdf1sdip/1930/07/15500/13001303.pdf). More details in I.F. Pimentel, 'A assistência social e familiar do Estado Novo nos anos 30 e 40', *Análise Social* 151–2, 1999, 477–508.

18. A.P. Ferreira 'Loving in the lands of Portugal: sex in women's fictions and the nationalist order', in S.C. Quinlan and F. Arenas (eds), *Lusosex: Gender and Sexuality in the Portuguese-Speaking World* (Minneapolis/London: University of Minnesota Press, 2002).

19. Ferreira, 'Home bound', 135–137 (quotation on 142).

20. Alves Ferreira, 'Mocidade Portuguesa Feminina', 196, citing M. Braga da Cruz, *O Partido e o Estado no Salazarismo* (Lisbon: Editorial Presença, 1988), 38–47. The 'construction phase' of the regime corresponded to 1933–45 and the 'diversification' phase took place during the years 1945–61.

21. D. Corkill, *The Development of the Portuguese Economy: A Case of Europeanization* (London: Routledge, 1999), 21.

22. T. Gallagher, *Portugal: A Twentieth-Century Interpretation* (Manchester: Manchester University Press, 1983), 137.

23. A. De Sousa, 'Os anos 60 da nossa economia', *Análise Social* 133, 1995, 613–30 (here 614–15).

24. Corkill, *The Development of the Portuguese Economy*, 25. For an overview on emigration from Portugal in this period, see I. Tiago de Oliveira, 'Emigração, retorno, e reemigração na primeira metade do século XX', *Análise Social* 184, 2007, 837–52. V. Pereira, 'Emigração e desenvolvimento da previdência social em Portugal', *Análise Social* 192, 2009, 471–510, argues that the limited 'social welfare' that was instigated in the late 1960s and 1970s came about in part as result of a regime response to emigration in light of social Catholic concerns articulated by Vatican II.

25. F. Almeida Garcia, 'A comparative study of the evolution of tourism policy in Spain and Portugal', *Tourism Management Perspectives* 11, 2014, 34–50 (Figure 1 on p. 37).

26. Ibid., 41.

27. D. Machado, *The Structure of Portuguese Society: The Failure of Fascism* (New York/Westport/London: Praeger, 1991), 32, citing C. Almeida and A. Barreto, *Capitalismo e emigração em Portugal* (Lisbon: Prelo, 1976), 97.

28. Cova and Costa Pinto, 'Women', 133.

29. Birmingham, *A Concise History of Portugal*, 179.
30. A. Cañellas, 'La tecnocracia franquista: El sentido ideológico del desarrollo económico', *Stud. Hist., Cont.* 24, 2006, 257–88.
31. T. Pavlović, *The Mobile Nation: España cambia de piel (1954–1964)* (Bristol: Intellect, 2011), 3, draws on G. Tortella, *La revolución del siglo XX* (Madrid, Taurus, 2000), 441, to discuss Spain as 'Styling itself as a society of wellbeing'. The notion of 'sociological Francoism' is so widely used that Wikipedia includes a sound definition of the term and its extended use today in different realms. See http://es.wikipedia.org/wiki/Franquismo_sociol%C3%B3gico#cite_ref-27, accessed 16 March 2015.
32. The recent history of diversity in gender roles is still part of work in progress in Spanish historiography. We are currently working on a research project funded by the Spanish Ministry of Education, analysing not only gender but emo-sexual diversity during the 1960s.
33. J. Crumbaugh, *Destination Dictatorship: The Spectacle of Spain's Tourist Boom and the Reinvention of Difference* (Albany: SUNY Press, 2010).
34. Pablo Martin Aceña, Elena Martínez, 'The golden age of Spanish Capitalism: economic growth without Political Freedom', in Nigel Townson (ed.), *Spain Transformed: The Franco Dictatorship, 1959-1975* (London: Palgrave Macmillan, 2007), 30–46; J. De la Torre, M. García-Zúñiga, 'El impacto a largo plazo de la política industrial del desarrollismo español', *Investigaciones de Historia Económica* 9, 2013, 43–53; Cañellas, 'La Tecnocracia Franquista'.
35. Pavlović, *The Mobile Nation*, 14.
36. The gender shifts brought by consumerism and the changes in corporate culture were beautifully described at the time by Richard Yates (*Revolutionary Road*, 1961).
37. S. Coontz, 'Vientos de cambio: el matrimonio en las décadas de 1960 y 1970', in *Historia del matrimonio. Cómo el amor conquistó el matrimonio* (Barcelona: Gedisa, 2006).
38. M. Martín Serrano, 'Publicidad y sociedad de consumo en España', *Cuadernos para el diálogo. Suplementos* 15, 1970, 24.
39. During the same period in France the private ownership of washing machines increased from 24 to 42 per cent and of cars from 35 to 60 per cent. A. Cazorla Sánchez, *Fear and Progress: Ordinary Lives in Franco's Spain, 1939–1975* (Chichester: Wiley-Blackwell, 2010), 149–54.
40. A. De Miguel, 'Clases sociales y consumo en España', in A. Miguez (ed), *España: ¿una sociedad de consumo?* (Madrid: Guadiana de Publicaciones, 1970).
41. M.M. Ortoll Vintró, *Todos se han ido* (Barcelona: Juventud, S.A., 1961).
42. C. Álvarez Sierra, *La ciudad de los muertos* (Barcelona: Seix Barral, 1961).
43. P.N. Stearns, *Consumerism in World History: The Global Transformation of Desire* (London: Routledge, 2006).
44. Álvarez Sierra, *La ciudad de los muertos*, 15.
45. R. Ruiz Franco, *¿Eternas menores? Las mujeres en el franquismo* (Madrid: Biblioteca Nueva, 2007).
46. A.G. Morcillo, *The Seduction of Modern Spain: The Female Body and the Francoist Body Politic* (Lewisburg: Bucknell University Press, 2010).
47. Pavlović, *The Mobile Nation*, 106.
48. J. Pérez 'Vestida Para Medrar: Rocío Dúrcal y la Modernidad por debajo de las rodillas', in J Pérez, R Cornejo Parriego, A. Villamandos (eds), *Un hispanismo para el siglo XXI. Ensayos de Crítica Cultural* (Madrid: Biblioteca Nueva. 2011), 81–101.

49. W. Mitchinson, 'Educating doctors about obesity: the gendered use of pharmaceutical', in T.P Light, B. Brookes and W. Mitchinson (eds), *Bodily Subjects: Essays on Gender and Health, 1800–2000* (Montreal: McGill-Queen's University Press, 2014).

50. M. Tungate, *Adland: A Global History of Advertising* (London and Philadelphia: Kogan Page), 200; Martín Serrano, 'Publicidad', 21.

51. Baudrillard, *The Consumer Society*, 149.

52. D. Herzberg, 'Blockbuster drugs in the age of anxiety: from Miltown to Prozac', in *Happy Pills in America* (Baltimore, MD: The Johns Hopkins University Press, 2010).

53. F. Álvarez Ude, 'Psiquiatría y Farmacología en el mundo actual', *Actas Luso-Españolas de Neurología y Psiquiatría* 19, 1960, 119–33.

54. R. Domínguez-Martín and N. Sánchez-Sánchez, 'Los diferenciales salariales por género en España durante el desarrollismo franquista', *Revista Española de Investigaciones Sociológicas* 117, 2007, 143–60.

55. Morcillo, *The Seduction of Modern Spain*, 70, 213.

56. http://en.wikipedia.org/wiki/Meprobamate.

57. http://www.aemps.gob.es/informa/notasInformativas/medicamentosUsoHumano/seguridad/2007/NI_2007-18_carisoprodol.htm

58. R.M. Medina Doménech, *Ciencia y sabiduría del amor. Una historia cultural del franquismo* (Madrid: Iberoamericana, 2013) 87–123.

59. 'The set of normative emotions and the official rituals, practices, and emotives that express and inculcate them; a necessary underpinning of any stable political regime' were examined by W.M. Reddy, *The Navigation of Feeling: A Framework for the History of Emotions* (Cambridge: Cambridge University Press, 2001), 129.

60. S. Cayuela, *Por la grandeza de la patria. La biopolítica en la España de Franco* (Madrid: Fondo de Cultura Económica, 2014).

61. L. Álvarez, 'Prólogo a La Edición Española', in B. Friedan, *La mística de la feminidad* (Barcelona: Sagitario, 1965).

62. A. González Temprano, 'La modernización del sistema productivo y la apertura al exterior', *Política y sociedad* 29, 1998, 17–37.

63. R. Carr and J.P. Fusi, *España, de la Dictadura a la Democracia* (Barcelona: Planeta, 1979), 80.

64. X. Allué, 'Pediatría social'. Blog de la Sociedad Española de Pediatría Social. 'Amfetas para el cole', https://pedsocial.wordpress.com/2012/10/15/amfetas-para-el-cole/.

65. Herzberg, 'Blockbuster drugs'.

66. M.J. Wolf-Meyer, *The Slumbering Masses: Sleep, Medicine, and Modern American Life* (Minneapolis, MN: University of Minnesota Press, 2012).

67. P. Stearns, *American Cool: Constructing a Twentieth Century Emotional Style* (New York: NYU, 1994).

68. J. García Hortelano, *Tormenta de Verano* (Barcelona: Seix Barral, 1962).

69. F. Alonso Fernández,, 'El hombre neurótico hoy', *Archivos de Neurobiología* 25, 1962, 357–73.

70. S. Obrador, D. Diersen and E. Pelaz, 'Psicocirugía en el nivel diencéfalo-hipotalámico', *Archivos de Neurobiología* 30, 1967, 275–86.

71. Ibid, 281.

72. Although we do not necessarily share all the conclusions drawn by the author, see on this law and the 'queer threat' to the regime more generally, G. Pérez-Sánchez, *Queer Transitions in*

Contemporary Spanish Culture: From Franco to La Movida (New York: State University of New York Press, 2007).

73. On debates within Catholicism on the subject of the pill, see J.T. Noonan, *Contraception: A History of its Treatment by the Catholic Theologians and Canonists* (Cambridge, MA: Harvard University Press, 1965).
74. See the discussion of Goffman's *Gender Advertisements* (1976) by P. Corrigan, *The Sociology of Consumption* (London: Sage, 2008), 70–2.
75. W.H. Courtenay, 'Constructions of masculinity and their influence on men's well-being: a theory of gender and health', *Social Science and Medicine* 50, 2000, 1385–401.
76. See N. Rose, 'Becoming neurochemical selves', in N. Stehr (ed.), *Biotechnology, Commerce and Civil Society* (New Brunswick, NJ: Transaction Publishers, 2004), cited in J. Moncrieff, 'The creation of the concept of an antidepressant: an historical analysis', *Social Science and Medicine* 11, 2008, 2346–55 (here 2346).
77. A. Sampaio Tavares, 'Medicina e moral', *Acção Médica* XXV, 1960–1, 18–29.
78. Quotations from Sampaio Tavares, 'Medicina e moral', 18 and 19.
79. Ibid., 19, 21.
80. Ibid., 25–6.
81. Anon, 'Vinte cinco anos depois ...', *Acção Médica* XXV, 1960–1, no page.
82. A.R. Almeida, 'Problemas morais em ginecología', *Acção Médica* XXV, 1960–1, 172–211.
83. M. Júdice Halpern, 'A Castidade', *Acção Médica* XXVIII, 1963, 82–104.
84. Ibid., 83–4. For a similar argument see L. Castanheira, 'Instinto sexual e Sexualidade humana', *Acção Médica* XXX, 1965, 132–9, where a purely instinctual interpretation of sexuality was rejected.
85. The debacle over the writings of Jaime Brasil in the mid-1930s illustrates this conflict. See Freire, *Amor e sexo no tempo de Salazar*, 199, 203.
86. Anon, 'O problema sexual nos jovens', *Acção Médica* XXX, 1965, 23–32.
87. This pattern would appear to coincide with other countries in a similar period. See J. Prather and L.S. Fidell, 'Sex differences in the content and style of medical advertisements', *Social Science and Medicine* 1, 1975, 23–6. This trend was followed in later years. See D.L. Kleinman and L.J. Cohen, 'The decontextualization of mental illness: the portrayal of work in psychiatric drug advertisements', *Social Science and Medicine* 8, 1991, 867–74.

CHAPTER 4
GENDER AND CONSUMER BEHAVIOUR: A PORTRAIT OF PORTUGAL IN THE 1960s
Inês Brasão

Introduction

This chapter examines how Portuguese women's magazines mediated images and values of an emerging hegemonic American culture in the 1960s, with emphasis on lifestyle, private life, advertising and gender representations. Guided by the brilliant work of Victoria de Grazia, I discuss the way in which personal and social needs were (re)imagined by the influence of a new material culture of mass consumption.[1] The *American way* was introduced to women's magazines in the 1960s through new sales techniques, new consumer habits, a growing attraction for the 'star system' and a new world of products and techniques to change body appearance. The analysis of two fundamental primary sources, from 1960 to 1970 – *Flama* and *Modas e Bordados* (*M&B*) – enables me to discuss how the visual and literary content of these magazines collided with the social and political construction of a female's role.

Firstly, I discuss how the Portuguese dictatorship shaped the image of the ideal woman through a set of institutions and rules while stressing the role of the MPF (Portuguese Female Youth) in this process. Secondly, I analyse how the conflicting traditional and modern models of femininity unfold in these women's magazines and the ways through which marketing and publicity forms that were increasingly important in these magazines helped to create a positive atmosphere around the more modernizing models and share the burden of domestic life. But that was not all. Changes in consumption patterns extended to body care treatments, fashion or food consumption, thus illuminating the increasing cosmopolitanism of city life. Cosmopolitanism was expressed in the desire to absorb everything that was considered modern. As Timothy Brennan mentioned, 'A part of the rhetoric of cosmopolitanism celebrates the opportunities created by unity.'[2] Urban consumers wanted to take part in transnational flows affecting several regions of the globe, and wanted hopelessly to follow modern trends. Cosmopolitanism was spreading through immediate consumption, multitasking and new boundaries set between the public and private spheres. A certain fascination to publicly engage in mundane experiences is present in the content of *Flama* and *M&B*: women could slowly take pleasure in life not only through domesticity but also through having a social and cultural life. So, this sort of cosmopolitan attitude is compromised with the idea of being part of a world that is interconnected.[3] As Appadurai mentions in a testimony, the first form of cosmopolitanism arises with a strong link to the idea of modernity. The desire for modernity was present in lifestyle magazines, university catalogues, in A and B movies, but also in buying American jeans.[4]

In the last part of this chapter I provide an overview of the attraction of supermarkets in the 1960s and reveal some of the major urban Portuguese consumer patterns related to music, cinema and literature. I analyse two interviews that were obtained during the course of writing this chapter. These interviews try to confront social representations with people's memories, since I firmly believe that social history cannot resign from a methodological critique of sources. It is important to recognize that there is a high risk when historical analysis attempts to deduce social practices from the interpretation of textual content. The two testimonies show the challenges in assuming that a new consumer sensibility was fashioned without resistance, even in the case of middle-class women. In the Portuguese context, access to the written press was fundamentally a privilege of the literate and urban population. This does not mean that other media (e.g. radio), did not have a role in disseminating values and trends, especially in the fields of music and advertising. But the radio did not have the same impact in developing identification processes regarding, for instance, new socially acceptable bodily expressions, as the images placed in the press and television.

Between 1926 and 1974, Portugal lived under the regime called *Estado Novo* ('New State'). In the *Estado Novo*'s dominant representations of women that were primarily disseminated through organizations like the 'Portuguese Female Youth' (*Mocidade Portuguesa Feminina*) and 'Portuguese Catholic Action' (*Acção Católica Portuguesa*), they had natural attributes, such as motherhood, affection and care that they should embody and nurture.[5] Ideally, women belonged to the private space. This moral and social pressure became a legal rule at the beginning of the dictatorship. In 1933, the 'Statute of National Work' was approved, stating that 'the work of women away from home would be controlled by special provisions in conformity with the requirements of morality, physical defence, motherhood, domestic life, education and the social good'[6, 7] It is worth noting that many of the rights of citizenship (voting, legal and commercial capacity, passports and freedom of movement) were available to women only after the revolution in 1974.[8] Socializing instances also contributed to the regulation of female behaviour. Social institutions such as the family, school and the Catholic Church played a crucial disciplinary role.

Through the analysis of the role of physical education and outdoor activities at public schools, we can identify a set of instruments that tried to discipline the female body by emphasizing certain social activities and the need to curb some natural instincts and impulses. Gymnastics, such as the 'Ling Method', were fundamental for the social construction of a new body *habitus* because it helped control attitudes and postures. Despite this fact, and among many other restrictions, young women were not allowed to display their body in sporting events.[9] Also, their bathing suits and skirts had to be modelled in accordance with Christian modesty.[10] It is not difficult to find in these official models the disapproval of behaviour such as pretence, innuendo or *coquetterie*, since such attitudes were at odds with a project that valued mores such as sanctity and duty. The search for the balance between the need to nurture some natural talents and the necessity of disciplining the female body was mainly directed at a group zof young, urban and educated females; an elite hardly educated according to Catholic principles, and not always docile, obedient and uncritical.[11] Many of these predicaments were understood by some sectors of the female population, especially the most literate, as repressive and limiting their freedom to feel and think, and they started to be rejected.

The analysis of *Flama* and *M&B* magazines allows us to understand how the idea of the woman as a model of moral virtues was constructed. Their editorial lines were based on education for 'distinction',[12] for a cultured spirit and the acquisition of domestic skills.[13] The pursuit of distinction was achieved not only by a cultivated *body ethos* but also by investing in the acquisition of cultural and social capital.[14] Their commitment to modernity was rather fragile – although it increased over time – since they reiterated the principles of conformity and the traditional definition of the female role that was predominant, mirrored in the idealized vision of women as spouses, mothers and housewives.

Flama magazine was created in 1937 and was published uninterruptedly over a forty-year period. It was originally linked to the Catholic Youth Movement (*Juventude Escolar Católica*). Its ties with the Church and the values of the *Estado Novo* were especially evident when this editorial project was founded, as it focused its attention on a number of contexts dedicated to the notion of an ideal 'physical culture'; one of the core concepts of the regime. The use of the concept of physical culture is constructed and is particularly relevant to the first two decades of Salazar's rule. It is a notion commonly used by the MPF to highlight the adopted assumptions that guided the physical and moral education programmes pursued by the *Estado Novo*.[15]

Between 1940 and 1960, *Flama* became increasingly interested in the coverage of social events, news and the careers of public figures. In 1964, *Flama* reaffirmed that it was inspired by Christian principles, repudiating crass sensationalism or the sexualized content that other journalistic publications used as 'bait to increase circulation'.[16] Despite avowing its principles and being more adept at creating competent housewives than *cocquetes*, the magazine was open to a permanent updating of popular culture icons. In fact, it emerged as a channel to promote a national artistic class linked to music and theatre, as well as cinema and literature. Simultaneously, its editorial resources included a group of individuals who became journalistic and political references – namely Sarsfield Cabral (Minister of Foreign Affairs between 1985 and 1987), Cáceres Monteiro (co-founder of weekly newspaper *O Jornal* and magazine *Visão*) and Beça Múrias (who had a very strong presence in the various phases of Portuguese journalism). In 1948, *Flama* sold 17,000 copies per week. Between 1967 and 1971 it sold 30,000 copies, thus making the magazine reach its record sales and grow to sixty-eight pages with about half of them occupied by advertising.[17]

M&B was initially managed by Maria Lamas and then by Etelvina Lopes de Almeida. Both were associated with opposition to the *Estado Novo*. The case of Maria Lamas is a paradigmatic one, since she was forcibly removed from the magazine's direction by the regime and lived for a long time in political exile. Although other studies have highlighted the Portuguese print media's resistance to the American cultural hegemony, I will argue that the female press was vulnerable to those cultural interpellations.[18] *Flama* and *M&B* targeted a middle and upper-middle class audience that was open to American and Western European popular culture. A great number of covers were dedicated to Portuguese football stars, such as Eusébio, national and international pop music icons, movie actresses, actors and directors.

The greatest taboo

In the early summer of 1961, *M&B*[19] published a short article entitled 'Jeanne Moureau's Moustache'. The film *Jules et Jim*, by François Truffaut, had just been released in Parisian cinema theatres and the event was announced in publicity posters with the image of an actress, with a moustache, seated on an old stairway in the 'city of light' holding her clenched fists to her cheeks, looking up at the sky. The poster was removed shortly after, at Moureau's request. Moureau could take such a decision, despite Truffaut's immense stature, because she was already a French diva. The short notice that was published in *M&B* concluded that the residents of Paris had not been scandalized by the moustache because they were used to 'worse eccentricities'.[20]

Portuguese readers would have been unaware of the reaction to the image of a 'moustached Jeanne Moureau' but the comment capitalizes on the notion that Portugal was ill prepared to handle such 'eccentricities'. In foreign countries, 'eccentricity was normal'; this was one of the strongest ideas of the *Estado Novo*, which rested on the belief that everything abroad was out of normal parameters. In a way, the concept of normality opposed the concept of change, and so, the need to change hairstyle, clothes or traditional gender roles was assumed to be negative and eccentric.[21] If there is one iconic aspect that could represent the spirit of the 1960s it is the profusion of male and female hair. This was a generational response to the *clean-cut* model, personified by pointed shoes, ironed suits and gelled hair. These bodily signs are already visible in photographs of Portuguese troops leaving for the colonial wars, as an expression of a rebellious behaviour and as a concrete expression of an internationalization of a style that affected all social segments.[22] The mass popularity of beards and moustaches in the 1970s and 1980s was also a dominant masculine style in cinema, television and soap operas. In contrast, the reaction to Jeanne Moureau's moustache points to the existence of hidden barriers in the context of liberalizing behaviour – something which is as evident nowadays as in the past. The moustache evoked a fetish trait of masculinity and even a social construction linked to the idea of 'Latin-ness'. It is important to stress that normative masculinity was also under severe surveillance, yet less visible in everyday life.

The criminalization of male and female homosexuality during the *Estado Novo*, with penalties of up to two years internment in Mitra (criminal mental hospital), played an important role in this persecution, with resonances in the democratic period. In legal terms and in the dominant social morality, homosexuality was treated as a mental illness, as were prostitution, poverty and begging. The detention of homosexuals in the Mitra hospital ceased in 1952.²³ It is known, however, that the persecution continued until the decriminalization of homosexuality in the Portuguese Penal Code in 1982.²⁴ Thanks to the contribution of poets' and writers' oral testimonies, a plethora of historians and anthropologists are beginning to reveal contradictions between formal and informal political intervention. For instance, Octavio Gameiro states that Mario Cesariny²⁵ was repeatedly arrested in raids on urinals and subject to police humiliation in the late 1960s.²⁶ Also Yolanda Gonçalves, a retired university professor and co-founder of ILGA, reports that her uncle and classic dancer, Mário Goncalves, was arrested. 'He has often been caught in public toilets in the gardens, where undercover agents pretended to walk on the coupling.'²⁷

Flama and *M&B* reflected the panic over the 'masculinization' of women. They emphasized the fact that, 'On no pretext should we become "women that wear pants", who don't wear anything else any day of the year and who look like tomboys. [...] We should always choose skirts, with their qualities and that also confer femininity.'²⁸ The tension in (re)constructing the ideal role, the product of a greater openness to cultural references, is clearly evident in an article which questioned to what extent girls could do away with household chores, since many girls who sought to be modern viewed masculine traits as the only meaning of the term 'modern', thus becoming an amalgamation of the two.²⁹ Being masculine was also linked to the fact that women had begun to enter the labour market and that there was also great progress made in terms of access to schooling. According to official data, between 1961 and 1970, the number of women studying at comprehensive school grew from 4,885 to 11,104.³⁰ However, if the resistance to women's participation in the public sphere was quite evident during the 1940s and 1950s, it was less visible at a later stage, as a kind of response to the considerable growth in the economic significance of the female workforce; a consequence of colonial war and the social impacts of emigration. After 1960, the female workforce increased, particularly in the sectors of 'manufacturing', 'commerce' and 'public administration and defense'.³¹ In fact, the editorial line of *M&B* created a section examining work conditions for some 'feminine' professions: nurses, teachers, phone operators or stewardesses, using advanced reporting techniques such as photographs of diverse aspects of work environments that were always accompanied by first-hand accounts. For instance, in 1966 *Flama* published fashion tips for Portuguese girls so as to help them to be well dressed while attending university.³²

As mentioned at the beginning of this chapter, women's magazines were particularly interested in narratives of American and European lifestyles, especially the exploits of actors and musicians as well as those of political figures. When John Kennedy became the president of the USA, he was portrayed in *Flama* as a Catholic president and a 'great friend of Portugal'.³³ However, a closer look reveals that the focus was on *Jackie* Kennedy; a myth of a perfect wife was created around her, as someone who could combine style, charm and conformity to perfection: 'I will be a good housewife and I am happy to be one!' she was said to have confided to reporters. As for Hollywood's influence in constructing positive models of femininity, the covers featuring Audrey Hepburn are an excellent indicator of the key role this actress played in the creation of a new mind set. One only needs to recall how Hepburn's gamine short hairstyle, the *garçonnete*, created a stir. Simultaneously, the acceptance of Hepburn as a diva, celebrated in characters who adopted male traits such as the use of a cigarette holder, as in *Breakfast at Tiffany's*, cannot be understood without keeping in mind that her private life was considered to be exemplary.

M&B and *Flama* praised Hepburn for her dedication to a homely life, being 'one of the most notable examples of dignity and common sense that artists confer on the real world.'[34] Other film stars, such as Sofia Loren (whose qualities of mother and dedicated housewife were constantly admired), were also put up as female prototypes who were in stark contrast to actresses such as Marilyn Monroe or Jayne Mansfield. After successively criticizing the quality of Marilyn Monroe's work,[35] when she died *Flama* promptly classified her amid a set of Hollywood myths, 'without the courage to follow her own path' and 'a victim of herself and a moral climate',[36] reaching the extreme limits of human sadness.

The greatest fear voiced in *Flama* on how cinema could influence customs concerned Portuguese girls behaving like starlets.[37] A sarcastic article with the title 'What is a star after all?' averred that these professionals came from nothing, but were 'increasingly recognized due to their physical attributes – as models, "cover girls", airline stewardesses, beauty queens or [...] simply as maids at the mansion of millionaires in North or South Carolina'.[38] The magazine's *mépris* for social promotion by means of physical attributes is quite evident. When Brigitte Bardot visited Lisbon in May 1960, it was reported that 'Overcome by unbridled enthusiasm, film fans noisily and excitedly did their best to touch the incredible Brigitte Bardot'. Increasing its critical tone, *Flama* added: 'They imitate the gestures of actors, slavishly imitate models and copy hairstyles. Do you remember the lock of hair à la Veronica, the slim moustaches à la Errol and the recent trend for ponytails à la Bardot?'[39] The tone of disapproval that was evident in the negative view of noisy and excitable behaviour extended to other formats. Almost a year later, the same magazine, directly interpelating young girls, tried to warn them of the sad – and growing – tendency to establish standards for the beauty of female bodies. Films were having a negative influence, since they promoted an era of 'Marilyn Monroes, Lolobrigidas, Sofia Lorens, as well as Brigit Bardots or Debra Pagets', far removed from what the regime defined as the Portuguese model. The great mission of a woman's life was to be a good housemaid, wife and mother. It was close to the Nazi and fascist model of the woman of the three Ks: '*Kinder, Kuche, Kirche*' (children, kitchen, Church).[40] It is important to note that for women, sex before marriage was strictly censored as it was placed in the realm of absolute immorality. Girls could not walk alone in the streets, especially at night, without being chastised. The repression of sexuality was also demonstrated by the disapproval of certain movies. For instance, the film *Gilda* was included in the index of films censored, largely due to the 'shy' striptease of Rita Hayworth.[41]

Electric fairytale

In this section I discuss changes in private life mediated by women's magazines. We start with the following question: at what point was the consumer revolution in Portugal akin to what Victoria de Grazia described in her study on the 'Model Mrs Consumer'? Is there any similarity? In fact the proliferation of advertising for paraphernalia such as electric appliances, which helped reformulate and reduce time spent doing domestic chores, represented a big issue in the female press. These devices were the focus of an arguably visible advertising euphoria at that time. This was the case with advertisements for Singer sewing machines, which were uncommonly popular and were highly sought-after by many Portuguese women. It is important to keep in mind that in Portugal during the 1950s seamstresses were the third most representative category of female workers, only surpassed by agricultural workers and maids (this last category representing 29 per cent of the female working population).[42] Teachers appeared only in fourth place. It is also necessary not to lose sight of the incipient modernization of houses in Portugal, since electricity and sanitation were not always present in a significant number of Portuguese homes, particularly in rural areas. This fact is important when contemplating the impact of advertising devices requiring electricity in semi-urban and rural areas.

One can ask if the desire of Portuguese women to own a Singer machine was a sign of the modernization of consumption. In fact, learning how to sew was a cultural obligation for most women: it was not by free choice. By learning how to sew housewives became more self-sufficient and simultaneously shunned appeals to consumption. The machine kept women who came from underprivileged social classes away from clothing stores, shop windows and fashion trends. However, the advertising for the Singer brand in women's magazines accurately exemplifies the advertising and promotional techniques de Grazia identified in her study, namely home support and the invention of specialized techniques at sales outlets. Singer advertisements announced: 'She and He at the Singer service. She ... a smiling and amiable hostess, always ready to demonstrate, explain and advise you at any Singer centre. He ... You already know him well! He is the guardian angel of your Singer. He is a friend, who accompanies the life of each machine step by step, without ever leaving you stranded.' This service heralded a modern version of consumption in stores that was disseminated by the personalized nature of forms of assistance and interaction. In short, this is just an example to point out that access to appliance stores did not necessary mean a radical subversion of traditional female roles.

The progressive introduction of technology in domestic work, namely the 'laundry revolution', emerged in Portugal both through the appearance of washing machines in domestic spaces as well as what Roland Barthes dubbed a 'whiteness revolution'.[43] This theoretical approach is relevant because, in our perspective, the publicity for detergents and soap-powders created a kind of euphoria for domestic work and a competitiveness for the construction of a wonder world of cleanliness. According to Barthes, publicity established relations between the evil and the cure, between dirt and a given product.[44] Having home appliances represented a clear proof of happiness at home and helped to settle at least some domestic differences. Technology gave women free time, but not necessarily less time dedicated to work. This idea is clearly expressed in advertising for Miele washing machines: 'If you have a large family, you love to dance and you have lots of clothes to wash which require unexpected care ... go out! Have fun and let your Miele automatic washing machine do all the work!' Going out was allowed *after* taking care of domestic duties. The progressive mechanization of domestic chores was also evident in the growing use of other home appliances such as vacuum cleaners. In Portugal, Hoover advertised: 'It is extremely easy to use and doesn't require staff. It's useful for delicate pieces, which rough hands don't always treat with the necessary care. A Hoover washing machine is indispensable in a modern home. It easily substitutes household help and uses less soap.'[45] Washing machines, vacuum cleaners and other domestic appliances allowed housewives to get rid of the burden of a household help. The housewife became autonomous: the mistress of her space and queen of her kingdom. This is a critical aspect given that it produced a paradoxical phenomenon in the living standards of the emerging middle classes. If families no longer needed to hire domestic help, women were only artificially emancipated from their task of managing the house, since the responsibility for domestic chores was still naturally attributed to them. It is this very paradox that gave rise to a disturbing series of depictions which can be seen in various advertisements aimed at housewives; the latter appear dressed in aprons while wearing expensive necklaces or high heels while holding dusters. This was, after all, just the beginning of creating a model of a 'super woman', which became increasingly sophisticated in the world of advertising but was not necessarily a symptom of female emancipation.

With regard to consumption of a new residential style, urban Portugal was neither immune to the cult of hygiene and asepsis, nor to the social construction of a 'kitchen-laboratory'.[46] This quest for 'cleanliness' and 'sparkling white' as a symbol of purity and opposed to the idea of impurity and dirtiness, is best exemplified in advertising campaigns for clothes detergents, which promised 'sparkling whites while safeguarding your clothes'.[47] This gave rise to a new prototype unleashed by the advertising industry: the 'guilty mother': the mother who was not abreast of the main products ensuring domestic hygiene, which prevented diseases among children.

The myth of 'sparkling white' is also omnipresent in campaigns for soaps and toothpastes. An advertisement for Pepsodent that was widely published in periodicals during this time proved to be a triumphant success. Flashing sparkling white teeth, the model in the poster mimicked Hepburn's style, using dark glasses, a hat and a scarf knotted at her neck; a style that was soon followed by other stars such as Grace Kelly. Advertising was already taking advantage of the *star system* to promote mass consumption. The campaign for Lux soaps endured for quite a while, focusing on the slogan '9 out of 10 stars use Lux', and persuading Portuguese women that the seductive beauty of film stars such as Esther Williams, Romy Schneider, Jane Fonda or Elizabeth Taylor was also within their reach.

There was another area of consumption habits open to new forms of commerce. This area changed the relationship between everyday life and family routines, since it made it possible to reduce food preparation and cooking times. This was the time when the first soup cubes appeared, along with instant soup powder, milk powder and instant gruel. The last two products were promoted via arguments of ensured hygiene and food safety and were targeted at urban audiences. The milk was 'pure, healthy and processed in the most hygienic conditions'. In fact, it is important to keep in mind the context of this appeal: in most parts of the country, milk went directly from producers to vendors. Families needed to boil milk to avoid bacterial contamination. However, advertising did not just sell asepsis. It also sold concentrated energy. In the case of the Milo brand, this was an energizing mixture to be added to milk. Most of the written information that was made available in the advertisement referred to the product's chemical composition while emphasizing how it was rich in vitamins, proteins, organic phosphates and minerals. 'With nourishing Milo, you have twice the energy!' – and this appeal, of course, must be connected with the pressure to produce more and more ... Thus, with little resistance, women's magazines of the time adopted the maxim by which domestic science required discipline, method, economy, judgement and planning. In an age of electric home appliances, 'Women can live twice'.[48]

While advertisements in magazines encouraged buying ready-prepared food which could be cooked quickly, devised for the myth of the 'complete woman' (who had exemplary domestic and professional skills), it is also possible to discern a paradoxical movement in terms of expanding culinary creativity and talent by providing recipes and cooking tips. Bertha Rosa Limpo (1894–1981), author of the *Pantagruel*, the most popular recipe book in Portugal and currently in its seventy-fifth edition, was a weekly contributor to *M&B* magazine. She tried to internationalize cooking techniques and introduced flavours, utensils and techniques that went far beyond traditional Portuguese cooking.[49] Apart from her column, Rosa Limpo was also responsible for the section entitled 'Thaber consultations', where she gave advice about cosmetics and personal care while simultaneously promoting her own brand. At that time the first volume of the *Great Cooking Encyclopedia* was published by Maria Lourdes Modesto who was the first media chef in Portugal and also created the first culinary show for television, broadcast on RTP. This programme began in 1958, shortly after television was launched in Portugal, and aired for twelve years.[50]

How and where to buy

The 1960s also marked a change in consumption sites. In an environment where the first supermarkets appeared, the urban population demonstrated their superior storage, hygiene and organizational conditions. The dark face of consumerism was also highlighted, linked to thefts and the emergence of a 'hitherto unknown type of buyer', i.e. shoplifters in large supermarkets.[51] In 1962, it was estimated that every day about 5,000 consumers used supermarkets to purchase goods in Lisbon. After the first supermarket, 'Modelo' ('Model'), appeared in Portugal in October 1960,[52] and the Portuguese began to use supermarkets instead of traditional grocer shops, it became clear that the vast range of products available and a more impersonal and anonymous relationship between sellers and buyers had caught the changing taste of the urban population. Despite the visual ecstasy caused by the astonishing growth of supermarkets in Lisbon, reports on this new form of consumption noted the contrast between the areas where goods were acquired, with an attractive décor, and backstage areas, which functioned as warehouses 'funded by powerful financial groups' and where products were found – in sacks, bales and cardboard boxes waiting to be transformed into eye-catching displays. One article's tone revealed a new awareness of novel techniques being used to sell products without overlooking the fact that these marketing techniques created subaltern labour regimes, such as loaders and warehouse employees.[53]

In a previous study dedicated to understanding the role of domestic service in structures of Portuguese society during the dictatorship, memories of household staff who lived and worked in their employer's home revealed that it is necessary to be careful in diagnosing cosmopolitanism and a revolution in commercial and consumption standards.[54] According to their accounts, although the vast majority of their masters were socially distinct, most products and foodstuffs were still delivered to homes: bread, milk, vegetables, meat, petrol, newspapers or washed clothes. Even products that guaranteed the comfort of private homes, such as coal, were still sold in coal depots. Products were bought on a daily basis and only a small amount of them were stored. These first-hand accounts are important in assessing the impact of advertising and news in effectively transforming the living patterns of the middle and upper-middle classes. For example, until the end of 1950s, tasks associated with washing clothes were commonly carried out by washerwomen who went from rural areas to central squares (e.g. the Praça da Figueira, in Lisbon, collecting bundles of clothes every week that were then taken by ox-carts to peripheral areas).[55]

In 1969, *Flama* reported on the inauguration of the first mini mall in the Portuguese capital. It was housed in a basement on the Avenida da Liberdade, the city's main street, and the event represented an opportunity to highlight the advantages for consumers which were related to better prices, varied products, good quality and suitable storage, constant supplies and ambience.[56] Silva Pinto, the author of the article covering the inauguration of the first drugstore in Portugal, made it clear that these spaces were especially attractive for youth. At the height of 1969 and in the aftermath of the Paris student wars, Silva Pinto highlighted the sale of 'Make Love Not War' posters. It must be noted that Portugal was grappling with a colonial war that only ended after the 1974 revolution.[57]

It is thus possible to see signs of an emerging cosmopolitanism associated with the growing presence of consumer habits in Portuguese daily life. Although still rare, the number of automobiles had already reached one for every nine inhabitants in Lisbon. Between 1958 and 1964, television sales rose at the rate of 2,600 sets per month. In 1964 there were 150,319 legally registered television sets, about ten times more than when television broadcasts were first introduced in Portugal. Another indicator of the country's growing openness to the outside world was the substantial growth in tourist arrivals. According to Barreto, the 1960s represented the beginning of mass tourism in Portugal. The origin was essentially European (British, Germans and Spaniards).[58] These numbers increased in a very short period and had positive repercussions on the balance of payments, in the hospitality industry and in the domestic market. As a consequence of this growing industry, Lisbon started to offer 'typical restaurants' serving Portuguese food, accompanied by *fado*,[59] duly reported in *Flama*.[60]

Gender and Consumer Behaviour: A Portrait of Portugal in the 1960s

An approach to cultural consumption

One of the most popular initiatives promoted by women's magazines, particularly by *Flama*, was the creation of contests for radio and television 'queens'. To a certain extent they can be considered the genesis of the popular talent contests of our times. Then, as now, the public was responsible for choosing a winner. By sending a coupon to the magazine, the mass of voters chose their favourite singer. An analysis of popular tastes in contests while trying to elect the best light music (*música ligeira*) acts reveals two ideas that echo the age. Firstly, that radio was still capable of competing with television. It is necessary to keep in mind that television only arrived in Portugal in 1957 and hence it was still far from becoming a medium massively available in the Portuguese social space. Secondly, this competition between radio and television played an important role in creating a national 'star system'.[61] Two great rivals, Simone de Oliveira and Madalena Iglesias, vied with each other for the greatest number of covers and pages in *Flama*, as we can see below.

Their look reflected fashion trends, from hairstyles to mini-dresses and enormous sunglasses. *Flama*'s readers were tempted to participate in voting for these contests by the possibility of winning various domestic appliances, such as television sets, knitting machines or radios. Despite the growing popularity of television, radio continued to dominate for quite a while. Apart from its importance in disseminating information and sports news, especially news related to football, the everyday presence of the radio in the world of female domesticity was evident in broadcasts of the programme *Housewives Club* (*Clube das Donas de Casa* – CDC). The programme was broadcast every day for ten hours, using the slogan 'music, friendship and company'.[62]

Although paying enormous attention to national radio and television, these magazines did not neglect European and American pop music. In 1964, *Flama* dedicated its cover to The Beatles, highlighting the group's unprecedented sales of 12 million records in sixteen months.[63] It noted clashes between 400 fans and policemen, during attempts that were made to get closer to the group. It stated that the band dominated the stage, causing pathetic scenes in the crowd and proved to be a strange social phenomenon in the context of 'the wild anti-conformism sweeping through our youth'. This was reflected in the total disdain that the four lads from Liverpool demonstrated for the conventions of old England.[64] The tone of the adjectives used kept getting stronger, launching the idea that this was an artistic format dominated by an 'impulsive and creative Bohemian streak'.[65]

The 'Bestsellers' section in *Flama* provided statistics of record, books and film sales. The recording companies supplied the magazine with the aforementioned data. Unfortunately, this coverage did not encompass all years. In 1965 it was noted that The Beatles had smashed sales records in Portugal, as was the case in other countries, with The Rolling Stones also topping the charts.[66] In the field of national pop music, a song by António Mourão entitled '*Oh tempo, volta para trás*' ('Turn Back the Time') was a hit. This song topped the sales charts in 1966 despite the Anglo-Saxon pop rock influences and sold 180,000 copies.[67] Songs in French were also increasingly popular, especially music by Adamo and Mireille Mathieu. Joan Baez and Bob Dylan were the reigning favourites in the USA.[68] In 1968, the Top Ten record charts were headlined by The Beatles twice, with 'Magical Mystery Tour' and 'Hello, Goodbye'. Amidst this unmitigated enthusiasm for British pop it was nonetheless possible to find '*Aranjuez, mon amour*', sung by Amália Rodrigues, in the top sales.[69] At this time, the journalist Cáceres Monteiro published a survey entitled 'Youth and Music'. He attacked fashion trends and musical influences, affirming that the mentality of young people from certain, more privileged, classes of modern Portuguese society was a direct result of needless imports. According to his point of view, 'Portugal's bourgeois youth imitates, as it has always imitated, trends from outside'.[70] This was not an isolated argument: others had warned of a certain kind of blind bedazzlement caused by attractive posters promising films and records in scary quantities.[71] As always, young people were infantilized and their choices questioned. Another example of this so-called 'infantilization of youth' is provided by the extreme success of *yé-yé* musical movement. The *yé-yé* movement exploded in 1965 with the creation of a contest of bands that played in Lisbon, at the Monumental Theatre. This contest was organized by the National Women's Movement under the *slogan* 'youth can be joyful without being irreverent'. In fact, the *ié-ié* triggered an explosion of garage bands. The most representative example of this style was the band Quarteto 1111. Although this musical movement was not simply repressed by the government, it was far from being accepted by the elite.[72]

In terms of cinema, in 1965 *Zorba* was the biggest box office hit. In 1966, *The Sound of Music* was screened for forty-four weeks, becoming 'One of the greatest box office successes of recent times'.[73] According to the magazine's cinema critic, 'Mediocrity reigns supreme and has made 1966 a sad year for good cinema'. Portuguese audiences did not surprise sociologists and made their preferences quite clear, flocking to theatres to watch James Bond movies. Statistics for 1966 reveal that of the 14,209 seats available for matinees in Lisbon, only 4,880 were sold. At night, of 11,082 seats, only 4,900 were used. The same trend could be seen in Porto, although the evening shows had slightly larger audiences.[74] Sarsfield Cabral, a television critic, declared in January 1963 that television had a duty to educate viewers regarding their taste.

Although this is no more than a brief contribution examining cultural practices and consumption, this chapter will conclude with a summary of the memories of a couple who were teenagers at the height of the 1960s. These two testimonies are relevant since the couple's social trajectory placed them within the spectrum of the Portuguese urban middle class at the time, i.e. the main target audience of *Flama* and *M&B*. There is some juxtaposition between a set of cultural references disseminated by magazines and the cultural capital incorporated during that period. The variable of gender was not a significantly decisive factor in their choices, with the exception of the freedom to use public spaces and a broader scope of international references being always greater in the case of males. In an article published in *M&B* entitled 'The emancipation of women has dark consequences' we can find a good synthesis of this gender division in terms of what matters to private and public dichotomy. It asserts that the access of women to public life, in particular in the case of married women, is dangerous and seriously harms domestic life, not just on the material side, but also, and more importantly, in terms of morality.[75] On the other side, the ideal of masculinity was associated with the active role of rescuing and protecting the family from any kind of disorder. He was responsible for stability inside the house and she was expected to obey, cloistered in the universe of the house and the children. The men went to the coffee houses or to bars to be with their friends, or with women of 'easy life', whose company some preferred when compared to their wives. There was the group of 'honest' women whom it was necessary to marry, and the 'other'.[76] The 'other' referred to all women who had broken the 'respectability code'. Some of the most social discriminated categories were prostitutes, maids, single women and women with a job outside the 'moral standard'.

Glimpses into the reception of novel patterns of consumption

In 1966, Ana and Daniel[77] were sixteen and eighteen years old respectively. Ana attended the António Arroio School for Arts and then taught crafts until reaching retirement age. Her father worked in an advertising agency and her mother was a housewife. They had seven children but two of them did not survive. Daniel studied law and was the son of a commercial manager, while his mother was a housewife. He still practices law in a small town along the coast. They began to date when they were adolescents and grew up together as teenagers in Lisbon. Their favourite bands were British, including The Beatles and The Rolling Stones. At that time, top hits were already broadcast on the radio and both of them were avid listeners to the legendary radio programme *Atlantic Ocean*. Daniel was from a wealthier family and honed his musical knowledge thanks to the French editions of *Bravo* and *Rolling Stone* magazines. His preferences were guided by these two publications, available in kiosks and stationery stores, except when an edition was censored. They shared their musical taste in garage dances. Ana described how

> Garage dances were allowed, even for girls, because parents knew each other, but nonetheless mothers often accompanied us to keep an eye on us. We resorted to subterfuge even to go to the cinema, with the assistance of older sisters. I remember going to see a film even though I was underage, *Clockwork Orange!*, but they turned a blind eye and let me in to watch.

According to Daniel, 'Our manner of dressing was far more influenced by music than cinema.' In fact, said Ana, 'I remember that our moral studies teacher saw the marriage between Johnny Halliday and Sylvie Vartan as a positive example of love. I adored Sylvie Vartan! She was a role model for me.' Ana recalls that she wore her first pair of jeans when she was seventeen, in 1967: 'I was a hit!' None of her three sisters had a pair at that time. It was an age when make-up was still being bought in neighbourhood stores. Daniel added: 'Anyone who had money would go [and] buy clothes at Porfírios, where one could find the main international trends.' Moreover, *prêt a porter* was a mirage for most people. Evenings spent at home with the family already included television programmes. For this couple, *Cinema Nights* and the series *The Invisible Man* were indispensable. I asked them to what extent modernity had already penetrated their homes in terms of electrical appliances. However, in both cases, their families did not have any modern appliances apart from a refrigerator and an oven. 'A lucky day was when my parents took us to have dinner at the local fairground! That's what we loved', confessed Ana.

Conclusion

This study has identified a strong attraction to the American and Western European model of consumption in the editorial lines of the main women's magazines of the time in Portugal. This attraction does not mean a detachment from the prevailing structures of taste and ideal behaviour propagated by the *Estado Novo* regime. In truth, the 'Mrs Consumer' model that was defined by De Grazia was essentially a conservative one, given that the spread of American cultural patterns since the late 1940s in Portugal did not dispense with gender inequality; by contrast, the 'Model Mrs Consumer', as it appeared in Portugal at that point, involved a combination of roles which still ensured that women continued to be confined to managing domestic activities. For this reason, it was possible to have in the same editorial line a systematic appeal to the acquisition of objects of comfort and beautification without this being an obstacle to the housewife paradigm. Only behaviours that challenged domesticity and obedience in the private space were disapproved of or vanished from headlines. I have demonstrated that there was a lower resistance to consumption changes related to body care, a standardization of consumption and a mechanization of domestic work. Nevertheless, the public sphere, night-time leisure activities and sexual freedom remained male prerogatives. It was not yet an option for an irresistible empire to produce a decisive revolution in the role of women.

Notes

1. Victoria de Grazia, *Irresistible Empire, America's Advance through 20th-century Europe* (Cambridge, MA: Belknap Press, 2006).
2. Timothy Brennan, *At Home in the World: Cosmopolitanism Now* (Cambridge, MA: Harvard University Press, 1997).
3. Pheng Cheah, 'Cosmopolitanism', *Theory, Culture & Society* 23.2–3, May 2006, 486–96.
4. Arjun Appadurai, *Modernity at Large – Cultural dimensions of globalization* (Minneapolis, MN: University of Minnesota Press, 1996).
5. Inês Brasão, *Dons e Disciplinas do Corpo Feminino: os discursos sobre o corpo na história do Estado Novo* (Lisbon: O.N.G.C.C.C.I.D.M, 1999), Caderno 13.
6. Article 31° of Decreto-Lei n. 23 048, 23 September 1933.
7. Irene F. Pimentel, *História das Organizações Femininas no Estado Novo* (Lisbon: Círculo de Leitores, 2000), 39.

8. António Barreto, 'Portugal na periferia e no Centro: mudança social, 1960–1995', *Análise Social* 30, 134.5, 1995, 841–55.
9. Inês Brasão, *Dons e Disciplinas*, 140.
10. Ibid, 60.
11. Mario Belo, Ana Paula Adão and Iolanda Neves Cabral, 'O Estado Novo e as mulheres', in *O Estado Novo, das Origens ao fim da autarcia*, vol. 2 (Lisbon: Fragmentos, 1987).
12. *M&B*, 26 July 1961, 19.
13. Ibid.
14. Pierre Bourdieu, *La Distinction. Critique sociale du jugement* (Paris: Editions de Minuit, 1979).
15. *Boletim para Dirigentes da M.P.F.*, October 1953, 11.
16. *Flama*, editorial, 15 June 1964.
17. Patrícia Fonseca, 'A pioneira Flama', *Clube de Jornalistas*, July–September 2007, 54.
18. Rui Bebiano, *O Poder da Imaginação: Juventude, Rebeldia e Resistência nos Anos 60* (Coimbra: Angelus Novus, 2003).
19. *M&B* was a weekly magazine supplement of *O Século* (1880–1977).
20. *Flama*, 5 July 1961, 5.
21. Inês Brasão, *Dons e Disciplinas*.
22. Joaquim Vieira, *Portugal século XX – Crónica em Imagens, 1960–1970*, 10 vols (Lisbon: Círculo de Leitores, 1999).
23. Susana Pereira Bastos, *O Estado Novo e os seus Vadios: contribuição para o estudo das identidades marginais e da sua repressão* (Lisboa: D. Quixote, 1997).
24. Ibid; Fernando Rosa and Miguel Carmo, 'Há uma história Queer em Portugal? (Primeira Parte)', *Jornal Mapa*, 9 December 2013.
25. One of the most well-known Portuguese surrealist poets.
26. J.C. Octávio Gameiro, *Do Acto à Identidade: Orientação Sexual e Estruturação Social* (Lisbon: Instituto de Ciências Sociais/UL, 1998).
27. J. São Almeida, 'O Estado Novo dizia que não havia homossexuais mas perseguia-os', *Público*, 17 July 2009, http://www.publico.pt/sociedade/noticia/o-estado-novo-dizia-que-nao-havia-homossexuais-mas-perseguiaos-13922.57, accessed 10 May 2015.
28. *Flama*, 29 August 1962, 16–17.
29. *Flama*, 12 February 1961, 23.
30. Pordata website: http://www.pordata.pt/Portugal/Alunosatriculados+porivel+de+ensino+e+sexo-1005, accessed 10 May 2015.
31. Ana Bela Nunes, 'A evolução da estrutura, por sexos, da população activa em Portugal – um indicador do crescimento económico (1890–1981)', *Análise Social* 26, 112–13.3–4, 1991, 707–22.
32. *Flama*, 7 October 1966.
33. *Flama*, 20 January 1961.
34. *Flama*, 9 February 1962, 14.
35. Namely in *The Misfits*.
36. *Flama*, 17 August 1962.

37. This moral panic about 'juvenile delinquency' and deviance was extended to other countries in Western Europe, like Austria, Britain, Germany and Italy, as well as Australia and Japan and even the Soviet Union, as noted in Efi Avdela, 'Corrupting and uncontrollable activities: moral panic about youth in post-civil-war Greece', *Journal of Contemporary History* 43.1, 2008, 25–44. There was a widespread fear that American culture 'barbarized' teenagers through the influence of jazz, rock 'n' roll and 'sex appeal'. See Uta G. Poiger, *Jazz, Rock, and Rebels: Cold War Politics and American Culture in a Divided Germany* (Berkeley, CA: University of California Press, 2000).
38. *Flama*, 22 January 1962.
39. *Flama*, 6 May 1960.
40. Julieta de Almeida Rodrigues, 'Continuidade e mudança nos papéis das mulheres urbanas portuguesas: emergência de novas estruturas familiares', *Análise Social* 16.3, 4 5, 1983, 908.
41. Isabel Freire, *Amor e Sexo no Tempo de Salazar* (Lisbon: A Esfera dos Livros, 2010), 101.
42. Official data published by Instituto Nacional de Estatística, 1950, cit. in Inês Brasão, *O Tempo das Criadas: a condição servil em Portugal (1940–1970)* (Lisbon: Tinta da China, 2012).
43. Roland Barthes, *Mitologias* (Lisbon: Edições 70, 2012, Portuguese edition).
44. Ibid.
45. *M&B*, 30 April 1952.
46. Mira McDonald, 'Mrs Happyman to kissing chaps goodbye. Advertising reconstructs femininity', in Douglas Kellner (ed.), *Cultural Studies, Identity and Politics Between the Modern and the Postmodern Media Culture* (New York, London: Routledge, 1995), 73–102.
47. *Flama*, 734, 30 March 1962.
48. *Flama*, 24 January 1969, 60–3.
49. Isabel Drummond de Andrade and Inês Castro, 'Saberes e Fazeres de Berta Rosa Limpo. A Construção de um Êxito: o Livro de Pantagruel', *Faces de Eva* 29, 2013, 45–66.
50. *M&B*, 2 March 1960, 35.
51. *Flama*, 6 April 1962.
52. *Flama*, 'Supermercados: revolução com música de fundo', 7 March 1969, 52.
53. Ibid.
54. Inês Brasão, *Tempo das Criadas* (Lisbon: Tinta-da-China, 2012).
55. Ibid.
56. *Flama*, 'Drugstores', 1969, 20–1.
57. The Portuguese colonial war began in 1961 and ended in 1975. It involved wars with Angola, Guinea-Bissau and Mozambique.
58. Barreto, 'Portugal na periferia'.
59. *Fado* is a Portuguese melancholic song which is accompanied by a Portuguese guitar and a normal guitar. Its origins date back in 1820 in Lisbon.
60. Neves de Sousa, 'Fado, o problema da Indústria', *Flama*, 1 February 1963, 9.
61. Manuel Denis, '"O essencial e o acessório": práticas e discursos sobre a música ligeira nos primeiros anos da Emissora Nacional de Radiofusão (1933–1949)', in Nuno Domingos and Victor Pereira (eds), *O Estado Novo em Questão* (Lisbon: Edições 70, 2010).
62. *Flama*, 1966, 18.

63. *Flama*, 14 February 1964.
64. Ibid., 19.
65. *Flama*, 7 July 1967, 36.
66. *Flama*, 7 January 1966, 10–12.
67. *Flama*, 6 January 1967, 24–5.
68. Ibid.
69. *Flama*, 2 February 1968, 35.
70. *Flama*, 9 February 1968, 49.
71. *Flama*, 10 February 1967.
72. Paula Guerra, *A instável leveza do Rock: génese, dinâmica e consolidação do rock alternativo em Portugal (1980–2010)* (Porto: author, 2010).
73. *Flama*, 6 January 1967, 25.
74. *Flama*, 15 November 1967.
75. Maria de Castro, 'A emancipação da mulher tem resultados funestos', *M&B*, 1 April 1960, 23.
76. Freire, *Amor e Sexo*.
77. Interview on 8 September 2014. Ana and Daniel are pseudonyms.

CHAPTER 5
TOURISM, BODY AND SEASIDE RECREATIONAL PRACTICES IN POSTWAR GREEK SOCIETY UNTIL 1974

Michalis Nikolakakis

Introduction

In his groundbreaking work, *At the Beach,* Jean-Didier Urbain described the sea coast before the advent of mass tourism.[1] However, the Greek coastline remained a borderline between two contested worlds for the better part of the second half of the twentieth century, even after the 'Golden Hordes' of international tourism had discovered it. On the one hand, Greece was viewed as a Western country, having one of the highest GDP growth rates internationally during the 1960s and a booming expansion of its urban centres during the same period.[2] In this context, the social practices that related to the beach were part of the demand and aspiration for higher living standards of the new urban middle classes and an approximation of what was broadly conceived of as 'the West'. On the other hand, in keeping with international trends, Greece was gradually becoming a constituent part of what Lanfant has described as the system of international tourist operations.[3] An array of policies was pushing the country in this direction. The Marshall Plan and the tourist legislation that was being introduced during the civil war period[4] as a result of direct American intervention, the currency devaluation of the drachma in 1953[5] and a state-promoted project for the construction of a state-owned hotel chain[6] that was expected to ignite private investment in touristic enterprises, were all part of the same strategy to promote tourist development in postwar Greece. Like other Mediterranean countries, such as Spain or Morocco, that were developing similar projects during this period,[7] the country depended heavily on the exchange rate of its currency, its ability to adapt to changes in the international transportation network and the average wage level. Consequently, the abstention of its population from consumer habits that would inevitably result from foreign influence was an economic asset. Cultural clashes and tensions that resulted from the dissemination of Western social practices and new gender roles, as argued in this chapter, were an expression of the widespread demand for higher living standards and fairer distribution of wealth that was generated from the economic development of this time period.

The following contribution describes the gradual spread of beach-related mores and consumer practices among the Greek middle and lower social strata from increased tourism during the 1950s through to 1974. In critically interrogating the notion of the 'democratization of desire', this chapter focuses on the effect that tourism-related social practices had on consumer habits and gender roles in the hosting Greek population. In particular, while it demonstrates a democratization of travel that appeared in Greece in the period in question through practices such as sea bathing, it also shows that this process was contradicted by enduring social class hierarchies and was, simultaneously, premised on 'pedagogies of leisure' that reinforced gender inequalities. It uses material mainly drawn from the popular Greek weekly periodical press such as *Eikones*, *Tachidromos, Epikaira* and *Alpha*, magazines that imitated the layout and the subjects of similar magazines with international appeal such as *Life* in the US or *Paris Match* in France.

Theoretical considerations

Broadly speaking, we can categorize the contrasting opinions within social sciences tourist research of postwar beach recreational practices into two different approaches. Initial work on the dissemination of tourism social practices regarded sea bathing, sun tanning and sea sports as forms of socially signifying consumption. For example, one of the founding fathers of tourism sociology, John Urry, in his broadly influential *The Tourist Gaze*, sought to shed light on the postwar differentiation of tourism. According to Urry, the construction of postwar tourist space in its material specificity is due to the gradual massification of the new *petite bourgeoisie* or the service class that popularized recreational sea tourism[8] through new, package tours. Urry is mainly drawing his argument from Pierre's Bourdieu's *Distinction*. His account of the French sociologist's notion of *habitus* is that distinct social classes possess different volumes of symbolic, economic and cultural capital and are constantly engaged in forms of indirect struggle in order to impose their cultural mores, and as a consequence enhance their political hegemony in society as a whole. Following Bourdieu, Urry considers this antagonism to reveal itself beyond conscious treatment and extend to tastes, bodily dispositions, fashion and consumer and recreational practices.[9] We could add that for Bourdieu, this form of struggle is embedded in unconscious bodily dispositions[10] and this antagonism not only plays out in contrasting social practices but also in the limits of those practices and the degree to which they are appropriated by different social strata.[11]

Recent research, however, is moving away from the previously dominant views on structuralism, and is instead emphasizing the actual forms of bodily enjoyment and bodily experience as the driving force behind the transformation of social mores. This line of analysis is affiliated with the theoretical tradition that breaks with mind-body dualism in Western philosophical reason. For example, the social geographer Obrador Pons uses the Heideggerian metaphor of 'dwelling' in order to present the beach 'as a place where the body lives, experiments and desires, a place of embodied utopias and non-discursive pleasures'.[12] Elsewhere he describes different forms of human senses, such as haptic experiences, as mediums through which the tourist phenomenon can be accessed by social scientists.[13] Other works, such as those of Soile Veijola and Eeva Jokinen, focus on the absence of the body from our framework of understanding modern tourism,[14] while more historically oriented researchers such as Webb[15] or Löfgren focus on the utopian and wish-fulfilling aspects of the participation of modern subjects at the beach, as a form of an embodied participation in an economically regulated democratic regime.[16] What all of the aforementioned approaches have in common is that they seek to restore the transcendental qualities of seaside social practices. Earlier critical accounts regarding the increase of seaside recreation, such as those of Henri Lefebvre, consider 'the beach [as] the only space of enjoyment that the human species has discovered in nature [in which] the body tends to behave as a differential field. It behaves [...] as a total body, breaking out of the temporal and spatial shell developed in response to labour'.[17]

My interpretation of seaside social practices that are related to recreation and tourism tries to bridge the aforementioned traditions by using the approach of social geographer David Harvey that considers the body as an accumulation strategy. According to Harvey, 'the body is not a closed and sealed entity, but a relational "thing" that is created, bounded, sustained, and ultimately dissolved in a spatiotemporal flux of multiple processes'.[18] He calls attention to the fact that, although different theoretical traditions that draw upon the work of Michel Foucault and Gilles Deleuze tend to focus on mechanisms that try to inscribe themselves upon the physicality of the human body, the gradual development of the capitalist mode of production pushes the human body in radically different directions.[19] In that sense the human body is both transformed through labour, the conditions of production and reproduction of the labour force, the signifying practices that attempt to mobilize desires and wishes in order to coerce consumption, and the desire of various regimes of political power to exercise forms of control upon social subjects.[20] Crucial to Harvey's analysis is that these transformations lead to contradictory directions, and it is the task of social scientists to construe the way this conflict manifests in different historical and geographical regimes. This would imply that what is at stake is not only the gradual spread of different social practices that relate to tourism in host societies but also that those processes may produce conflicting final outcomes. At the same time, it would indicate a permanent tension between the populations in host societies. On the one hand, the hosts act as potential producers of tourist services and on the other they are entangled as consumers, as well as subjects, in the same mechanism of coercion and utopian desires of the consumers of tourist products.

The coming of the Golden Hordes

The gradual process of appreciating the coastline and scenic tourism in the cultural aftermath of the romanticism movement that led to sea bathing[21] appears to begin at the end of the nineteenth century in Greece. The pacification of the beach[22] and its establishment as a space of physical enjoyment can be already discerned during the interwar years and this in limited areas and among specific segments of the local bourgeoisie.

The main practice that introduces sea bathing in Greece during the nineteenth century is the use of mineral springs in spas for health reasons. The examples of the popular spas in Aidipsos and Loutraki, in Euboea[23] and the Corinthian gulf respectively highlight the forms by which the sea is introduced as a means of social interaction for the rising bourgeoisie. However, the first beaches used solely for recreational purposes were those of Neo Faliro and Palaio Faliro in the Attica region, developed along with the creation of the first urban railway in the Greek capital.[24]

Despite these developments, sea bathing was still regarded as an activity for the upper and upper-middle classes during the early years after the Second World War and the Greek civil war, and was imbued with connotations regarding its effect upon health and physical rigour.[25] Its dissemination to the lower classes was the outcome of mimicry of the middle classes to the upper classes, as seen in most Western European countries.[26]

The postwar dissemination of foreign tourism truly began to solidify the form and structure of the beach as a space of enjoyment and entertainment for Greeks and tourists alike. Given the fact that the tourist industry was being promoted by a combination of state investments that were supposed to fuel private, mainly foreign investments, the new tourist resorts and organized bathing facilities that opened after the war drew extraordinary media attention. In the 1950s, two such examples stand out due to their cultural importance as places of new Western European leisure practices: the Corfu Club Med and the *Asteras* Glyfadas establishment in the Attica region.

The Corfu Club Med began its operations in 1953 and was one of the initial resorts that the prolific French company operated. Copying the first Club Med in the Balearic Islands, the Corfu Club Med functioned as an all-inclusive 'village' with small, furnished straw huts or tents as dwellings.[27] The Corfu Club Med followed the parent company's international code of conduct in which full dressing was discouraged, sports activities were organized and presumably, as with other Club Med villages, a 'tolerant attitude toward casual sexual encounters'[28] was practised. The international success and booming demand of the parent company was very much dependent on what Urbain later coined and credited to Club Med – its theming of *polynesianism*.[29] According to a 1956 article in *Eikones* magazine, the manager of the local branch who had been groomed by Gerard Blitz, Club Med's founder, stated that inside the establishment, 'slowly, the town-personality of the customer is rejected in favor of the vacation-personality'.[30]

Despite the fact that few Greeks had access to this establishment, it stands to reason that the abundance of related articles in the local as well as the national press made the Club a prototype for the country's nascent tourist industry. The Corfu Club Med clearly showcased that sea leisure activities were the future of the business, and included a process of constructing, in terms of policy-making as well as in terms of habits and mores, the beach.

Local agents and entrepreneurs were progressively imitating the few seaside recreation resorts scattered throughout the country, such as the Club Med. For example, the Touring Club of Greece (*Periigitiki Leschi*), created in the 1960s during the middle war period, sought to establish its first camping site.[31] More importantly however, the physical allocation of Club Med's buildings and facilities became the model for the new seaside recreation resorts. The architects of the new hotels that were being constructed at the time used this prototype, opting to distance themselves from big urban hotels or the grand hotels typical of the late nineteenth century and the early twentieth. Aris Konstantinidis, the pioneer architect who oversaw the construction of the state hotel chain Xenia[32] after the late 1950s, favoured a form of hotel design of distinct, low-floored and functionally-separate buildings that later was imitated by the private sector as well.

The Greek state introduced the concept of the 'organized beach', together with the hotel chain Xenia, as the main vehicle to propel investment in the tourist sector. The construction of the *Asteras* establishment in the mid-1950s, a venture owned by the National Bank of Greece, was seen as a major step in the modernization of the country.[33] It is interesting to note that the establishment of an organized beach in Glyfada became the first site in the wider region that introduced the practice of sea bathing to all strata of Greek society. By the end of the decade, the density and abundance of local swimmers captured the attention of the press, whose comments reflected irony or cultural elitism.[34] John Urry aptly recognized that sea bathing contributed to the process of the democratization of travel,[35] and that this democratizing process was inevitably and unintentionally affecting the local middle and lower classes within hosting societies with unexpected results. Despite the fact that the Mediterranean beach signified, as Turner and Ash commented, the tourist's 'pursuit of hedonism and expressivity [that] takes place in a controlled, artificial environment and in strict isolation from his society',[36] this form of isolation was literally taking place in the centre of another society or, in the case of Greece, in the country's capital.

Pedagogies of the sea

From the early 1960s, it is safe to assume that unlike the traditional idea by which sea bathing practices were being transited by the upper strata to the lower strata of society, as in the classical model introduced by Alain Corbain,[37] the Greeks were being introduced to sea leisure practices through the effects of the foreign tourism industry. However, the creation of this consumer sphere did not appear out of thin air, or without any degree of coercion or active construction of consumer demand.[38] Greek magazines during this period were rife with articles mixing lifestyle journalism and pure advertisement, presenting new leisure practices together with the specific product being promoted. This form of journalism began to take shape by the end of the 1950s and is naturally related to the evolution of women's magazines that were promoting new forms of postwar consumption. Notable in this sense is the case of the publication of *I Ginaika*, which resembled foreign popular women's magazines, such as *Elle* in France or *Vogue* in US. This form of fashion journalism was found even in the mainstream popular press, from which we will be drawing our examples.

What is notable about postwar fashion journalism is its wholesale introduction of leisure practices as part of the process of demand construction. This process was not limited to sea bathing, of course. A discernible trend in the popular magazines of the time is what we could call 'pedagogies of leisure' or in other words, a systemic introduction of new practices to enhance the pleasures of activities done in one's free time. Photography was continually promoted as such an activity, as were new forms of mobility – such as the use of cars by middle-class women, along with advice regarding camping accessories or the right types of brochures or information one must have to plan for a trip abroad. What is distinct about sea bathing is the peculiar way that those pedagogies targeted the body – and mainly the female body – as a space of desirable transformations and gender performativity; the press explicitly passed on and transmitted the requisite knowledge to enable such transformations.

Let's take for example a May 1957 article from *Tachidromos* magazine simply called 'Bathing Suit'. This piece of popular journalism begins by offering advice to girls on how to choose the appropriate swim-wear in order to look attractive. After describing how different types of bathing suits flatter different body types, the anonymous columnist provides extremely explicit instructions:

> If you follow the aforementioned advice, you will surely choose the bathing suit that best suits you. Waist test: stand straight without stretching your body. Pinch you stomach right above your lower rib – the one not attached to your sternum. If you grab two cm of flesh, this means that you would be advised not to wear *deux pièces*. Favour a lastex swimming suit or one with battens, if it is made out of soft fabric. In this manner your waist will appear lean. Belly: Lie down on the floor and place a walking stick touching both your chest and your belly. If the stick is not horizontal purchase a bathing suit with a small skirt to hide your belly. Arms: Stretch your hand and inspect your skin under your arm. If it is not stiff choose a light coloured swimsuit. Thighs: Stretch a strip above the fattest part of your thighs. Now tighten it. If flesh protrudes from the strip, avoid straight narrow swimsuits. Prefer a bathing suit with small knickers. Back: If you are able to pinch your back without hurting yourself this means that your skin is flabby. Choose a swimsuit with a lower back and avoid lastex. Chin: If you have a 'dewlap', avoid closed and dark swimsuits. A 'V' neckline will appear more flattering.[39]

What is novel about this article compared to earlier forms of fashion journalism is the way in which the body itself is being instructed to conform to a specific stereotype *in absentia* of the consumed object. Swimsuits don't just match different body types as other forms of fashion garments do, according to the fashion columnist. Bathing suits, and the discourse that surrounds them, organize the exposure of the body in accordance with specific stereotypes. Interestingly, yet not surprisingly, such discourses appear mainly in reference to the female body. Men are instructed in the ways of the new social practices but their bodies are not supposed to be exposed through preconceived procedures or strict rules.

This process of consumer regulated bodily exposure, underway in Europe from the time of the interwar period,[40] became dominant in Greece in the early 1960s. In this sense, fashion was educating specific segments of the upper middle classes that read those magazines in a particular code of bodily conduct while at the seaside. Fashion and the pedagogies of the sea were constructing what Tim Enderson has described as the tourism taskscape[41] for non-tourist locals, namely, forms of social conduct compatible with the usage of public space as a place of regulated consumption by tourists.

This newly found fashion discourse was met with a degree of uncertainty in Greek society, colliding with mainstream ethical and moral principles. Therefore, it could only establish itself by being presented as urgent and obligatory. In an article in the same magazine that was also published in 1967, the columnist gave the following advice regarding sea leisure practices: 'two points should be considered as rules: swimsuits serve your beauty and should not irritate your body. And they should always be according to fashion. You can never appear at the *plage* without knowing the fashion – and specifically the latest fashion'.[42] The symbolic capital ascribed to leisure practices could only be assured if these practices were presented as being an ethical obligation that social subjects pursued with strict discipline. This sense of obligation made leisure appear less as a right and more as a mandatory practice suited to fit the desire for upward social mobility for the urban middle classes.

Symbolic struggles by the coastlines

By the early 1960s the beach had become a melting pot for Greeks and tourists, as well as for Greeks of different social strata, even if it only existed near the main urban centres and in areas with noticeable tourist activity. This made a distinct impression on the periodical press at the time. A symbolic struggle was taking place regarding the eligible meanings and functions of the beach, as more and more people were storming the shores. On the one hand, the symbolic effect of the public display of nudity had strong egalitarian[43] effects upon the host population. On the other, the same process was stripping the urban-centre upper classes of one of the spaces considered to be a symbol of their hegemony. The underlying tensions related to the advent of the masses at the beach were both territorial, whether or not one was allowed in certain areas, and conceptual, whether or not certain practices were acceptable at the beach.

During the 1960s, summertime articles describing the mass presence of Greeks at the beach became a common feature. During the summer of 1967, an *Eikones* magazine columnist noted: 'Never before had the beaches appeared so crowded, never before did they leave us with the impression of a concrete surface of fried victims, never before did the sea resemble so much a soup, never before . . .'.[44]

Territorial segmentation based on social milieus went hand in hand with an evolving differentiation of the material cultures of the beach despite egalitarian perceptions regarding nudity and leisure. Commenting on the newly found leisure hierarchies of the beach, a columnist for *Eikones* magazine wrote in August 1960: 'the audience of the beaches in Scaramanga [. . .] is different than the one in Varkiza',[45] noting the difference in vehicles, such as Jaguars versus pick-up trucks, or different cutlery used at the beach by different social classes. As was the case in most Western countries even in the nineteenth century,[46] the massification of the beach was accompanied by the differentiation of various beaches for people of distinct social milieus. The specific seaside resorts on the coast of Attica that constituted the crux of the country's tourist efforts were to a large extent accessible only to a limited part of the local population. However, during this same period, the expansion of the road network on the Argosaronikos coast increased the opportunities for access to non-organized beaches for the masses.

But it was the existence of differences regarding how one is supposed to act while at the beach that best highlights the rising tensions. The lower classes were portrayed as being unaware of the hygienic usefulness of the sea and unable to appreciate its nature and effects on the human psyche, and were often described as grotesque imitations of 'real' sea bathers.

As the tourism industry was slowly addressing concerns regarding ecological sustainability in the mid-60s, the lower classes were portrayed as polluters, and unable to comprehend the dangers stemming from uncontrolled usage of natural resources. The magazine *Alpha* presents us with an interesting example: in July 1967, right after the military junta came to power, the columnist describes the tendency of Athens' urban dwellers to bath near the sewage drains:

> They are insane, they are potentially suicidal, self-punishing masochists or complete illiterates – our fellow citizens that swim in the estuary of the capital's sewers and pose with smiles full of bliss in front of the lenses of photojournalists underneath a huge sign saying 'Danger, polluted waters. Swimming is forbidden.' Men, women and children root about with their feet in the horrendous materials in front of the mouth of the underground septic tubes of the capital, sail in the green-yellow, viscous seawaters and swallow with pleasure millions of germs of typhus and dysentery. Who has responsibility to oversee this bizarre swarm of [...]? Is it to the domain of nearby police stations, of neurologists or of psychiatrists?[47]

This form of semi-covert moral outcry regarding the usage of the sea by the lower classes was accompanied by both symbolic and actual forms of penalization of young tourism practices. For example, in 1961, articles regarding the cosmopolitan and libertarian atmosphere in Hydra island led to the state prosecutors' intervention and prohibition of swimwear more than fifty metres away from the beach. During the years of the military dictatorship incidents of state intervention multiplied, beginning with the initial restriction that the junta regime imposed upon incoming tourists in an effort to monitor youth and hippie mobility that the newly established colonels found threatening.[48] As the seaside was increasingly recognized as one of Greece's prime economic assets, the more likely it became that forms of socialization relating to the beach were frowned upon or met with hostility.

Everyday life by the sea

Over time, however, obstacles of a political or ideological nature were set aside as the social practices of tourists began affecting everyday life in Greece. The endorsement of recreational sea practices by the indigenous population was done in a uniquely local way, transforming them in order to suit their desires and the country's conditions. The spread of recreational sea practices reflected a real increase in living standards and, henceforth, consumer expectations. For example, in 1964 there were approximately 500 owners of recreational boats, while by 1970 there were well over 3,000.[49]

The main peculiarity one notes while examining the way these practices were being introduced in Greek society was the proximity and the abundance of beaches. After all, Greece is a country with enormous stretches of coastline accessible to most of its citizens. This simple geographical feature was transforming the rhythm[50] of sea recreation as opposed to the rhythm of the tourist industry. As such, going to the beach was becoming part of Greek citizens' everyday life and constituted a rupture of daily – rather than annual – time. As opposed to the rhythm of the tourist, in which sea bathing constitutes a rupture to each citizen's biography, or a breach between labour and non-labour, Greeks were appropriating the same practices that were embedding themselves in their daily lives. This was becoming more obvious in urban centres with access to beaches during the years of the military junta, but it was also relevant for the citizens of the southern municipalities of Attica and, progressively, for the country's agricultural provinces. For example, as early as 1963, *Eikones* magazine ran an article on how families of farmers were being introduced to sea bathing in various villages near Ilea in the region of Peloponnese and featured a photo spread about young children who had tried to convince their donkey to join them in the sea.[51]

The notion that the construction of an explicitly tourist space would become a melting pot for hosts and guests and a sphere of cosmopolitan socialization can be seen in the plans of the architects of the first hotels of this type. Aris Konstantinidis, commenting on the design of the Xenia hotel chain, noted: 'living spaces – lounges and restaurants etc. have been developed so as to serve a large number of patrons [...] this is so as to take part in the everyday life of the hotel passerby's – locals and foreigners – and so that inside the hotel the residents will come in contact with outside elements and local residents of the area'.[52] Later anthropological and sociological research would confirm the disruption of the local networks of sociability in tourism areas that their initial architects had in mind.[53]

By the beginning of the 1970s the beach had been transformed into one of the main spaces for socialization for most members of Greek society. Three functions seem to stand out in the commentaries of the periodical press: the beach as the site of flirting and socialization for young Greeks, the beach as a site of public family life and the beach as a space of rest for the elderly.

For example, in July 1971, *Tachidromos* magazine featured an article titled 'Our coasts are filled with incidents and brutes'. It begins by recounting how an old man who was attempting to enjoy the sea in his downtime was disrupted by small children playing ball. In keeping with the moralistic tone, the article lists a number of inappropriate practices that take place by the sea and were becoming increasingly popular with middle- and lower-class Greeks, such as small children chasing each other, picnics, romantic rendezvous, swimming lessons and various other games, as well as using the sea for hygiene purposes: 'What seriously stirs me is the bathing – literally – of several elderly people; they enter the sea, proceed until the seawaters reaches their waist and start to [...] clean themselves. They clean their ears, their nose and their necks – in and out – this public bathing is something that disgusts me and makes it impossible for me to enter the sea.'[54] As noted by various tourist studies commentators,[55] the beach in this context functioned as a type of stage, a form of publicized everyday life whereby what was formerly considered private was now exposed to the prying eyes of strangers, be it of other Greeks or foreign tourists. At the same time, everyday household routines, such as cooking, cleaning or children's learning, were being exported to the beach.

An excluding hedonism

Naturally, the beach's most prominent and popular socializing function was flirting among younger Greeks. This occurred simultaneously with the familiarization with public nudity that was underway, namely the public nudity of foreign women and their romantic socializing with Greek men performing their gender identities.

By the early 1960s, weekly magazines were rife with articles satirizing the relations of young Greeks with tourists, often categorizing the sexual practices of foreign women by nationality.[56] In 1964, the popular comic strip writer and *Eikones* columnist Kir (Κυρ) noted:

> The difference between a Greek and a foreigner is this: the foreigner [...] that has enjoyed for 11 months a free and without obligations erotic life, wants during his 12th month to rest, see the sun, the ancient ruins and to breathe fresh air. On the contrary the Greek, that has been resting, seeing the sun and the ruins and has been breathing fresh air for 11 months, wants in the 12th month to have a free and without any obligation erotic life. And he thinks, who can present me with such a life? And he answers: a foreign tourist.[57]

Female tourists were often being presented as opportunities or playthings for young male Greeks in the public discourse, with no small degree of disguised sexism. This discourse also contained moral panic regarding instances of tourist rape by 'disillusioned' Greeks[58] or cases of indirect male prostitution, also known at the time both in Italy and Greece as the phenomenon of 'papagay'.[59]

The same discourse, however, had a negative impact on young Greek women. Displaying their bodies was considered an indirect form of prostitution and was heavily criticized by the same magazines that were featuring the newest trends in bathing suit fashions and giving advice on sea practices. This criticism seemed to question even the most fundamental ideological preconditions of tourist development, such as its progressive and modern connotations. In 1964, for example, the humoristic columnist and writer Dimitris Psathas noted the following with irony:

Given, as it is well known, that the progress of humanity, lies underneath the bras of women and inside their various other underwear, it is unacceptable for humanity to be deprived of its fruits. Undeniably, therefore, there should be a fight not of topless bathing, but on the contrary for women to be encouraged to expose all of their progress. And not only the progress of their breasts, but also other progresses that topless – besides all of its progressiveness – continues to hide, harming aesthetics and civilization alike.[60]

Although sexual libertarianism and the cosmopolitan atmosphere that surrounded the tourist industry was more or less socially acceptable for male Greeks, especially of the middle and upper classes, Greek women, on the other hand, were to be excluded from what was seen as a hedonistic lifestyle.

Contrasting and conflicting meanings were being projected on the female body due to the increase in recreational sea practices, and the process of restricting the female body was not limited to sea recreation. After all, the discourse regarding shrinking bathing suits was an international phenomenon, as news of topless swimming in St Tropez in 1964 began to spread.[61] This international trend, later labelled 'cultural sexualization'[62] became mainstream and brought into public life the individualized nature of sexual discourse and preference. However, what was distinct to Greece regarding sea recreational practices was the nationally specific nature of this discourse. Mainly, the interaction between an international tendency towards consumerism and bodily self expression and the specific insistence in Greece in which tourism tended to idealize and commoditize the lack of modernizing social structures, gender roles and everyday life. New forms of body-centric social mores were therefore the outcome of this unique spatiotemporal fusion.

Conclusion: the body and its symbolic functions

John Urry has commented on the shift that occurred during the nineteenth century regarding beach recreational practices from a 'medicalized beach' to a 'pleasure beach'. According to Urry, 'the grotesque body was shamefully uncovered and open to the gaze of others'.[63] However, according to Jean Claude Kaufman, this gradual procedure of exposure could not have been possible unless followed, for upper and lower social strata alike, by a procedure of internalization of rules of social conduct that enabled socializing without the existence of external restraints such as clothes.[64] Kaufman, following Norbert Elia's understanding of the civilizing process,[65] indicated that the gradual reduction of beach wear doesn't necessarily imply fewer rules regarding bodily conduct, but rather an increase introduced through both direct and indirect processes of education and coercion.[66] We have already seen how, in the case of Greece, magazines were both educating young Greek women on how to act and dress properly at the beach and, at the same time, using moral arguments to affect female sexuality and mores. The problematic of Elias and Kaufman seems to indicate that a wider shift regarding the functions of the body was taking place through those changes. Even if the body functioned as a sort of repository of different social strata habits and conventions according to Bourdieu,[67] the process of gradual exposure of the naked body at the beach functioned over time as a paradigm shift. The difference here is that although bodily dispositions and fashion have always been considered a form of expression of a certain individual social milieu, the beach introduced a form of communication or a way of addressing social signifying practices through the naked physicality of the body. As Urbain has commented, it is through the beach that the body replaces external signs of wealth or social status as the prime signs of sublimation and social recognition.[68] In accordance with this notion, in the period that this contribution is assessing, beach bodily social practices were being transformed as the main strategies through which individual citizens were trying to enhance their social status.[69]

In postwar Greece, the introduction of sea recreational practices through tourism resulted in two different contrasting systems of signification. On the one hand, social commentators of various political affiliations were calling for the containment of the spread of habits and practices connected with tourism. This process was evident in the public discourse, but during the military dictatorship there is evidence even of public services responsible for issues of economic planning, such as KEPE (Center for Programming and Economic Research) having concerns regarding the social effects of tourism.[70] On the other hand, different social and economic agents favoured the widespread popularization of Western consumer practices and used the appeal of modernization due to tourism as a vehicle for their promotion.

As a result, women faced conflicting forms of signification due to the symbolism bestowed upon the female body. The view of the body, most often the female body, as a labouring device, relating to dowries or privileged consumption, was transformed by the obvious shifts in sexuality and the public display of nudity. Eventually, the fall of the military junta would give rise to a politicization that momentarily seemed to liberate the processes of the 'democratization of desire' and shifts in gender hierarchies in Greek society from those that had previously interlocked gender roles with consumer habits. The effects however of this process would persist through time.

Notes

1. Jean-Didier Urbain, *Stin akrothalassia* (Athens: Potamos, 1999), 59.
2. Panos Kazakos, *Anamesa se kratos kai agora: Oikonomia kai oikonomiki politiki stin metapolemiki Ellada* (Athens: Ekdosis Pataki, 2006), 228.
3. Marie-Françoise Lanfant, 'Introduction: tourism in the process of internationalization', *International Social Science Journal* XXXII, 1, 1980, 22.
4. Angelos Vlachos, *Touristiki anaptixi kai dimosies politikes stin sinchroni Ellada (1914–1950)*, (PhD diss., National and Kapodistrian University of Athens, 2013), 331, 409–14.
5. Kazakos, 165.
6. Margarita Dritsas, 'Tourism and business during the twentieth century in Greece', in Luciano Sergeto, Carles Manera and Manfred Pohl (eds), *Tourism at the Seaside: The Economic History of Mass Tourism in the Mediterranean* (New York: Berghahn, 2009), 58.

7. See for example the case of Spain in: Sasha D. Pack, *Tourism and Dictatorship: Europe's Peaceful Invasion of Franco's Spain* (New York: Palgrave Macmillan, 2006), 83–103.
8. John Urry, *The Tourist Gaze* (London: Sage, 2002), 81.
9. Ibid., 79.
10. Pierre Bourdieu, *I Diakrisi* (Athens: Pataki, 2002), 118–19.
11. Ibid., 360.
12. Pau Obrador-Pons, 'Being-on-holiday: tourist dwelling, bodies and place', *Tourist Studies* 3.47, 2003, 55.
13. Pau Obrador-Pons, 'Building castles in the sand: repositioning touch on the beach', *Senses and Society* 4.2, 2009, 199–204.
14. Soile Veijola and Eeva Jokinen, 'The body in tourism', *Theory, Culture & Society* 11, 1994, 148–9.
15. Darren Webb, 'Bakhtin at the seaside: utopia, modernity and the carnivalesque', *Theory, Culture and Society* 22.3, 2005, 132–5.
16. Orvrar Löfgren, *On Holiday: A History of Vacationing* (Berkeley, CA: University of California Press, 2002), 271–3.
17. Henri Lefebvre, *The Production of Space* (Oxford: Blackwell, 1991), 384.
18. David Harvey, *Spaces of Hope* (Berkeley, CA: University of California Press, 2000), 98.
19. Ibid., 104.
20. Ibid., 111.
21. Urry, *The Tourist Gaze*, 20.
22. Urbain, *Stin akrothalassia*, 43.
23. Margarita Dritsas, 'Water, culture and leisure: from spas to beach tourism in Greece during the nineteenth and twentieth centuries', in Susan Canderson and Bruce H. Tabb (eds), *Water, Leisure & Culture: European Historical Perspectives* (Oxford: Berg, 2002), 196–203.
24. 'Se megali plage tha metavlithi to Neo Faliro', *Tachidromos*, 14 June 1968, 14–15.
25. 'Thalassini omorfia kai igia', *Tachidromos*, 6 July 1957, 24.
26. Löfgren, *On Holiday*, 123–4.
27. 'I vavel tis charas', *Eikones*, 6 August 1956, 34.
28. Ellen Furlough, 'Club Méditerranée, 1950–2002', in Luciano Sergeto, Carles Manera and Manfred Pohl (eds), *Tourism at the Seaside: The Economic History of Mass Tourism in the Mediterranean* (New York: Berghahn, 2009), 176.
29. Urbain, 163.
30. 'Hawaii? Samoa? Kerkira!', *Eikones*, 10 September 1956, 21–2. Author's translation.
31. 'Fthines diakopes gia tous neous', *Tachidromos*, 12 July 1968, 57–62.
32. Vassilis Kolonas, 'Tourist facilities in Greece 1950–1974', in Yannis Aesopos (ed.), *Tourism Landscapes: Remaking Greece* (Athens: Yannis Aesopos, 2014), 68.
33. 'Ta "Asteria", mia apolausi gia kathe politismeno anthropo', *Tachidromos*, 16 November 1957, 27.
34. 'Glifada', *Eikones*, 12 August 1957, 12.
35. Urry, 17.
36. Louis Turner and John Ash, *The Golden Hordes: International Tourism and the Pleasure Periphery* (New York: St Martin Press, 1976), 91.

37. Alain Corbain, *The Lure of the Sea: The Discovery of the Seaside 1750-1840* (London: Penguin, 1995), 250–81. The reverse argument, the idea that lower social strata had a tradition of sea bathing is argued in Hartmut Berghoff, 'From privilege to commodity? Modern tourism and the rise of the consumer society', in Hartmut Berghoff, Barbara Korte, Ralf Schneider and Christopher Harvie (eds), *The Making of Modern Tourism: The Cultural History of the British Experience, 1600-2000* (Basingstoke: Palgrave Macmillan, 2002), 160–4.

38. According to Thurot and Thurot recreational practices in tourism are not disseminated from the social elites to the lower classes but rather from a strictly advertising social milieu towards the rest of society. Jean-Maurice Thurot and Gaitane Thurot, 'The ideology of class and tourism: comforting the discourse of advertising', *Annals of Tourism Research* 11.3, 1984, 178–9.

39. 'Magio', *Tachidromos*, 31 May 1957, 24–5, author's translation.

40. Fred Inglis, *The Delicious History of the Holiday* (London: Routledge, 2000), 134–9.

41. Tim Endensor, 'Sensing tourist spaces', in Claudio Minca and Tim Oakes (eds), *Travels in Paradox: Remapping Tourism* (Lanham, MD: Rowman & Littlefield Publishers, 2006), 24–5.

42. 'Esis kai I thalassa', *Tachidromos*, 21 July 1967, 27–34, author's translation.

43. Jane C. Desmond, *Staging Tourism* (Chicago: University of Chicago Press, 1999), 257–8.

44. 'I thalatta ton neon mirion', *Eikones*, 30 August 1963, 15–2, author's translation.

45. 'Athina tin kyriaki- Panigyri sti thalassa', *Eikones*, 26 August 1960, 26–35, author's translation.

46. Urbain, 140; Urry, 22.

47. 'Thalata, thalata', *Alpha Reportaz*, 15 July 1967, 43.

48. Kostas Katsapis, *To 'provlima neolaia': Modernoi neoi, paradosi kai amfisvitisi stin metapolemiki Ellada* (Athens: Aprovleptes, 2013), 403.

49. 'Kalokairi, thalassa, spor', *Tachidromos*, 6 June 1970, 63–6.

50. Henri Lefebvre, *Rhythmanalysis* (London: Bloomsbury, 2013), 23–5.

51. 'I agapi gia ti thalassa kerdizi tora tous agrotes', *Eikones*, 20 September 1963, 24–7.

52. Aris Konstantinidis, *Gia tin architektoniki: dimosieumata se efimerides, se periodika kai se vivlia* (Athens: Agra, 1987), 187, author's translation.

53. See for example Maria Kousis, *Tourism as an Agent of Social Change in a Rural Cretan Community* (PhD diss., University of Michigan, 1984), 168.

54. 'Oi aktes mas einai gemmates apo aprepeis kai vanausous', *Tachidromos*, 2 July 1971, 48–9.

55. See for example: Simon Coleman & Mike Crang, 'Grounded Tourists, Travelling Theory', in *Tourism: Between Place and Performance*, eds Simon Coleman and Mike Crang (New York: Berghahn Books, 2002), 1–17; Urbain, 248.

56. See for example: 'Koritsia tou kalokairiou', *Epikaira*, July 14, 1972, 36–39.

57. 'Idra kai oi erastes tis', *Eikones*, 7 August 1964, 44–9, author's translation.

58. 'Oi oraies kai ta ktini', *Tachidromos*, 25 April 1964, 30–1.

59. 'Oi erastes tou kalokairiou', *Tachidromos*, 8 August 1969, 34–5.

60. 'Pros "toplesofrona"', *Tachidromos*, 1 August 1964, 7, author's translation.

61. Jean Claude Kaufmann, *Somata gynaikon, vlemmata andron: koinoniologia tou toples* (Athens: Marathia, 1997), 47.

62. Brian McNair, *Striptease Culture* (London: Routledge, 2002), 8.

63. Urry, 29.

64. Kaufmann, 25.
65. Norbert Elias, *I exelixi tou politismou, tom. 'A* (Athens: Nefeli, 1997), 302.
66. Kaufmann, 227.
67. Pierre Bourdieu, *Glossa kai symvoliki exousia* (Athens: Kardamitsa, 1999), 177.
68. Urbain, 320.
69. Ibid., 331.
70. Epitropi Ethnikou Protypou Anaptyxeos, *Schedion protypou makrochroniou anaptyxeos tis Ellados, meros 'A* (Athens: KEPE, 1972), 16.

PART II
CONSUMPTION AND GENDER THROUGH THE MOMENT OF TRANSITION

CHAPTER 6
REPRESENTATIONS OF SEXUALITY AND GENDER IN PORTUGUESE CINEMA DURING THE LATE *ESTADO NOVO* AND THE CARNATION REVOLUTION

Érica Faleiro Rodrigues

This chapter rethinks the relationship between cinema and politics in Portugal, from the early 1960s to the Marcelist Spring and the Carnation Revolution of 1974, by contextualizing the status quo in the years preceding and following the coup, by investigating a number of cultural contradictions inherent to the revolutionary process and, finally, by seeking to identify transformations in politics, and in aesthetic production and dissemination. It evaluates the triangle of revolution, sexuality and gender in film, as well as the outright absence of regulations in the Portuguese cinema exhibition market between 1974 and 1976. It examines consumer culture employing film as the example of a commodified cultural product.

This analysis is divided into two parts: the first focuses on the political circumstances just before the revolution and the second on what arose in its aftermath. The former investigates the clash between hegemonic masculinities, subordinated masculinities and femininities in the *Estado Novo*, focusing on how Portuguese law dealt with gender, sexuality, race and class, from basic rights to film censorship and the circumstances of a heavily hierarchical society. It is followed by the dissection of the promises of the Marcelist Spring and the Gulbenkian Golden Years during which films were overtly being made to face censorship and Portugal started to open up to cultural transformations occurring in the 1960s.

The second part focuses on the end of censorship and how this sudden catharsis shaped the post-revolution market. I concentrate on the consequences of the sudden permeability of capitalism and market forces and the effect and meaning of pornographic and erotic film distribution in Portugal from 1974 to 1976 – bracketing this chapter at a time when, as stated by Kostis Kornetis, there was a 'fascination with third world independence movements [that] had an enormous impact both in the United States and Europe, especially in countries under authoritarian regimes such as Greece, Spain and Portugal',[1] and waves of change seemed to sweep the Western world. In the aftermath of the revolution there was a utopia of free film distribution. This, however, did not swing open the doors of film production and distribution away from heteronormativity. This utopia soon came to an end with the introduction of film classification in 1976.

Consumption and Gender through the Moment of Transition

The clash between hegemonic masculinities, subordinated masculinities and femininities in the *Estado Novo*

Prior to the revolution, most films screened in Portuguese cinemas had been deeply shaped by the controlling morals and the aesthetic programme of a conservative regime with a dense Catholic morality. In addition, colonial Portugal relied strongly on a stratified society that confined every citizen to a place and a stratum, where race and gender determined social position and aspiration, with the white male at the top of the social pyramid. ID cards clearly stated whether a person's race was white or mixed, while social codification was used as a means of control: in the various interviews carried out by this author, interviewees mention how they were categorized and perceived as second-class citizens, for being mixed race or predominantly 'black' and born outside Portugal. The African woman was doubly downgraded: first, as a woman and second, as an African. António Ferro, the cultural patriarch of the regime, had been one of the most influential personalities during this period; he was also someone who would define the form and ideas of Portugal's national cinema. Ferro is quoted as saying that 'Beauty – from moral beauty to fine art beauty – must be the supreme aspiration of men and of the races'.[2] This phrase encapsulates an ascetic, quasi-mystical sense of how art should be construed; one that warns against, and sets out to avert, the distortion of beauty by any art form that is considered degenerative or decadent. It is also important to note that the State definition and categorization of what *acceptable* beauty should look like is not solely a feature of the dictatorship, but also a 'trait' somehow regained by the democratic revolutionary state two years after the revolution, in 1976. The cultural forms that became available after the revolution had a major impact on what and how Portuguese society consumed, what it aspired to and how it behaved; hence, inevitably, these started to come under political control.

From the outbreak of the colonial war in Africa, in 1961, the main taboos of Portuguese cinema had been the jurisdiction of war itself and pacifism. Films that promoted the war were screened, but films that, by any means conceivable, could reverberate a questioning of the war were heavily edited or categorically banned. Also censored was everything that could be considered offensive to the morals of the day. Severe cuts were applied to sexually explicit imagery and to the female body: breasts, mouths, flesh and skin. The filmmaker Manuel Mozos has recently completed a trilogy of films on Portuguese censorship; a series made entirely from footage cut out by the censors. The third film in Mozos' trilogy, *Alguns Cortes: Censura III* (*The Devil is a Woman – A Few Cuts From the Censorship III, Cinema*), focuses on the female subject precisely to unveil the dictatorship's heavy-handed censorship of the female body and female sexuality. This film, made entirely from the negation of female presence and released in 2014, provides a spellbinding insight into the thought processes and dynamics of the dictatorship's censorship machine. Mozos mentioned to this author that the idea for the title (*The Devil is a Woman*) came from realizing that so much of the female presence and sexuality had been cut out by the dictatorship. There is clearly a strong Catholic morality influencing these cuts and a certain representation of the female that is not solely specific to Portugal's *Estado Novo*.[3]

Luis Buñuel's *Simon of the Desert* (1965) mirrors remarkably the perception of women around this time: a woman embodies a tempting Satan; the reverberations of Eve echoing across time and space in the Western world.

Another of Manuel Mozos' films, the first in his trilogy (*Censura: Alguns Cortes, Censorship: A Few Cuts*), directed in 1999, is an eclectic compilation that showcases everything that could be cut. Most of the cuts will look puerile nowadays: a kiss here, a slight joke at the expense of the Church there. But all these details were part of a mélange which was perceived as a danger to the status quo. Dogma, as the devil, is in the detail. This is why the comb of censorship needed to be as strong as it was fine.

In this void, in the vacuum left by what was censored, one notes the sexuality that was being denied to women, the repudiation of sexual awareness and the fear of emancipation contained in the actualization of female desire.

> Therefore, the Portuguese cinema of the dictatorship is a portrayal of its time, not solely for what it shows in its films, but also for all that it omits and therefore – as the image of a negative – reveals of the existing climate of censorship, that started with political power and ended with the film critics, through the sieve of producers and the self-censorship of directors and scriptwriters.[4]

Portuguese cinema under the control of the dictatorship was a cinema of female oppression, where women were excluded from feature filmmaking, but were also made the object of a controlled male gaze. It will always be a difficult task to scrutinize the full impact the censorship apparatus had on what is now a part of Portuguese cinema's history. One can survey the archives, but the major damage (far more than the official records will ever tell us) will always be with what is unwritten and absent from any documentation: the 'panoptical' self-censorship of creators, the unrecorded actions and conversations that led to cuts, the fading memories only partially preserved by the testimonies of those who were, on either side of the barrier, the executors and the victims of censorship.

Gender hierarchies in the *Estado Novo* did not only affect heterosexual femininity, but also male and female homosexuality. Back in 1923, before the *Estado Novo*, it had been known across the land that the modernist poets Judith Teixeira, António Botto and Raul Leal had been persecuted for being homosexuals. However, despite the interdictions imposed by the dictatorship, what one realizes is that not all homosexuals were treated equally by the regime and that their fate could be at significant variance depending on their social status. Although homosexuality was always something to be kept well under wraps, we know from a few upper-class scandals that the social elites somehow always escaped the morality imposed upon, and often willfully adopted by, the petty bourgeoisie and society at large. While some gay women, such as the writer Irene Lisboa, the feminist Olga Moraes Sarmento, the writer Edith Arvelos or the painter Maluda, managed to enjoy same-sex partnerships so long as these were camouflaged as friendship, the fate of most other gay women was to have to conceal their relationships entirely or end up in an 'institution'. It would also help if you were a partisan of the regime, like the poet Virgínia

Vitorino. The dictatorship had early on created legislation for the prosecution of homosexuals, however this was mainly used against the poor roaming the streets; many of those accused of homosexuality would, at least until 1952, be confined to an emblematic psychiatric institution called 'A Mitra', as discussed in Ines Brasão's chapter.

Actually, class was a key factor in how sexuality was concealed or expressed during the *Estado Novo*, not only in the case of homosexual relationships (both male and female), but also for heterosexual women. Women of the upper classes could continue their education as far as university level, especially from the 1960s onwards. It was during their time studying at college that most became acquainted with leftist perspectives and with the contraceptive pill. Specifically, homosexuality was commonly perceived as a pathology and therefore 'treated' as such, with leading medical figures (e.g. the Portuguese Nobel Prize winner Egas Moniz), developing 'remedies' to rid patients of their condition, to eradicate what was considered a disease. For the medical profession, homosexuality was a perversion, a type of insanity. This led to homosexuals being locked up in hospitals; a famous case was that of ballet dancer, Valentim de Barros, who was held in the Miguel Bombarda hospital from 1938 (at the age of twenty-two) for over fifty years: 'The homosexuals leave the prisons to be placed in hospitals'.[5] It is documented that the same Miguel Bombarda had also become the destiny of choice for the 'treatment' of upper-class adulteresses[6] – female desire and homosexuality affixed together as *diseases of the nerves* and both attended to by such methods as internment and 'the electric shock'.[7]

Out of fear, homosexuals were compelled to marry, have children and keep up appearances, thus often living a discreet second love life on the side. If in film the topic was taboo, in other art forms some manifestation was allowed – for example, the 1954 song by Pedro Homem de Mello 'Boy of The Green Shirt' ('O Rapaz da Camisa Verde'), which had music that was composed for it by the cleric Frei Hermano da Câmara Pereira, in 1965, and which was sung by *Fado* diva and darling of the regime Amália Rodrigues. Remarkably, the lyrics make it a song about a gay pick-up; a country boy's rendezvous with the Lisbon docks' underworld of male prostitution which was a well-known gay hotspot of the time – a song about the encounter between sexual and economic exclusion. It is also interesting to note that, according to what is listed in the archives of the dictatorship's political police, the PIDE never used homosexuality as a prosecution argument, as with the example of well-known homosexual members of the Portuguese Communist Party Júlio Melo Fogaça, Fernanda de Paiva Tomás and Maria Julieta Guimarães Gandra. As the historian José Pacheco Pereira remarks: 'In the archives of PIDE there are references to several homosexual communists arrested in Tarrafal. But this was not politically used.'[8] It is relevant to point out that female homosexuality had to be doubly invisible, because female sexuality was already meant to go chiefly unnoticed, hence making the transgression of something that ought to be kept concealed a deeper taboo.

It is very difficult to trace any homosexual perspectives in cinema during the *Estado Novo*. The topic was fundamentally taboo. There were gay writers and playwrights, but their sexuality had to be kept well under wraps, for fear of repudiation and incarceration. The openly gay surrealist poet, Mário Cesariny de Vasconcelos, was one of a few exceptions to this regime of secrecy. The number of films that were censored for containing scenes or shots of characters naked or half exposed was ten in 1968, sixty-one in 1969 and seventy-three in 1970. In what concerns censorship of homosexuality, or hints of homosexuality, the present study reveals the existence of two processes in 1968 and the same number in 1969, but in 1970 the number rose to seven.[9] The Portuguese State had undertaken that a virile, strongly heterosexual image of the Portuguese man would serve as the iconic base for its power. John Schlesinger's *Midnight Cowboy* from 1969, with a narrative that is propelled by the errands of a naive male prostitute and his sickly friend trying to survive on the streets of New York, had every hint of homosexual ambiguity cut by the censors' scissors. Once again, what was being cut was the illustration of what the establishment feared above all: desire and homosexuality (as was the case with women). What was happening in Portugal was part of a wider repressive direction, with similar taboos triggering censorship cuts in Greece and Spain. Yet while the regime had wanted little change in perpetuity, the world around it was evolving as the 1960s and 1970s were ushering in a new wave of sexual exploration that would change the narratives of international and of Portuguese cinema.

In addition to war and sexuality, another constant taboo was imagery that exposed poverty in Portugal and in the colonies. 'The process of brutal censorship inflicted on *Catembe* is a symptom of a system that systematically and paradoxically exposes the fragility of a regime that aimed to showcase itself as strong and triumphant to pass through'.[10] *Catembe*, a film that intermixes documental footage with a fictional narrative centered around the life of a mixed race prostitute, touched on quite a few of the regime's interdictions: depicting the sexual encounters between Portuguese men and African women (an affair of unbalanced power), and also candidly exposing the poverty that afflicted the overwhelming majority of Maputo's (then Lourenço Marques) black population. Research focused on this period of censorship in Portugal points to the fact that, as Ana Bela Morais states, '. . . [there is] a greater emphasis on the censorship of love than on the censorship of violence. . .'.[11] And nothing seems to entice the desire to cut as much as the sexuality of the underprivileged. *Catembe*'s censored material gives us quite a compelling image: in the rather banal shots of black women flirting and dancing with white men in bars, one gets a clear sense of the coalescing of race and gender power imbalances. In the colonies, and in contrast to the gender imbalance that seemed to spread from Portugal to the frontiers of its empire, homosexuality was at least circumspectly tolerated and therefore benefited from the turn of an obvious blind-eye: 'male homosexuality, at least from the start of the colonial war and female homosexuality from the seventies, were allowed to exist with a certain degree of freedom by the colonial elites'.[12] These are idiosyncrasies of a colonial power at war.

The Marcelist Spring and the Gulbenkian Golden Years

Women becoming filmmakers was a utopia; only one dictatorship entry exists in the annals, for the feature director Bárbara Vírginia, and her 1946 film *Três dias sem Deus*

(*Three days without God*) which is a work that was unfortunately lost (just a few excerpts remain in the *Cinemateca Portuguesa*). The regime had mythologized the domestic habitat as women's natural environment. And so, all types of limitations intruded into careers and, by extension, the female self. Any mention of contraception was absolutely forbidden, even in medical journals. The repercussions of this situation severely limited women's prospects of becoming professionals in all fields of work. There is not a single woman director among the filmmakers of the Gulbenkian Golden Years of the Marcelist Spring – between 1968, which is the year Marcelo Caetano replaces Oliveira Salazar, and the revolution (a period that starts with great expectations of reform and ends with these largely failing to materialize). Although this lack of women *auteurs* is far from specific to Portugal or to film, it is still remarkable that it was occurring from within movements that trumpeted intellectual and artistic progressiveness.

Also, from the 1960s onwards, the regime could no longer keep a closed lid on the awareness that was starting to rise about the expansion of sexual behavior and exploration happening outside Portugal. Information was starting to pass in the gaps between the regime's fingers, like sand leaking from a hand seeking to contain it. 'We verify in Portugal an explosion of tourism from the early 1960s. This phenomenon brought great economic benefits but, more than everything, it contributed to a change in people's mentalities.'[13] This moment in the history of Portugal serves as a beacon for the questionable capitalist belief that the force of economics will always be a force for freedom. The profit that had started to drip from the tourism tap had become such a vigorous stream that it could no longer simply be closed by the regime; and with the waves of tourism came the waters of sexual revolution. António José Telo points out that:

> [T]he regime tries to resist in every way it can, going to the point of forbidding the first Jazz or Pop music concerts, and 'censoring' the American press. From 1969, it is obvious that this effort is pointless. It is practically impossible to control the arrival of foreign cultural media in a country with 1.5 million tourists.[14]
>
> Despite all the institutional control and censorship, the flow of information was happening. It is an entire generation that becomes 'foreignized [sic] and that, as a means of reacting to a traditionalist and closed society, adopts the cultural perspectives that come from abroad in all manner of ways.'[15]

Disconcerting the dictatorship were also the protests organized by university student unions that were aware of and influenced by May '68 and other protests transpiring around the world during those years. At one point, student protests had become so subversive as to turn the dictatorship's famous phrase 'Angola is ours' on its head, by having a black student hold a billboard with this same sentence.[16] These students were influenced by the books they were reading illegally in Portugal and by the films they could watch and texts they could read when travelling or studying abroad (a similar situation to what was happening in Greece); an example of the intensification of transnational cultural change in the 'Long 1960s', as analysed by historian Arthur Marwick.[17] A generation was being motivated not solely by what was happening in its own country, but also by what was taking place elsewhere: 'Undoubtedly, students were among the main actors of the "long sixties" all over the world'.[18]

This was also the moment when the dictatorship opted to soften its tone on the economic front and open up to foreign investment, which brought with it economic growth and a feeling of prosperity, hand in hand with the insecurities precipitated by exposure to consumer society, as shown in Richard Cleminson's and Rosa Medina-Domenech's chapter in this volume. The echoes of this reverberated heavily in the Portuguese film *The Siege* (*O Cerco*, 1970) by director Cunha Telles (the godfather of Portuguese *Cinema Novo*).[19] In this film, Marta, the main female protagonist, is trapped by economic necessity into seeking relationships with men who, in turn, see her as an object to be consumed. Consumer society had arrived to stay.

These films were clearly an authorial product and the cinema of a new generation that had studied abroad in France and in the UK. In parallel, in 1970 and 1974, filmmakers from the Gulbenkian Golden Generation (the *Cinema Novo* wave that was largely sponsored by the Gulbenkian Foundation)[20] made films that they consciously knew would never survive the censors' feverish cutting (e.g. Fernando Matos Silva's *Unloved* or João César Monteiro's *Fragments of an Alms-Film*). Both films were banned from the cinemas as they featured male protagonists with a certain level of fragility vis-à-vis their female partners.[21] These were defiant projects, made to survive as statements against the repressive perversions of the regime – films that were provocative from the outset, produced with an awareness of the censors' scissors, but with a strong sense of urgency and an absolute demand to be printed for the eyes and ears of the future generations. In these narratives, gender roles are questioned by changes in the power balance between men and women; we suddenly start to find depictions of women in control of their sexuality and of vulnerable men supplanted by fear and insecurity. Most of the work by the (male) filmmakers of this period is, as such, paradoxically, an object made with the hope of a better future, but also one that often problematizes and even disrupts the patriarchal sanctitude of the regime.

O Mal-Amado, in particular, is key to understanding the pre-revolution censorship and post-revolution exhibition: it was the last film to be banned by the *Estado Novo* and the first to be released after the revolution. In the film, the protagonist, João, embodies the antithesis of the alpha male. João is the object of a woman's desire (Inês) – an empowered woman. João is seduced and professionally below; a fragile man, somehow lost in the newly arrived consumer society. Inês, his manager, drives her own car; João uses public transport. Inês is the sexually demanding alpha in a film that does not stay shy from portraying female desire and male entrapment. Simone de Beauvoir said of a young Brigitte Bardot that she was no longer the prey, but rather the hunter[22] – this is the case with Inês. In a key scene, João is forced to accept Inês' incestuous fantasies, dressing up in her brother's military uniform and holding his gun, before a rapturous love scene. The abyss between past and present representations of Portuguese men and women could not be wider than in this scene that is fostering women's sexual empowerment and the questioning of the colonial war. João is represented on the screen with devices that were previously used for female representation; his objectification undermines the traditional role of the male in Portuguese society. This era witnessed the dawn of the 'fragile male' in Portuguese screens. Gender stereotypes seemed to be eroding in anticipation of the revolution due to come.

Revolution and eroticism

So far, this chapter has examined the heavy cuts to sexually explicit imagery in cinema during the *Estado Novo* due to the gender hierarchies that the regime promoted and the extent to which these tendencies were reversed during the Marcelist Spring. The following sections address the spread of erotic films during the revolution in Portugal as a clear manifestation of the support of the revolutionaries for a culture unbound. They demonstrate, however, that such movies did not really represent a rupture in terms of representations of gender, since they privileged the male heterosexual gaze.

In April 1974, straight after the revolution, one of the first political actions of the *Movimento das Forças Armadas* (Movement of the Armed Forces) was the abolition of censorship as a measure considered to be paramount to safeguard freedom of thinking and expression. However, an ad hoc commission was created in the following days by the information and tourism delegate so as to control press, radio, television, theatre and cinema and avoid disturbances to the political order. This commission would define a provisional structure of film classification interdicting erotic and pornographic films to viewers under the age of eighteen. The process of democratization and the concurrent availability of sexual content triggered a discussion about the role of erotic and pornographic cinema that would last from 1974 to 1976, spreading from the general to the specialized press. According to Luís de Pina, on 29 April 1974, a commission of antifascist filmmakers occupied the Portuguese Cinema Institute (*Instituto Português de Cinema*), the Cinema Professionals Union (*Sindicato dos Profissionais de Cinema*) and the state department responsible for the overseeing public shows (*Inspecção dos Espetáculos*) and 'managed to abolish film censorship and create an ad hoc commission for public shows to replace it'.[23] What can be observed in the aftermath of this event is an outcry given that such a measure would lead to an upsurge in the distribution of erotic and pornographic cinema in Portugal. And indeed, a downpour of 'adult' cinema quickly plugged the distribution channels and flooded the cinemas. But this was not an isolated phenomenon. As Regina Silva observes, 'the wave of porn cinema, "cine pornô", is part of an international trend, happening in France, Italy or Brazil – sexual liberation is manifested also in the cinema'.[24]

In Portugal, as in other countries, revolution equalled freedom in the minds and mouths of the population. Revolution was in the air, but interestingly, the case of Portuguese cinema is one of a far greater influence by the *Nouvelle Vague* and French *auteur* cinema (modes and perspectives that had been nursed by pre-revolution exposure) than any revolutionary zeitgeist that would sweep all cinematographic production before it. Work by *auteurs* seems to have taken a stronger hold and left a more lasting imprint. It is as if the most precious commodity revolutionary freedom could bring to Portuguese cinema was freedom of authorship.

A similar phenomenon of upsurge in sexuality also occurred in the cinema screens in Spain during the *Transición* which was the seven-year-long period following the end of the Franco dictatorship in November 1975 and is mentioned by historian Daniel Kowalsky, in his seminal article 'Rated S: softcore pornography and the Spanish transition to democracy, 1977–82'.[25] However, in contrast to Portugal, in Spain, '[d]ue to internal political indecision and strife among parties vying for power, in the wake of the Generalíssimo's[26] demise, no prompt decision was taken on the issue of acceptable film and media content. Only with Royal Decree 3071, signed on 11 November 1977, did the newly elected government of Adolfo Súarez formally abolish all media censorship'.[27] Also by contrast, while in Spain this newly found freedom led to a boom in national film production of what were called 'S films' '(the S rating was attached to products that, due to their content, might offend the sensibility of the spectator),[28] in Portugal audiences were consuming erotic and pornographic films produced in other countries. What is important to ascertain is whether or not the erotic cinema screened in Portugal can be categorized as 'S Films' and is 'ultimately conservative'.[29]

Meanwhile, immediately after the revolution, Portuguese audiences' craving for the sexual literacy and erotic fantasy that had been forbidden to them for so long invigorated the newly found erotic or pornographic screenings, with the distributors who were ogling a quick buck jumping at the opportunity. It is also relevant that a quarter of the Portuguese population was illiterate and that this had an obvious impact on the types of narrative film audiences could enjoy. Paulo Cunha states that on 20 June 1974 the ad hoc commission would publish its film classification legislation (*decreto Lei* n. 281/74), responding to the 'utmost necessity to avoid an improper use of a freedom that must go hand-in-hand with responsibility, and so that the country would not plunge into anarchy, thanks to the incitement to disorder and violence'.[30] Notwithstanding, this legislation merely established a criterion for classification according to age. No other bills were passed to regulate the growing volume of erotic and pornographic films in the cinemas. Many newspaper articles of the time would give the impression that 'pornography was everywhere', but the scholar and filmmaker Lauro António reminds us that this is an 'argument that could only exist and have apparent consistency in the mouths of those who did not attend the cinema and were not aware of new releases'.[31] Lauro António's research contextualizes the phenomenon and makes the point that 'During five decades accustomed to seeing things safely, movies previously scrutinized by others, others who would consider whether or not these films would be fit for the spectators' "candid" eyes, the Portuguese cinema audience lived as a child always protected from dealing with fire'.[32] Lauro António argues that with the end of censorship came a rise in conscious and responsible viewership: 'Therefore the spectator will have to proceed like this: to read the row of different shows that are available in his daily newspaper and to discern what is relevant to him and what does not interest him, what he does not want to watch, what he refuses to watch'.[33] It is easy to sympathize with Lauro António's idealism. However, the flipside of that same coin is whether or not cinema audiences (a population with limited cultural resources) possessed enough of the cognitive tools necessary to make sense of the sociopolitical forces behind this reality. In its edition of 1 June 1974, the magazine *Cinéfilo* included the following:

The truth is that more than one month after the abolition of censorship, the films that can be seen in the cinema screens are as bad or worse than the ones we used to watch prior to the revolution of 25th April. It is easy to conclude that aside from some 'sexual audacities' in mediocre and reactionary films that usually would remain in the private film reels of the censors, the films that we used to watch in the cinema, coincide with the average taste of the Lusitanian[34] distributor.[35]

This points to the fact that cinema consumption was not defined as much by the intervention of state institutions, but rather more because of the entrepreneurship of distributors. It is clear that a great degree of control was given over to distribution and that the resulting market was largely driven by profit and a cheap thrill – usually of a sexual nature. It is worth noting that immediately after the revolution, the State took control of banks and the overall economy so as to consolidate progress towards the socialist society it envisaged. This was considered of vital importance to the underpinning of revolutionary ideals and the protection of a revolutionary society. However, the control of cultural production and distribution was perceived as somehow not that vital for the materialization and safekeeping of those same ideals. The revolutionary process and the Portuguese population needed safeguarding from capitalism and the free market, however through the uninhibited distribution of a wealth of cheap cultural commodities that same market found a relatively trouble-free inlet where it had otherwise been the subject of a degree of control. It is true, also, that a revolutionary state emerging from the toppling of a dictatorship could not be seen to be implementing any measure of cultural control that could resemble the old ways of the *Estado Novo*.

In this vein, the magazine *Cinema 15* published an article in 1976 with the title 'The sexual themes in cinema: hypocrisy, frustration, the erotic and pornography'. From it, a few considerations on the economic relevance of porn can be drawn: 'Small provincial towns manage to successfully exhibit for days in a row films such as "Emmanuelle" [. . .] That the film "that dares" in sexual themes is more profitable than any other is what tells us the box office statistics of the Portuguese Institute for Film'.[36] With the wave of post-revolution 'sexual cinema' (1974 to 1976), a demarcation that was erased for audiences and critics alike was the distinction between eroticism and pornography, with the word 'erotic' receding and vanishing. In most debates and reviews, what can be observed is a differentiation between moral and amoral, normal and perverse. In the same magazine, a government statement (via the Procuradoria Geral da República) was published on 7 October 1975, with the denouncement that 'If, in principle, we must consider pornographic the publications that showcase and describe shocking and vicious sexual acts, it won't be necessarily the ones that exhibit full nudity, above all when dominated by the worry of beauty and the development of a normal sexuality.'[37] Thrown into this discussion about beauty and perversion, normality and abnormality, were such iconic films as Ralph Baskshi's *Fritz the Cat* (1972), that dealt with racism, class struggle, drugs and the sexual revolution; Bernardo Bertolucci's *Last Tango in Paris* (1972), about the sexual revelry of a modern cosmopolitan couple; and Pier Paolo Pasolini's *Decameron*

(1971) which was an adaptation of nine stories by Boccaccio. My research across the databases[38] on film distribution in Portugal from 1974 to 1976 points not so much to a wave of pornographic films, but rather to a stampede of erotic cinema. 'Almost 69% of the cinema audiences in Lisbon have opted in 1975 for films where sex and violence preponderated, 25% preferred other kinds of film and 6% watched films for children.'[39] Among the films with sexual and sometimes violent content one can find the work of key international filmmakers jumbled up with ordinary films.

Consequently, even with the sudden availability of sexual cinema or cinema that contained sexual explicitness, the majority were crowding to see what can be depicted as erotic films (and in many instances mainstream films) and not pornography. Many such films should be considered erotic because they went further than focusing solely on blunt sexual imagery and stopped short of explicit depiction: most contained a narrative (although very often mediocre), and worked by suggestion and titillation more than by offering sexual consummation on the screen. Pornographic cinema had a presence, but above all it was the erotic that attracted the audiences. Questions as to what is considered pornographic or erotic were also shifting and the boundary between the two, and had been the focus of international debate for a while, from the US to Brazil, to Spain and to France. These were the 1970s and *Emmanuelle* (1974) as well as *Deep Throat* (1972) were great cinema box office successes around the world. For instance, in Greece, 'Pornographic films were immensely popular in the initial post-dictatorship period, as is made evident by *Emmanuelle*'s sale of 337,485 tickets in Athens and Piraeus in 1974–5, the box-office runner up at that point.'[40]

What took place in the aftermath of the revolution was less the product of the State controlling culture and gender perceptions and more a laissez-faire relaxation. Nevertheless, this allowed a certain hegemonic perspective to creep in and take over. Soon, the Orwellian adage *all equal but some more than others* started to seep into the revolutionary process: a prominent case in point being heteronormativity.

Homosexuality and revolution

The revolution witnessed ambiguous developments with regard to gender and sexuality. Women became increasingly active in politics; this allowed the creation of several women's organizations by the end of the 1970s. Nevertheless, it is telling that, in contrast to women's groups elsewhere in Western Europe, they did not put emphasis on abortions, since most of these organizations construed this issue as too divisive. In fact, an abortion decriminalization law was approved only in 1984.[41] Meanwhile, the status of homosexuals did not change substantially. On the gay rights front, if up to 1974 homosexuality was a disorder subject to rectification, afterwards the revolution simply did not deliver a legal frame of recognition and protection. It was only in 1982 that homosexuality ceased to be a crime, taking until 2010 for gay marriage to be legalized. The collapse of the dictatorship did not bring with it the legalization of homosexuality. Even after the revolution, Portuguese society remained centered on the values of the traditional family and the sovereignty of heterosexuality. São José Almeida's investigation makes reference to testimonies about middle-class homosexuality somehow previously tolerated, but now being suppressed by the revolutionaries, as something incompatible with the revolutionary process: 'With the 25th of April, democratization did not allow that these behaviors [sic] would last. They represented the image of the decadent bourgeoisie of the fascist families, when before it had been the eccentric boys of well-to-do families, from whom everything was allowed.'[42]

A number of gay organizations, such as the Action Movement of the Revolutionary Homosexuals (Movimento de Acção dos Homossexuais Revolucionários – MAHR), were obliterated shortly after their creation. The catalysts for the crackdown on the revolutionary gay movement were the publication of a manifesto by the MAHR on 13 May 1974 in the newspaper *Diário de Lisboa*, and a revolutionary gay gathering in the city of Porto straight after. This led

> Admiral Galvão de Melo (paradoxically, a counter-revolutionary character), member of the governmental Junta de Salvação, to proclaim on Portuguese state television, to reassure the population, that the morality and decency of the revolution would be safeguarded, and to state that the revolution had not been achieved for the benefit of prostitutes and homosexuals. It was the end of any utopia that the revolutionary moment had created, as the arrival of a democracy equal for all and with legalized individual rights for all members of society.[43]

Under these circumstances, there was little space left for any gay perspectives in the cinema. Across the arts, Jorge de Sena's novel *Sinais de Fogo* (*Smoke Signals*), published in 1979, was the first and one among only a few to openly discuss homosexuality. Female homosexuality was invisible: '... lesbianism [was] crushed, reduced to the dimension of a ghost, for a double stigmatization: that of homosexuality itself and that inherent to the female condition'.[44]

The revolutionary process did not entirely revoke the dictatorship's hostility towards homosexuality; most sexually explicit films in the cinemas catered to male heterosexual fantasies, with female and gay viewpoints muzzled by the merry-go-round of distribution. One of the films that was most fiercely debated at the time was Italian gay filmmaker Pier Paolo Pasolini's *Saló, or the 120 days of Sodom* (*Salò, o le 120 giornate di Sodoma*) from 1975. It made the then minister, Almeida Santos, state (after a private viewing) that 'While I'm in power, this film will never be shown to the public!'[45] What transpired was that gay men and women watched the cinema intended for heterosexual audiences, as homosexuality was still illegal.

Controversies and rollback

This blossoming of erotic film did not go uncontested. It came under fire, not from advocates of gay and lesbian rights, but, rather, from more conservative sections of society: a voice of concern was regularly expressed by a media portal of the Catholic Church, the Secretariat for Film and Radio (Secretariado do Cinema e da Radio). The following excerpt is from a text published in no. 1222 (1-VI-1974) of the *Film Journal* (*Boletim Cinematográfico*):

> But, in defence of good cinema, we do not want to see cinemas invaded, like the example of other countries, by films that are worthless, aimed at an easy profit by exploiting a degrading pornography, of a sadistic violence, with contempt for the dignity of humanity, with the resulting disappearance of a cinema that is culturally and aesthetically relevant for the formation of an audience and that will contribute to a conscious public.[46]

The Secretariat for Film and Radio had as its mantra, 'the development of a cinéphile culture for everyone, within a Christian perspective'.[47] But what can bring us this Christian perspective? In the list of 'condemnable' films published by the Secretariat for 1975, one can find, among others, Jacques Rivette's *The Nun* (*La Réligieuse*, 1966), along with Anna Karina and Walerian Borowczyk's *Immoral Tales* (*Contes Imoraux*, 1974), with Paloma Picasso.

In a debate in Rádio Renascença (a radio controlled by the Church) in April 1976, Almeida Santos, the then Social Communication Minister (Ministro da Comunicação Social), stated that 'In what regards films, I suggest that the board of film classification grades them also as pornographic or non-pornographic (although the terms must be other) and upon these [pornographic films] may fall an extra taxation that will act as a discouragement to the tendency of bad films of evicting the good ones'.[48]

Eventually, on 7 April 1976, via legislation in Decreto-Lei n. 154/76, the Ministry of Communications published a law on the polemic question of pornography in Portuguese society:

> Despite understanding the hunger for films of pornographic content due to 'almost half a century of sexual mystification and a total lack of sexual education', the government decided to intervene by advancing a law, because it realized that 'the freedom that followed repression's containment has always the price of a certain level of excess', favouring 'the commercial exploration not of the erotic or of the artistic nude, but rather the pornographic and obscene'. Contrary to previous governments that just 'witnessed without intervening' the executive power believed that the time has arrived to intervene, as a response to the 'manifestations of protest against what [several sectors in the society] consider, not without reason, intolerable abuses'.[49]

The government established the code of film classification at the same time as the counter-revolutionary movements were starting to take a firm hold on Portuguese institutions and society. These counter-revolutionary forces took the shape of organized structures that defended the control of personal freedoms at several levels and the discontinuation of socialist perspectives on a variety of issues – for instance, film classification or workers' rights. Yet, it is clear that the revolution had engendered a space for freedom and equality that was now irrevocable – although this remained limited in scope and slow in its progress. Portuguese film distribution was structured around this time as the purveyor of a certain 'product' catering chiefly to a heterosexual male market (as it is today). Still, the revolutionary process gave rise to the principle, harboured in the concept of freedom of speech, that no film, regardless of merit or topic, should be censored, partially or entirely but that it instead should fall under a system of classification. This opened the doors to the screening of all kinds of fringe cinema which, although at the margins of the mainstream, played a significant role in the shaping of important sections of Portuguese society and influenced *auteur* and political cinemas in Portugal.

Conclusions

Undoubtedly, the circulation of erotic and pornographic cinema between 1974 and 1976 was the manifestation of a space of freedom; of the utopia of a culture unbound, freed from (or wanting to free itself from) the chains of the old Catholic morality that had reigned supreme during the *Estado Novo*. The State chose, in these years, not to define a narrative for the cinema. However, no country can remain an island, especially a relatively small country like Portugal. So the largest slice of distribution came in the form of specific types of foreign cinema, shaped with a narrative that catered mostly for hegemonic masculinity, for the heterosexual male gaze, aiming at a quick and easy profit. Film distribution freedom did not contribute to values of equality. The utopia of a free distribution market turned out a relatively homogenized stream that was defined by a few individuals holding particular market-driven prescriptions. Revolutionaries, in the meantime, had to concentrate on trying to shore up the values that were starting to crack and collapse around them. It is undeniable that with the revolution came also a cultural revolution, as shown in Giulia Bonali's chapter in this volume, a profound change in gender roles and, in the long term, the recognition of the rights of homosexuals and a greater degree of gender equality. But in its immediate aftermath, it did not engender a society that would promote full sexual and gender equality. The revolution was not for all.

Notes

1. Kostis Kornetis, '"*Everything Links*"? Temporality, territoriality and cultural transfer in the '68 Protest Movements', *Historein* 9, 2009, 34–45.
2. António Salazar Ferro, *O Homem e a sua Obra* (Lisboa: Empresa Nacional de Publicidade, 1933), 225.
3. *Estado Novo* (New State) was one of the terms used to describe the Portuguese dictatorship.

4. Leonor Areal, 'As Imagens Proibidas – A Censura ao Cinema Português in Cabrera', in Ana Cabrera (ed). *Censura Nunca Mais!* (Lisboa: Alêtheia Editores, 2013), 115.
5. São José Almeida, *Homossexuais no Estado Novo* (Lisboa: Sextante Editora, 2010), 50.
6. Ibid, 57.
7. Ibid.
8. Ibid, 146.
9. Ana Bela Morais, *Tensões entre Marte e Vénus – Reflexões sobre a censura ao amor e à violência nos primeiros anos do Governo de Marcelo Caetano*, in Ana Cabrera (ed.), *Censura Nunca Mais!*, 180.
10. Maria do Carmo Piçarra, *Do Minho a Timor somos todos . . . pássaros de asas cortadas* in Cabrera, *Censura Nunca Mais!*, 245.
11. Ibid, 265.
12. Almeida, *Homossexuais*, 209.
13. Morais, *Tensões*, 271.
14. António José Telo, 'Portugal, 1958–1974: Sociedade em Mudança', in João Medina (ed.), *História de Portugal. Dos tempos pré-históricos aos nossos dias*, vol. XIII, O, 'Estado Novo', II: opressão e resistência (Amadora: Ediclube, 1993), 328.
15. Ibid.
16. Miguel Cardina, *Memórias incómodas e rasura do tempo: Movimentos estudantis e praxe académica no declínio do Estado Novo* [https://www.academia.edu].
17. Arthur Marwick, *The Sixties. Cultural Revolution in Britain, France, Italy and the United States, c. 1958– c. 1974* (Oxford, New York: Oxford University Press, 1998).
18. Guya Accornero, 'The Revolution Before the Revolution, Student Protest and Political Radicalization at the End of the Portuguese Estado Novo', paper presented at the 46th ASPHS.
19. Akin to the *Nouvelle Vague*, Portuguese *Cinema Novo* was characterized by a generational eagerness to break with what was considered the conservative moulds of filmmaking and bring a new language to the screens. This generation studied in France and the UK and was profoundly influenced by the experiences they lived in these countries. Paulo Rocha and Fernando Lopes are also key names in this movement.
20. It was established in 1956 as a foundation to foster the arts, charity, science and education, using the fortune of the deceased Calouste Sarkis Gulbenkian. Calouste Gulbenkian was one of the wealthiest individuals of his time and he played a major role in making the petroleum reserves of the Middle East available to Western investment.
21. In the case of *Unloved*, the film was banned outright, while *Fragments of an Alms-Film* was not screened because its director refused to screen a cut version of the film.
22. Simone de Beauvoir, *Brigitte Bardot and The Lolita Syndrome* (London: New English Library, 1962).
23. Luis de Pina, *A Aventura do Cinema Português* (Lisboa: Vega, 1977), 199.
24. Regina Silva, 'O Cinema Brasileiro em Portugal. Contexto e Análise da Crítica Acerca de Filmes Brasileiros publicada na Imprensa Lisboeta (1960–1999)', PhD thesis, Universidade Nova de Lisboa, 2006.
25. Daniel Kowalsky, 'Rated S; softcore pornography and the Spanish transition to democracy, 1977–82', in Antonio Lázaro Reboll and Andrew Willis (eds), *Spanish Popular Cinema* (Manchester: Manchester University Press, 2004).

26. General Franco.
27. Kowalsky, 'Rated S', 188.
28. Ibid.
29. Ibid, 196.
30. Paulo Cunha, *A Censura depois da Censura: O caso dos filmes eróticos e pornográficos (1974–76)* in Cabrera, *Censura Nunca Mais!*, 183.
31. António, Lauro, *Cinema e Censura em Portugal* (Lisboa, Biblioteca Museu República e Resistência, 2001), 14.
32. Ibid, 14.
33. Ibid.
34. Lusitanian here equals Portuguese.
35. Cunha, *A Censura*, 187.
36. *Cinema* 15.I, 1976, 6–8.
37. Cunha, *A Censura*, 196.
38. Archives of Cinemateca Portuguesa e Torre do Tombo in Lisbon.
39. *Cinema* 15.IV, 1976, 9.
40. Nikolaos Papadogiannis, 'Between *Angelopoulos* and *The Battleship Potemkin*: cinema and the making of young communists in Greece in the initial post-dictatorship period (1974–81)', *European History Quarterly* 42, 2012, 286.
41. Ana Prata, 'The Portuguese women's movement struggle for bodily citizenship rights: the issues of abortion and prostitution', in Joyce Outshoorn (ed.), *European Women's Movements and Body Politics: The Struggle for Autonomy* (Houndmills, Basingstoke: Palgrave Macmillan, 2015).
42. Almeida, *Homossexuais*, 222.
43. Pina, *A Aventura*, 199.
44. Almeida, *Homossexuais*, 222.
45. Cunha, *A Censura*, 203.
46. Ibid, 185.
47. Ibid, 183.
48. *Cinema* 15.IV, 1976, 7.
49. Cunha, *A Censura*, 200.

CHAPTER 7
THE SPANISH HOUSEWIVES IN TRANSITION (1959–80)
Elena Díaz Silva

Introduction

The role of Spanish women in the transition to democracy after Franco's death in 1975 has been somewhat neglected in traditional historiography that until now has been centred on political aspects, on the institutional development of the new regime and on the role of the founders of the democracy. Recent approaches try to demystify the Spanish Transition, highlighting the importance of the so-called secondary characters: working class, students and social and grassroots movements.[1] However, in the literature on social Transition, an issue on which there is still much to be written, the contribution of women remained unexamined.[2] This fact changed when new researches from a gender perspective appeared and revealed the role of women and feminism in this process.[3] Writing about women during the Transition implies, firstly, recognizing the importance of the social and cultural transformation process in the period preceding the Transition; secondly, dwelling on the study of the implications for gender identities. These transformations were more than just the backdrop of the Transition and the political events that delimit it; they enabled it, which is why they should form a fundamental part of any study on the Transition.[4]

The maintenance of traditional and patriarchal family structures had been a priority of the regime from the very beginning. The policy on women was very similar to the one developed by the fascist regimes in Italy and Germany.[5] Women's magazines helped to consolidate and maintain these structures during the dictatorship through the production and transmission of a feminine model of behaviour.[6] They constituted a vehicle of ideological indoctrination and a complement to the informal education of young women and girls received from the *Sección Femenina*, the women's branch of the Phalange political movement.

During the first stage of the Francoist era (1939–45) the most widely propagated feminine stereotype was the 'angel of the hearth': an abnegated woman-mother-wife. The isolation of Spain during this period, from the end of the Second World War to 1959, made easier the consolidation of this gender model. The adoption of new policies for the development of the economy from 1959 brought a new chapter in the history of Francoism. The autarky was replaced by the developmentalism, an economic theory brought by the technocrats that took control of Spanish economic policy. The changes in the Spanish economic structure during this era introduced a new model of femininity influenced by North American culture, which arrived at the same time as appliances to Spanish homes.

Consumption and Gender through the Moment of Transition

At that point, magazines like *Ama* began to educate and orient women towards new practices of consumption and family budgeting which introduced Spaniards (mainly the rising middle class) to the mass consumption society. New discourses of domesticity emerged as technology began to mechanize domestic tasks. The 'economic miracle' brought about by tourism, foreign investment and emigration contributed significantly to the growth of the economy and the modernization of social mores and values, as well as to the transmission and dispersion of new ideas and aspirations among Spaniards.

The transition to democracy after Franco's death further contributed to the evolution of gender roles. As a result, the existing hegemonic model of masculinity and femininity was altered. Legislative changes and reforms to family rights meant that during the Transition the notion of the family began to evolve and to become more democratic. These changes slowly began to be reflected in the more traditional feminine press where, despite the conservative nature of these publications, the question of women's rights began to be addressed: from the 'eternal minority of women' (because of discrimination in law and practice), to the right to abortion or to the use of contraceptives.

The housewives' associations, created since 1963 in the context of political openness, provided new spaces for debates and discussions about the issues that affected women collectively such as the rising prices of consumer goods and services, the low salaries and the lack of infrastructures in new neighbourhoods. Although they defended private or particular issues, these associations allowed an increase in the limits of domesticity towards the public sphere, and gave women freedom from the socialization imposed during the early stages of Franco dictatorship. However, as Pamela Radcliff recognizes in her works, there has been a certain reticence in established historical accounts to recognize housewives' associations as 'schools of citizenship' and to include them in accounts of the democratic Transition in Spain.[7]

What has been even more neglected by historians, however, is the collective role of housewives more generally as agents of change in the modernization and democratization process in Spain, perhaps due to the complexity of this role. In order to understand this, it is necessary to overcome the established association between housewives and traditional models of femininity which were spread by the women's magazines at the time. Therefore, on the basis of Joan Scott's theory, gender is considered not only as a cultural construction of sexual difference but as a 'primary way of signifying relationships of power'.[8] Thus, changes in the model of femininity lead to changes in the model of masculinity, considering that gender is a relational category.

This chapter analyses the evolution of gender models disseminated by *Ama* for twenty years, mainly the housewife stereotype, to confront it with the discourse and practices of the associations of housewives in the same period. The press and associations had been controlled by the regime from the beginning due to their importance for political indoctrination and the socialization of Spaniards. The new association and press laws approved in 1964 and 1966 were the pillars of the *apertura* ('political openness') in the late Franco dictatorship. They allowed the emergence of critical positions in the press from a progressive ideology, and a certain freedom of gathering in 'democratic' spaces open to discussion, in spite of the limits imposed by the authorities. The evolution of

Ama regarding the content, as well the changes in, the aims and strategies of housewives' associations reflects the process of shaping gender identities in these spaces during the last years of Francoism, and during the Transition. It also reflects the tension between the different models of femininity that appeared during this period.

In addition, the acknowledgement of these cultural and social changes allows a reintegration of Spain in the international context. From a gender perspective, the 'cultural revolution' in Spain started shortly after that in France or Italy. The 'silent' revolution of women was not only a reaction against authoritarianism, but also part of a transnational movement: the second wave of feminism that first began in the early 1960s in the US. The Long Sixties, an idea elaborated by Arthur Marwick in *The Sixties: Cultural Revolution in Britain, France, Italy and the United States, 1958–1974*, may well be used in the case of Spain.[9] However, in Spain the Long Sixties lasted more than in those countries, covering virtually the whole decade of the 1970s. The 'cultural revolution' implied more than a simple opposition to Franco's regime. Cultural changes opened a deeper generational gap in Spanish society, also implying changes in the strategies and discourses of the anti-Franco opposition movement.[10] Furthermore, the demands of democratization in Spain assumed the proposals defended in Europe in order to re-found Western democracy. Despite the efforts of the regime, Spain and Spaniards were not so different as the Minister of Tourism tried to make believe with his famous slogan: 'Spain is different'. Recent scholarly works suggest that both immigrants who returned to Spain from France or Germany and tourists contributed to the modernization of Spanish society, as well as to the reshaping of gender identities.[11]

The adoption of the 'Model Mrs. Consumer' in the late Franco dictatorship (1959–75)

In her work, Victoria de Grazia analyses the arrival of the 'Irresistible Empire' from the US and the assimilation of modern consumption practices in European households through their main representatives: housewives.[12] However, this phenomenon requires closer examination in the case of Spain. The adoption of the model of woman consumer during the late Franco dictatorship is linked to the cultural influence of the US in Spain as a result of a closer relationship between the two countries after signing the bilateral agreements in September 1953. The 'Pacts of Madrid' allowed the US government to install military bases in Spain in return for financial support. However, although its relationship with the US allowed the Franco regime to emerge from international isolation, it did not contribute directly to Spain's democratization in later years. The purpose of the American intervention in Spain was always to secure its role as a geostrategic ally.[13]

As part of the public diplomatic efforts to strengthen relations between the two countries and ensure the leadership of the US, the North American model of femininity began to be promoted in Spanish culture. The purpose of diffusing this model was to counter the negative image that many Spaniards had regarding American women, mainly the female protagonists of Hollywood films who appeared on the first television screens in Spanish households, and regarding the 'decadent' American society.[14] The truth is that the postwar model of the American woman was not far away from the feminine ideal propagated by National Catholicism in Spain. The domesticity ideology of the postwar period had reinforced the role of breadwinner and homemaker. War and Cold War had contributed to define the household as a safe place in which to face the menace of communism.[15] American diplomats reiterated the message that differences between the two societies were not as irreconcilable, nor divorces as common, nor American homes as disorderly as many Spaniards believed.[16]

The ideology of National Catholicism in Spain had imposed a conservative, traditional model of femininity, based exclusively on the roles of mother and wife.[17] At that time, social norms and the sexual division of labour dictated that most middle-class married women were responsible for the care of the children and the dependent family members, carrying out domestic tasks and administering the domestic economy. The values of sacrifice, abnegation and frugality were the pillars upon which isolation and political autarky were maintained in the early stages of Francoism. Journals like *Teresa* or *Medina*, published by the *Sección Femenina* from 1940 onwards, showed women as consumers who cut costs and practised austerity. These models were replaced in the 1960s when consumption, particularly in the domestic sphere, became an engine for Spanish economic development.

The arrival of the 'Model Mrs. Consumer' and consumer standards are important phenomena in the analysis of the influence of the American way of life in Spain. Women's magazines and particularly advertisements demonstrate the transition towards a consumer society where women were a focal point, because they were the main consumers within households. This fact coincided with the regime's *apertura* and the economic liberalization that inaugurated a new stage in Francoism. The magazine *Ama, revista de las amas de casa* that emerged in 1960 with a print run of 225,000 copies every two weeks was promoted by the public organism responsible for transport and supplies (CAT). Created in the style of the women's magazines imported from North America that had become so popular in Europe, this and other similar magazines became the main source of information on Western consumer standards. Their message helped to diffuse the notion of a 'professional' housewife whose sphere of work was at the centre of the home and particularly in the kitchen, where work was mechanized and rationalized almost as if it were a factory.[18]

The arrival of a new imported consumer model benefited from the new socioeconomic reality that was extensible, however, to the whole of Europe. At the same time, the arrival of consumer culture in Spain was beneficial to Francoism because it offered a positive image of development to the outside world, which fitted with the regime's desire to break out of political isolation, mainly in Europe.[19] As well as generating a sense of desire/need among consumers, advertisements also reflected the social and cultural changes that were taking place and the process of modernization in Spanish society. Changes were gradually inserted into the messages transmitted in the press and particularly in women's magazines that used this new stereotype of the 'modern woman' as a 'political insignia'.[20] The re-signification of the role of housewives redefined the social function of women.

Now they were the chief household administrators as well as wives and mothers. In order to exercise their role in the consumer culture, *Ama* educated its readers on new techniques of consumption and shopping, on the distribution of family budgets without neglecting the importance of saving, and warned them of the dangers of misleading advertising.

The advent of the supermarket in Spain provides an example of the success of these interventionist policies, which complemented the American technical and financial aid that had contributed so much to the rapid development of the Spanish economy, the 'Spanish miracle', as well as to the legitimization and perpetuation of the regime. *Ama* dedicated its first issues to the advent of the supermarket in Spain, highlighting the virtues and benefits of this new system of supply and demand, which had been imported directly from the US and was associated with the new model of economic productivity.[21] However, even if this brought an end to earlier consumer practices in which shopping was limited by the scarce supply, variety and quality of products, not all the effects were positive. As *Ama* warned, although the introduction of supermarkets brought many benefits to sellers, they also required greater intellectual efforts on the part of customers who now needed to evaluate different products.[22] This, in turn, led to new shopping habits and behaviours in a customer base that consisted almost exclusively of women. The selection of products and decision-making, which had been previously the prerogative of the shop assistant, was thereafter the responsibility of women. Although it was not the initial intention, in some ways the introduction of the supermarket in Spain led to a certain empowerment of housewives by turning them into more demanding customers.

Women were the main consumers in the domestic and family sphere, the 'home professionals', and the adverts that filled the pages of women's magazines were addressed mainly to them. Phrases such as 'The way to a man's heart is through his stomach. A well-fed husband is a happy husband',[23] used by a kitchen manufacturer in one of its advertisements, exemplify the association drawn between the product and its consumption (or use) and the effect of immediate happiness. These adverts also assured marital and familial harmony, encouraging consumption as a means of solidifying and preserving love between partners.

Men were also indoctrinated in the traditional and Catholic gender model. After the Spanish Civil War, the Francoist masculine ideal suffered a metamorphosis.[24] The model of warrior, inspired in the fascist ideals of masculinity, was replaced by a different one influenced by the Catholicism and paternalism which emphasized the roles of men as fathers, husbands and workers. As a result, the 'breadwinner family model', that implied the recognition of a gender division of labour, was reinforced. In response to his wife's obedience, a husband was expected to protect and support his wife, as established in the legislation of the Spanish Civil Code until its reform in 1975. *Ama* helped to indoctrinate young people in these models of behaviour:

> Those of you young ladies who have just gotten married you should know well that you must practise serenity, patience, goodwill, and self-sacrifice in order to ensure the happiness of your 'hubby'. Over time you will be surprised to see that this

happiness and peace that you have achieved will make your life better as the one of your husband.²⁵

Advertisements complemented this task through statements that praised the traditional family model as the only valid one, and 'perfected' thanks to the arrival of household appliances and other consumer products that raised the standard of living for Spaniards in general, despite the social inequalities created. In 1965, the advertisement for a washing machine's manufacturer stated: 'She is a woman of today. She loves the perfection in the wash but she is not willing to waste her time on this. She goes on with an active working and social life, the SUPERMATIC-2 takes care of the laundry.'²⁶

In addition to appliances, advertisements encouraged women to buy cosmetic products such as make-up or weight loss products, sometimes in a manner which was sexist by the imposition of a new beauty canon. Advertisements pressured women to consume products in order to maintain attractiveness, happiness, youth, marriage and even social position. Although it is true that the pressure for women to remain desirable and young had existed before, the progressive eroticization of their image in advertisements represented a new phenomenon. As Aurora Morcillo stated in *The Seduction of Modern Spain*, women's bodies had played a central role in the political imagination of Francoism. The new facet of femininity that emerged in the press and media was part of the new discourse of gender, a symbol of modernity, the 'Spanish model of modernization'.²⁷

At that time, *Ama* began to publish reports in its social chronicles about the private lives of famous actresses, singers and other artists, which did not adhere to the social norms and restrictions of the time. Some articles also unreservedly exposed the most 'scandalous' details of their romances. This new feminine model was very different from the Falangist and even the National Catholic ideal. At that time, even the magazine itself struggled to maintain a balance between the representation of the model of 'modern' and sexually liberated women, and the old one identified with the 'modern' housewife, that is, the 'home professional'. The evolution of the ideal of femininity was influenced by the appearance of new women's magazines, mainly *Telva*, addressed to modern, cultivated and upper-class women. In fact, the publisher of *Telva*, which appeared in 1963, was very close to the Opus Dei Roman Catholic organization that helped to design the programmes to modernize the Spanish economy. While it is true that *Telva* was not only addressed to housewives, but also to young unmarried women, the magazine insisted that the main responsibility of women was the family and housework. Both models struggled to represent the modernization of 'true Catholic womanhood'.

Throughout the 1960s, this model was reinforced thanks to the entry of Spain into a consumer society. However, behind this phenomenon that drew Spain closer to Europe, were hiding the inequalities and imbalances caused by the economic policies of the regime. Labour and social protests that hardened from the late 1960s questioned the developmental policy, the stillness of the regime. However, none of this was reflected in *Ama* which continued with the same editorial line until Franco's death.

The political socialization of women during the Transition through *Ama, la revista de las amas de casa* (1975–80)

The widespread use of home appliances also had an effect on the standard of living of Spanish women, because it allowed housewives, according to their socioeconomic class and new technological advances which mechanized household tasks, to be progressively freed from most of their domestic obligations.[28] Women had more time to devote to activities beyond the sphere of their homes, as reflected in *Telva*, or in the Spanish version of *Cosmopolitan* and *Marie Claire* that appeared between 1976 and 1977 without much success.[29]

From 1975 onwards there was a change in the editorial management of *Ama*, which began to be edited by a private firm (Distribuciones Hogar SA) in place of CAT. The advertisements, the inclusion of political messages and the expansion of the subjects of interest for readers reflect the influence that the Transition had on the magazine, which sought to adapt itself to a changing society:

> The ideal woman, who is capable of sharing her life with a man and standing at his level, is not just a woman who can manage her household, care for her husband, and care for their children in a traditional domestic sense [...] In order to reach her potential, today's woman must also be aware of other aspects of life in order to equip herself for the world of men and in order to truly be man's equal as well as his companion.[30]

Adverts for home appliances, which had become increasingly sophisticated, were progressively replaced with adverts for consumer products tailored to a more individualistic society, one that was less invested in the desires and aspirations of family unity. Beauty products began to replace food adverts. The automobile industry, which until then had been limited to taking advantage of the rise in the standard of living of Spaniards and the consolidation of a majority middle class, found a new target audience: the woman born of *desarrollismo*. Driving cars, which had always been a masculine habit and prerogative, was no longer considered a gender transgression, and adverts began to encourage women to buy and drive cars as a means of liberating themselves.[31] The slogan used by the French car manufacturer Citroën read 'You, free woman, modern woman', encouraging women to buy a car of this make.[32]

New articles kept in step with the interests of the new woman and housewife. The incorporation of women into the labour force and higher education was an issue that could no longer be ignored by the women's magazines.[33] In 1977 a new section of the magazine devoted to male and female users and consumers published an article dealing with 'the issue of prices, rights, rules, and codes that should be recognized by consumers'.[34] This reflects the magazine's effort to open itself up to a more participatory audience, including men. The reference to 'rights' leaves no doubt about the influence of a democratic language.

As the sections devoted to domestic issues and to the consumption habits of housewives began to disappear, new sections appeared such as '*Derecho*' (Rights) and the series '*La Española ante la ley*' (the Spanish woman and law), which warned Spanish women in a series of issues about sexual discrimination in law, particularly in the family. 'How far do your rights extend?' asked the magazine. 'Is our legislation undeveloped in comparison with the rights which women and men themselves [are] enjoying abroad?'[35] The magazine praised the fact that, although it arrived later than in other countries, the feminist movement had 'entered' Spain. The editorial expressed its approval of the movement: 'At last! The Spanish woman has (finally!) realized that she is just as human as the Spanish man, just as much a citizen, and consequently, deserving just the same rights as him.'[36]

In 1977 and 1978 the magazine echoed the debates surrounding the legalization of contraceptives,[37] abortion[38] and divorce,[39] positioning itself for its regulation, and consequently, towards changes in legislation. Despite the criticism received from some of its conservative readers, the magazine no longer concealed its editorial board's changing views.[40] *Ama* seemed to be in favour of family planning after recognizing that Spanish legislation against contraceptives was 'really out-of-step' with contemporary social values. The reports were accompanied by statistics and opinion polls, mostly in favour of these changes mainly among youth. Despite this fact, in regard to sexuality, changes in sexual morality were not included in *Ama*, which continued to view this as a taboo topic. However, *Cosmopolitan* as well as *Vindicación feminista*, the first feminist magazine in Spain that appeared in 1976, included this topic.[41] The inclusion of this issue in *Ama* was however limited to the advertisement that continued in the style of the late Franco dictatorship with sexual references and/or content that became increasingly explicit. The advertising of lingerie is a clear example of this. During the 1960s, drawings were replaced by suggestive photographs that focused on the nudity of women's bodies. These advertisers took advantage of the misnamed 'sexual liberation' which had been expressed profusely in films since 1960 and which only served to reinforce traditional gender roles.[42]

Lastly, in these years *Ama* showed an interest in political socialization. A political section, although sporadic, provided information designed to inform readers on the changes that had taken place since Franco's death. In '*De la cosa democrática*' (on the subject of democracy), the magazine's director, Rafael Andreu, who was confident and hopeful about the development of democracy in Spain, took the opportunity to petition the government for greater transparency and full political freedom. This meant the legalization of all political parties. As a result of this commitment, during these years the publication began to include in its pages adverts for the main political parties that had been legalized and were launching their campaigns, mainly the Union of the Democratic Centre (UCD), the Spanish Socialist Workers' Party (PSOE) and the Popular Allianz (AP). These political messages were not targeted specifically at women, nor did they include instructions with the objective of mobilizing them. Both AP and UCD aimed to attract conservative and centrist voters, respectively, by appealing to the traditional Christian family model, which needed to be defended and protected, especially after the legalization of the Communist Party in 1977. The role of women, specifically of housewives, was very important because they assured the transmission of familiar and

Christian values. The images that accompanied their proclamations and electoral promises included representations of a new model of the family, less hierarchical, inclined to the collaboration and participation of all its members, reflecting an effective change in the power dynamic existing in the relationship. For that reason, *Ama* decided to publish a series of reports entitled 'The wives of politicians speak out', in which the wives of the main political leaders of the time were interviewed.[43]

The inclusion of their testimonies seems to reflect the magazine's interest in introducing changes in the Spanish model of femininity, masculinity and family, as well as its desire to adapt itself to social and political transformations and to the current political climate. It promoted a model of a woman who was interested and immersed in the social and political issues of her country, even though she was constrained by her domestic obligations. However, ignoring the experience of the female political activists, *Ama* promoted a model of a man devoted to politics, still seen as a masculine prerogative, as a 'full citizen'. Despite this fact, *Ama* was ambiguous with regard to its approach to masculinity. A new version of masculinity was introduced in its pages that reflected changes in power relations in a male-female relationship. Asked about their 'ideal men' the readers of *Ama* cited the most important values and attitudes in a man as being comradeship, responsibility, non-sexism and trustworthiness.[44]

Ascensión Sedeño and the first Spanish housewives' association (1963–81)

Although a large part of society still regarded politics as a man's profession, the participation of women in social activism and in the formation of associations was increasingly valued. The regime favoured the formation of family-oriented organizations, such as neighbourhood, housewife and parent associations from the 1960s. Far from contradicting Francoism's fundamental principles, they helped the reinforcement of the existing social structures and channelled the population's participation in politics through corporative organizations that underpinned a fiction of democracy, the 'organic democracy' of the late Franco dictatorship. The Law of Associations of 1964 was designed to meet the demands of democratization of the international community, particularly the European Economic Community (EEC) which Spain aspired to join, without much success. The first housewives' association in Spain appeared between 1963 and 1965, founded by Ascensión Sedeño, who was a trained teacher and housewife. The phenomenon arose in Spain later than in the rest of Europe, although again it was influenced by the US and by the women who pioneered new housekeeping and household efficiency in America in the 1920s.[45]

The context in which these associations were formed, however, was very different in Spain. Although one of their main objectives was to guide women in the administration of household budgets, particularly shopping budgets, they prioritized protesting against inflation in the prices of basic products, which had occurred as a result of the government's liberal economic policies. The initiatives of this organization did not question the political system. They channelled their complaints and petitions through the limited official channels that were open to them. Their activism was carried out in the name of 'female conscience' as defined by Temma Kaplan, demanding the right to carry out their roles according to the gender division of labour.[46] Their campaigns had the protection, if not the support, of the public authorities, and as a result they played an important role in the simulation of democratic normality. Apart from contributing to the politicization of gender relations in everyday life, as Temma Kaplan has noted, they also helped update the behavioural expectations of model housewives, which until then had been characterized by obedience and passivity. Apart from protesting against price inflation, in the later years of the Franco dictatorship and the Transition, the Spanish Housewives' Association promoted an image of a professional woman who was committed to her home and to her domestic obligations – a model addressed again to middle class and urban women. Ascensión Sedeño believed that it was at a local level that housewives could make a greater contribution to society. In this sphere that was located somewhere between the complex dichotomy of the public and the private spheres, and which was reinterpreted as an extension of the home, women extended their role as mothers and wives for the benefit of their families and their communities. As an example of this role, in the local elections in Madrid in 1966, she presented herself as a candidate to the city council as a representative of the 'familial third', according to Franco's rules.[47] Ascensión Sedeño stated that her intention was to 'open up a venue for women to have a role in the future of Spain', and she also declared her candidature independent of any ideology or political affiliation, reaffirming the right of women to participate in local politics because of their role as wives and mothers, 'a valuable contribution to the family unit, an indisputable foundation in the social structure of the nation'.[48]

Her role in the struggle for women's rights has been the subject of much controversy. Although it opened up new channels for women, the Spanish Housewives' Association did not make a significant contribution to the democratization of society. At all times, the Association separated itself from politics under the pretext of defending its apolitical and independent character, a discourse that it maintained throughout the Transition. From a feminist perspective, the defence of women's role as housewives and the campaigns to dignify and revalue this social role helped to perpetuate sexual segregation and to consolidate the unequal gender division of roles which was not in accordance with the calls for the equality of a democratic society.

Responses to the traditional housewife model from the women's movement in Madrid: from the female conscience to the feminist conscience (1969–80)

The stance adopted by the women's movement in response to the regime's efforts to monopolize these new spaces of socialization is particularly significant. Simultaneously with the creation of the first official and predominantly pro-Francoist Housewives' Association, various associations – born out of a clearly anti-Francoist vocation – were legalized in Madrid, as well as in other cities all around Spain. In Madrid, the housewives' associations of the working-class neighbourhoods of Tetuan, Getafe, Ventas, Chamartin and Moratalaz, as well as the *Castellanas* (Castilians) housewives, shared interests and objectives that reached far beyond those of the National Association. One of the aspects that distinguished them was their connection to and identification with other forces of resistance to the regime, mainly with the neighbourhood movement.

The rise of the neighbourhood movement thus signified the creation of a new urban social movement, which joined the political parties, unions and student movements in order to fight against the dictatorship. The convergence of a variety of social agents and the emergence of a new generation of Spaniards born after the Civil War meant that the opposition movement to Francoism became associated with a new 'cycle of social protest', a concept developed by Sidney Tarrow in his work.[49] In this new cycle of protest, Spanish women played a very important role through their participation in political parties and unions, and due to the progressive inclusion of sexual equality values in the political culture of anti-Francoism. In addition to generational relevance, the existence of a gap in the regime, the crisis of the dictatorship and its progressive deterioration propelled the development of the movement. The contradiction of the regime's adoption of a liberal and open policy in some areas while maintaining an immobile and reactionary posture in others gave a special character to this new cycle of protests. In particular, the intensification of repression and terror by the State had a boomerang effect on protest by radicalizing it even more and causing the emergence of armed movements in response to disproportionate violence. Although it coincided at the time with other youth revolutions in the Long Sixties, the truth is that student movements during later Francoism were noticeably different because of their repressive and authoritarian context. For some historians, Spaniards saw consumer society as a distant horizon to reach, an escape from the frustrations and unmet aspirations of many years of dictatorship.[50] Despite the criticism of the left-wing, more than symptoms of a new form of authoritarianism imposed by capitalism and mass consumer culture, consumption and advertising came to represent cultural opposition and resistance to Francoism,[51] in particular to the Falangist ideology and its austerity policies and values. *Sección Femenina* warned women about the dangerous effects of the consumer society, mainly among youth, because, in combination with their 'emotional emptiness', it could lead to political subversion.[52] However, we cannot deny the role of consumption and tourism in legitimizing the dictatorship and its progressive international acceptance, in line with Spanish specialist Justin Crumbaugh's argument. Both indicators were symbols of the integration of Spain in Western capitalist society.[53]

These more critical housewives' associations not only facilitated the incorporation of women into the public sphere, but also provided legal cover for political activities in an era when political parties were illegal. The most important illegal women's organization was the Democratic Women's Movement (MDM), formed in 1965 under the influence of the Spanish Communist Party (PCE). At that time, in Spain there also existed other women's associations such as the Spanish Association of University Women (refounded in 1953) or the Seminary for the Sociological Study of Women (founded by intellectuals in 1960). However, the campaigns of MDM against price inflation and the rising cost of living, and in favour of salary increases, gave the militants an excuse to approach women with no political and social conscience: housewives as well as wives of left-wing militants. The activists of MDM started to infiltrate legal housewives' associations early on and, progressively, began to include criticisms in their campaigns directed at the regime, which highlighted the absence of democratic rights and liberties. Sheltered by the legal umbrella of the housewives' associations, they organized various campaigns in favour of the release of political prisoners and in opposition to the repressive policies of the regime, including via illegal strikes and protests. Progressively, these associations paved the way for the development of a feminist consciousness by addressing issues that specifically affected women under the dictatorship. As a result, their campaigns began to include gender demands and criticisms of the patriarchal character of the Franco regime with a very different version of the 'liberated woman' from what appeared in the media. The process of convergence of women's collectives from different backgrounds was accelerated during the International Women's Year in 1975. At the end of that year, shortly after Franco's death, took place the first Conference for the Liberation of Women in Spain, organized in Madrid and, a few months later, in Barcelona.

This heterogeneous women's movement also participated in the public debate that led to the approval in December 1976 of the Law of Political Reform, which opened the doors to a new regime and constituent process. In the lead-up to the first democratic elections in 1977, both the *Castellanas* and the independent housewives' associations encouraged women to participate 'overwhelmingly and consciously in elections, being well-informed and avoiding manipulation', voting for the political parties that were committed to the issue of women's rights.[54]

In 1978, after having overcome some significant bureaucratic obstacles, the delegations and independent housewives' associations merged into a single association that was given the name of a Peruvian nineteenth-century feminist, Flora Tristán.[55] The association was lead by Mercedes Comabella who had been, until that time, the president of the housewives' association of the neighborhood of Tetuan in Madrid, and a militant, in turn, of MDM. The organization – notwithstanding maintaining the defence of 'the interests of housewives' in their statutes – showed a clear reorientation regarding its objectives. From that moment onwards, its campaigns were focused on the defence of women's rights, particularly regarding the legalization of contraceptives, abortion and divorce, and the de-penalization of adultery.[56] These aims were in line with Spanish feminism, which emerged in those years as an independent movement from left-wing and neighborhood associations.[57]

In 1980, the Flora Tristán Association changed its statutes again, definitively abandoning the label that it had carried since it was founded. This was a highly important step in terms of reaching a wider audience of women, not just housewives. The first conference of the Association, which was held the same year, explored ideological self-reflection and developed a new position on various issues. Consequently, it identified itself clearly with the feminist struggle and distanced itself definitively from the specific interests of housewives. At this conference, the participants first rejected the idea that the education of women was 'limited to the domestic sphere'. The liberation of women, they argued, could only be achieved through economic independence and remunerated work, hence their insistence on child care facilities.[58] In terms of consumerism, they were also the first to point out and condemn the objectification of women in the media and to promote a different and more responsible model of advertising and consumption based on information.

Conclusions

The media in the 1960s and especially the women's magazine *Ama* contributed to the adaptation in Spain of the 'Model Mrs. Consumer', a cultural product that came from the US. However, it presented considerable differences with respect to other countries where it was implanted, mostly due to the political situation in Spain. The adaptation of this model, which 'improved' the already existing traditional role of the housewife in Spain, allowed its assimilation with the models that dominated Europe and the US. The great success of *Ama* magazine during these years shows the general acceptance of this model, identified by the regime and media as 'modernity'.

Franco's death in 1975 caused a change in editorial policy resulting in the inclusion of new content, allowing housewives to become part of the democratic process. In spite of changes, the female model promoted in *Ama* was the antithesis of the left and of feminism, and even more different from the models that appeared in the 1980s thanks to the countercultural movement *Movida madrileña* ('The Madrilenian scene') that took place mainly in Madrid at the end of the Spanish Transition.

The first housewives' associations, on the other hand, allowed women to become integrated in public life and to familiarize themselves with democratic practices and discourses. Although they declared themselves apolitical and focused on defending and perpetuating the traditional role of women, they contributed to the politicization of the domestic sphere. The more radical housewives' associations developed a much stronger feminist and political awareness against the dictatorship, running like true 'schools of citizenship'. These organizations began to question the domestic role of women, which was rejected from 1980 onwards by a women's movement aspiring to the recognition of full citizenship.

Both changes in the representation of gender roles in *Ama* magazine, and new militant practices in which housewives were involved, reflected the sociocultural transformations experienced by Spaniards throughout their unique Long Sixties. They further demonstrated that Spanish society had overcome the 'Model Mrs. Consumer' tendency that was linked to the last stages of Francoism. Spanish women rejected the model of housewife as the only one that was valid, embracing other gender models more in line with democratic political culture.

Notes

1. See, for instance, Rafael Quirosa-Cheyrouze (ed.), *La sociedad española en la Transición: Los movimientos sociales en el proceso democratizador* (Madrid: Biblioteca Nueva, 2011).
2. Pamela Radcliff, 'La historia oculta y las razones de una ausencia. La integración del feminismo en las historiografías de la transición', in Carmen Martínez (ed.), *El movimiento feminista en España en los años setenta* (Madrid: Ediciones Cátedra, 2009), 53–70.
3. Pamela Radcliff, 'Imagining female citizenship in the "New Spain": gendering the democratic Transition, 1975-1978', *Gender and History* 13.3, November 2001, 498–523; Monica Threlfall, Christine Cousins and Celia Valiente, *Gendering Spanish Democracy* (London: Routledge, 2005).

4. Pamela Radcliff, 'Associations and the social origins of the Transition during the late Franco Regime', in Nigel Townson (ed), *Spain Transformed: the Franco Dictatorship, 1959-1975* (Basingstoke, New York: Palgrave Macmillan, 2007).
5. Carme Molinero, 'Mujer, franquismo, fascismo. La clausura forzada en un "mundo pequeño"', *Historia Social* 30, 1998, 116–17.
6. María del Carmen Muñoz, 'Las revistas para mujeres durante el franquismo: difusión de modelos de comportamiento femenino', in Gloria Nielfa, *Mujeres y hombres en la España franquista: sociedad, economía, política, cultura* (Madrid: UCM, 2003), 95–116.
7. Pamela Radcliff, 'Citizens and housewives: the problems of female citizenship in Spain's transition to democracy', *Journal of Social History* 36.1, 2002, 77–100.
8. Joan Scott, 'Gender: a useful category of historical analyses', *American Historical Review* 91.5, December 1986, 1053–75.
9. Arthur Marwick, *The Sixties: Cultural Revolution in Britain, France, Italy and the United States, 1958-1974* (Oxford: Oxford University Press, 1998).
10. Kostis Kornetis, 'Let's get laid because it's the end of the world!': sexuality, gender and the Spanish Left in late Francoism and the Transition', *European Review of History* 22.1, 2015, 176-98.
11. Juan B. Vilar, 'Retornos y retornados en las migraciones españolas a Europa en el Siglo XX: Su impacto sobre la modernización del país. Una aproximación', *Anales de Historia Contemporánea* 22, 2006, 185–202.
12. Victoria de Grazia, *Irresistible Empire. America's Advance through Twentieth-Century Europe* (London: The Belknap Press of Harvard University Press, 2005).
13. Charles Powell, 'The United States and Spain: from Franco to Juan Carlos', in Nigel Townson (ed.), *Spain Transformed: The Franco Dictatorship, 1959-1975* (New York: Palgrave Macmillan, 2007), 227–48.
14. The model of *femme fatale* was personified by the actress of Spanish origin Rita Hayworth (born Margarita Carmen Cansino) in the film *Gilda*. The film, screened for the first time in Spain in 1947, provoked a big scandal and the intervention of the censors.
15. Elaine T. May, *Homeward Bound: American Families in the Cold War Era* (New York: Basic Books, 1988), 5. See also the analysis of the postwar model of femininity elaborated by Betty Friedan in 1963 in 'The feminine mystique'.
16. Elena Díaz Silva and Francisco Javier Rodríguez, 'Recepción, conflictos e influencias del "American Woman Model" en España, 1945–60', in Josefina Cuesta, María Luz Prado and Francisco Javier Rodríguez (eds), *¿Mujeres sabias? Mujeres Universitarias en España y América Latina*. (Limoges: Presses de l'Université de Limoges, 2015), 301–34.
17. Aurora G. Morcillo, *True Catholic Womanhood: Gender Ideology in Franco's Spain* (DeKalb, IL: Northern Illinois University Press, 2000).
18. De Grazia, *Irresistible Empire*, 445.
19. A new manoeuvre adopted to 'neutralize and depoliticize' Spanish society. See José Reig, *Identificación y alienación: la cultura política y el tardofranquismo* (Valencia: Publicacions de la Universitat de València, 2007), 94.
20. Carmen Romo Parra, 'El desorden de la identidad persistente. Cambio social y estatus de la mujer en la España desarrollista', *Arenal* 12.1, 2005, 98.
21. *Ama*, 1, 15 January 1960.
22. *Ama*, 2, 1 February 1960.

23. *Ama*, 9, 15 May 1960.
24. Mary Vincent, 'La reafirmación de la masculinidad en la cruzada franquista', *Cuadernos de Historia Contemporánea* 28, 2006, 131–15.
25. *Ama,* 122, 15 February 1965.
26. *Ama,* 131, 1 July 1965.
27. Aurora G. Morcillo, *The Seduction of Modern Spain: The female body and the Francoist body politic* (Lewisburg, PA: Bucknell University Press, 2010).
28. In 1960, only 1 per cent of Spanish homes had TV, 4 per cent had a refrigerator and 19 per cent a washing machine. In 1971 these percentages had increased considerably: 56 per cent of homes had TV, 66 per cent had a refrigerator and 52 per cent had a washing machine. See Enrique Moradiellos, *La España de Franco (1939–1975): Política y sociedad* (Madrid: Síntesis, 2000), 147.
29. Isabel Menéndez, 'Prensa femenina internacional en la transición española: el fracaso de Cosmopolitan y Marie Claire', *Ámbitos: revista internacional de comunicación* 23, 2013, http://ambitoscomunicacion.com/2013/prensa-femenina-internacional-en-la-transicion-espanola-el-fracaso-de-cosmopolitan-y-marie-claire, accessed 30 January 2015.
30. *Ama*, 368, 1 April 1975.
31. Films such as Juan Antonio Bardem's *Muerte de un ciclista* (1955) in which the main female character, a *femme fatale*, drives a car (and smokes) throughout the movie, had reinforced the idea that driving a car was a male issue. Adultery of the female character reinforced the gender transgression in the plot that could only end in tragedy.
32. *Ama,* 430, 1 November 1977.
33. According to Foessa's reports, the feminine labour market participation rate in Spain in 1977 was 26.5 per cent of the employable population, while for the European Economic Community (EEC) it was 35.3 per cent. However, this implied an increase from 16 per cent in 1950. In regards to university education, women represented in 1970 a modest 4.5 per cent of the total, increasing to 19 per cent in 1977.
34. *Ama*, 412, 1 February 1977.
35. *Ama,* 411, 15 January 1977.
36. *Ama*, 414, 1 March 1977.
37. *Ama,* 442, 1 May 1978.
38. *Ama,* 413, 15 February 1977.
39. *Ama,* 435, 15 January 1978 and *Ama*, 436, 1 February 1978. In regard to this issue, *Ama* included references to the legalization of divorce during the Second Republic (1931–9) that did not result in an increase in the number of divorces but rather the regulation of an already widespread practice.
40. *Ama*, 412, 1 February 1977.
41. '... y si tengo vaginitis ¿qué hago?', *Cosmopolitan*, 3, 1977, and 'Encuesta: la sexualidad femenina. El placer es mío, caballero', *Vindicación Feminista*, July 1979.
42. The 'liberated woman' represented in adverts as *Comedias sexy celtibéricas* and in *Destape* films, was a hypersexual woman but, after all, heterosexual, a sexual instrument in the service of patriarchy and of the consumer society. This stereotype emerged due to the relaxation of censorship regarding the nude female body, and was sometimes linked to the indecency of female tourists.
43. *Ama*, 462, 1 March 1979.

44. *Ama*, 445, June 1978.
45. Janice Williams Rutherford, *Selling Mrs. Consumer: Christine Frederick and the Rise of Household Efficiency* (Athens, GA, London: University of Georgia Press, 2003).
46. Temma Kaplan, 'Luchar por la democracia: formas de organización de las mujeres entre los años cincuenta y los años sesenta', in Ana Aguado (ed.), *Mujeres, regulación de conflictos sociales y cultura de la paz* (Valencia: Institut d'Estudis Universitaris de la Dona, 1999), 91.
47. During the dictatorship, electoral participation for Spaniards was limited to the two referendums celebrated in 1947 and in 1976 and the voting for city councillors in the municipal council elections, which were designated 'by thirds'. In the case of the 'familial third', married women were excluded from the electoral corps through the application of gendered criteria and recourse to the sexual division of labour. Only the 'head of the family' could vote in these municipal elections. Even if married women could not vote, they could submit themselves as a candidate. This happened in the case of Ascensión Sedeño. In all cases, however, the participation, and the electoral behaviour of Spanish citizens, was characterized by an absence of rights and freedoms, the absence of an alternative candidate list to the official one, as well as the pressure, coaction, ideological control and manipulation by the authorities during the whole process.
48. *ABC*, 1 November 1966.
49. Sidney Tarrow, 'Cycles of collective action: between moments of madness and the repertoire of contention', in Mark Traugott (ed.), *Repertoires and Cycles of Collective Action* (Durham, NC: Duke University Press, 1995), 89–116.
50. Jaime Pastor, 'El movimiento estudiantil bajo la dictadura franquista y el 68 español', in M. Gari, J. Pastor and J. Romero (eds), *1968. El mundo pudo cambiar de base* (Madrid: Los Libros de la Catarata, 2008), 285.
51. L.E. Alonso and E. Conde, *Historia del consumo en España: una aproximación a sus orígenes y primer desarrollo* (Madrid: Debate, 1994), 84.
52. Speech of Pilar Primo de Rivera in the National Council of Feminine Section, San Sebastian, March 1970. In General Administration Archive (AGA), Feminine Section papers, (3) 51.41, 635.
53. Justin Crumbaugh, *Destination Dictatorship: The Spectacle of Spain's Tourist Boom and the Reinvention of Difference* (Alberny, NY: State University of New York Press, 2009), 15–40. See also: Sasha D. Pack, *Tourism and Dictatorship: Europe's peaceful invasion of Franco's Spain* (New York: Palgrave Macmillan, 2006).
54. *El País*, 8 March 1977.
55. Documents relating to the change of the name of associations and statutes, February 1977. Provincial Federation of Women Flora Tristan Papers. Feminist Research and Training Center (CIFFE), 1, 2. In Historical Memory Documentation Center (CDMH).
56. Contraceptives were legalized in Spain in 1978 but it was not until 1982 that the law legalizing abortion in some cases was approved. On the other hand, the de-penalization of adultery in 1978 was followed by the legalization of divorce in 1981 in spite of the opposition from the Catholic Church.
57. Led by the Women's Liberation Front founded in 1976 that proposed the collectivization of child care and of home tasks. The foundation of the first feminist political party in Spain by Lidia Falcón took place in 1979.
58. First Federation Congress: documents of debate and conclusions, February 1980. Provincial Federation of Women Flora Tristan Papers, CIFFE 71, 1. In CDMH.

CHAPTER 8
DOCUMENTING POST-AUTHORITARIAN SUBCULTURES IN THE EUROPEAN SOUTH: THE CASES OF PEDRO ALMODÓVAR'S *PEPI, LUCI, BOM* AND NIKOS ZERVOS' *DRACULA OF EXARCHIA*[1]

Kostis Kornetis

In the mid- and late 1970s Spain and Greece began experiencing a post-authoritarian politics and significant social change. The transition to democracy from dictatorship – Franco's regime (1939–75) and the Colonels' rule (1967–74), respectively – was the last chapter of the long post-civil war periods. In both cases, transfer of power to the politicians was engineered and implemented from 'above', by the elites. Spanish and Greek political life in the transitional years was anything but peaceful or elite-dominated, however, as both processes took place against a background of intense mobilization. Worker activity and industrial conflict experienced an upsurge. Violence was pervasive too: police shootings ripped through the fabric of Spanish and, to a lesser extent, Greek political life, with a death toll outstripping that of revolutionary Portugal. Numerous assassinations and kidnappings by the Basque separatist organization ETA (*Euskadi Ta Askatasuna*) went hand-in-hand with government reprisals. Similarly, though for different reasons, the Greek leftist terrorist group 17 November belied peaceful transition, aiming at destabilization and jeopardizing the shaky democratic edifice. Organizations of the extreme left like GRAPO and FRAP in Spain, and ELA in Greece killed policemen and former torturers, and were largely seen as avengers for past repression. They capitalized on political disenchantment at the 'pacted' transitions, shuttering hopes for retroactive justice in Spain, and the entirely unsatisfactory trials of the torturers in Greece. Extreme right-wing violence was present too, especially in Spain with the brutal murder of communist lawyers in the Calle Atocha in 1977 and the firebombing of the queer hub 'Vaquería'.[2] Similarly in Greece the following year a central Athenian cinema was attacked with explosives during the screening of a Soviet film.[3]

At the same time, non-violent movements mushroomed in the mid- and late 1970s, experimenting with new, essentially post-authoritarian, political forms. This new contentious politics sprang from a youth quite isolated under the dictatorships, and included 'second wave' feminism and homosexual militancy.[4] After years of social conservatism and political authoritarianism, the transitions to democracy were also reflected in cultural politics. In Greece, this was expressed in the occupations of the Athens University in 1979, the apogee of a May '68-like libertarianism.[5] In Spain, it was expressed through 'neighbourhood movements' reacting against rapid urbanization.[6]

This was a protest cycle, following Sidney Tarrow's definition,[7] that although connected to the previous phase of contention had an entirely new dynamic and radicalism. One could say that a new generation of Greeks and Spaniards was experiencing, over a short period of time, an abridged version of what in the rest of Europe had taken place throughout the course of thirty years – an accelerated change that condensed successive stages of development.[8]

Abortion, birth control and sexual education – all illegal in authoritarian Spain and Greece – were gradually openly discussed and practised.[9] However, until the mid-1970s laws in both countries persistently criminalized adultery and homosexuality.[10] Democratization did not bring immediate revocation of these bans; rather it brought a gradual liberalization and an eventual relaxation. Yet the processes of liberalization were unequal and often discontinuous: for instance, influential groups such as the Communist Youth of Greece (KNE) endorsed a socially conservative language regarding sexuality and traditional institutions such as marriage.[11] As far as Spain was concerned, gay and lesbian activism that had experienced an upsurge in the late Francoist and early transitional years were surprisingly halted by the victory of the socialists in the early 1980s.

The two cases differ on a number of issues, including local micro-nationalisms but also an anti-religious, secularist tendency, which were present in Spain but not in Greece. In terms of sexual, gender and consumer practices, Greece experienced a tamer and less hedonistic explosion than did Spain, with the emergence of the *movida madrileña* (the Madrid 'scene') in the late 1970s and up to 1985. *Movida* chronicler José Luis Gallero recalls that 'from one day to the next, a worn-out city became the maximum emblem of modernity in the do-it-yourself spirit of British punk'.[12] The *movida*, which took its name from the drug subculture, caused a plethora of new trends in fashion, music, design, art and film, building up on tendencies dating back to the late Francoist period.[13] The emerging counterculture and its artistic production were comparatively tempered in Greece.

Revolutionary politics were read as obsolete as the left came to power, at least in as far as concrete political objectives were concerned: a year after Colonel Tejero's abortive coup in 1981 in Spain, Felipe Gonzalez's PSOE won the general election. Andreas Papandreou's PASOK, Greece's first socialist government, had been in power since 1981. Yet despite the optimism of democratic change, the abandonment of radical politics and the socialists' rise to power created immediate disillusionment to segments of the radicalized youth and former militants who had expected a more radical break from authoritarianism. This disillusionment from the original bliss ('*encanto*') and the fall to '*desencanto*' (disenchantment) was more accentuated in Spain, which also witnessed '*pasotismo*' in the 1980s, namely a drastic withdrawal of youth from politics.[14]

Post-authoritarian cinema

Art-house films of the initial transitional period belong mostly to the so-called 'cinema of social concern', connecting to cinematic developments of previous times in terms of political filmmaking, including 'New Greek Cinema' and 'New Spanish Cinema' respectively. The post-authoritarian condition, however, allowed filmmakers to take advantage of more liberal production values and the fact that relative 'freedom' replaced strict censorship – for many years a defining factor for cinematography. In Spain, films with a strong regional autonomist component, such as Imanol Uribe's *El proceso de Burgos* (1979), dealing somewhat favorably with Basque nationalism and ETA, would have been unimaginable in previous years. Even so, directors such as Theodoros Angelopoulos in Greece and Pilar Miró both faced severe censorship. Angelopoulos' film *The Travelling Players* (1975) was withdrawn as Greece's official selection for the Venice film festival for promoting a one-sided, propagandistic left-wing version of recent history, while Miró almost faced court-martial for incendiary politics in depicting the *guardia civil* torturing two farmers falsely accused of a crime at the beginning of the century in *El Crimen de Cuenca* (1977).[15]

Many films of the late 1970s and early 1980s began to incorporate the new spirit of subversion, in essence challenging the same norms (family, nation, religion, heteronormativity) despite contextual differences. In both countries rigid politics were mocked while authoritarian residues like arbitrary police forces and conservative sexual mores were criticized. A new kind of filmmaking based on sexual explicitness was now promoted via alternative channels. Deviation from sociocultural and aesthetic norms is particularly relevant in these films as they coincide with newly acquired freedoms and a new, transgressive mode of representation. The permissiveness accompanying the fall of the regimes allowed for a more graphic cinematic depiction of these trends – and not only in art-house cinema. Typical of post-authoritarianism, Spain and Greece saw an explosion in pornography; so-called 'S'-rated softcore films and hardcore genres proliferated. Despite the convincing critique of the Spanish comic soft-porn *destape* films that inundated Spanish theaters at the time, especially by scholars such as Justin Crumbaugh, I share Daniel Kowalsky's view that these genres were often much more sophisticated than they seem. Quite often they involved an indirect – or even direct – criticism of the sexual repression of the authoritarian years.[16] Likewise in Greece, soft- and later hardcore erotic films of the early and late 1970s paved the way for more open attitudes vis-à-vis nudity and sexual practices, not only in cinematic representations but in society as a whole.[17]

Other films of the period display a strong homosexual component. Filmmaker Eloy de la Iglesia, for instance, politicized marginality and repressed homosexual desire, locating it within its sociopolitical context in films like *El Diputado* (1978);[18] Uribe, too, marries the political with the (homo-)sexual in *La muerte de Mikel* (1983).[19] Thus in Spain, films with homosexual protagonists and the general issue of homosexual liberation became of prime cinematic concern. Still, these directors' interest in social and political emancipation and their active involvement in politics – Iglesia was a member of the Spanish Communist Party (PCE) – greatly differentiate them from Pedro Almodóvar's depiction of alternative lifestyles and sexuality, habitually stripped of their sociopolitical milieu, as we will see later on.

By contrast Greek cinematography was not involved in queerness; the appearance of films reflecting the emerging dynamic identities of sociality and sexuality – such as

Consumption and Gender through the Moment of Transition

Andreas Thomopoulos' *Aldevaran* (1975), Nikos Nikolaidis' *The Rugs are Still Singing* (1979), Nikos Panayotopoulos's *The Indolence of the Fertile Valley* (1978) and *Sweet Bunch* (1983) or Thanasis Rentzis' experimental films – lacked such subject matter. They nevertheless depicted the post-authoritarian generation of '*amfisvitisi*' (contestation) and its malaise. This sort of unconventional filmmaking – political but in an entirely new way, differing from the *engagé* militant cinema with a Marxist twist, focused on young people in the margins: hippies, dropouts, drug addicts, petty criminals, misfits – an entire category of youth henceforth either ignored or caricatured. Such films had a committed, albeit limited, audience.[20] Historian Nikolaos Papadogiannis quotes an interview with a young contemporary activist reflecting the general feeling among a segment of contemporary left-wing youth about these films: 'We glorified the marginal'.[21] In Spain too, so-called 'kinki' cinema on juvenile delinquency and drugs had a long genealogy, going back to such classics as Carlo Saura's *Los Golfos* and even Luis Buñuel's *Los Olvidados*.

This chapter focuses on films that are representative of the post-authoritarian cinematic tendency: *Dracula of Exarchia* (henceforth *Drakoulas*) by Nikos Zervos (1983), and Pedro Almodóvar's *Pepi, Luci, Bom and other girls on the heap* (henceforth *Pepi, Luci, Bom*) (1979). By exploring the overarching leitmotifs and connecting threads between them, the chapter attempts to demonstrate the semantic affinity between post-authoritarian Spain and Greece in social realities, artistic avant-gardes and the way in which consumption was conceptualized and represented in cinema. It further highlights the films' provocative, but not necessarily subversive, nature in terms of gender politics. The vulgar, punky flair that characterizes this cinematography, always provocative, at times absurd and occasionally brutish and violent, is ultimately quite problematic for their representation of gender and sexuality.

Two directors, two films

By 1983 Nikos Zervos, now known as a cult director of farcical comedies, had made some quite political films including *Black and White* with Thanasis Rentzis (1973) and *Attempt at Sociological Research in Greece* (1974), on rebelling art students and women working in factories, respectively. He had already faced censorship: his experimental film *Catch 76* was censored for insolence and insult to the Greek national character, as it questioned the authorities of Church and State. Although censorship was officially lifted after the Junta, it was not entirely absent from cultural productions, which often faced state intervention.[22] Zervos noted in 1976 that: 'We are not allowed to make statements against religion, or strong statements against the family. The army cannot be insulted, and things Greek-sacred, such as ancient history, must be treated with respect. The sexual act is not permitted. We produce some pornos but it is not supposed to be permitted.'[23] It is precisely such elements that Zervos tried to document in the two films prior to *Drakoulas*, with which they form a trilogy of sorts: *Exiled on the Central Highway* (1979) and *Skewer Them!* (1981) – all about dropout artists, moving in the crossroads between the underground and the avant-garde. These three films commented on the contested relationship between art and politics, juxtaposing the local scene to what was happening abroad. In depicting the artist protagonists as 'artsy fartsy' countercultural hippies, the director castigated the supposed apolitical stance and the aping tendencies of Greek artists to developments in the West. Moreover, the young protagonists' post-materialist tendencies are presented, notably, as a decadent feature. Next to all this, Zervos was particularly interested in counteracting what he viewed as severe sexual inhibitions within Greece.

Pedro Almodóvar, on the other hand, began shooting Super-8 shorts in the newly liberated Spain of the late 1970s. Almodóvar's own part in the culture of the postpolitical *movida* included work on *fotonovelas*, fanzines, comics, writing and performing punk music.[24] In contrast to politically radicalized segments of youth and the disenchantment with politics, Almodóvar 'seemed to espouse a radical apoliticism and practiced a kind of 'cultural transvestism'', typical of the *movida*.[25] His comment about Francoism is quite telling: 'My films were never anti-Franco. I simply didn't even recognize his existence. In a way, it's my revenge against Francoism. I want there to be no shadow or memory of him.'[26] Evidently, the fact that Almodóvar does not refer to Franco does not expunge his presence from his films. It was Franco's dictatorship that had deprived Spanish cinema – as the repressive democracy of the 1950s and 1960s and the dictatorship had in Greece – of a genuine sex, drugs and rock 'n' roll phase, though certain circles did experience a certain *yé-yé* and rock scene and a sexual liberation of sorts.[27] These were precisely the features introduced ad extremis by the *movida*, challenging the iconography of the old regime through a camp aesthetic. Borja Cajani, publisher of the most influential magazine of the *movida*, *La Luna de Madrid*, commented on the sense of being somehow responsible for a 'cultural transition' of sorts, shared among young people at the time:

> International media was following Spain as a very particular case because it was perhaps an experiment of global relevance in that moment. How do you happily and merrily go from a totalitarian to a democratic regime? Journalists came to see how it had happened. And it was great for the government, for politics and for the country that we not only had a fabulous, charming, democratic and very polite king or a government full of young people who could speak French, but also a dynamic cultural movement.[28]

The transgressive spirit of the *movida* can be clearly discerned in *Pepi, Luci, Bom*. The film was loosely based on a comic strip, a medium very much in vogue among *movida* aficionados – in fact, a comic strip precedes each sequence in the film. Its overriding comic-book quality shows in the plot itself: in the opening scene, a plain clothed policeman rapes Pepi (Carmen Maura), threatening to expose her for marijuana possession. She seeks revenge, using Luci, the rapist's wife; Luci for her part swaps knitting and housewifery for independence, golden showers, sadomasochism and lesbianism with Bom, a punk singer. The fact that Bom is played by Olvido 'Alaska' Gara, a real life rock star of the time, marks an interesting link with mainstream culture.

Zervos on the other hand made *Drakoulas*, a film containing the very elements censored until the late 1970s: insults to the triptych of family, fatherland and religion, plus a vehement disavowal of the police and army. Through a rather schematic plot, the film marries Dracula with Frankenstein together in early 1980s Athens. The protagonist is Viktor Papadopoulos, a Dracula-like doctor, played by cult actor Konstantinos Tzoumas. Papadopoulos, homonymous with the primus inter pares of the Greek Colonels, has clear fascist inclinations, a portrait of dictator Metaxas hangs in his living room; he speaks in a German accent – probably a reference to collaborationists during the German occupation – and listens to Nazi marches. Working for a record company he decides to form the perfect rock band using dead legends: a postmodern mix of Jimmy Hendrix, Greek *rembetika* master Manolis Chiotis and influential composer Manos Hadjidakis, a pivotal figure in the post-authoritarian cultural setup and, humorously, still alive at the time. The inclusion of the latter two, and especially Hadjidakis, an influential cultural producer, was a direct assault on some of Greece's 'sacred cows'. Predictably, something went wrong and the Frankenstein group formed from the dead bodies was the Music Brigades, the band of the ascending alternative rock-star of the period, Jimis Panousis.[29] Panousis, after establishing a love affair with Dracula's daughter, goes on to play with the Brigades at a giant concert for the necrophiliacs of Athens, dubbed the 'Zombie Festival'. The entire film contains performances of the Brigades' songs, characterized by outspoken verses and melodies that blended reggae with folk songs, and funk with *rembetika*. It portrays several absurd, surreal and unconnected situations – with cameo appearances of heroes of the Greek underground rock scene, such as Nicolas Asimos, Johnny Vavouras, Sakis Boulas and Dimitris Poulikakos. According to Hellenic Studies scholar Vrasidas Karalis, the film is a 'marvelous example of trashy, nonsensical, outrageous, raw and freakish cinema, in the manner of Ed Wood, celebrating the anarchist culture of an Athenian suburb through parody, satire, and over ridiculing of national symbols'.[30]

Despite the transparent differences between the early films of Zervos and Almodóvar, *Pepi, Luci, Bom* and *Drakoulas* share many similarities: both were shot under unorthodox conditions, they contained a trashy quality, and did not aim at mass attendance. The two movies are a mixture of several genres: pure comedy, musical, and horror. In these tentatively postmodern creations,[31] hybridity, intertextuality and bricolage, namely the reordering and recontextualization of objects to communicate fresh meaning,[32] are omnipresent. Fragmentation of genres, mixing different styles and radical eclecticism are used at length by both directors, testifying to a newly discovered delight in freedom of expression leading to the total disintegration of fixed artistic forms. As film critic Alberto Fernández Torres put it bluntly in the art movie journal *Contracampo* at the time, it is the triumph of 'ugly aesthetics, ungainly camerawork, and disrupted continuity'.[33]

These irreverent films fall clearly into the category of underground cinema, defined not so much by their formal properties as by their marginal relation to mainstream production and distribution networks and their tendency to break down social and particularly sexual taboos.[34] Sequences seem improvised and are characterized by absurd or grotesque humor and parody – making them easily classifiable as B-movies or 'crazy comedies' – while the centrality of 'alternative' sexual encounters and a weak narrative form follow notable cinematic prototypes. Their underground ethos is not dissimilar to that which flourished in New York in the 1960s. Almodóvar's early cinematography, in particular, is close to Andy Warhol and Morrissey, sexploitation and the punk attitude of the American underground, including a powerful influence by John Waters' amoralism and scatological humour. *Drakoulas*, on the other hand, draws on the tropes of *Rocky Horror Picture Show*, featuring a combination of vampirism and drag. *Pepi, Luci, Bom* also refers to *Rocky Horror* through its opening pop song 'Do the Swim' sung by Little Nell, the singing co-star of Jim Sharman.[35] This fact testifies to the contemporary popularity and impact of Anglo-Saxon culture among underground circles experimenting with new social and aesthetic codes and at the same time practising but also documenting cultural ones.[36] In fact, Warhol himself visited Madrid in 1983 and met Almodóvar, who was introduced to him as the 'Spanish Warhol'.[37] As we shall see, this encounter had wider symbolic implications for the meeting point between the avant-garde and the mainstream in Spanish art.

Documenting subcultures

Pepi, Luci, Bom and *Drakoulas* documented the burgeoning youth subcultures, characterized by punk aesthetics, political irreverence and an anarchical spirit.[38] Here, I am using the term 'subculture' as it was coined by the Centre for Contemporary Culture Studies, Birmingham University, whereby the rejection of 'mainstream' culture by the protagonists of contestation did not imply political coherence.[39] This is differentiated from the 'new social movements', to quote E. Dimitris, insofar as their protest was 'confined to a nebulous attitude of rejection of "mainstream" culture without corresponding (explicit) demands or a unified political entity'.[40] The gradual fusion between these groups, the new socialization of the 1980s and the more politically radical groups of anarchist tendencies brought about a synergy between the libertarian, anarchist, countercultural and autonomist tendencies, usually referred to in the Greek case as *Anti-Authoritarian Chóros*.[41] Almodóvar, on the other hand, rather than documenting the disenchantment with the fact that the era of radical politics seemed to be over in Spain, documented young people – like himself – who were delighted by the new possibilities that this new era signified in terms of personal liberation.

Zervos typically approached all this often in a 'cinema-verité' manner, both staging but also obsessively documenting – ethnographically almost – these emerging subcultures. In fact, film historian Mel Schuster remarked that 'he may conceivably become one of those dropouts in which he is interested'. His collaborator in the 1970s, director Thanassis Rentzis, talks of Zervos' 'teenager-like subversive feeling': 'He liked to put screams on the loudspeaker. He had a pirate radio station, Zervos. What a character. Anarchist-rightwing-something.'[42] Almodóvar was himself very much involved in the subculture he depicted.

The 'documentary nature' of the two films immortalizes the clearly defined urban spaces of the subcultures they portrayed: the urban landscape of the centre of Athens as well as the urban highways and the desolate atmosphere of Madrid's suburbs. Like Exarchia in Athens – the avant-garde anarchist neighbourhood in which Zervos' film is situated, a 'cultural and social kaleidoscope' according to a 1985 article[43] – the Rastro neighbourhood in Madrid was the site of the burgeoning subculture that hosted the *movida*.[44] Both films thus eternalize these alternative loci: the anarchist scene of Exarchia in Athens and the 'new wave' *demimonde* in Madrid and their protagonists. Fabio McNamara, at the time performing a punk duet with Almodóvar, like Alaska, Costus and, of course, Almodóvar himself was a very real and key figure of the *movida*; likewise Jimis Panousis, Nikolas Asimos, Dimitris Poulikakos, Sakis Boulas and Johnny Vavouras for the Athens scene. Self-referentiality was pivotal as cameos by key figures of the Madrid *movida* and the Athenian scene render the films of topical interest. Both are powerful documents of an era, especially as some of its youthful underground protagonists (like director Vangelis Kotronis and musician Nikolas Asimos in the Greek case, or Costus in the Spanish one) met early deaths. In short, both *Drakoulas* and *Pepi, Luci, Bom* relied on the spectator's knowledge of an actual referent (those very *demimondes*) that lied 'beyond the camera'.[45]

In terms of the cultural geography of these subcultures, whereas the *movida* was clearly not connected to high society or elite art, in *Drakoulas* Zervos and Panousis make fun of Hadjidakis, who is referred to only in terms of his voluminous body and not his genius. Same for the Nobel-winning poet Odysseus Elytis, whose influential 'Heroic and Elegiac Song for the Lost Second Lieutenant of Albania' is satirized, its protagonist appearing as a zombie (played by actor Antonis Kafentzopoulos). Filmmaker Theodoros Angelopoulos is equally mocked for the slow-pace sequence shots of his films, mostly involving the civil war (1946–9) – a taboo subject until the mid-1970s, but almost saturated by the early and mid-1980s. At a certain sequence Panousis, the protagonist, uses the following line as a lullaby for Dracula's daughter: 'Angelopoulos is a director who makes movies about partisans who walk slowly, slowly, very slowly'. Only to add, looking straight at the camera when she falls asleep: 'Don't get me wrong, I think Angelopoulos is cool.' Mockery and satire of well-established tropes of learned and so-called *koultouriaris* ('artsy-fartsy') culture is what dictates these punchlines.[46] Typically the Communist Youth was very critical of the overt intellectualism of artists whose work was all too cryptic for the masses to decipher.[47] Here, however, the same attitude is applied from another vantage point, equally rejective of the Communist trope. In other words, the film seems to be saying 'neither with the one, nor with the other'.

Post-politics

It would be unwise to look for direct connections between discrete events in films as chaotic and corrosive as *Drakoulas* or *Pepi, Luci, Bom*. But as Paul Julian Smith argues, it is surely legitimate to ask 'what ideological investments are to be found in the comic cacophony of film[s] made at a time characterized by such dramatic historical changes'. There is a clear political difference between the two: the dictatorship, seemingly absent in

Almodóvar due to his aforementioned negation, is omnipresent, though fiercely satirized, in *Drakoulas*. The Music Brigades' 'Festival Zombie' concert at the end of the film clearly alludes to the festival mania of post-1974 Greece, especially in the Left and the Greek Communist Youth (KNE).[48] This is but one of the many parodic references to the conservatism of left-wing politics and of Greek society in general. Zombies for Zervos represent the monolithic, old-fashioned dogmatic Marxists and as such they employ the jargon used in debates between the pro-Soviet (KKE) and Eurocommunist (KKE-Esoterikou) debates that emerged from the 1968 split within the Communist Party (KKE). In an earlier scene, the Mousikes Taxiarchies sang 'Disco Tsoutsouni' (Disco Weenie), with the intertextual refrain: '*sti steria den zei to psari, oute Knitis me frikia*' (just as a fish cannot live out of water, a KNE member cannot coexist with freaks), referring to the age-old vendetta between the Communist Youth and the so-called 'freaks', a codename for anarchists.[49] In 1979 Nikos Zervos commented on the rising anarchist tendency – to which this film ascribes – and on the plethora of Marxist youth organizations, which he considered a fashion of sorts:

> What I see most is young people who want to fight, for lack of a better word, the system. The biggest numbers go into the communist party. But lately, most of the students have begun to think of themselves as anarchists. I don't know if they fit theoretically, but it is a kind of general reaction against things. Of course, the junta time played a big part in it. And young people, in order to act organized, they find the … well, I don't want to say the 'easy' way, but they don't really examine what Marxism is all about, they just get into a group so they can fight the establishment. That is why it is such a big thing now. I don't believe it is out of a consciousness of Marxism. It is fashionable.[50]

'Necrophiliac' in the film is a codename for a communist or follower of the left-wing canon in music: *andartika*, the 1940s guerrilla songs very much in fashion in the early transition years, and the songs of Mikis Theodorakis. Theodorakis, former dissident composer during the Junta, had become a national composer of sorts after the fall of the regime, standing for the legendary resistance against oppression through his persona and epic music. In fact, Theodorakis was a typical target of mockery both by established alternative artists such as Dionysis Savopoulos in his *Acharnians* and by the underground scene of the time.[51] As literary theorist Gail Holst-Wahraft notes, 'it was chic to criticize Theodorakis and Ritsos, [and] it was also radical, for the students and intellectuals […] to abandon the Left wing camp'.[52] Accordingly, in the final scene of the film, the zombies sing a famous Theodorakis song 'of the struggle', habitually performed by signature artist Maria Farandouri. Not surprisingly, and despite Theodorakis' having broken with the Communist Party, Dimitris Danikas, the film reviewer of the party's organ *Rizospastis*, scolded Zervos 'for promoting identification with drug consumption, pessimism and individualism' in his films.[53]

Almodóvar shared with Zervos a rejective stance of leftists: if for Zervos the rejection is of the *Knites*, for Almodóvar it is of left-wingers in general, known as *progres* in Spain.

Consumption and Gender through the Moment of Transition

Much like Zervos, he seems to show preference for suburbanites and hooligans. What is more, the dialogue in *Pepi, Luci, Bom* is thick with references to contemporary history and politics: the policeman who rapes Pepi is a fascist caricature complete with dark glasses, who complains that he doesn't know what the country is coming to 'with so much democracy'; he reads the far right newspaper with the somewhat ironic title *El Imparcial*, containing headlines on ETA's activities – offering up these issues for comic redirection; further on, when Luci walks out on him for Bom, she claims to be a victim of 'the wave of eroticism sweeping Spain', reverberating General Franco's obsession with this issue.[54] More importantly, in a famous scene – the penis contest – Almodóvar himself appears, baptizing the bar contest 'general erections' (*erecciónes generales*), a clear allusion to the general elections (*elecciónes generales*) of 1977, the first since the transition to democracy. With irreverence typical of the *movida* Almodóvar thus turns the game of politics into satire on public life, an alternative culture to the extravaganza of Spain's new democracy. In addition, the violence that Luci and Bom seemed to be drawn to stands as a metonymy for the entire Spanish society trying to act out the trauma of the forty years of Francoist repression.

Commodifying marginality

State institutions – the state repressive apparatus, to quote Louis Althusser's famous label – are mercilessly attacked and satirized in the two movies. The police – in both countries one of the most feared and hated groups, still associated by the youth of the time with dictatorship, is depicted in a critical or derisory way. Franco's *Policia Armada* or the Greek *astyfylakes* and *chorofylaki* are ridiculed. However, the attitude towards the policemen differs: in *Pepi, Luci, Bom* the policeman is predatory, while, on the contrary, in *Drakoulas* the chief of police – mockingly played by Poulikakos, a rock singer with a long history of drug abuse and arrests during the Junta period – is actually raped by female groupies when he storms a concert. In both cases the police and what is described as their sexual deprivation are ridiculed.

Religion does not, of course, escape the general assault. In *Pepi, Luci, Bom*, Bom and her Luci engage in a golden shower in the midst of a knitting lesson. While Bom urinates on the repressed housewife, who derives pleasure and acquires a certain liberation from it, a Catholic liturgy plays in the background. Similarly in *Drakoulas*, Panousis sings the equally infamous '*Ki ego s'agapo, gamo ton Christo mou*', which translates to the more suave 'I love you too, Christ dammit', whereas the Greek original literally refers to copulation with the figure of Christ. This is probably one of the most notorious verses ever written in Greek, earning Mousikes Taxiarchies a lawsuit after a concert in 1980 for 'blasphemy', which did not stop them from using it in the film, this time with no legal repercussions.[55] In this respect, both films are comprised of elements and topics that would have been banned from cinema screens a few years earlier. Cinema appears, thus, to be a powerful condenser of the subcultural undercurrents that had emerged and were being consolidated during that time.

Mass consumption was not spared in this tear-it-all-apart filmic tendency, while both Zervos and Almodóvar show little respect for the medium of television. In both films fake, farcical TV commercials play with artifice and the functions of advertising. According to Almodóvar commercials are for television what furniture is for town apartments: part of the decor. 'Commercials are also, in principle, the genre most open to comic delirium, to humor and surrealism' – in this case, mimicking the register and subverting the real commercials.[56] *Pepi, Luci, Bom* features sample adverts designed by Pepi, including a commercial for anti-flatulence knickers and one for urine-absorbing ones, both typical of Almodóvar's scatological humour,[57] that appears even more clearly in one of his following *movida* films, *Labyrinth of Passion* (1982). These absurd and ridiculous commercials mimic the standard style of countless others (the sensuous tone of the female first-person narrator in Almodóvar, the romantic music, and so on) – all devices used to expose the emptiness and exaggerated claims of advertisement in general. This way the filmmaker undermined the medium and upset the social decorum.[58]

In a similar way, in *Drakoulas* a journalist tries unsuccessfully to stage a commercial with the standard trope of offering a shopper a double portion of detergent to check product loyalty. When the woman stubbornly refuses to make the exchange, he takes it by force, mumbling an irritated 'don't you people watch television?' Panousis' lyrics sung at the end of the film feature, moreover, an unmistakable attack on consumer values:

Consumerist pigs
We got bells hanging down our necks
If you ain't part of the flock
Tarring and feathering

However, one does not discern an overall rejection of consumption, hence rendering the distinction that Trentmann makes between consumerism and consumption quite pertinent.[59] And this because those involved in the *movida* were still involved in a variety of consumer practices involving galleries and shops.[60] Moreover, both films relied very much on the sympathies of contemporary audiences, who partook in the respective subcultures or were sympathetic towards them, thus being both producers and consumers of said subcultures.[61] Considering that Alaska and Panousis and the Brigades were real life stars, attracting large audiences, these figures possessed what Sarah Thornton has termed – paraphrasing Pierre Bourdieu – 'subcultural capital'.[62] This term highlights the empowering contradictions within the subcultural universe, as it corresponds to the cultural knowledge and commodities that certain members of the given subcultures acquired. As far as the filmmakers themselves are concerned, they did not manage to develop a militant anti-consumerist discourse, but rather an ambivalent relationship with consumption – since they too commodified and commercialized marginality, in a way. In other words, and going back to the initial distinction between subcultures and new social movements, these films, and the subcultures they document, were visually, and maybe *culturally*, subversive, but not so much *politically* so; and they did not even aspire to be.

Consumption and Gender through the Moment of Transition

Gender, pleasure, frivolity

Gender features prominently in all sorts of critique levelled in these films. Both are exponents of the post-authoritarian frivolity prevalent as a youth trend, which was at times overly politicized, and at others seemingly dropout.[63] Trying on and casting off the range of different identities, which suddenly became possible after the end of the dictatorship, made some commentators regard post-Franco Spain as 'the epitome of the postmodern, the incarnation in practice of European theory – from its multilingual, multicultural mix to its alleged toleration of drugs, pornography and homosexuality'.[64] In Paul Julian Smith's accurate description, it was 'a blatant assertion of the *autonomy of pleasure* and of the triumph of *libidinal anarchy* over the pieties of political progressives'.[65] The predominance of *jouissance* over all else is evident in the Greek case too and is exemplified by Panousis's provocative verse in a song at the Zombie Festival: 'Get laid, otherwise we're lost' (*gamate, giati hanomaste*) – a verse based, in fact, on an anarchist slogan.[66]

Furthermore, in both movies one senses a lack of gender fixity, a certain sexual fluidity and a playful attitude regarding sexual identities. It is an approach contesting heteronormativity, close to what Joan Wallach Scott calls 'highly unstable' gender identification – in lieu of a coherent and fixed one.[67] This all implies mutable gender roles, again a standard feature in both Almodóvar's and Zervos' cinematography. The two films feature a parody of a beauty pageant, with male nudity and genitalia in the spotlight. The penis-size competition takes place in *Pepi, Luci, Bom*; a male body-building show and strip-tease (by Panousis himself) in *Drakoulas*. Both sexualize and objectify the males involved, thus 'invert[ing] the traditional female role as specularized, passive sex object'.[68] Panousis performs and strips in a female club where women appear half-naked and homoerotic but also very much excited by this male performer on a pedestal; a woman-leader, dressed like a dominatrix, gives a fiery speech on 'vaginocracy', the danger from the men's liberation movement, and new-technology cooking pots to save time. This is a clearly parodic discourse on feminism, the same we find in Almodóvar's film in which women's sexual liberation seems satirical. Bom, the singer in the band *Bomitoni*, sings, for instance, in total exuberance, typical of the time, the song 'Murciana', dedicated to her housewife lover. The lyrics contain clear political pointers to the time, such as the left-wing terrorist organization GRAPO:

> All I think about is you, Murciana.
> Because you're a dirty pig.
> I stick my finger in your slit.
> I give you a couple of slaps
> I make you wank me
> I'm more violent than the GRAPO
> I'm like the ring on your finger
> With me you reach orgasms
> If I fart in your mouth
> You applaud me with enthusiasm

Transvestites – a typical trait in underground cinema – are prominent in both movies, reflecting to a great extent the appearance and strengthening of their presence in the late 1970s and early 1980s in the two countries. Jean Baudrillard famously argued that

> what transvestites love is the game of signs, what excites them is to seduce the signs themselves. With them everything is makeup, theater and seduction. They appear obsessed, first of all, with play itself; and if their lives appear more sexually endowed than our own, it is because they make sex into a total, sensual and ritual game, an exalted but ironic invocation.[69]

This 'total, sensual and ritual game' is omnipresent in *Pepi, Luci Bom*, with the transvestite Roxy, played by Fabio McNamara. The exuberant transvestism of McNamara – who is given more screen time in *Labyrinth of Passion* – went beyond individual identity statements; it stood for 'radical apoliticism' and '*cultural*', other than simply sexual, transvestism, to paraphrase Vernon and Morris.[70] Similar ingredients are present in *Drakoulas* with instances of cross-dressing, men appearing in drag, with make-up and lipstick and homoerotic embraces. In sociologist Panayis Panayotopoulos words, Jimis Panousis' artistic gaze is most penetrating when it deals with gender identity, cross-dressing and homosexuality[71] – and in *Drakoulas* he is actively involved in all three.

As in Zervos' film none of the characters is properly developed, it is impossible to speak of the function of gender in any full sense. In Almodóvar, on the other hand, women appear dynamic, energetic, seductive and emotionally confused – but above all, they are given center stage. However, the gender politics of both films are far from unproblematic. Rape scenes are habitually humorous, and abundant sexist jokes are in the vein of male adolescent humour. As feminist scholar Louise Davis has suggested, under the guise of feminism Almodóvar continues to perpetuate patriarchal stereotypes about women and female sexuality rather than liberating women. For Davis, female characters who are sexually perverse lesbians or neurotic bisexuals are subjected to the dominating power of men who constantly prove their male superiority over them.[72] Moreover, the lack of gender fixity does not necessarily imply a challenging of prevalent versions of masculinity in the two societies, but a more ambiguous attitude, whereby at times provocation reproduces sexism, despite the overall subversiveness and transgressiveness. As historian Nikos Bozinis puts it convincingly '[Zervos'] intended subversion and mockery deconstructed in the end [his] films themselves, despite the interesting and well-known characters and the interesting subjects and images they included'[73] – a conclusion that applies to a great extent to Almodóvar's early features too.

A gradual cooptation

The two films mark the apogee of the respective subcultures in the two countries. In both cases these cultures suffered greatly from drug excesses, which led to a substantial diminishing in their demographics. The gradual cooptation, which especially in the case of the *movida* became rather official, the passage to a less radicalized political sphere and the advent of a certain lifestyle, greatly diminished the mass appeal of these groups. Additionally, heroin and AIDS led to their rapid disintegration, particularly that of the *movida*. Concomitantly, the depiction of these groups on camera, and a willingness to experiment with the medium also diminished. In this respect, both films act as powerful mementos of the time in which they were made and the countercultural explosion that characterized it. A cycle of protest ended and alongside it came the decline of the countercultural dynamism of those years.

In later years, *Pepi, Luci, Bom* acquired a cult status as, according to Graham and Labanyi, Spain's youth subculture was eventually welcomed by Spain's political elite as the 'official image of Spain'.[74] This opinion is shared by historian Giulia Quaggio, who cites the socialist Minister of Culture Javier Solanas, claiming that he was himself a great fan of the *movida* as it was unfolding.[75] It is no coincidence that *La Luna de Madrid* quickly turned into the first and main source for the mainstream media. In the end, a major part of the *movida* was about 'controlled excess, compatible with respected responsibilities, in which there was no conflict between working effectively by day and having fun at night'.[76] Its connection to mainstream media, culture and politics proved to be a powerful link to commercialism.[77]

To paraphrase cultural theorist Alberto Medina, this was a clear moment in which the Andy Warhol syndrome of coexistence between the underground avant-garde and the mainstream came to the fore. This worked out to perfection in the case of Almodóvar and his career, going hand-in-hand with the eventual full institutionalization of *movida* – or at least a part of it that became codified and accepted. The same does not apply so much to the case of Zervos, who ended up directing insignificant farcical comedies, although it does apply to some extent to Panousis' career. While in the Greek case no direct institutionalization of the anarchist subculture could be discerned, like its Spanish counterpart it became more mainstream in later years, through a large number of similar comedies. More importantly, perhaps, some of *Drakoulas*' protagonists, like Sakis Boulas and Johnny Vavouras even had their own television show (*Grafiti*) – not surprisingly, just like Alaska's *Bola de cristal* and general promotion of punk music on Spanish television (*La edad de oro*); and all this despite – or maybe because of – their critique of the medium and the mocking of its poetics. One can only think of the Birmingham School of Cultural Studies and the idea of subcultures becoming eventually incorporated in and coopted by the dominant culture; in other words, their extant links to the mainstream intensify and become firmly established.

Conclusions

This chapter focused on two representative filmic exponents of the new subcultures that developed in Greece and Spain during the immediate post-authoritarian period and their manifestation of individual autonomy and cultural diversity. Nikos Zervos' *O Drakoulas ton Exarchion* and Pedro Almodóvar's *Pepi, Luci, Bom* both documented and portrayed the respective youth experiencing post-authoritarian excess. It demonstrated how these films attacked some of the most long-lasting taboos of both societies, ridiculing the grotesque features of the respective transitions. The chapter also argued that the films testify to and document the subcultural periods of each country and its universe. Subcultural elements, including drugs, punk rock and an underground attire undermined in multiple ways the official political discourse of both the contemporary right and the left and their puritanism. All these elements are present in the films, which partake of what Umberto Eco has famously termed 'semiotic guerilla warfare'[78] with a parallel use of transvestites as central figures in this semantic confusion.

Although cultural transvestism and radical apoliticism were elements to which both films aspired, national-mindedness, family values and religion were not spared either. Gender features prominently in these films too, as they introduced novel elements, attacking social taboos and promoting fluidity and excess. They did not introduce a sophisticated or reflexive stance that would problematize on gender, however. Almodóvar's representations contain a crawling misogynism, while Zervos' depiction of the feminist movement of the time is sheer caricature. Even less reflexive is the fact that the two films, albeit underground, were consumer items, commodifying to a certain extent contestation and anarchy. It is no coincidence that two of the protagonists in the films, Jimis Panousis and Alaska, were symbols of this alternative culture, both recognizable rock singers at the time, thus possessing 'subcultural capital'. Nevertheless, the films documented subcultures in post-authoritarian Spain and Greece and the disenchantment of a segment of the radical youth, which, albeit connected to a cycle of protest that had started in earlier years, did not constitute a social movement in themselves. Still, the films highlight in a paradigmatic way the culturally subversive tendencies and irreverence of these subcultures which were caught off the hook between tradition and modernity, authoritarianism and democracy, conservatism and libertarianism, and, ultimately, the underground and the mainstream.

Notes

1. This chapter is based on a paper first presented at the conference 'Greek Cinema: Texts, Histories, Identities' in Liverpool, 23–4 May 2008. I would like to thank the participants of the conference for their useful comments. I am also grateful to Nikolaos Papadogiannis, Ursula-Helen Kassavetes and Alberto Medina for their extremely detailed feedback.
2. Pepe Ribas, *Los '70 a destajo. Ajoblanco y libertad* (Barcelona: Destino, 2011), 451.
3. Dimitris Psarras, 'Tyfles vomves, aorates arches', *Arxeiotaxio*, 15 September 2013, 24–8.
4. Gracia Trujillo Barbadillo, 'Deseo y resistencia. Treinta años de movilización lesbiana en el Estado español (1977–2007)', in Javier Ugarte Pérez (ed.), *Una discriminación universal. La homosexualidad bajo el franquismo y la transición* (Madrid: Editorial Egales S.L, 2008).
5. Nikolaos Papadogiannis, 'From coherence to fragments: "1968" and the making of youth politicisation in Greece in the 1970s', *Historein* 9, 2009, 76–92; Dimitris E. Kitis, 'The anti-authoritarian chóros: a space for youth socialization and radicalization in Greece (1974–2010)', *Journal for the Study of Radicalism* 9.1, spring 2015, 1–36.

6. Manuel Castells, *La Cuestión Urbana* (Madrid: Siglo XXXI, 1977); Pamela Beth Radcliff, *Making Democratic Citizens in Spain. Civil Society and the Popular Origins of the Transition, 1960–78* (London: Palgrave Macmillan, 2011).

7. Sidney Tarrow, *Power in the Movement: Social Movements and Contentious Politics*. (Cambridge: Cambridge University Press, 1998).

8. Jo Labanyi and Helen Graham, 'Democracy and Europeanization: continuity and change 1975–1992, editor's introduction', in Jo Labanyi and Helen Graham (eds), *Spanish Cultural Studies. An Introduction. The Struggle for Modernity* (Oxford: Oxford University Press, 1995), 312.

9. Abortion was not unknown in authoritarian Greece. In fact, often seen as the best solution for an undesirable pregnancy, an 'abortion syndrome' appeared in the 'Long 1960s'. See in this respect Nikolaos Papadogiannis, *Militant Around the Clock? Left-Wing Youth Politics, Leisure, Sexuality in Greece 1974–81* (Oxford and New York: Berghahn Books, 2015), 157. Yet as Papadogiannis clarifies it remained illegal, only being decriminalized in 1986, and thus practised in far from ideal conditions. Spain, by contrast, legalized abortion in 1981.

10. Donatella Della Porta, Celia Valiente and Maria Kousis, 'Sisters of the south. the women's movement and democratization', in Richard Gunther, P. Nikiforos Diamandouros and Hans-Jürgen Puhle (eds), *Democratic Consolidation in Southern Europe: The Cultural Dimension* (Baltimore, MD: Johns Hopkins University Press, forthcoming), 7. R. Montero, 'The silent revolution: the social and cultural advances of women in democratic Spain', in Labanyi and Graham (eds.), *Spanish Cultural Studies* 381.

11. Papadogiannis, *Militant Around the Clock?*, 280.

12. José Luis Gallero, *Solo se vive una vez – splendor y ruina de la movida madrileña* (Madrid: Ardora Editores, 1991), 9.

13. Mark Allinson, *A Spanish Labyrinth: The Films of Pedro Almodóvar* (London: I.B. Tauris, 2001), 14.

14. For a critique of the notion of 'pasota' as an empty signifier constructed by mainstream Spanish media, see Pablo Sánchez Leon, 'Estigma y memoria de los jóvenes de la transición', in Emilio Silva et al. (eds), *La memoria de los olvidados. Un debate sobre el silencio de la repression franquista* (Valladolid: Ámbisto, 2003, 163–79), cited in Alberto Medina, 'Over a Young Dead Body. The Spanish Transition as a Bildungsroman', *MLN* 130.2, March 2015, 309.

15. Giulia Quaggio, *La cultura en transición. Reconciliación y política cultural en España, 1976–1986* (Madrid: Alianza Editorial, 2014), 119.

16. Justin Crumbaugh, *Destination Dictatorship: The Spectacle of Spain's Tourist Boom and the Reinvention of Difference* (New York: State University of New York Press, 2010). Daniel Kowalsky, 'Rated S: Softcore pornography and the Spanish transition to democracy, 1977–82', in Antonio Lázaro Reboll and Andrew Willis (eds), *Spanish Popular Cinema*. Manchester (Manchester University Press, 2004).

17. Maria Komninou, and Ursula-Helen Kassavetes, 'Idiotiki mou zoi'. Mia apopeira eikonografias tou ellinikou erotikou kinimatografou tis periodou 1971–1974', in Katerina Sarikaki, Liza Tsaliki (eds.), *Mesa epikoinonias, laiki koultoura kai viomihania tou sex*, (Athens: Papazisis, 2011), 167.

18. Marsha Kinder, *Refiguring Spain: Cinema, Media, Representation* (Durham, NC: Duke University Press: 1997).

19. Marvin D'Lugo, 'Re-imaging the community: Imanol Uribe's *La muerte de Mikel* (1983) and the cinema of transition', in Peter William Evans (ed.), *Spanish Cinema. The Auteurist Tradition* (Oxford: Oxford University Press, 1999), 196.

20. Likewise Elias Petropoulos developed an idiosyncratic ethnography of the margins, with prostitutes, homosexuals and even thieves. Anarchist subculture publications coming out of the Exarchia quarter of Athens tended to deal with these matters as well.
21. Papadogiannis, *Militant Around the Clock?*, 215.
22. Peter Besas, *Behind the Spanish Lens: Spanish Cinema under Fascism and Democracy* (Denver, CO: Arden Press, 1985).
23. Mel Schuster, *The Contemporary Greek Cinema* (London: Scarecrow Press, 1979), 108. Besas, *Behind the Spanish Lens*.
24. Allinson, *A Spanish Labyrinth*, 15.
25. Barry Jordan and Rikki Morgan-Tamosunas, *Contemporary Spanish Cinema* (Manchester: Manchester University Press, 1998), 114.
26. Frederic Strauss (ed.), *Almodóvar on Almodóvar* (New York: Faber & Faber, 1996), 18.
27. Kostis Kornetis, '"Let's get laid because it's the end of the world!:" Sexuality, gender and the Spanish Left in late Francoism and the Transición', *European Review of History* 22.1, 2015, 176–98, 179.
28. Medina, 'Over a Young Dead Body', 305.
29. The Music Brigades referred directly to the Red Brigades in Italy, at about the time in which the terrorist organization was reaching global notoriety due to its kidnapping and ultimate assassination of Aldo Moro. This choice of name testifies to Panousis' steady willingness to be provocative beyond limits.
30. Vrasidas Karalis, *A History of Greek Cinema* (New York: Continuum, 2012), 204.
31. Here I take a different perspective from Labanyi's and Sevastakis' view of postmodern as juxtaposed to subversive. I do see it, however, in light of Hall and Jefferson's more recent analysis, as the transitional heterogeneous phase between the subcultures of the 1960s and the present day dislocation, with the 1980s typically being the faultline. Stuart Hall and Tony Jefferson (eds), *Resistance through Rituals: Youth Subcultures in Post-War Britain* (London: Routledge, 2nd ed., 2006), xxix, xxv.
32. Dick Hebdige, *Subculture. The Meaning of Style* (London and New York: Routledge, 1979), 103. See also Claude Levi-Strauss, *The Savage Mind* (London: Weidenfeld & Nicolson, 1966).
33. Alberto Fernández Torres, '"Pepi, Luci, Bom y otras chicas del montón", de Pedro Almodóvar (España, 1980)', *Contracampo: ensayos sobre teoría e historia del cine*, cited in Smith, *Desire Unlimited*.
34. Richard Dyer, *Now You See It* (London: Routledge, 2002), 102.
35. Jean Claude Seguin, *Pedro Almodóvar: filmer pour vivre* (Paris: Ophrys, 2010), 12.
36. Influences were not solely American: European films such as *Captain Berlin* by Jörg Buttgereit shared elements with these films.
37. Medina claims that as Warhol stood for this harmonious coexistence between mainstream and avant-garde underground, velvet or not, this was a crucial moment symbolizing *movida*'s potential to do the same; Warhol became its role model. See Medina, 'Over a Young Dead Body'.
38. Hamalidi, Nikolopoulou and Walldén call them 'counter-cultures'. Elena Hamalidi, Maria Nikolopoulou and Rea Walldén, 'A second avant-garde without a first: Greek avant-garde artists in the 1960s and 1970s' in Sascha Bru et al. (eds), *Regarding the Popular: Modernism, the Avant-garde, and High and Low Culture* (Berlin: Walter de Gruyter, 2012), 425–45.
39. Hall and Jefferson, *Resistance Through Rituals*.

40. Dimitris E. Kitis, 'The anti-authoritarian chóros: a space for youth socialization and radicalization in Greece (1974–2010)', *Journal for the Study of Radicalism* 9.1, spring 2015, 6.
41. Mallet et al. compellingly call it a collective of 'individuals either advocating serious anarchy, alternative lifestyles or merely mischievous fun'. Mark Mallet, Adriana Florez-Borquez, Costas Paris, 'Exarchia. An in depth report on its history, the people and the scene', *30 Days: Greece this Month*, July 1985, 44.
42. Thanasis Rentzis, interview to the author, June 2011.
43. Mallet et al, 'Exarchia', 44.
44. Gallero, *Solo se vive una vez*, 8.
45. Paul Julian Smith, *Desire Unlimited: The Cinema of Pedro Almodovar* (London: Verso: 2014).
46. Kostis Kornetis, *Children of the Dictatorship. Student Resistance, Cultural Politics and the 'Long 1960s' in Greece* (Oxford and New York: Berghahn Books, 2013), 215.
47. Papadogiannis, *Militant Around the Clock?*, 128, 246.
48. Ibid.
49. It is important to note here, however, that the *Knites* (members of KNE) tended to describe as anarchists people who would not necessarily describe themselves as such.
50. Schuster, *The Contemporary Greek Cinema*, 109.
51. Underground musician Pavlos Sidiropoulos wrote a song called 'Mickey Mouse' (1985) – playing with the identical sound of the names Mikis and Mickey, concluding: 'O Mickey Mouse eyfyi, o Miki Miki axion esti' ('Oh Mickey Mouse the genius, oh Mikis Mikis, Axion Esti' [worthy it is]). See Kostis Zouliatis, 'Mous(e)i(a)ko Underground', 91–100 (95) in Thanasis Moutsopoulos (ed.), *To Athinaiko Underground* (Athens: Athens Voice, 2011).
52. Gail Holst-Warhaft, 'The lion and the jackal: song as protest during the Greek Dictatorship', unpublished paper presented at the conference on 'Balkan Literatures of Dissent', Brown University, 20 April 2007.
53. Papadogiannis, *Militant Around the Clock?*, 214–15.
54. Smith, *Desire Unlimited*, 27; Kornetis, 'Let's Get Laid', 192.
55. Manolis Daloukas, *Elliniko rock. Istoria tis neanikis koultouras apo ti genia tou Haous mehri to thanato tou Pavlou Sidiropoulou, 1945–1990* (Athens: Agkyra, 2006), 372.
56. Strauss, *Almodóvar on Almodóvar*, 46.
57. This was a standard feature in the *movida*: Alaska, for instance, was involved in a fanzine and a punk band called Kaka de Luxe. On the general scatological obsession of Spanish counterculture during the democratic transition, see Germán Labrador Méndez, *Letras Arrebatadas*, 216–19.
58. Allinson, *A Spanish Labyrinth*, 33, 55.
59. Frank Trentmann, 'Knowing consumers: histories, identities, practices: an introduction', in Frank Trentmann (ed.), *The Making of the Consumer: Knowledge, Power and Identity in the Modern World* (Oxford: Berg, 2005).
60. Emma Dent Coad, 'Designer culture in the 1980s: the price of success', in Labanyi and Graham (eds), *Spanish Cultural Studies*, 377.
61. In Greece, *Drakoulas* sold 500,000 tickets, a remarkable achievement for a trashy B-movie, while *Pepi, Luci, Bom* sold 216,214 tickets.
62. Sarah Thornton, *Club Cultures* (Polity, 1995), 11.
63. Gallero, *Solo se vive una vez*, 12.

64. Kathleen Vernon and Barbara Morris, *Post-Franco, Postmodern: The Films of Pedro Almodóvar*. Westport, CT: Greenwood Press, 1995.
65. Smith, *Desire Unlimited*, 16, my emphasis.
66. Filippos Filippou, *Oi Knites. Tekna tis anagkis i orima tekna tis orgis?* (Athens: Pyxida, 1983), 57. Interestingly, this exact phrase was reiterated to me by a Catalan interviewee on the post-1968 liberalization of mores in Barcelona and a popular phrase of the time, 'follem, follem, qu'el mont s'acaba', or 'let's get laid because it's the end of the world'. See Kornetis, 'Let's get laid'. In terms of the Greek case, it should be noted that this slogan, alongside 'Besides imperialism there is also loneliness', 'The Aegean Sea belongs to its fish' and others, were all anarchist or freaks' slogans written on Exarchia or university walls at the time of the film or earlier. See, in this respect, Filippou, *The Knites*, Papadogiannis, *Militant Around the Clock?*
67. Joan Walter Scott, *Gender and the Politics of History* (New York: Columbia University Press: 1999), 38.
68. Alinson, *The Spanish Labyrinth*, 85.
69. Jean Baudrillard, *Seduction*, trans. Brian Singer (New York: St. Martin's Press, 1990), 13.
70. Vernon and Morris, *Post-Franco, Postmodern*, my emphasis.
71. Panayis Panayiotopoulos, 'Jimis Panousis', in Vassilis Vamvakas and Panayis Panayotopoulos (eds), *I Ellada sti dekaetia tou '80. Koinoniko, politiko kai politismiko lexiko* (Athens: To Perasma, 2010), 422.
72. Louise H. Davis, 'High heeled sexualities: representations of femininity and masculinity in four films by Pedro Almodóvar', M.A. Thesis, Department of English, University of Michigan, 1999, 186–8.
73. Nikos Bozinis, *Rock pagkosmiotita kai elliniki topikotita. I koinoniki istoria tou rock stis chores katagogis tou kai tin Ellada* (Athens, 2007), 170.
74. Jo Labanyi and Helen Graham, 'Democracy and Europeanization: continuity and change 1975–1992. editor's introduction', in Labanyi and Graham (eds), *Spanish Cultural Studies*, 312.
75. Quaggio, *La cultura en transición. Reconciliación y política cultural en España, 1976–1986* (Madrid: Alianza Editorial, 2014).
76. Medina, 'Over a Young Dead Body', 303.
77. On the plethora of debates around the nature of the *movida* and the function that it came to play in Spanish society and culture, in general, see William J. Nichols et al. (eds), *Towards a Cultural Archive of la Movida. Back to the Future* (Madison, WI: Fairleigh Dickinson University Press, 2013).
78. Umberto Eco, 'Towards a semiotic enquiry into the television message', *W.P.C.S.* 3, University of Birmingham, 1972.

CHAPTER 9
'NAKED PIAZZA': MALE (HOMO)SEXUALITIES, MASCULINITIES AND CONSUMER CULTURES IN GREECE SINCE THE 1960s
Kostas Yannakopoulos

After the collapse of the dictatorship in 1974, Greek society witnessed the proliferation of new sociopolitical movements that had emerged in Western Europe several years earlier. One of them was the gay movement, the emergence of which is connected more with the broader liberty of political expression and the expansion of radical ideas after the collapse of the dictatorship rather than with the legitimacy of the Left (especially that of Communist Party in Greece). Leftist parties, with the exception of the small Eurocommunist[1] party ('Communist party of Interior') and its youth 'Rigas Feraios', were reluctant – if not hostile – towards the newly emergent gay movement (AKOE) and homosexuality in general.[2] The emergence of a gay identity, movement and culture – i.e. gay bars – was linked with the broader changes that occurred in Greek society regarding the conceptualizations of homosexuality, sexuality and gender. The aim of this study is to explore these changes regarding male homosexuality and masculinity and to analyse how these shifts reflected on, but were also produced by, the new consumer practices regarding the gendered public space and the body. As Voulgaris argues, it seems that the shifts in male homosexuality and masculinity could be associated with the explosion of consumerist expectations and political claims regarding gender and sexuality after the fall of the dictatorship period (*Metapolitefsi*).[3] These expectations – along with the overall social and cultural modernization – were repressed by the 'Greek-Christian' cultural politics of the dictatorship. The episode that Loukas Theodorakopoulos – a writer, spokesman for AKOE[4] and editor of its magazine *AMFI* – narrates in his book *Kaiadas* is indicative of the dictatorship's repression of new consumer practices regarding the male body and homosexuality.[5] *Kaiadas*[6] is a chronicle of the arrest of a company of homosexual men who gathered in the house of one of them celebrating his birthday. The arrest was followed by a public castigation – i.e. display of their names and photos in the daily newspapers, and a trial. During the interrogation the policemen wanted to check out who was 'homosexual' or not, and demanded the arrested men show them their underpants. If they wore a modern brief slip they were perceived by the policemen as 'effeminates', i.e. 'homosexuals'; if they wore the traditional underpants (*sovrako*) they were perceived as 'men', i.e. non-'homosexuals'.

Following the spatial and material turn in contemporary studies on space and material culture, I argue that space and gendered/sexual bodily appearance are not a container, an epiphenomenon of sexual relations between men and an inner gendered/sexual self.[7] As I will demonstrate, they play a considerable and active role in constituting the gendered/sexual self and the sexual desire, even orientation, towards men or women. References made to mid-1970s Greek society, along with the articulation of a new consumer culture and the emergence of different conceptualizations of sexuality and gender, are not to be interpreted as an argument for 'pure' masculinity being spoiled by a culture of commodification prior to widespread consumerism. Instead, my point of view is that different male (homo)sexualities and masculinities are shaped by different materialities. In addition, a moralistic, anti-materialistic approach to consumption that is widespread in social sciences[8] constitutes a basic part of the political ideology by which intellectuals – who lived with their homosexuality between the 1950s and the 1970s – have interpreted the shifts that occurred in Greek society. This ideology is partly suggested in the following verses from Dinos Christianopoulos' poem:

> [...] And yet, everything changed within a few years. The cafeteria rendered the parks useless. Television emptied out the movie houses. Females became a dime a dozen. Studs, lousy rich. Soldiers, kept men. We were knocked out by wheels, the efficiency apartment and dough. [...][9]

The poet himself is one of the prominent representatives of the old generation of Greek homosexual intellectuals. The writings of Christianopoulos and other intellectuals combined with my own research reveal that in Greece a widespread queer[10] cuture or, to use the conceptual category deployed by my interlocutors, a culture of *poniroi*, existed which was significantly different from the hegemonic, Western perception of contemporary gay culture. As the researchers of the new queer history put it, instead of turning to the past to discover the origins, to trace the history of a modern 'homosexual consciousness' as the early gay history did, we have to reconsider our categories of identity and desire which are of limited use in understanding this history.[11]

The following text is based on the research that I conducted on male homosexualities of the 1950s to 1970s, in order to better understand the contemporary masculinity, male homosociality and homosexuality[12] in the areas of Athens and Piraeus which were the main topics I researched for my doctoral dissertation.[13] Both my past and ongoing research is based on interviews with men who lived, or experienced their homosexuality, during the 1960s and 1970s in Athens. In this chapter I also use literary writings, testimonials, published interviews and a collection of photographs of the homosexual intellectuals mentioned above, not to confirm or enrich my 'data' but rather to better grasp the perceptions of masculinities and male sexualities. In other words, these sources were valuable for revealing not so much the 'facts', the 'truth of correspondence' but rather the 'truth of unveiling' – i.e. the gendered/sexual imaginary.[14]

Conceptualizations of gender and male sexuality from the 1950s to the 1970s

In Greek society of the 1950s to 1970s, the sexual behaviour and identity of a man – but also of a woman – was conceptualized based on the gender with which he or she identified, and not on that of the sexual partner of choice.[15] More specifically, men were not broadly categorized as 'heterosexual' and 'homosexual' but as 'masculine' and 'feminine' (*andras* i.e. man – *poustis/adelfi*).[16] A 'masculine' man could have sexual relations with either a 'feminine' man or a woman without being stigmatized. Moreover, many 'masculine' men had relationships with women. The gender identities of *andras* and *poustis/adelfi* are defined according to the 'masculine' or 'feminine' bodily appearance, performance and the sexual roles during intercourse: the one who penetrates is 'active' either with a man or with a woman and is regarded as *andras*, while the one who, like a woman, 'suffers', undergoes the penetration, is *poustis/adelfi*. The access of *andres*[17] to sexual relations with other men is connected with a masculine perception of male sexual desire. This is perceived as a 'natural' sexual need which is characteristic of the male physiology. More specifically, the male sexual organ is considered as the site of a sexual instinct which is called *kavla* in the 'male' slang.[18] In periods of sexual deprivation, *kavla* is becoming more intense and sometimes painful because of the hyper-concentration of sperm in the testicles. So, men need urgently to discharge by penetrating whomever, woman or man. Overall, in rural but also urban Greek sites, sexuality was perceived as a 'natural' action aimed at either reproduction or the satisfaction of the 'biological' needs of men. Tenderness and love were not considered essential, constitutive elements of the heterosexual couple, or of marriage.[19] Contrarily, men expressed publicly intense tenderness and sensuality to their homosocial partners through embraces, ambiguous looks and verbal expressions without these relationships being characterized or stigmatized as (homo)sexual or erotic in the modern, Western sense of the term, but, rather, as non-sexual – friendly.[20] Thus, by limiting their (hetero)sexual relations to just sexual activities, men could experience intense sentimentality and sensuality for individuals of the same sex. For some men this sensuality extended to erotic, sexual relationships that often were long-term and were characterized by an intense, often vehement emotional devotion between two men. Despite the fact that these relations included homosex,[21] they were not perceived as erotic or (homo)sexual. In addition, the 'masculine' men who were the subjects of these relationships were not identified as *poustides/adelfes*[22] but as *andres* or rather as *poniroi*. *Poniros*,[23] a term generally used for the men having homosex, is a man with 'manly' appearance who 'understands', i.e. intuits, the implicit erotic character of an explicit non-sexual communication, a meeting between two men. In this way, a *poniros* 'understands' that another man is susceptible to his erotic advances and the reverse: the other man 'understands' that someone is making erotic advances and responds to them. *Poniros* refers only to men who present a manly appearance and not to the 'effeminate' ones, since the appearance of the latter would make male communication sexual. However, *poniros* can be active or passive but always 'masculine'. Therefore, the term includes *andres* and *adelfes* as well. The majority of *adelfes* were of a conventional masculine appearance since only a small portion of courageous queer men were 'effeminate' in appearance. It is important to note that 'effeminacy' had a different meaning from what we mean nowadays. As we will see in the following section, it seems that 'effeminacy' was not a lifetime performance due to an 'inclination' but was performed by the actors according to the sexual and social context.

Consumption and Gender through the Moment of Transition

Class/gendered differences, male body and desire

During the first three postwar decades, Athens had the biggest growth of its population due to the migration of workers from rural areas. In the postwar period, the urban agglomeration of Athens represented the 43.3 per cent of the total Greek population with migrants populating 56 per cent of the city.[24] The majority of these migrants worked as specialized or unspecialized manual labourers (for example, as construction workers) and represented the 11.7 per cent of the migrant population.[25] According to David Close, half of the population in Athens and Thessaloniki was working class.[26] These ex-peasant workers were living in conditions of poverty. Even in 1974, 31 per cent of the households in Greece were living below the poverty line while in Athens, 57 per cent of the households had three or four people living in one room which was considered their home.[27]

Working-class men, especially construction workers, *betatzides*, peasants who visited, or were soldiers in Athens, known as *laika tekna* – i.e. young working-class studs – originated either from rural areas or Athens and were a significant portion of the men who participated in sexual encounters with other men. This participation was validated socially by their gendered/sexual performance as *andres* and their state of *kavla*.[28] Their 'physical' sexual needs could be satisfied or, better yet, relieved, only by *adelfes* because of the scarcity of premarital sexual encounters with women. The taboo loss of virginity for unmarried women was widespread in the villages[29] and was strong especially among the immigrants from rural areas and the working-class neighbourhoods of Athens, even in the early 1970s.[30]

The *adelfes*, the erotic partners of *andres*, were usually men who worked in sedentary white-collar occupations. This class difference was interpreted as a gender difference,[31] because the white-collar occupations were considered womanlike compared with physical labour.[32] In her study, Dimitra Lambropoulou notes that construction workers who were living in Athens in the 1960s participated in a male culture of pride at the core of which was the robustness of the body.[33] The possibility of a male body being damaged or injured due to physical labour is what distinguishes male from female bodies. *Betatzides* would often exhibit their naked upper bodies by taking off their shirts in their political demonstrations.[34] The robust bodies of the working men were the focal point of desire for middle-class queer men. The literature of writers who lived their homosexuality from the 1950s to the 1970s and middle-class homosexual research participants describe the masculinity of working men and peasant men as 'natural', 'spontaneous', 'tough'.[35] The beauty of these *andres* was considered the outcome of a life of difficulties and material deprivation – poverty. In a collection of men's photos taken in 1950s and 1960s by the homosexual intellectual Thanos Velloudios (1895–1992) and the editor and poet Yorgos Chronas there was an exaltation of the 'naturalness' of the photographed male naked bodies, the 'Greek statues' as the latter would call them, noting that – contrary to the contemporary fat and ill bodies of affluence – these bodies were the outcome of poverty, of malnutrition, due to a diet consisting of 'potatoes, bread and beans, legumes'.[36] In other words, deprivation of material, consumer goods leads to a 'natural' masculinity in the same way as sexual deprivation accentuates the 'natural' male instinct *kavla*. According to this perception, the 'natural' masculinity is rather a matter of the soul than of the body. The testimonial of Miltos, a seventy-year-old university professor, sheds light on the contrast between the contemporary male body and the 'natural' masculinity of the past, noting that the latter reflected the soul and adding that this difference is between body and flesh. Yorgos Ioannou, a well-known writer (1927–85) also notes: 'And the beauty is a matter of the soul and not only of the body. And, unfortunately, it presupposes a hardened soul'.[37]

Consequently, the *poniroi* middle-class intellectuals rejected the beautification, the care of the body which included wearing fancy clothes and using cosmetics, because these spoiled the peasant and working-class 'authentic' masculinity. Christianopoulos, in his poem entitled 'To a working-class friend', writes:

Please don't wear perfume.
I like the odor of your body.
There's no perfume lovelier than your sweat.
I want to savor the saltiness of your chest,
to drink in the fragrance of your armpits,
to soak myself in the moisture of your loins.

Please don't wear perfume.
Why are you in such a hurry to forget your village and auto repair shop?
What do you want with perfumed soap?
They will treacherously wreck your virility.

Please don't wear perfume.
It was all I could do to find a man among all these pansies.
So remain what you are:
an unspoiled working-class boy.[38]

As for perfume, Andreas, a 72-year-old Greek-American businessman, recalls that in the late 1960s he brought as a gift a perfume for a middle-class *poniros*, owner of a bar in which many Athenian *poniroi* hung out. He looked at the gift with disgust – as if it was a 'bag of shit', Andreas characteristically says – and of course never used it. In general, perfumes were not considered as compatible with masculinity but as a sign of bourgeois elegance[39] and, therefore, of 'effeminacy'. The only perfume that existed from the 1960s and was used by all family members was the cologne 'Myrto' which was made in Greece.

As for clothing, only the military uniform was considered, exalted, by my *poniroi* interlocutors and intellectuals in their writings and paintings[40] as a 'masculine' accessory. But perhaps due to its compulsory character, the military uniform was not perceived as an 'accessory' but rather as a cloth that reflected and highlighted the toughness and aggressiveness of peasants and working-class soldiers. Moreover, the military uniform constituted a component, a constitutive element of masculinity and, consequently, of the desire of middle-class *poniroi* towards lower-class young studs, *tekna*.[41] Matt Houlbrook reflects on the relationships between 'men' and 'queans' in London from 1918 to 1957 by stating that 'rather than being erased by sexual desire, class difference *actuated* that desire, eroticized in almost gendered terms'.[42]

However, the majority of *adelfes* had a more or less conventional masculine appearance, at least for the most part of their everyday life. Yannis, a seventy-year-old actor, recalls that the hippy look spread throughout Athens in the 1970s, with a lot of young men wearing bell-bottom trousers and tunics – i.e. embroidered shirts with soft patterns. Both a*delfes* and *andres* wore bell-bottoms and tunics but *adelfes* were distinguished from *andres* by the fact that the bell-like shape of the trousers was a little wider and the tunic hung out of the trousers, while *men* tucked it into their trousers. In other words, *adelfes* 'reworked rather [than] rejected' the conventional masculine appearance.[43] Their dress code and attitude were more eccentric rather than effeminate. Kostas was the legendary barman of a bar in which *poniroi* hung out in the 1970s. Although he was called and was known by his eccentric, 'feminine' nick-name *i*[44] 'Tsin-Tsin', my interlocutors were impressed by the fact that he would have two cigarettes in his mouth which he smoked simultaneously. Moreover, he wore a shirt that had two different types of sleeve. In addition, 'Tsin-Tsin' and the majority of *adelfes* seemed to exhibit their eccentricity/'effeminacy' in the moments and places of their encounters with *andres*[45] and lived as 'masculine', 'normal' men the rest of their life. This happened also in the cases of more 'effeminate', 'open', publicly recognized *adelfes*, which is close to what is now considered to be the prevailing perception regarding transvestites. My interlocutors remember that these *adelfes* wore wigs and make-up and used inflated preservatives as substitutes for female breasts. One of these seems to be the famous *fterou*; a man who sold plumes for dusting (*ftera*) in the streets of the centre of Athens saying loudly in an effeminate manner '*ftera, ftera*' (plumes).

Sexual and consumer pleasures in all-male public places

When asking my *poniroi* intrelocutors to mention which were the specific places where they met their sexual partners they start naming some but after a while all said: 'Everywhere!' Andreas – who represents some of my interlocutors who were born and had lived in a Western society such as the USA where they could meet a sexual partner only in the specifically 'gay' places – was impressed and excited when he first came to Athens in 1968 by the 'total freedom', as he perceived it, of homosexual encounters.

In Athens, from the 1950s to 1970s, a man could meet a male sexual partner in almost all public spaces. Even the most central streets of Athens such as Stadiou, were ideal places for erotic encounters between men. Strolling in Stadiou, exchanging glances with other men, a *poniros* could easily start a sexual encounter because many, especially lower-class, men responded to his erotic advances. The same happened in central places such as Syntagma and Omonia but also on the buses or even at political, public gatherings. This diffusion in space of male-to-male sexual encounters is connected to the fact that almost all public places were male-dominated except for upper-class neighbourhoods such as Kolonaki. Women, especially the unmarried ones, were restricted when going out in public if they were not accompanied by a man, or better yet a relative.[46] This restriction was due to the surveillance of female chastity. So, the women's exclusion and the all-male character of public spaces was accentuated in areas where only men, or mostly lower-class men hanged out. These were the male urinals in several central areas in Athens (Syntagma, Omonia, Kotzia, Kannigos), the big parks in Athens such as the National Park, Zappeion and Pedion Areos at night, as well as cinemas. The latter were mainly cinemas near Omonia where most lower-class men would hang out. During the 1950s and 1960s cinemas were very popular and were considered as places of corruption and moral danger for the youth who went to watch films that were officially labelled as inappropriate (*akatallila*) for minors.[47] This moral danger included homosexuality. As Efi Avdela notes, there are many cases recorded in the reports of juvenile probation officers of minors who were persecuted for having sexual encounters with older men in such places. My interlocutors note that it was in the 1950s that many *kolomparades* approached and had sexual encounters with minors. These cinemas usually showed films with cowboys and in the 1970s soft and hardcore porn films called *tsontes*.[48] Also, the all-male cafes (*kafeneia*) and *tavernes*, especially in Omonia Square but also near military barracks in which soldiers[49] would hang out, were places of the *poniroi*'s erotic encounters. A considerable part of these encounters were taking the form of a sexual economic exchange. *Andres* offered their 'masculine' sexual favours not so much for money but usually for consumer goods offered by the middle-class *adelfes*. Even the small amount of money given in some cases to *tekna* was called *hartziliki*[50] or *doraki* – i.e. a small gift. In the majority of the relationships, *adelfi* usually offered a dinner or a lunch, food and drink in a taverna, a treat (*kerasma*), or even a bath in a house.[51] The more affluent *adelfes* offered clothes, watches and other material goods. Andreas remembers that in the late 1960s he and other American gay tourists[52] offered American cigarettes such as Marlboro that were not sold in Greece nor were very expensive. The appearance of a well-dressed man, especially in the Western manner, attracted lower-class studs. 'They were stopping me in the middle of the street to ask me where I bought my shoes' recalls Andreas. All the aforementioned suggest that working men were interested in consumer goods and that new modes of distraction such as going to cinemas became very popular among youth in the 1960s. As the reports of the juvenile probation officers suggest, many minors committed misdemeanours such as robbery or panhandling for fulfilling their desire to acquire such goods.[53] In his study on consumption from 1960 to 1975, Vassilis Karapostolis argues that the working-class population would not tolerate any more its material deprivation and had consumerist aspirations.[54] Despite the fact that part of the population did not manage to achieve a social ascendance through change of profession (for instance by becoming civil servants), social mobility through consumption and consumerist mobility were espoused by all. Nevertheless, according to Close it was only after the early 1970s that the results of this mobility and overall economic growth were evident.[55] Karapostolis notes that – due to economic uncertainty – the working classes was deprived of consumerist mobility, at least concerning luxury goods.[56] In addition, my interlocutors emphasized the poverty that existed mainly within the working classes in the 1960s and even in the early 1970s. When asked to describe his long walks in the centre of Athens while cruising for a*ndres* Yannis stated: 'that's why we were doing all these walks because we were penniless'. Not only for Yannis, who was a beginner actor at the time, but even more for the working-class men and soldiers, strolling – in Omonia, the National Garden or Syntagma – was their main distraction. However, it seems that consumption patterns were changing even among working-class men. In this way – as Schofield notes for the commercial homosex in 1950s' London – sexual pleasure and the material, consumer goods offered by *adelfes* constituted a way into a world of consumerist pleasures.[57]

Nevertheless, offers of material goods made by *adelfes* were not, at least in all cases, the necessary sine qua non condition for having an erotic relationship with a working-class *tekno*. Or, the latter – according to the male code of reciprocity between male friends – compensated for the offer in the degree he could afford it, especially when the relationship was not limited to a pure sexual encounter but had sentimental dimensions.[58] While describing his first encounter with a young peasant man doing his military service in the navy, Andreas emphasizes that he was a 'sweet boy': 'he had his pride, he wanted to pay the tickets of the tram, he was very sorry when I left him to go to the islands'. As mentioned, the sexual encounter between an *andras* and an *adelfi* could change into a sentimental attachment taking the form of a friendship between men. In other words, middle-class but also working-class *poniroi* men exploited and reworked the affective ties and the sensuality of male homosociality. In this way, they created homoerotic bonds diffused into male public space.

The emergence of new, modern, Western conceptualizations of gender and sexuality

From the end of the 1970s onwards, modern, Western conceptualizations of homosexuality and of sexual identity gradually emerged on a broader scale. More specifically, although the gendered categories of *andras* and *adelfi/poustis* continued to coexist with the modern ones, men were divided into 'homosexual/gays' and 'heterosexual/straights'.[59] In other words, the sexual behaviour and identity of a man was conceptualized based on his choice of sex partner and not on the gender to which he considered he belonged. Moreover, *sexoualikotita* – i.e. sexuality, a Western neologism – became the main subject of daily discussions after being perceived not only as a sexual male need, or a necessity for reproduction, but as a constitutive element of the self and personal happiness.[60] The most prominent form of expression of 'sexuality' was the couple, even outside of marriage. This emergence of the 'couple' as a preferential place for sentimental expression is directly connected to the decline, or even destruction, of homosociality. There was a shift in sentiment/tenderness from homosociality to forming couples; a privatization, as I call it, of tenderness in the modern Greek society.[61] The new ideal of couple was also prevalent among 'homosexuals/gays'.[62]

Shift in masculine desires and new consumerist masculinities

The new distinction between heterosexual/homosexual gradually spread within the working class and got connected with the withdrawal of young working-class studs from sexual encounters with *adelfes*. In the 1980s, these *tekna* were replaced with young immigrants from the Balkans – e.g. Albanians – who were arriving in Greece at that time. More specifically, if a young man responded to the sexual advances of an *adelfi*, or even worse was looking for homosex, he would be considered as, and therefore stigmatized as, 'homosexual'; a category which at that time also included a man having an active role in homosexual intercourse. Moreover – despite the fact that *kavla* remained a valid cultural category – it could no longer justify the participation in homosex. This was due to the fact that young women could have premarital sexual relationships as long as these took place in the context of 'serious' (i.e. emotional and stable) relationships. In other words, sentimentality replaced the taboo of the loss of virginity, which in turn enabled young women to have premarital sexual intercourse.[63] This tolerance towards the premarital sexual activity of women has often been exaggerated and viewed negatively, mainly by older Greeks, as a sexual liberation. Thus, it is supposedly more probable for young men to have heterosexual intercourse. In addition, the new widespread normative ideals of the tenderness and the couple set the rules for the expression of masculinity. In order to attract women, young heterosexual men ought to present themselves as possessing a 'softer' masculinity – i.e. sentimental, 'well-mannered', 'civilized'. The heterosexual man who expresses a hypersexual, aggressive, tough masculinity is considered and, therefore, degraded, as ravenous and backward. In the 1990s, the sexual aggressiveness that was caused by sexual deprivation was no longer considered a characteristic of the Greek man but of young immigrants (such as young Albanians). Consequently, a sexual encounter with an *adelfi* would be a sign of a sexual deprivation which was perceived as a characteristic of an impoverished Greek past, or of other, arguably backward, societies.

In addition, the offers of material and consumer goods made by an *adelfi* in the 1960s and even 1970s would now leave peasants and working-class young men utterly indifferent. In the 1980s, Andreas told of another Greek-American gay who came to Greece with a lot of packs of American cigarettes (as he himself used to do in the past) so as to entice working-class studs to have casual sexual encounters with him. This man returned to the US with his baggage still full of packs of cigarettes as he did not manage to give any away. Apart from the fact that young men could by then buy American cigarettes, offers of material, consumer goods could be perceived as degrading, portraying them as impoverished and challenging their potential upward social and, especially, consumerist mobility.

According to Close, there was a considerable improvement in the Greek standard of living during the 1980s due to the increase of salaries, social protection benefits, social services and the funding of agricultural products by the European Union, despite unemployment and socioeconomic inequalities.[64] This social mobility and ascendance was expressed mainly through consumption.

In this context, labour was no longer considered as prestigious, even among working-class young men. In Perama – a working-class neighbourhood of Piraeus where I conducted part of my fieldwork in the 1990s – a lot of young men refused to work in the dockyard even if some of them were unemployed. They were keen to buy motorcycles, cars, clothes, and wear gold bracelets on their neck or hands even when playing football. These consumerist practices were connected with a new widespread model of the man who was professionally successful, consuming ostentatiously and paying attention to his appearance.[65] Even if professional success was not achieved, a lot of young men would spend a considerable amount of money from their salary, or mainly their *hartziliki* given that this time it was not from *adelfes* but from their parents, on buying motorcycles, clothes, accessories, gadgets and for their entertainment. My young interlocutors in Perama considered these accessories of the new masculinity as necessary for seducing girls. Consequently, robust 'natural' masculine physical appearance shaped by labour was no longer valued as a source of male pride because it embodied deprivation. Young men were exhibiting their social ascendance and status by taking care of their bodies and appearance mainly by the selection of clothes, adornments, accessories, cosmetics and workout sessions in the gyms. From the 1980s onwards, gyms were in most neighbourhoods of Athens and became very popular among young men who engaged in muscle training.[66] Shopping and wearing clothes of well-known brands became very popular even among young men who could not afford them but who would save up money to buy them.[67] Perfumes and cosmetics were no longer considered as a sign of effeminacy; from the mid-1980s onwards, cosmetics for men were made available on the Greek market.[68] This commodification of the male body was perceived by the old generation of *adelfes*, *poniroi*, as a decline of masculinity; a feminization of contemporary young men. Contrary to the 'natural' body of the past, this new masculine body was perceived as 'fake, raw, sweat less, artificial'.[69] Moreover, the military uniform – the erotic fetish of old *adelfes* – was not worn by soldiers in public (since around the mid-1980s soldiers were allowed to wear their civilian clothing). In addition, the uniform that was worn when one was granted a pass, or was taking leave of absence from the barracks changed in order to become more comfortable. This change of the uniform has been interpreted as a loss of masculinity.[70] In other words, not only was the desire of *tekna* taken away from *adelfes* but also that of the older *adelfes*. This split of old *poniroi* and new *tekna* desire strengthens the distinction between male heterosexuality and homosexuality. This also happened among the new homosexual men: the desire of the new middle-class *gays* was directed towards other gay men since gays were considered as masculine as heterosexual/straight men. The emergence of this new gay masculinity was connected, among other things, to the emergence of a commodified masculinity. Weston analyses gender performance based on Benjamin's classic study on art and mechanical reproduction.[71] According to Benjamin, mechanical reproduction erodes the meaningfulness and prestige of the original. The exhibition value of the copies of works of art comes to override the value placed on uniqueness. In a similar way, people in the age of mechanical reproduction – from the Harley to cummerbund to the gold lamé – gender themselves as copies of former copies through a pronounced reliance on machine-produced goods that are reproductions themselves. In the same way, once the meaningfulness and prestige of the 'authentic' male body shaped 'naturally' by physical labour had been eroded, all Greek men could gender themselves as masculine copies relying on machine-produced masculine goods. In other words, the emergence of a new 'artificial', made by clothes, masculine accessories, physical activity in the gyms[72] and weight-loss programmes, allowed middle-class gay men to become masculine in the same way as heterosexual men. In March 1988, in an article entitled 'Hymn to the Boot' that was published in the gay magazine *Pothos* (desire/lust) edited by a gay political group in Thessaloniki – which was in turn inspired by Salonician Christianopoulos' homonymous poem[73] – the writer concludes with the following: 'The contemporary tough gays, with muscled arms, shaved heads, military boots, tattoo, piercings and aggressive glances, are overwhelming with masculinity. Nevertheless, in contrast to the unaware *tsolia*,[74] they are fully aware that they constitute drag queens- from the opposite side.'

Heterosocial and homosexual/'gay' places

The destruction of male homosociality was connected directly with the gradual disappearance of homosocial places. The all-male places *kafeneia* were seen by modern young people as obsolete and were degraded as lower-class places. Urinals in central squares of Athens were demolished when these squares were gentrified in the 1980s. Cinemas near Omonia no longer attracted young working-class men since television and videotapes became very popular in the 1980s. As Panayis Panayiotopoulos notes, the popularity of movie rentals viewed at home was connected with the transformation of the home into a place of consumerist and individual pleasures for each family member.[75] So, in the context of general privatization of sexual and consumerist pleasures – since the projection of hardcore porn movies in cinemas but also the circulation of videocassettes containing such movies were permitted in the 1980s – many young working-class men were renting and watching *tsontes*.[76] For these men, strolling around the central squares, parks and streets of Athens became meaningless. They preferred to hang out in *kafeteries* – i.e. the modern cafes that replaced the *kafeneia* first in the big cities (1970s) and then in all of Greece (1980s), or later in the evening – and after dressing up – to drink and dance in discos (popular in the 1980s) and in bars (mostly from the 1990s onwards).[77] *Kafeteries*, discos and bars were places of a mixed, heterosexual sociability where young men and women could meet and mainly, as Jane Cowan puts it, 'show who they are by spending and consuming'.[78] If the heterosexual young men and women preferred to go to modern, sophisticated heterosocial[79] leisure places, their gay counterparts had their own modern, Western leisure places to hang out in; the gay bars.[80] One such place was the legendary bar 'Mykonos' that was considered by many of my interlocutors as the first Greek 'gay' bar. Mykonos opened during the dictatorship (in 1969) in the neighbourhood of Plaka; its owners and bartenders were two friends, a man and a woman, Alekos and Nora. Mykonos – despite the majority of its clientele being queer, *poniroi* men and the connotations of its name[81] – was not identified as a 'gay bar' at least in the contemporary, Western sense of the term. In his interview, Alekos focuses more on the famous international artistic clientele and the Cycladic and also European aesthetic of his bar rather than its 'gay' character. Besides, he himself was at the time a *poniros*, having both heterosexual and homosexual relationships. In 1979 Alekos moved his bar to Kolonaki under the name 'Alekos' Island'. This new bar was like a typical Euro-American gay-bar[82] in which the first Greek 'gay clones'[83] appeared. The gay bars that emerged in the 1970s and 1980s were either in cosmopolitan, tourist neighbourhoods – e.g. Plaka, Makriyianni, Thisio, or in the upper-class ones such as Kolonaki. In the early 2000s, Alekos closed down Alekos Island and opened a new bar near the new gay neighbourhood, the so-called 'gay village' of Gazi. This new bar was a commercial failure and was also closed down.

Anti-conclusion

From the 1950s to the 1970s, a significant world of male to male sexual, erotic relationships existed in Athens and generally in Greece. This diffused 'homosexuality' refutes the widespread perception that – prior to the advancement of gay liberation in Greece – there was only oppression, culpability, almost the 'inexistence' of homosexual relationships, especially among the Greek gays who lived their homosexuality from mid-1970s onwards. According to this hegemonic perception, the mid-1970s and the 1980s were the turning point of a linear evolution from an era of murkiness to the luminous years of gay liberation. On the other hand, *poniroi* intellectuals, more or less, severely criticized the ascendance of 'Western' gay culture in Greece and were opposed to the 'new gay'.[84] Many of these criticisms were focused on the distinction heterosexual/homosexual, commercial 'Western' gay 'ghetto' and grieved, as we have seen, the commodification of Greek masculinity. Nonetheless, this decline of the old *poniroi*'s culture was the result of broader and more complex shifts concerning gender, sexuality and the entire Greek economy and society. Nowadays, new 'queer', anarchist and far Left groups make criticisms which resonate with those of *poniroi* – about the commercialization of gay culture and the 'nonetheless-political' character of the LGBT 'Athens Pride'. Nevertheless, at the time of AKOE and the magazine *AMFI*[85] the number of its members was very limited and only very few gays would participate in its demonstrations. Following a broader Leftist cultural attitude at that time,[86] militants of AKOE who adopted an 'alternative' style of clothing mainly listened to rock music or songs of Manos Hadjidakis and distanced themselves from, abstained from going to, the commercial gay discotheques where disco music was played.[87] Only decades later was the gap between gay militants and the commercial gay world bridged, with many gay bars serving as sponsors and participating in 'Athens Pride', which thousands of young gays and lesbians attended. I by no means suggest that there is a straightforward causal link between commercialization and the expansion of gay community but, certainly, the growth of a visible gay community corresponds with the visibility of gays and lesbians in a growing gay commercial world. However, as Pellegrini points out, lesbian, gay, but also heterosexual, identities have always been marked from capitalism: 'So what? This [i.e. the relay capital-identity-community] is not the end of politics homosexual, queer, or otherwise, but among its operating conditions and constraints [....] the commodification [...] may actually constitute the starting point for contemporary lesbian and gay politics.'[88]

Acknowledgements

I would like to thank the editors and especially Nikos Papadogiannis and Eirini Kotsovili for their accurate and useful comments. I am also grateful to Dimitra Lambropoulou, Yannis Ntiniakos, Elia Petridou and Mary Leontsini for our discussions on sexuality, working-class masculinity and material culture issues.

Notes

1. Eurocommunism was a political tendency dominant in several Western European communist parties, especially the Italian one. Eurocommunist parties criticized the Soviet model of communism and were in search of a democratic and national path to socialism. It was given official currency by the Secretary-General of the Spanish Communists, Santiago Carillo, in his 1977 essay 'Eurocommunism and the State'. The 'Communist Party of the Interior' was created in 1968 after the split of the Communist Party of Greece and endorsed Eurocommunism in the 1970s.
2. The stable heterosexual couple was the framework of 'normal' and 'healthy' sexual relationships and was promoted by Communist Youth of Greece affiliated with the Communist Party of Greece. See Nikolaos Papadogiannis, 'Between *Angelopoulos* and the *Battleship Potemkin*: cinema and the making of young communists in Greece in the initial post-dictatorship period (1974–81)', *European History Quarterly* 42.2, 2012, 296.
3. Yannis Voulgaris, *I Ellada tis Metapolitefsis, 1974–1990. Statheri Dimokratia Simademeni apo ti Metapolemiki Istoria* (Athens: Themelio, 2001), 126–8.
4. In the late 1970s and early 1980s.
5. Loukas Theodorakopoulos, *Kaiadas. Chronicle of a Siege* (Athens: Eksantas, 1976), 42, 55.
6. The book was published two years after the fall of the dictatorship and its subtitle 'chronicle of a siege' was a reference to the famous movie of the Leftist director Costas Gavras, *State of a Siege* (1973).
7. About the spatial and material turn, see, for instance: Henri Lefebvre, *La production de l'espace* (Paris: Anthropos, D., 2000); Edward W. Soja, *Postmodern Geographies. The reassertion of space in critical social theory* (London, New York: Verso, 1989); Daniel Miller, *Stuff* (Cambridge: Polity Press, 2010).
8. Daniel Miller, 'Consumption' in Eleanna Yalouri (ed.), *Ylikos Politismos. I anthropologia sti chora ton pragmaton* (Athens: Alexandria, 2012), 319–53.
9. Dinos Christianopoulos, *The Naked Piazza*, translated by Kostis N. (Peania: Bilieto Publications, 2000), 4.

Consumption and Gender through the Moment of Transition

10. I use the term 'queer' in the sense of all erotic and affective ties between men and all men who engaged in such interactions. See Matt Houlbrook, *Queer London. Perils and Pleasures in the Sexual Metropolis, 1918–1957* (Chicago and London: Chicago University Press, 2005).
11. Houlbrook, *Queer London*, 265.
12. For the 'continuum between homosocial and homosexual' and the 'male homosocial desire' see Eve Sedgwick Kosofsky, *Between Men. English Literature and Male Homosocial Desire* (New York: Columbia University Press, 1985).
13. I conducted my first research for my doctoral dissertation between 1990 and 1992 and I have continued the research specifically on male homosexualities of the 1950s to the 1970s from 2013 onwards. See Kostas Yannacopoulos, *Jeux du désir, jeux du pouvoir: corps, émotions et identité sexuelle des hommes au Pirée et à Athènes* (unpublished doctoral dissertation, Paris: Ecole des Hautes Etudes en Sciences Sociales, 1995).
14. Tzvetan Todorov, 'Fictions et vérités', *L'Homme* 1989, 111–12, 7–33.
15. Kostas Yannakopoulos, 'Amis ou amants? Amours entre hommes et identités sexuelles au Pirée et à Athènes', *Terrain* 27, 1996, 59–70.
16. Another term used broadly in the 1950s and 1960s instead of *poustis* was *toioutos* (someone of this kind) a term of the archaic language *katharevousa*.
17. *Andras*, in plural.
18. Kostas Yannakopoulos, 'Corps érotique masculin et identités sexuelles au Pirée et a Athènes', *Gradhiva* 23, 1998, 101–8.
19. M.-E. Handman, *La violence et la ruse. Hommes et femmes dans un village grec* (Aix-en-Provence: Edisud, 1983); Renée Hirschon, *Heirs of the Greek Catastrophe. The Social Life of Asian Minor Refugees in Piraeus* (Oxford: Clarendon Press, 1989).
20. Yannakopoulos, 'Amis ou amants?'
21. Homosex: I use this term in the sense of 'an amalgam ... [that] indicates sexual activities of various sorts between two males'. See: Houlbrook, *Queer London*.
22. *Poustis*, *adelfi* in plural.
23. *Poniros* in singular; *poniroi* in plural, means cunning.
24. Bernard Kayser, Anthropogeografia tis Elladas, translated by T. Tsaveas and M. Meraklis (Athens: EKKE, 1968), 115; Dimitra Lambropoulou, *Construction Workers. The People Who Built Athens 1950–1967* (Athens: Vivliorama, 2009), 20–1.
25. Lambropoulou, *Oikodomoi*, 20–1.
26. David Close, *Ellada 1945–2004* (translated by Y. Mertikas, Thessaloniki: Thyrathen, 2005), 121.
27. Ibid.
28. This 'masculine' gendered/sexual performance was demonstrated mainly in public. According to my interlocutors, in private sexual encounters the gendered/sexual performance of *andres* was more fluid and included even the 'passive' role when having coitus.
29. Handman, *La violence*.
30. Hirschon, *Heirs*.
31. In addition to class difference, age difference was also a constitutive element of these relationships. In some relationships *adelfes* were older than *tekna*. The age difference was the principal constitutive element in the relationships between *kolomparades* and even minors. In these relationships *kolomparades* were masculine, *andres*, and active regarding their role in

sexual intercourse. The figure of *kolomparas* (in singular) and the danger he presented was also widespread in provincial cities and villages. Many parents gave warnings to their young boys on how to avoid the advances of *kolomparades*.

32. See note 39.
33. Lambropoulou, *Oikodomoi*, 228–9.
34. Lambropoulou, personal communication.
35. Christianopoulos, *The Naked Piazza*; Yorgos Ioannou, *The Trapdoor* (Athens: Kedros, 1989).
36. Yorgos Chronas, 'Some words for the naturalness of postures,' in Yorgos Chronas, *Greek Statues. Photos of Men 1950–1960* (Athens: Odos Panos, 1992), 6.
37. Ioannou, *The Trapdoor*, 180.
38. Christianopoulos, *The Naked Piazza*, 73.
39. In the poem cited above, dedicated to a 'working-class friend', Christianopoulos uses the term *floroi* (translated as 'pancies' by N. Kostis) to describe men who use perfumes. *Floros* (in singular) means mainly the bourgeois mannered and well dressed, elegant man and, therefore, the effeminate. In other words, it is the bourgeois – sometimes, excessive – elegance that constitutes *floros* as 'effeminate'. In addition, *floros* might be someone who has sexual relationships only with women without, nevertheless being considered as *andras*.
40. Such paintings depicting soldiers and young working-class men are those of Yannis Tsarouhis (1910–89) who is one the most well-known Greek painters and set designers.
41. The military uniform as a component of this desire is very well depicted in the poem of Christianopoulos 'Laces and Elastic Bands' and 'Hymn to a Boot'. Christianopoulos, *The Naked Piazza*, 58–9 and 20–1.
42. Houlbrook, *Queer London*, 211.
43. Ibid, 146.
44. 'i' represents a version of the gender specific article 'the', (η) in Greek.
45. Yannis says that there were doubts if Tsin-Tsin was a 'real' *adelfi* – i.e. that he had sexual relationships with men. Besides, according to Yannis, Tsin-Tsin was married.
46. Efi Avdela, '"Neoi en kindyno"': *Epitirisi, anamorfosi kai dikaiosyni anilikon meta ton polemo* (Athens: Polis, 2013), 310.
47. Ibid.
48. These films were called *tsontes* (*tsonta* in singular) which refers to a small piece of a larger item. So, *tsonta* was a scene of heterosexual intercourse which included penetration and which interrupted the projection of a soft, often Greek, porn film. This scene was usually from another movie.
49. It is not by change that the photos of Velloudios depicted naked soldiers. Velloudios was a high ranking officer, one of the first pilots of military aircraft, and so he had free access to the barracks. Among soldiers *tsoliades/euzonoi* – i.e. an elite unit of Greek army, guards of the king and later of the president of the republic, were known as sexual partners of *adelfes*.
50. *Hartziliki* is an amount of money given for buying something; it could be translated as pocket money.
51. The bath seems to be very significant given that in 1964 only 35 per cent of urban households in all Greece had running water. See Avdela, 'Neoi', 291.
52. Andreas came for the first time in Athens with a gay 'tour'. Gay Americans often travelled in groups to Athens and the Greek islands because they had read in American homosexual

magazines that they could easily find sexual partners who were masculine, handsome young Greeks, the 'Greek Gods'. On their part, local young men in the islands – as soon as they learned that the homosexual Americans had arrived – would go to the places where Americans would hang out, to meet them.

53. Avdela, 'Neoi'.
54. Vassilis Karapostolis, *Katanalotiki Symperifora sti Neoelliniki Koinonia, 1960–1975* (Athens: EKKE, 1983).
55. Close, *Ellada 1945–2004*.
56. Karapostolis, *Katanalotiki*, 279.
57. Houlbrook, *Queer London*, 177.
59. Evthymios Papataxiarchis, 'Friends of the heart: male commensal solidarity, gender and kinship in Aegean Greece', in Peter Loizos and Evthymios Papataxiarchis (eds), *Contested Identities. Gender and Kinship in Modern Greece* (Princeton, NJ: Princeton University Press, 1991), 156–79.
59. The term 'gay' – and to a lesser degree the term 'straight' – were used broadly from the late 1980s onwards.
60. Michel Foucault, *Histoire de la sexualité 1. La volonté de savoir* (Paris: Gallimard, 1976).
61. Yannacopoulos, *Jeux du désir*.
62. Kostas Yannakopoulos, 'Cultural meanings of loneliness: kinship, sexuality and (homo)sexual identity in contemporary Greece', *Journal of Mediterranean Studies* 18.2, 2010, 265–82.
63. At the same time the eroticization of sentimentality renders the expression of tenderness, sensuality between men, suspect of 'homosexuality'.
64. Close, *Ellada*, 304.
65. This model was promoted by the media magazines addressing a masculine, mainly middle-class readership, which were published from the mid-1980s onwards. See Panagiotis Zestanakis, 'Ekdoches tou andrismou sta ellinika lifestyle entypa tis dekaetias tou '80: Playboy, Status, Klik (1985–1990)' (unpublished postgraduate diploma, Rethymno, University of Crete, 2008).
66. Vassilis Vamvakas and Yiannis Karayannis, 'Gymnastiki. I narkisistiki epimeleia tou somatos', in Vassilis Vamvakas and Panayis Panayiotopoulos (eds), *I Ellada sti dekaetia tou '80. Koinoniko, politkco kai politismiko lexiko* (Athens: To perasma, 2010), 93–5.
67. Vassilis Vamvakas and Tatiana Michailidou, 'Endymatologikoi kodikes. Ekdimokratismos tou styl kai apotheosi tis markas', in Vassilis Vamvakas and Panayis Panayiotopoulos, *I Ellada*, 187–90.
68. Zestanakis, 'Ekdoches', 125–7.
69. Ioannou, *The Trapdoor*, 180.
70. Christianopoulos, *The Naked Piazza*, 44–5.
71. K. Weston, *Gender in Real Time. Power and Transience in a Visual Age* (New York, London: Routledge, 2002), 86–7; Walter Benjamin, 'L'Oeuvre d'art à l'époque de sa reproductibilité technique' (dernière version de 1939), in Walter Benjamin, *Oeuvres III* (Paris: Gallimard (folio), 2000).
72. From the mid-1980s onwards gyms become very popular among young homosexual men.
73. 'Hymn to a Boot' in Christianopoulos 2000. In this poem Christianopoulos considers that only tough, 'natural' young *andres* should wear boots.

74. *Tsolia* in the homosexual slang are the *tekna* who are violent towards the *adelfes,* stealing from them, beating or even killing them.
75. Panayis Panayiotopoulos, 'Gia tin ereyna tis oikiakis katanalosis kai tin optikoakoustiki koultoura stin Ellada tou '80. Prologikes skepseis se mia simantiki meleti', in Orsalia-Eleni Kassaveti, *I elliniki videotainia (1985–1990)* (Athens: Asini, 2014), 8–10.
76. The term *tsonta* lost its initial meaning. It is now used to describe a hardcore porn movie.
77. Jane Cowan, 'Going out for coffee? Contesting the grounds of gendered pleasures in everyday sociability' in Loizos, Papataxiarchis (eds.), *Contested Identities,* 190.
78. Ibid, 202.
79. By the term 'heterosocial' I mean the sociability, sexual and non-sexual, between male and female individuals.
80. Except for the bars where the majority of their clientele are gays and lesbians, there are also heterosocial, apparently 'hetetosexual', leisure spaces known as 'gay-friendly'. In these spaces men and women self-identified as gays/lesbians or with more fluid sexual identity can create enclaves of homosexual encounters and sociability. Such a place is described in Kirtsoglou's study regarding female homosexual relationships in a Greek provincial town in the late 90s. In the provincial towns, except for some specific open-air places, these bars and cafes are the only leisure places where queers can meet each other without being stigmatized as 'homosexuals'. See Elisabeth Kirtsoglou, *For the Love of Women. Gender, Identity and Same-Sex Relations in a Greek Provincial Town* (London, New York: Routledge, 2004). The emergence of these gay leisure places does not contradict the shift in sentiment, tenderness, from homosociality in a couple, a privatization of tenderness, mentioned above. In agreement with Houlbrook, I regard these places as semi-private, in the sense of becoming physically separated from the sites of 'normal' urban life and being marginalized in comparison with the 'straight' places. See Houlbrook, *Queer London,* 270.
81. At the time and especially in the 1970s the Cycladic island of Mykonos was already known as a tourist destination for gay men. See P. Bousiou, *The Nomads of Mykonos* (New York, Oxford: Berghahn Books, 2008).
82. This spatial transformation was accompanied by a change in the erotic life of Alekos. From 1973 he stopped having heterosexual relationships and started having a stable, long-term relationship with a French man.
83. 'Clone' is a term in gay slang that was widespread in the USA during the 1970s, and described the homosexual man who appeared in dress and style as an idealized version of the working-class man.
84. Yannacopoulos, *Jeux du désir.*
85. In the period from 1978 to 1984 in which *AKOE* and *AMFI* flourished see Kostas Yannakopoulos, 'Omofylofiliko kinima', in Vamvakas and Panayiotopoulos, *I Ellada.*
86. Manos Hadjidakis (1925–94) was a famous Greek composer who mixed classical with folk music and belonged to the generation of *poniroi* intellectuals.
87. Nikolaos Papadogiannis, 'Greek communist youth identities and rock music in the late 1970s,' in Timothy Brown and Lorena Anton (eds), *Between the Avant Garde and the Everyday: Subversive Politics in Europe from 1957 to the Present* (New York/Oxford: Berghahn Books), 77–91.
88. Ann Pellegrini, 'Commodity capitalism and transformations in gay identity', in Arnaldo Cruz-Malavé and Martin F. Manalansan IV (eds), *Queer Globalizations. Citizenship and the Afterlife of Colonialism* (New York: New York University Press, 2002), 141.

PART III
CONSUMPTION AND GENDER BETWEEN THE TRANSITION TO DEMOCRACY AND THE FINANCIAL CRISIS OF THE 2010s

CHAPTER 10
TELEVISION CULTURE AND SOCIAL CHANGE IN POST-REVOLUTIONARY PORTUGAL
Luís Trindade

Introduction

Television is often used as a marker in the political history of the transition from dictatorship to democracy in Portugal. The creation, in 1957, of *Radiotelevisão Portuguesa* (RTP), the State-owned broadcaster, was part of what many historians see as the beginning of a permanent state of crisis (including the colonial wars, political radicalization and urbanization of society) that would afflict the *Estado Novo* (New State) – the authoritarian regime institutionalized in 1933 in the context of the wave of fascisms in the period between the two world wars in Europe – until its end in 1974.

More specifically, the attitude of politicians towards the new medium seems to indicate a shift inside the regime itself, from conservative isolationism to a late, and failed, attempt to open up and liberalize: whereas António de Oliveira Salazar, the long-standing leader of the *Estado Novo*, looked at television with suspicion and tried to avoid it, his successor between 1968 and 1974, Marcello Caetano, used it to get closer to the public with his own TV show, *Conversas em Família* (*Family Chat*).[1] Later, television played a key role in the 1974–5 revolutionary process by giving a previously unavailable visibility and rhythm to events. Finally, both the form and the content of broadcast are often seen as an important aspect of the democratization and opening of Portuguese society towards the end of the 1970s.[2]

This chapter will focus on this late, post-revolutionary, period (between 1976 and 1983). It will be argued that we can identify the emergence of an autonomous television culture, with its own historical temporality. The first consequence of this is methodological: when the medium reached a certain degree of specialization, its social and historical function also gained a logic of its own. In other words, rather than looking at television in post-revolutionary Portugal as an illustration of the political process or merely a symptom of social change, my analysis will assume a different historical context; that of postmodernism as a moment during which cultural media become central agents in economic production and social reproduction.[3] In this context, television has to be treated as a decisive historical actor in its own right, not only because it simultaneously intervenes in and documents social change – in the reconfiguration of subjectivities and practices – but also, and mainly, because it is a prism that mediates the perception of all other phenomena. In particular, I will show how the Portuguese television culture signals the consolidation and reconfiguration of middle-class values and aspirations in the new democratic context, which will pave the way to the development of late capitalism and consumer culture in Portugal.

And yet, the formation of these cultural forms and social aspirations around television and the cultural *distinction* of an emergent middle class[4] can neither be separated from the cultural isolation and conservatism of the dictatorial period, nor from the forms of political radicalization that marked the revolutionary period of 1974–5. This is because they were born, to a large extent, in opposition to both authoritarianism and revolution. In this sense, post-authoritarian and post-revolutionary culture oscillates between a sense of economic progress and social change typical of all processes of modernization, on the one hand, and new aspirations related to individual fulfillment and non-ideological subjectivities, on the other. In other words, contrary to other (and in many ways close) processes of democratic transition, in the Portuguese case it does not seem possible to separate a sense of social modernization (and indeed a narrative of historical progress towards both democratization and economic wealth) from a new culture of leisure and hedonism.[5]

This raises a particular form of ambivalence within our object in which the perception of social transformation towards a wealthier society, as seen from the perspective of TV programming (and the debates around its content by critics and a new type of magazine dedicated to television), entailed both a sense of emancipation and a sense of depoliticization. This was particularly visible in the relations between gender – especially femininity – and consumerism, or, more specifically, in the ways the new audiovisual culture was organized around television, pointing to new opportunities for women while simultaneously submitting the female body to the male gaze. The chapter will thus start by presenting the role of television in the Portuguese transition to democracy so as to then contextualize the formation and social meaning of this new television culture. Finally, the last section will read the society 'imagined', or presupposed, by TV content, in order to grasp the abovementioned ambivalence between social and gender emancipation and the new economic order.

Post-revolutionary television in Portugal

With the end of the revolutionary period, from 1976 onwards the country's politics focused on the establishment of a parliamentary system in which the main parties agreed on a minimal programme of social democracy, economic modernization and rapprochement with the European Economic Community (which would eventually lead to full membership in 1986). However, the drive towards Western standards of political democracy and social welfare had to reckon, at least until the early 1980s, with a strong revolutionary culture that did not just disappear with the end of the revolution as such. In fact, the whole of the 1970s were still under the strong influence of a concept of culture – developed in the resistance to the dictatorship – that saw it as a tool of historical transformation and political emancipation.

Some of the figures and contents of immediate post-revolutionary Portuguese television, as well as the most influential television critics, bear witness to this. The first programme director after 1975, Mário Dionísio, was a prestigious poet and literary critic of neo-realism; the dominant cultural movement in Portuguese anti-fascism. His successors in the post, at least until 1978, and some of those chosen to give cultural cachet to what was shown on TV were all renowned intellectuals with impeccable credentials not only as members of the resistance, but also as representatives of some of the most modern, or 'progressive', trends in the arts and humanities (such as the Portuguese *Cinema Novo* of the 1960s, experimental theatre and structuralism).

Classic and modern cinema, high quality TV series (the BBC is presented as the model to follow) and programmes with strong didactic content were seen by these programme directors as key instruments (which were as important as free information) in the democratization of a society that had lived under censorship and political isolation for almost five decades and that still presented high levels of illiteracy.[6] But democratization also meant that previously censored forms of entertainment could finally see the light and become more accessible to wider audiences. The explosion of pornographic films in Portuguese movie theatres was one of the most visible manifestations of a broader aspiration to see everything that authoritarianism had hidden.[7]

In short, RTP was well aware that the audiences expected a democratic medium to broadcast three types of previously forbidden, or at least limited, content: transgressive humour (in the tradition of theatrical comedy, a genre with strong roots in the country); foreign series dealing with everyday life in modern societies; and a more liberal approach to sex, which entailed more autonomy, and visibility, for women in society and the public sphere, especially when compared with the strict patriarchal code inherited from the dictatorship. And yet, RTP's most successful shows in the second half of the 1970s suggest that, along with freedom and democracy, Portuguese audiences also aspired to modernized television. When programme director Maria Elisa Domingues presented her plans for RTP according to European standards, she was explicitly equating her idea of television with what were perceived as the emergent values and aspirations in Portuguese society at large at a time when 'Europe' stood for everything that was modern, wealthy and sophisticated: 'I am not trying to come up with something fundamentally different from what already is done in other Western European countries, which are those with whom we should become more similar in terms of our European option'.[8]

In particular, TV was expected to work as an autonomous medium, with its own codes, and to broadcast a sense of modernity through language, image and rhythm.[9] This was apparent, for example, in the choice of TV presenters Raul Solnado (who was also one of the leading figures in theatrical comedy) and Fialho Gouveia to host *A Visita da Cornélia* in 1977, the first big hit after the revolution. Both Solnado and Gouveia had already been the authors of *Zip-Zip*, another enormous success just before 1974, and by 1977 still remembered by the public for its political boldness and the way it broke new ground – because of its relaxed atmosphere and its subversion of rigid TV codes – in the way Portuguese television came into people's homes.

In other words, along with the end of censorship over speech and images, the new free television also had to loosen up its style in line with the aspirations of a society released from the constraints of authoritarianism. *A Visita da Cornélia*, a talent show whose participants were distinguished by their pronounced middle-class profile[10] reinforced this tendency and confirmed the audiences' preference for an audiovisual language that did not pose a strong mediation between what was happening in the studio and the comfort of the domestic household. The social sophistication of the participants, as well as the cultural content of most challenges on the show, on the other hand, created a very interesting balance between entertainment and the pedagogic role still expected from RTP.

This same combination of cultural legitimacy and home entertainment was also provided by the other hugely popular show that, with *A Visita da Cornélia*, made 1977 a turning point in the history of post-revolutionary Portuguese television: *Gabriela, Cravo e Canela*, a Brazilian *telenovela* that RTP bought from TV Globo, by then an already well-established producer of very popular television formats in Latin America and beyond. The impact of the Brazilian format in Portuguese society is interesting, as it reverses the traditional relation between a former colonizer with its former colony and helps nuancing the position of both countries within the world-system, in which Brazil would be closer to the centre while Portugal would somehow fall in the European periphery.[11] But *Gabriela* quickly became part of the everyday life and imaginary of Portuguese society for a number of very specific reasons: the sensuality of the protagonists, the exoticism and historical appeal of the script (based on a novel by an important author of the Brazilian literary canon, Jorge Amado) and the daily broadcast of episodes, which led to a reorganization of everyday life of many Portuguese families.[12]

The ambivalent place of TV shows like *A Visita da Cornélia* and *Gabriela*, lying somewhere between cultural legitimacy and entertainment, immediately raised a number of questions. The impact of these programmes on the everyday was closely linked with the changing political mood of Portuguese society in the second half of the 1970s, in moving the realm of conflict from political struggle to entertainment – in the case of *A Visita da Cornélia* – or by keeping people at home in the evening rather than, say, encouraging them to go to political meetings or other forms of public participation. More specifically, in the still strongly politicized post-revolutionary period, the tension between culture and entertainment seemed to replace the more overtly political conflicts between left and right or revolution and reform in the debates around the best model of television for Portuguese democratic society. This made every option by RTP in relation to its structure and content sound like an affair of State, or at least one in which the limits of revolutionary transformation were being negotiated.

Nowhere was this more visible than in the appointment of programme directors and the announcement of the new season's schedules. As we have already seen, during the revolutionary period and immediately after 1975 (when the RTP was under military tutelage or seen as an instrument of revolutionary transformation), the meaning of these appointments and the rationale of broadcasting could be given a direct political translation. But from 1977–8 on, the period where I locate a shift towards the emergence of an autonomous television culture, the politics of RTP will become more difficult to grasp.

Accordingly, when television became an autonomous field with its own rules – rather than an instrument at the service of external political forces – its 'politics' shifted to more specific issues, like the internal management of content, and in particular the decisions concerning the above mentioned balance between culture and entertainment. What makes this more difficult to analyse can be seen at two levels. First, the divide ceases to be overtly political to become one between politics proper and depoliticization. TV critics, for instance, mostly still aligned with the left, kept a close eye on a process where they equated the mounting weight of entertainment in TV listings with the political defeat of revolutionary ideals.[13] As a result, though, what was earlier seen as the consequence of political choices became a question of programming based on what seemed to be purely technical, rather than ideological, issues related to the specialized know-how required by television management in an increasingly professionalized field. The gradual specialization of Portuguese television and the depoliticization it entailed can be said to go along with a similar process in Portuguese society at large (revolutionary politics giving way to technocracy) and can be seen in the proliferation of a specialized press – with magazines like *Se7e* and *TV Guia* – that helped in creating a new television culture.

Television culture

We can start to untie this knot between entertainment and depoliticization by looking at the discourses and managerial choices of the two programme directors appointed from 1978 to the early 1980s, when a more autonomous model of television consolidated in Portugal: Carlos Cruz and Maria Elisa Domingues, two young but already experienced TV professionals and, in that sense, people with a profile that was clearly distinct from that of their predecessors. Cruz took office in the beginning of 1978, almost a decade after *Zip-Zip*, the groundbreaking talk-show he had also helped to create with Raul Solnado and Fialho Gouveia (the presenters of *A Visita da Cornélia*). He was thus familiar with some of the most successful moments in the history of RTP.

In 1978, the responsibility inherent to the job had been increased by the company's decision to bring the programming of Channels 1 and 2 together under the same direction, which would centralize the strategy behind the line up of both channels.[14] The choice of someone familiar with the ins and outs of television seemed, in these circumstances, decisive. However, the previous director of Channel 2, Fernando Lopes, an important name in the new Portuguese cinema of the 1960s and in the militant cinema of the 1970s, was highly critical of the decision. According to him, to merge the strategy of both channels would undermine the autonomy of the second channel and his own efforts to fill it with cultural content and thus to guarantee some form of alternative broadcasting to mainstream entertainment.[15] What seemed like a simple managerial choice had, from this perspective, concrete political consequences in the narrowing of cultural diversity.

Moreover, Lopes denounced the choice of a TV professional like Carlos Cruz as a political strategy to depoliticize RTP and open it up to commercial and private interests. These accusations seemed to bring the company in line with what, according to Lopes and the left, was happening in other sectors of Portuguese society and economy, with the dismantling by the Socialist Party government of many of the State and collectivized structures created during the revolution. The process would accelerate towards the end of the decade, with the victory of a centre-right coalition in the 1979 elections. As before, the impact of the political situation was immediately felt in RTP, where a new programme director, journalist Maria Elisa Domingues, was appointed to replace Carlos Cruz. Domingues was immediately accused by TV critics of being close to the new conservative government,[16] and of promoting the return of TV presenters and journalists who had been recently dismissed for their close collaboration with the dictatorship.

Be that as it may, what was most striking in the discourses of Cruz and Domingues in their new functions was less their overt political views (which both explicitly avoided making public) than a new way of talking about television, its social mission and the technical challenges of the medium. Contrary to the politically committed intellectuals and artists who had preceded them, both spoke like managers, and their discourse about RTP impressed by its technical know-how. In the interviews they gave to several newspapers and magazines (particularly to *Se7e* and *TV Guia*) at the time of their respective appointment, this display of specialization was apparent at two levels.

To start with, both felt that Portugal had failed to keep up with the dramatic changes experienced by television in the previous two decades. This was due to the political conservatism of the dictatorship, but also to the revolution, as the subordination of the content of TV to an exclusively political and pedagogic rationale, they argued, had failed to see how the medium had become both a complex technical issue and an international industry, and how every national broadcasting company, in order to survive, had to produce and negotiate with competition in mind. Accordingly, and again in line with the country's own political evolution, the future of RTP lay in abandoning its nationalist and/or revolutionary past and definitively embracing international, in particular European, standards of management and programming.

RTP's cultural mission was not completely abandoned, though, as both programme directors accepted the role of television in social modernization and democratization. And yet, their concerns evolved very significantly: whereas for Cruz it was still important not to fill the listings with foreign shows, given Portugal's large illiterate population,[17] Elisa Domingues was particularly worried about the impact of Brazilian *telenovelas*, whose plots she considered shallow, and the need to broadcast shows addressing more contemporary issues.[18] In any case, both agreed on the need to prioritize the audiences in any consideration of TV content, not only to match what public expectations were perceived to be (the RTP starts publicizing polls that seemed to back up their choices and *TV Guia* has a weekly top of the most popular programmes), but also because it became clear, especially after *Gabriela*, that Portuguese families were increasingly organizing their everyday life around the broadcast schedule.

This brings us to the second level of technical know-how the two directors brought to the fore: the line up of TV listings was now thought of as a whole, or better still, as a structure that not only adapted to people's everyday life but was in fact conceived as an instrument to divide the contents into specific parts of the day and according to different target audiences. The considerations involved in this new art of programming affected decisions on whether to broadcast Portuguese or foreign programmes in specific time slots (and the need to increase national production of audiovisual content), and on the cultural demands of certain shows vis à vis different social and age groups, as well as the need to entertain and the requirements of national cohesion. Evenings were not to be treated like afternoons and weekends demanded shows with a different profile than weekdays: in short, every social stratum and cultural standard, every region, day and hour was given a profile that should be reflected in the choice of content.

According to Cruz and Elisa Domingues in interviews provided in 1980, a brief survey of what an ideal line up should contain may then give us an interesting perspective on the changing structure and habits of post-revolutionary Portuguese society, or at least on the ways television perceived social transformation.[19] Culture was still seen as a major guarantee of the quality of broadcasting (though any references to the social mission of RTP tended to wane with time), but the intellectuals in consideration for presenters of programmes on art and literature needed to combine cultural legitimacy with good communication skills (in the case of Maria Elisa Domingues, this also included a visible shift towards political conservatism).[20] Foreign TV series, on the other hand, seemed to allow the perfect combination of cultural value and entertainment. As we have seen, BBC series were always invoked as the model to follow, but *Buddenbrooks*, a West German production of Thomas Mann's classic novel probably constituted the period's major success in this category.

Another important concern was with the total percentage of national production in the content of broadcasting. In 1981, for example, Maria Elisa could proudly announce that 80 per cent of the content on Channel 1 and 60 per cent on Channel 2 in the following season would be Portuguese.[21] Fiction and music were here the major challenges, for whereas the in-house production of contests or information shows was relatively inexpensive, the fees charged by local musicians and the costs involved in the production of fictional series were often prohibitive for RTP's budget. This helps to explain the success of the Brazilian *telenovela* in the schedule of Portuguese television in the first decades after the revolution, to such an extent that Portuguese TV gave priority to and became dependent on it. The *telenovela* was an imported format (it did not involve the costs of production) but its original language was already Portuguese.

And yet, the permanent presence of Brazilian *telenovelas* in RTP's listings from 1977 on raised a number of problems of their own: despite the literary quality of *Gabriela*, subsequent series had proved much less interesting and soon critics and other figures in the cultural field started to express concerns about what they saw as the colonization of the public by the Brazilian Portuguese and above all by the cultural impoverishment of poor plots in low quality productions.[22] To abandon Brazilian *telenovelas* was already unthinkable by the early 1980s, so the solution would have to be for RTP to raise standards in its negotiations with TV Globo. A good compromise seemed to have been achieved with *Malu Mulher*; a Brazilian series on the everyday life of a woman who, after her divorce, had to juggle raising her daughter with her return to college so as to finish off her interrupted sociology degree.

The example of *Malu Mulher* is important as it illustrates a subtle shift, increasingly noticeable in the early 1980s, from the traditional cultural mission of television as the educator of an illiterate society to a new focus on contemporaneity, or, more specifically, on the need to tackle the emergence of new social problems and forms of subjectivity, namely through women's emancipation and the challenge to patriarchy. This explains the emphasis given to a new concept of information that could not only cover more social ground and bring into the news more aspects of people's lives, but also one that, in line with the specific aesthetics of this television culture, could use the instruments of entertainment to address important and pressing questions. Carlos Cruz's call for imagination as the main trait of TV communication, 'even when one tells a story or writes a piece of news',[23] could be seen as a new golden rule to consider when making decisions on any type of content.

This brings us to the last item in this short survey of the ideal TV schedule that was imagined by the new line of programme management in the late 1970s and early 1980s: entertainment. Music and comedy would prove the key elements at this level. On the one hand, one of the most visible signs of social transformation in the period was the emergence of a new pop culture and in particular the popularization of rock music in Portuguese. Comedy, on the other hand, not only benefited from a long and popular presence in the broadcast schedules of RTP, but also constituted the ideal form to critically reflect upon that same transformation in Portuguese society.

In the summer of 1981,[24] Maria Elisa announced a new concept for Sunday afternoons: a four hour-long show with games, music and humour. The show's title was *O Passeio dos Alegres* and its host was Júlio Isidro, a young but by then already popular TV and radio presenter.[25] Júlio Isidro and *O Passeio dos Alegres* would prove instrumental in the explosion of Portuguese rock, by giving visibility to new and still largely unknown bands. But it was as midwife to the birth of a new comedian that the show would gain its place in the history of Portuguese television. The comedian, still a very familiar figure in Portugal today, was Herman José, and his impact represented a true revolution, not only in the relation between the public and television, but indeed in the definition of RTP's vision of its audiences and, in that sense, early 1980s Portuguese society.

Television's imagined society

Herman José's performances in *O Passeio dos Alegres* were not, at first sight, very different from the familiar forms of humour used in the theatrical tradition (which, as we have seen, were among the most popular shows of RTP). As in the latter, the comedian created a number of characters that would then punctuate the programme with a series of gags. Here, one could see the woman with a strong working-class accent but the attitude of the *arriviste*, the boy whose impeccable sailor suit contrasted with his naughty behaviour, or the tacky crooner with a Spanish accent (to whom I will return at the end of this chapter). All these types resonated, in different ways, with contemporary social issues, in particular forms of social mobility and cultural capital.

What made this humour special, then, was not in its originality, nor even the unanimously recognized talent of the actor (whose experience had been gained in the theatre). The reason why Herman José's performance in *O Passeio dos Alegres* was such a turning point lay entirely within the logic of TV aesthetics. More specifically, what made those familiar characters so shocking and innovative was their awareness, and comical subversion, of TV codes. Herman José proved, in this sense, to be perfectly up to date with the emergence of the autonomous television culture we discussed in the previous section, in which televised forms of communication became clearly distinguishable from, for instance, those of the theatre. Dialoguing with the camera, or deliberately running away from it; repeating the questions back to the host and forcing him to follow an improvised dialogue; or simply interacting informally with the audience at the studio, Herman José took the language of television in Portugal to another level, in which the medium became its own content.

A couple of years later, in clear recognition of his success, José was given the opportunity to host his own comedy show. As before, the show followed the traditional structure of the theatrical comedy, a bird's-eye view of society through some of its most recognizable contemporary figures and situations. What was new, or in line with the comedian's own ongoing revolution of TV codes, was that the microcosm chosen as a backdrop for those figures and situations was a television channel. *O Tal Canal*[26] was structured as the line up of any normal day at RTP, with its children's, youth and sports programmes, with its news, musical show and even its own *telenovela*. One should insist on the meaning of this metanarrative, for *O Tal Canal*'s huge popularity[27] suggests that to laugh at television was no longer like laughing at any other social phenomenon. When viewers were watching the show they were indeed laughing at themselves through a medium that, as we have seen, to a large extent already filled their imaginary and organized their everyday lives.

The technique used by Herman José to achieve all this was, as in *O Passeio dos Alegres*, to deconstruct and subvert the codes and rules of TV language. Some of the characters became hugely popular, like José Estebes, the drunken sports presenter who spoke directly to the director (and called him by his real name). The news, on the other hand, entered into dialogue with RTP's own *Telejornal*, not only because Herman José created a character inspired by the period's most familiar news anchor but also because it reproduced the style of communication in TV journalism; a new language in its own right, thus creating amusing episodes where the event being reported completely disappeared from sight and all the viewer was left with was a group of journalists nonsensically talking to each other.

Such comedy technique, as I have suggested, presupposed a close intimacy with the medium. Viewers were supposed to recognize the structure of the programmes and the rules of its language – otherwise they would not understand its comical subversion – but also the figures of artists, journalists, presenters and announcers who entered their homes. But this was not only, and not even primarily, a relation the viewer established with her or his TV set. Obvious as it may seem, it is important to insist that such proximity was already at work in the form of the broadcast, in the way the informality of TV language matched the relaxed mood of the domestic household. And what makes this structure of communication so decisive is that through it we can grasp the ways in which RTP imagined contemporary Portuguese society and interpret its content as responses to the perception it had of how dominant social aspirations looked like.

In this sense, it is interesting to note how this relation between television and its viewers brought centre stage a figure that looked secondary at first sight, but that ultimately proved instrumental in assessing how television imagined the way in which viewers wanted to be reached: the continuity announcer, one of a group of young, good-looking and friendly faces, mostly women, who guided audiences through the day's schedule and its different programmes. Between the viewer and the broadcast content, they encapsulated the true spirit of this television culture. They were, according to television's own internal processes of self-promotion, the 'faces' of RTP. As such, the continuity announcer could not fail to play an important role in the line up of Herman José's programme. Played by Helena Isabel, a young actress and singer, who hopelessly tried to cope with the permanent technical problems affecting the channel's broadcast, *O Tal Canal*'s continuity announcer was deliberately conceived to match, in her image, outfit and gesture, the stereotype of the 'dumb blonde'.

And yet, in that historical context, nothing could be further from reality. In fact, since 1978 the continuity announcer had been an important element of the strategy developed by RTP to modernize its profile and outlook, along with all the other figures who, as we have seen, developed its autonomous culture. Given the importance of their image for the job, it could even be said that they were given much more visibility than programme directors and other high profile TV presenters.[28] But if we take a closer look at the real continuity announcers who were then being recruited by the company, we can see that not only were they the exact opposite of the hapless character of *O Tal Canal*, but they also contradicted the image of submission and passivity traditionally ascribed to women in Portuguese society – the role of women in social reproduction (through motherhood and religious transmission) was instrumental in the preservation of the family as the base of Salazarist society. Indeed, in the interviews they give to *TV Guia* (in 1979, for example, this happens almost on a weekly basis), it becomes clear that their profile was much closer to the cultural standards, or distinction,[29] of the emergent middle-class values we have already seen in other protagonists involved in the modernization of Portuguese television (particularly in the way they embraced an idealized image of Europe as modernity and sophistication).

Hence, I believe the public figure of the continuity announcer – the way in which it was promoted as the 'image' of RTP – may allow us to take a step further in our analysis and finally grasp in its profile how RTP idealized the contemporary Portuguese. More specifically, rather than being simply a particular representation of contemporary society, the figures, fictions and practices this television culture promoted presupposed an ideal image of what the aspirations and new values of that society were. This is the idea I will now explore until the end of this chapter. The contents and figures that were dominant in television throughout the period were more than a representation of society, accurate as it may have been: what they did was to represent the horizon of expectations[30] of a country eagerly trying to leave a traumatic past behind.

It is hence very interesting to notice how close these young women were to the managerial sophistication and spirit of expertise shown by programme administrators like Carlos Cruz and Maria Elisa. Their personal and professional background was remarkably homogenous and, as such, easily identifiable with emergent social values. They all came from middle-class or lower-middle-class families (most of their parents worked in the tertiary sector); the majority had been to college, mostly in traditionally feminine degrees such as languages and literature (but in the emergent English and German, rather than French and classical languages); and they all had short professional experiences in teaching, administration or tourism. But besides the clear urban, late capitalist[31] character of these backgrounds, what is most impressive here is the relationship they established between their ambitions and gender. They all seemed to be perfectly aware that in a profoundly patriarchal society like that of Portugal, women had to overcome imposed limits and seize the new opportunities promised by the 1980s.[32] In a process that is not uncommon in a broader European context,[33] women's emancipation, after the profoundly politicized feminism of the revolutionary period, now seemed a simple question of professional achievement.

Taking the group as a whole, we get a coherent picture of people who believed in the values of dynamism and ambition, who were open to new personal and professional experiences, and who consequently paid close attention to every social transformation occurring around them, in a context where society and economy were experiencing intense modernization and becoming closer to European standards and lifestyles. That is why, one could argue, they all ended up working in RTP in the first place, as television had clearly become the cultural expression of this evolution towards social mobility and more liberal mores. More than their professional skills as such (familiarity with modern languages, managerial experience and personal ambition), their combination of good looks (at least according to the dominant beauty standards at that point) and sophistication symbolized what it meant to be modern in the given context. This synthesizes the ambivalence that is at play in this process of modernization: while a more liberal profile provided women with new opportunities, the focus on their image simultaneously set a limit by reinforcing their (largely aspired) exposition to the male gaze.[34]

The signs of the ways in which these values were crystallizing into new lifestyles were pervasive in all sorts of cultural forms, but I propose we look for them, before concluding, in two rather contrasting sources where, I believe, we can find a clearer picture of how they were differently perceived by distinct sectors of society. This will also allow us to go back to our initial distinction between cultural value and entertainment and reframe that key post-revolutionary question at the beginning of the 1980s.

Only three years after *Gabriela*, a very different Brazilian *telenovela*, *Dancin' Days*, became a similar, if not greater success. The setting of *Dancin' Days* was the easygoing everyday life of Rio de Janeiro's middle class. The show was initially promoted for dealing with the same forms of moral relaxation and sexual suggestiveness, which, only a few years earlier, had had a major impact on the RTP audience. Soon, however, it became clear that viewers were more interested in the signs of urban sophistication they could see in the everyday life of people going to the gym, attending psychoanalysis and dancing in nightclubs. These were, in short, the 'dancing days' that the *telenovela*'s title refers to, and which increasingly larger segments of Portuguese society (a stratum significantly enlarged by the fact that the show was in Portuguese without subtitles) equated with their own aspirations. In it, personal happiness and achievement depended on hedonistic values, physical wellbeing and less rigid family structures. The banalization of divorce played a very important role in these fictions. If we take the already mentioned *Malu Mulher*, for instance, we can see how empowering divorce could be to the traditional balance of power of married couples. The way divorce initiated a reflection and critique on traditional identities of masculinity, on the other hand, is less obvious, as the latter was not put into question so radically as femininity. However, the success of *Kramer vs. Kramer* – an American film where Dustin Hoffman plays a single father – suggests some sectors of Portuguese audiences were increasingly open to imagine alternative family structures including different male roles as well.

But where some saw an example of cultural hybridity[35] and thus a promise of the democratic opening of sophisticated lifestyles to virtually every social segment, others seemed to identify the emergence of a new social norm and the impoverishment of cultural standards. In a very interesting article written by playwright and intellectual Luís de Sttau Monteiro for the cultural magazine *Se7e* (in itself, a privileged source for these social transformations), it becomes very clear how, to some observers, the imagined society represented by television (in figures like continuity announcers) and in television (in *telenovelas* like *Dancin' Days*) signalled the emergence of a new culture where social legitimacy was entirely defined by what people owned and looked like, that is, a lifestyle entirely colonized by commodification:

> I don't need to know them better to understand how they live and what they want from life. Good carpets; 'posters' on the walls; pillows lying on the ground, like on *Playboy* covers [...]; stereos that would make any music lover happy, full of the sounds of dance; bad whisky everywhere; [...] a 'très moderne, very sophisticated'[36] style, with that sophistication they learned in 'art house' films; [...] and, to sum it all up, small talk that by itself could define that sad imitation of a bourgeoisie those people had never met: 'where did you buy that skirt', 'where did you buy those appetizers', 'where are we going this week' [...][37]

The affinity between the fictional plot of *Dancin' Days* and the social setting described by Sttau Monteiro is more than one of reality and its representation, or even one of a form of (fictional) encoding which TV viewers would then subsequently decode.[38] The coincidence between the social context of a certain middle-class formation and a contemporary fictional representation of middle-class values and aspirations (even if originating in a foreign society) is simultaneously more simple and complex: it is 'merely' the recognition that both fictional representations and social aspirations cannot but be part of the same historical context, a proximity that makes them share the same language and imaginary – or *political unconscious*³⁹ – and thus establishes a closer relation between the two, which, as such, become much harder to disentangle.

In this sense, the deeper meaning of this extract lies beyond the immediate conservatism of the critique (in itself, quite redolent of the impact this new TV culture had on social classes whose cultural legitimacy was based on the written word). The key thing in the resolute ambition of continuity announcers, in the sophistication of the everyday life of *Dancin' Day*s and in the gadgets of a new urban lifestyle described by Sttau Monteiro, was a set of social aspirations (that could be positively or negatively defined) already very clearly shaped around specific images and objects. More specifically, what pervades all these figures and narratives, throughout fiction and television culture, is a single code of middle-class taste and values, not necessarily available to everyone, but in the process of becoming the norm shaping the majority's social aspirations.

Epilogue

To conclude, Herman José's success may help us understand this process more clearly, and in particular the ways these forms of social aspiration, and social distinction, became crystallized around the notion of taste.⁴⁰ While promoting *O Tal Canal*, José had to come to terms with some of the things he had done in the beginning of his career, a period when he had condescended with what, according to his own words, was 'artistic bad taste'. He was referring in particular to some comedies and musical records that had made him popular among the lower classes but also earned him the contempt of the more 'intellectualized segment' of the audience. Now, in the early 1980s, 'these are the people I want to keep close to, [...] because quality is what I am most nostalgic for'.⁴¹ Apparently, then, all he wanted was to be a good professional, in line with the specialized skills and increasing know-how of all the other agents involved in television culture. And yet, this new competence had a strong social dimension, for to produce quality was to conform to the new criteria of middle-class taste. 'Taste', in these circumstances, encapsulated a very complex web of references where the central role of cultural capital specific to postmodernism corresponded to a new status of social sophistication, in which the realignment of gender relations was being dramatically negotiated.

Herman José's most popular character in both *O Passeio dos Alegres* and *O Tal Canal*, Tony Silva – the tacky crooner with the Spanish accent I mentioned before – may, in this sense, be seen as a symbol. The remarkable skills used by Herman José to compose the figure, with his exuberant clothes and the *arriviste*'s affected manners, may have been acquired during his experience in theatrical comedy and as a popular singer. However, the risks taken in choosing such a character to be the star of his programme (*Tony Silva's All Star Show* was the highlight of *O Tal Canal*), indeed to be the actor's alter ego, already presupposed an audience with enough *taste* to understand how ridiculous Tony Silva was. An audience already sufficiently immersed in a world of cultural sophistication to recognize in the character the exact opposite of how it wanted to be seen.

Notes

1. Francisco Rui Cádima, *Salazar, Caetano e a Televisão Portuguesa* (Lisboa: Presença, 1996).
2. Cf. Mário Mesquita, 'Os Meios de Comunicação Social', in António Reis (ed.), *Portugal. 20 Anos de Democracia* (Lisboa: Temas e Debates, 1996).
3. Fredric Jameson, *Postmodernism, or, The cultural logic of late capitalism* (Durham, NC: Duke University Press, 1991).
4. Pierre Bourdieu, *Distinction: A Social Critique of the Judgement of Taste* (Cambridge, MA: Harvard University Press, 1984).
5. Accordingly, it is hard to grasp in the Portuguese case a similar match between democratic transition and postmodernism as the one Jo Labanyi points to in Spain. Cf. Jo Labanyi, 'Postmodernism and the problem of cultural identity', in Helen Graham and Jo Labanyi (eds), *Spanish Cultural Studies. An Introduction* (Oxford: Oxford University Press, 1995). As José Rebelo suggested in his study of Salazarism (the dominant political culture in authoritarian Portugal), the succession of dictatorship, revolution and democracy in a very short span of time created a sense of overlapping, rather than transition proper, between different historical periods: 'With the exception of April [revolution], when some signs of late modernism are still visible, one could argue that Salazarism did an economy of modernity. With and because of Salazarism, post-modernism appears, in Portugal, as an extension of pre-modernity.' Cf. José Rebelo, *Formas de Legitimação do Poder no Salazarismo* (Lisboa: Livros e Leituras, 1998), 346.
6. Edite Soeiro, 'Fernando Lopes ao *Se7e*. "Vamos ter uma Televisão morna"', *Se7e*, 12 March 1980, 2.
7. On the impact and meaning of pornographic cinema in post-revolutionary Portugal, see Érica Faleiro Rodrigues's chapter in this volume.
8. Edite Soeiro, 'Manter as emissões de pé é quase um milagre', *Se7e*, 31 December 1980, 2.
9. John Fiske, *Television Culture* (London: Methuen, 1987).
10. As people to whom wealth also meant cultural capital and as such stood as the exact opposite of the imaginary of poverty and isolation of authoritarian Portugal. Cf. Jean-Claude Passeron and Pierre Bourdieu, *Reproduction in Education, Society and Culture* (London: Sage, 1990).
11. Joseph Straubhaar and John Sinclair, *Latin American Television Industries* (London: BFI, 2013).
12. Isabel Ferin da Cunha referred to the impact of *Gabriela* as a 'revolution' of its own, not only because of its power to transform the everyday life of many families, but also because it introduced questions of gender and sexuality often ignored during the revolutionary process. Isabel Ferin da Cunha, 'A revolução da *Gabriela*: o ano de 1977 em Portugal', *Cadernos Pagu* 21, 2003.
13. The articles of the communist TV critic Mário Castrim in the evening newspaper *Diário de Lisboa* will echo this in a particularly critical way. Mário Castrim, 'Foram à Horta e Colheram um Nabo', in *Diário de Lisboa*, 8 March 1980, 15.
14. The second channel was created in 1968 with a stronger cultural profile than RTP1.
15. Soeiro, 'Manter as emissões de pé é quase um milagre', 2.
16. The theatre community, increasingly excluded from television, was particularly emphatic about the cultural implications of Domingues' political affinities: 'in the same way you said in an interview, while you occupied a political post, that you didn't recognize any quality in most Portuguese theatre, so we, the people involved in the theatre [...], don't

recognize any authority for you to evaluate our work' (Comuna, 'Carta a Maria Elisa', *Se7e*, 7 January 1981, 11).

17. Carlos Cruz, ' "Aceito o desafio" – Carlos Cruz de volta à RTP', *Se7e*, 18 January 1978, 10. Normally, foreign films and TV series are not dubbed in Portugal and audiences have to read subtitles.
18. Clara Pinto Correia, 'Maria Elisa apresenta – o Mapa-Tipo da grande viragem', *Se7e*, 30 September 1981, 2.
19. Edite Soeiro, 'Vou ter de responder perante muitos mais juízes . . .', *Se7e*, 5 March 1980, 12, and Soeiro, 'Manter as emissões de pé é quase um milagre', 2.
20. This was apparent in the invitations made to some authors with connotations with authoritarian culture.
21. Correia, 'Maria Elisa apresenta – o Mapa-Tipo da grande viragem', 2
22. Eduarda Dionísio, *Títulos, Acções, Obrigações. A cultura em Portugal (1974–1994)* (Lisbon: Salamandra, 1993).
23. Soeiro, 'Vou ter de responder perante muitos mais juízes . . .', 12.
24. Correia, 'Maria Elisa apresenta – o Mapa-Tipo da grande viragem', 2
25. 'Passeio dos Alegres' (The stroll of the happy ones) is a pun inverting a popular expression (the stroll of the sad ones) describing people killing time on Sundays with nothing to do.
26. Something like 'The Special Channel' or 'The One Channel'. The show was to be called 'The Third Channel', but the RTP resisted the idea.
27. *Tal Canal* was chosen as the best show in the history of Portuguese television in an opinion poll organized by the newspaper *Diário de Notícias* in 2007.
28. Their photos fill most of the covers of *TV Guia*, the weekly magazine created by RTP in 1979 and dedicated exclusively to its programmes, throughout this period. For some issues where these photos can be found, see note 32.
29. Bourdieu, *Distinction*.
30. Reinhart Koselleck, ' "Space of Experience" and "Horizon of Expectation": two historical categories', in *Futures Past: On the semantics of historical time* (New York: Columbia University Press, 1985).
31. In the sense defined by Jameson in his *Postmodernism*, a stage in the development of capitalism in which economic activities linked with the tertiary sector (and the culture industries in particular) start playing a much more structural role in society and economy than before.
32. For 1979 alone, cf. *TV Guia* 1, 10 February; 3, 24 February; 22, 7 July; 27, 11 August; 29, 27 August; 35, 5 October; 38, 27 October; 41, 17 November.
33. Angela McRobbie, *In the Culture Society. Art, Fashion and Popular Music* (London: Routledge, 1999), 8.
34. Laura Mulvey, 'Visual pleasure and narrative cinema', *Screen* 16, 1975.
35. Nestor Garcia Canclini, *Hybrid Cultures: Strategies for entering and leaving modernity* (Minneapolis, MN: University of Minnesota Press, 2005).
36. In French and English in the original.
37. Luís Sttau Monteiro, ' "Opções" ', *Se7e*, 28 November, 11.
38. Stuart Hall, *Encoding and Decoding in the Television Discourse* (Birmingham: Centre for Cultural Studies, 1973).

39. Fredric Jameson, *The Political Unconscious. Narrative as a socially symbolic act* (Ithaca, NY: Cornell University Press, 1981).
40. The question of taste is inextricably linked to the new horizons of consumerism and fashion in 1980s Portugal analysed by Giulia Bonali in this book.
41. Maria João Duarte, '"Tony Silva é o meu ídolo"', *Se7e*, 18 November 1981, 6.w

CHAPTER 11
LEAFING THROUGH THE 1980s IN PORTUGUESE FASHION MAGAZINES
Giulia Bonali

Introduction

Salazar's forty-year dictatorship ended in 1974 with the April Revolution reinstating democracy. In the following decades, Portugal's political, social and cultural structures underwent a series of transformations as the political stabilization began. The 1980s was critical for Portugal as it came to define itself as a post-authoritarian and post-revolutionary state. A key development here was its relationship with the rest of Europe and its desire to join the European Economic Community (EEC).[1]

Popular European fashion magazines proved to be highly influential as Portugal became increasingly attuned to European customs in the 1980s. This chapter demonstrates that fashion images played a key role, shifting economic and political identities as seen through the lens of fashion theory and history. Seen as semi-symbolic signs of social change, these magazines turn into cultural tools that disseminate and contextualize views on how Portugal's national identity can be successfully integrated with that of a more desirable pan-European identity. By examining the way in which the magazines presented Portuguese fashion to a wide geographical audience and a growing market in the 1980s, I investigate the representations of 'Europe' that played an increasingly important role ahead of and after the country's entry to the EEC.

The chapter is divided into three sections: it begins with an examination of secondary sources and the analysis of the texts and images found in the primary sources. The first section focuses on the historical context of fashion and its consumption in Portugal during the 1970s – just after the revolution. The emergence of shops selling 'unconventional' clothes encouraged new forms of pleasure and desire, emphasizing consumerism and public appearance. It created ideal conditions for the rise of a new generation of female fashion designers and sowed the seeds of a national fashion identity with products and garments identified as essentially 'Portuguese'. The second and third sections analyse a selection of texts featured in Portugal's two most influential European fashion magazines that were published towards the end of the 1980s: *Elle* and *Marie-Claire*. These were the Portuguese versions of the well-established French magazines, which targeted mostly female Portuguese consumers with an array of images.

By analysing the magazine editors' letters, the columnists' writing and editorials,[2] I illustrate how these magazines provide what Rebecca Arnold defines as 'narratives of a culture, clues, and revelations of the way a social group or indeed a nation envisions itself, particular to time and space'.[3] These magazines are valuable sources for tracing the emerging signs of modernity in Portuguese society, which, until that time, had often been perceived as traditionalist and backward-looking. By developing a narrative based on a selection of four editorials from the two magazines, it is my intention to map out the growing tension between the desire to establish a strong Portuguese identity and the increasing pressure to adopt a more European identity. The latter arguably constitutes one of the prevailing tensions found in Portuguese culture during the 1980s. As a result of this tension, these emerging fashion images allowed the predominantly female Portuguese readers to re-imagine the cultural landscape of Portugal via their symbolic language of dreams and desires. In doing so, I claim that the magazines attempted to compensate readers for this perceived loss of national identity by presenting Portuguese fashion as a modern artefact and sign of tradition. As Luis Trindade also suggests in his contribution to this volume, rather that clashing, Europeanization and national identity complemented each other.

In the ensuing sections, 'modernity' refers to a historical process entailing both economic and social development, as well as political emancipation. Accordingly, when referring to twentieth-century Portugal, it is possible to state that the decisive time in the country's economic, social and political modernization corresponds to the period of cultural postmodernism, seen here as the cultural logic of late capitalism,[4] a set of phenomena closely related to consumerism and social and cultural perceptions of leisure, hedonism and desire, to which fashion contributes in a decisive way.

It is important to mention that the Portuguese case needs a chronology of its own and should not be subsumed in global chronologies putting modernity and postmodernity in succession in a linear way. In Portugal there is arguably an overlap of what is usually considered postmodernist culture and a process (and perception) of social and political modernization. As Luís Trindade explains: 'the succession of dictatorship, revolution and democracy in a very short span of time created a sense of overlapping, rather than transition proper, of different historical periods'.[5]

The emergence of popular fashion in Portugal

It is difficult to discuss popular Portuguese fashion during the forty-year long dictatorship, because it was mainly anything 'French' – i.e. Parisian *haute couture*.[6] As a result, fashion – as a symbol of social contextualization – was limited to only the wealthiest sections of Portuguese society and rarely indulged in. As Ines Brasão explains, women's magazines that emerged during the Regime of *Estado Novo* were mainly addressing middle- and upper-middle class readers who were more interested in European culture.[7]

In the late 1920s, Lisbon was a city where one could find various ateliers specializing in French *haute couture* with the use of French fabrics.[8] Their influence on Portuguese dress became very important throughout the 1930s and the 1940s. This is well documented in writings about Madame do Vale and Ana Maravilhas.[9] These two ladies were the most well-known designers for women, having both succeeded in adapting and popularizing Parisian couture for their clients. Ana Maravilhas remembers being the first one to make 'a Dior' in Lisbon.[10] Her professional name defined her as a 'modista', which differs from the 'costureira' who usually made less expensive garments. The habit of commissioning clothing was widespread in affluent Portuguese society because this was the only way to acquire such clothing.[11] Ana Maravilhas continued to produce expensive, fashionable clothing until April 1974; according to her, no one would order or buy clothing any more, because ready-to-wear was both more affordable and readily available. Young female customers were now buying their clothes from Loja das Meias, Eduardo Martins and Porfírio; shops introducing Portuguese youth to ready-made clothes, international brands and trends.[12] These stores sold 'gangas' (jeans) and mini-skirts. However, it was still not possible for everyone to purchase brand-new clothes. For most young Portuguese women, everyday dress consisted of wearing outfits similar to those of their mothers and grandmothers. Many could simply not afford to adopt what was considered to be a more 'fashionable' look.[13] And even for those who could, fashionable clothes were still very difficult to find.[14]

Reflecting on early 1970s fashion the Portuguese editor of *Marie Claire*, Helena Redondo, wrote in the 1990s that Lisbon was a 'suspended' place; a city 'where people made resignation a way of living' and in which only a minority of people were interested in having an original look.[15] My focus on the city of Lisbon does not imply that I intend to leave out other parallel realities in the country.[16] Instead, it is meant to bring attention to particular cases as a starting point for questioning how and when Portuguese fashion began.

Shops would sell ready-to-wear clothes, especially pieces from other countries where the youth fashion market was already established, and carried certain cultural kudos. An example is 'Maçã', a shop that was opened in 1972 by a young woman named Ana Salazar. The legacy of and memories from the shop and its 'English' look still feature prominently in the stories of many.[17] The design of the logo evoked the aesthetic style associated with a hippy subculture, which in turn drew upon elements of Pop Art and Art Deco. It was reminiscent of logos used for the independent clothing stores in London in the 1960s. Maçã (apple) was the place to buy clothes sourced in London; a shop where young people could buy English brands, like Miss Mouse, and find 'gangas' that were not readily available elsewhere in Lisbon.[18] Those who remember Maçã still recall the sense of novelty and strangeness associated with their clothes; the awareness that they were participating in a global but arguably more exotic fashion scene.[19]

In this context, the appearance of Maçã can be viewed as one of the first successful attempts to import young men and women's fashions to Portugal. After the opening of her first shop in the new – and middle-class – residential area of Alvalade, other shops followed (e.g. Alice in Blues, which was on the same road; a place that sold nothing but gangas).[20] The arrival of such shops arguably had an impact on the neighbourhood, not only bringing new people into the area but also transforming the habit of shopping in the city into a new experience. Perhaps for the first time in Portugal, consumption became, as Angela McRobbie noted, 'a grand gesture of will, an act of opposition or an expression of identity'[21] – the possibility of choosing a particular stylistic look transformed the act of buying into a true moment of pleasure. Being more than a new cultural form, the trend promoted by such a pattern of consumption can be described as a form of subculture with its own forms of expression and representation. The style of subculture opposes the mainstream, which, in this case, can be seen in the way the younger generation invested these commodities with a strong social, cultural and even political meaning. If subculture is about the 'objections and contradictions' that an alternative culture is able to express, the sense of deviance and resistance that normally characterizes it was reinterpreted, in this context, as a form of distinction acquired through appearance.[22]

The new Lisbon scene allowed fashion to acquire a role in the process of social, but also political, transformation. Prior to 1974, access to new products and fashion trends was limited but the political change that was brought on by the revolution came with new perspectives in terms of consumerism and access to fashion trends. This made it possible for new designers to become examples of national talent and allowed their clothes to become potent symbols of Portugal's cultural heritage.

In 1984, the success of Maçã encouraged Ana Salazar to launch her own label, 'Harlow', and to begin exporting her designs to foreign markets. Other names that emerged in the post-revolutionary period were Manuela Gonçalves, one of the first Portuguese designers with formal training in fashion design in London, and Manuela Tojal, who started out as a teacher of fashion before becoming a designer herself in the late 1970s.[23] These women were the first generation of female designers to contribute to a national corpus of fashion design, which would later be internationally recognized as intrinsically Portuguese. It is important to note that male designers also emerged during this period, but this chapter focuses on women's fashion and female designers in order to highlight the stronger role that women had in the field of fashion as makers, entrepreneurs, promoters and consumers. It is also worth noting that in the 1980s, Portuguese versions of fashion magazines – including *Maxima*, *Elle* and *Marie-Claire* – would become important vehicles for spreading and promoting Portuguese fashion across national and international markets.

There are also other agents that contributed to the emergence of this fashion scene. New organizations were created in what can be described as an effort to institutionalize a national fashion industry. In 1974, the National Costume Museum was founded in Lisbon in order to build a collection (mainly through private donations) and promote the work of contemporary designers. Fashion education became the object of economic and social investment; new schools like the CITEX were created in Porto, while manufacturing associations like the Portuguese Textile Association supported each other to prepare young fashion designers for employment in the industry sector.[24] This increasingly professionalized scene was also supported by contemporary fashion events located in Lisbon, thus making the city a fashion capital that could match others in Europe, for example, *Manobras de Maio* (May Manoeuvres), a show held in the city centres of Lisbon and Porto that promoted new designers.[25]

The above indicate that fashion became an important protagonist for Portuguese urban youth from the early 1970s, and offer a different perspective regarding the revolutionary process. The emergence of a youth fashion market brought new attitudes towards people's personal appearance in the city; fashion encouraged new commodity buying behaviour, helping people express their identities via their clothing.[26] Furthermore, it allowed for the establishment of a new profession that was embraced by a generation of female designers, which, while identifying with international fashion trends, worked to create a Portuguese fashion identity. Ana Salazar's challenge to the 'desert of fashion' in the early 1970s can serve as an act of rebellion before the political revolution, and reveals the highly direct way in which fashion acts to spread new ideas far quicker than conventional media. As Elizabeth Wilson points out, fashion can be a 'site of struggle, as an arena in which the conflicts of society are played out in semi-symbolic forms that may heighten rather than drug the consciousness of oppression'.[27]

From a historical perspective, it must be acknowledged that the end of Salazarism and the emergence of democracy through revolution was at least as much the result of deep social changes as of political radicalization. In other words, there were two revolutions within that of 25 April 1974: first, the ideological upheaval of Marxist inspiration while carrying the project of a socialist society, and second, the explosion of a new affluent urban middle class tired of the colonial wars, dictatorial isolation and censorship. This moment mirrors the 1960s as a historical period broken between political rebellion and individual emancipation, which, in Portugal's case, came about with a certain delay. Forms of social transformation such as women's emancipation and the rise of an autonomous youth culture could only be manifested in the 1980s, when the political circumstances of the 1960s (political rebellion) were no longer in place.[28] The latter revolution shaped and was influenced by the fashion industry in Portugal, which gained momentum in the 1980s. Thus, what appeared was the era of 'Long 1980s'[29] that had began already in 1974 and affected notions of memory and national identity.

Notions of memory and national identity in Portuguese magazines

Following the development of the fashion scene from the early 1970s to the 1980s in Portugal, this section now turns to a selection of texts featured in two of the most influential fashion magazines that were printed in Portugal towards the end of the 1980s so as to examine the fashion scene from the early 1970s to the 1980s. The examination of the editors' letters, columns and editorials sheds light onto the way these reinforce a sense of Portuguese fashion among female readers. The letters are of interest because they serve as data on the language used at that time and can also allow one to trace the impact of fashion in the context of the 1980s while conveying emerging signs of modernity in a society that was worried about its national identity in light of European integration.

When *Marie-Claire* appeared in Portugal in 1987, with *Elle* following in 1988, it was the first time the Portuguese public could flick through the pages of an international fashion magazine. Both magazines had an established history in France (*Marie-Claire* was first published in 1937, followed by *Elle* in 1945), after the war. According to Tereza Coelho, director of Portuguese *Elle*, when these magazines were first published the aim was to surprise and epitomize the emerging fashion scene for the young people.[30] Both Tereza Coelho and Maria Elisa Domingues,[31] who was *Marie-Claire*'s director, introduced the magazines to their readers by pointing out that their editorial priority was to be 'Portuguese' and to reflect Portuguese culture in the magazines' content. Both editors made reference to the stability of a specific Portuguese identity, which was a poignant reminder, given that those same readers were experiencing first-hand the socioeconomic changes that were taking place at that time.

The first issue of *Marie Claire*'s Portuguese edition opened with a letter in which the director listed all the sociopolitical events that had recently occurred in the country, such as the revolution, the legalization of divorce and the increase in employment opportunities for women:

> More than that, we thought it was time to reflect the reality of Portuguese women. Several changes have occurred in our society over the last few years: we have experienced the feminism of the 1970s, the revolution of April 25th, divorce, the entry of thousands of women into the work market. All of this has profoundly changed the traditional image of women and relations between genders.[32]

As a result, the magazine recognized the importance of acknowledging the 'new woman' who was emerging as a result of contemporary historical events. According to Maria Elisa Domingues, the traditional image of women had been replaced by a 'new' female subject who wanted to know about fashion, beauty, shopping as well as the daily social and political news: 'There is a new female public interested in issues like fashion, beauty, decoration, and cooking, yet at the same time these women are closer to the transformations of the world, and more aware of their role in society. These young women need real information without prejudice.'[33] In the opening issue of the magazine, the title of the main article was 'Viva Portugal' and emphasized how good it felt to live in Portugal in 1988. Journalist Helena Torres interviewed several VIPs asking them what they liked about Portugal, requesting things that could be praised and shared. The text was accompanied by a rich, vivid graphic inventory mapping the 'history' of Portugal through a range of consumer symbols: *Água das pedras*, a famous brand of sparkling water; *a bolacha maria*, the traditional brand of biscuits; *Português Suave*, the cigarettes smoked by several generations.[34] Yet, the issue also included an image of the recently built shopping centre *Amoreiras* that, with its distinct postmodern architectural style, showed that Portugal was also the height of modernity, embracing contemporary design movements.

All these objects seem to be part of a 'pastiche of stereotypical past'[35] that celebrated history through the images of a 'glossy mirage.' In this sense, these pieces seem to remind readers that modernity did not do away with the past. On the contrary, traditions could be kept alive through forms of reification and commodification under the codes of postmodernism. In short, all these commercial objects were to be turned into national symbols. Although such a process was compatible with other facets of modernization,[36] Portuguese society of the 1980s struggled to represent contemporary experience and to celebrate it while it was undergoing this transition. Ironically, this inability to experience the present without the mediation of artefacts from the past seems to be keeping with Jameson's 'symptom of the waning of our historicity', which he identifies in postmodern culture.

In the same article, under a section titled 'Clima de Euforia' (euphoric atmosphere), economist and financial consultant Helen Gray de Castro highlighted the 'euphoric climate of the moment' which the country was experiencing during its first years in the EEC. She compared Portugal to a sleeping beauty, awakened from a long and deep sleep, while all around her everything was changing:

> Portugal is a kind of 'Sleeping Beauty' who has woken after a long sleep and is flattered by the attention from European princes. Everything is coming to the boil in a good way; for the first time we are experiencing the new Common Market, new companies, and products from all around the world. People are buying goods as if they had never seen consumer goods.[37]

The word 'euforia' evokes one of the most 'interesting historical symptom[s]'[38] of the period, one very closely related to the impact of consumerism. Both *Elle* and *Marie Claire* worked as suitable vehicles for this negotiation between present and past in a period when European integration had become a real challenge to Portuguese national identity.[39] The drive towards cultural homogeneity brought on by globalization can be seen as the other side of the coin in this context. However, the arrival of new international products and the growing tide of change were, above all, experienced with intense excitement. In a way, these symbols promoted and reinforced feelings of national identity, while simultaneously representing the new branded identity ready to be consumed and sold both nationally and internationally.[40]

In a recent article that was published in the blog *Malomil*, the Portuguese historian Antonio Araújo remembers how a sense of nostalgia was prevalent in Portugal during the 1980s and manifested itself in several cultural trends.[41] Araújo's main point is that revivalism in the 1980s was given a strong political meaning as it opposed the memory of the 1974 revolution. The pages of the magazine *Kapa*,[42] for instance, were populated by reproductions of old advertisements featuring products belonging to the dictatorial period of *Estado Novo*: from the popular toothpaste *Couto* to *Encerite* wax, which featured a maid dressed in uniform while waxing a wooden floor on her knees. There is also a reference to the combination of nostalgia and nonsensical irony in the use of these materials by the magazine's director, writer and journalist Miguel Esteves Cardoso:

> in an appropriation that explored *nonsense* [...] but also nostalgia and revivalism. Only in this way Miguel Esteves Cardoso used a form of humour which was soft and naïve, although slightly hurtful, so the imagery and iconography of Salazarism could be retrieved without provoking a commotion among people on the left, who, by being reactive, ran the risk of becoming reactionaries.[43]

Consumption and Gender Post-Transition

By imbuing this nostalgic imagery with nonsense, one can conclude that the magazines managed to somehow depoliticize nationalism.[44] Antonio Araújo notes that by making a strong connection with the past, this revivalism also works as a place where the objects lose their ideological meaning through a process of depoliticization during which they become totally commodified. I would argue that the magazines become celebratory vehicles of 'memory' and 'national pride', while capturing the transformation of everyday life. The nostalgia emerging in such a process helped to re-imagine and re-represent the past, with the risk of depoliticizing its symbols.

The magazines, with their editorials, articles and advertisements, act as an effective mediation by instilling confidence in the national market and reframing national identity.[45] The tension between the national and international, the reinforcement of traditional values and the need to move towards European uniformity, is expressed in a vital tension that animates the period's visual language. A sense of national identity emerges through the nostalgia that animates certain images and the way it pervades the landscape, the style of the editorial, and finally the type of clothes. Within this context, fashion takes on a playful role in this period of transition, as it manages to speak many languages: it simultaneously expresses the values of modernity and a 'fragmented sensibility – its obsession with surface, novelty and style for style's sake – highly congruent with this sort of post-modernist aesthetic',[46] all encapsulated in a specific national imaginary.

Fashion editorials

In order to illuminate notions of memory and identity that circulated in Portuguese fashion magazines in the era in question, it is important to address fashion editorials.[47] These constitute a decisive part of the magazine edition because they are mainly conceived for commercial purposes. Their aim is to sell clothes, draw readers in and get them to fantasize about fashion. Editorials instil readers with the desire to buy and create aspirations by making them available and accessible as consumable images.[48] In producing new needs and desires, they helped shape the aspirations of a new middle class that was emerging at that time in Portugal, especially for women. In this section I analyse some fashion editorials in both *Elle* and *Marie Claire* to illustrate the way fashion is portrayed, its role in revealing how society imagined itself and what its main aspirations were.

The featured editorial of Portugal's first edition of *Elle* in October/November 1988/9 includes six images shot by Portuguese photographer Paulo Nozolino. The first two images open with a large sign made out of two letters, 'T' and 'Z' standing against the sky while two silhouettes placed behind the letters are holding them. When looking at the 'T' and 'Z' the reader realizes that they are the final letters of the big sign standing on the top of the RITZ hotel. They look like giant billboards recalling '[Las] Vegas with all its excess and pastiche, the paradigm of rampant consumerism and celebrity';[49] the famous landscape celebrated by the architects Venturi and Scott Brown during their journey through the desert in 1966. And yet, we are not in a desert, but on the top of a luxury hotel dominating central Lisbon, which in the photo remains concealed, leaving the reader to imagine any possible futuristic landscape that seems to announce a new kind of architectural space and a new era. The editorial, in fact, promotes a new kind of Portuguese design that had not as yet been featured in national media. In this sense, it deploys fashion as an appropriate medium to express the values of modernity and identity through a process that celebrates a postmodernist design that brings to the present a future mediated by a past imaginary.

The third image is named after the three fashion designers appearing in that same issue, labelled as new suggestions for the forthcoming winter season. As before, three shadow silhouettes are seen standing on a roof while their clothes are kept hidden and all you can see is their pure geometrical cut. The three designers are Ana Salazar, Manuela Tojal and Manuela Gonçalves; the new generation of Portuguese women designers who began to emerge in the 1970s. The editorial dedicates an image to each designer, with the shoot set in the Modernist interior of Lisbon's Hotel Ritz that was built in 1952; the title of the editorial is 'O Futuro no Retrovisor', literally the 'Future in the rearview mirror', as if the future can only be seen by looking backwards. All three designers are presented as icons of Portuguese design, which suggests that they are no longer restricted to a small circle, but are part of an emerging fashion scene in Portugal. The new style they promote conforms with the dominant one – i.e. the one existing in 1980s European fashion elsewhere: geometrical shapes, asymmetrical cuts, large necks and abundant sleeves, shoulder pads, zips and dark colours. The models' poses are rigid, expressing seriousness and confidence. Along with their postmodernist aesthetic, they also enact symbols of modernity. 'Modernity' as a the way of representing the ongoing desire for something new which is highly characteristic of any postmodern, capitalist society, in that it 'enacts symbolically the most hallucinatory aspects of our culture'.[50] This combination of different temporalities reflects the way Portugal's process of economic modernization (and the adhesion to the EEC in 1986) was negotiated in different spheres of Portuguese society.

The second fashion editorial I would like to analyse was published in the January edition of *Marie Claire* in 1988. The issue's general theme for that month was '*valores seguros*' (safe values) and the editorial was titled '*viva azul*' (long live sky blue). The female model that was used for the shoot had Nordic features, blue eyes and blonde hair that seem a little strange in a Portuguese context. In the first image, she stands in a square in front of a church on a misty day, wearing a white trench coat with a pair of Levi's, and a light blue bandana in her hair. She looks like a smart but casually dressed city woman, with the appropriate outfit for a trip to the country. In the images that follow, the same model stands in front of a typical Portuguese wall-fountain that frames the entire image (see Figure 11.1). She is now wearing a white wool jumper covered by a light blue dress that looks like an apron, while her head is covered with a blue handkerchief. On one side, she holds a traditional straw basket full of tomatoes while wearing white woolen gloves. She is styled like a woman from the countryside, but with a glamorous, urban spin and both the make-up and her pose give a certain allure. In the next shots she sits at the

Consumption and Gender Post-Transition

Figure 11.1 'Viva Azul', from *Marie-Claire* n. 3, 1989, photographer Patrick Wilen. Reproduced by permission of the photographer.

seaside, next to a white tower. This time she is wearing more casual clothes; a masculine blue jacket paired with a white pair of jeans. In the last shot, she is standing underneath the *Cristo Rei* (see Figure 11.2), the large sculpture of Christ, which dominates the south bank of the Tagus River in front of Lisbon.

All these images express a romantic mood reinforced by the architectural symbols of old Portugal populating the landscape. The fountain, the church, the square and the monumental statue of Christ are the protagonists of the scene, as much as the model and her clothes, and no single element would work without the other. The colours chosen for the clothing are, as the title says, blue and white, which are typical colours of the Portuguese image of the sky, the sea and the bright white walls of the country's cities.

One is left wondering whether the 'safe values' are aspects of the landscape or of the classic style of these clothes; elements that tend not to change for each new season, as the editorial captions remind the readers. The landscape is surely a constant in these images, one that becomes 'an instrument of cultural power', in the sense used by W.J.T Mitchell who describes how landscape works as a medium. According to Mitchell, landscape is able to represent itself and to 'make [...] that representation operational by interpellating its beholder', which often happens in fashion photography.[51] The images in *Marie Claire*'s editorial in January 1988 are there to sell the clothes as much as the landscape itself. In this sense, it produces a strong reference to the reader, where both landscape and clothes somehow become fashionable. Romanticizing the country and the Portuguese woman is crucial in creating a nostalgic place to aspire to, in which one can fantasize about an old past re-enacted and project a future vision.

A similar editorial used the Quinta da Ermida mansion as its location, inside the Portuguese porcelain manufacturer of Vista Alegre, opening with a close-up of a yellow chiffon bow with an eighteenth-century religious medallion attached to it. Under the title '*Colonial Romantic*', it features a sequence of images in which a woman dressed in a 'romantic' white night gown is wandering around a garden in front of the farm. The green around her evokes an exotic landscape, while framing the 'Colonial style' of the model's clothes: a white Sahari dress, beige shorts and embroidered white clothes. The model looks like a lady of leisure resting in front of her colonial possessions. In another image, a model with 'southern' features sits on the roots of a big tree in front of the farm; while in another, a pale red-haired model sits comfortably in a straw chair to one side of the garden.[52] The 'colonial' imagery is introduced through the references to leisure and the linen clothes as well as the atypical skin and hair colours, while the nostalgic style recreates a romantic atmosphere. As before, fashion shows its ability to act as 'a vehicle for fantasy'[53] and to play with the ambivalence of meanings. In this case, however, the achievement is far more problematic, as to make colonial imagery into a fashion statement in a country that had only recently lost its five century long empire brought up very sensitive issues for Portuguese society.

Finally, in the March 1989 edition of *Elle*, we have one of the first editorial studio shoots curated by Isabel Branco. The style of the editorial distinguishes itself in comparison to the ones previously analysed by not making reference to any particular place in Portugal apart from showing clothes by Portuguese designers, like Manuela

Figure 11.2 'Viva Azul', Cristo Rei, Lisbon, from *Marie-Claire* n. 3, 1989, photographer Patrick Wilen. Reproduced by permission of the photographer.

Tojal and Ana Salazar. The editorial shows a model in different poses highlighting the style of her clothes in the studio. The scene, contrary to the other editorials analysed so far, is completely decontextualized by the absence of any background. A few pages later in the same edition, another editorial shot by iconic 1980s photographer Oliviero Toscani shows a similar photographic style but in this case features clothes from the two most influential cities in fashion at the time: Paris and Milan. The similarity in the composition of both editorials suggests to the reader that fashion only has one language, not only in terms of design but also in the way it is communicated: fashion shares the same 'landscape', the studio, where the national and the international merge into a single language, bringing readers towards a more European context. In this case, Portuguese fashion ceases to be represented through its romantic past or through a national modern-futuristic scenario, and becomes absorbed into an international stage. The creation of the narrative of the four editorials highlights the complexity of the organizing tension in Portuguese culture throughout the 1980s. It reveals how fashion images can mediate the process of reimagining new identities and new values that one can aspire to, and most importantly in creating new dreams which one can believe in. The last editorial makes one wonder how the magazines will look like throughout the 1990s; whether the dialogue between national and international will continue or will be totally absorbed into a more globalized imaginary. In the editorials of the late 1980s, I believe that what clearly appears is the overlap of aesthetic female ideals revealed by the representation of women with autochthonous features and other models of beauty, i.e. the blonde and Nordic woman featuring in the 'safe values' editorial. Such coexistence anticipated a new globalized imaginary in which the 'European woman' is induced to recognize herself.

Conclusion

Transformations are often a central theme of the study of popular culture. Furthermore, as Stuart Hall argued, popular culture is the ground upon which such transformations take place. To comprehend the complexity of the social, political and cultural layers that occurred in Portugal is no easy task, especially when looking at a period that is relatively close to the present day. The visual analysis of fashion magazines allows us to view this period using fashion as a kind of alternative protagonist whose role has often been overlooked.

This analysis has revealed how the country saw itself during this critical period of transformation and, more importantly, how Portugal wished to be seen by others during this time. The fashion magazines celebrated the present while dreaming about the future. This is why they worked as the perfect vehicles to shape the new aspirations and desires of a society rebuilding its own identity. The growing confidence acquired by Portugal during this period shows the key role played by fashion in helping the Portuguese hold onto their national identity at a time when the country was ostensibly hoping to become ever more European. The emergence of a young fashion market during the 1970s was supported by the appearance of independent shops such as Maçã, which served as a seedbed for trends that contributed to the formation of a new national fashion. This situation favoured the rise of young female designers who established themselves through the creation of national design that was recognized at home and abroad. During this time, the growing desire in Portuguese society to its identity in tune with what were viewed as European standards in the 1980s placed magazines in a position to mediate between a sense of loss of national identity, and a way forward, via the international representation of Portuguese fashion as one which stood for tradition. This cultural transformation that unfolded during the 'long 1980s' in Portugal was intimately linked with developments in gender representations and relations: women were both the main targets and the protagonists in the emerging Portuguese fashion industry. Furthermore, the latter often offered gendered metaphors of the Portuguese identity, which it aimed to help reconfigure.

In conclusion, this chapter demonstrated the extent to which the study of fashion in Portugal is key when it comes to understanding the complexity of the transformations undergone by this country. It also reveals a more nuanced insight into what happened. The privileged lens of fashion allowed us to zoom in on the 'fabric' of society 'to gain a new understanding of cultures, and individual lives, as well as the mechanics regulating the cultural and economic production of the past and the present'.[54] While leafing through the pages of the 1980s we find a future that in some ways still looks towards the past. The re-emergence of nationalism across the diverse phenomena of the 1980s is especially interesting when it comes to the world of fashion, which, instead of clashing catastrophically while the country began to assimilate its values with the rest of Europe, proved to be a moment which was complementary, and in many ways helped to reinforce the country's national identity.

Acknowledgments

I would like to express my gratitude to Emma Davenport and Alison Bron for editing and helping me to develop the chapter. A special thank you to the editors for their great support.

Notes

1. Portugal would join the EEC in 1986.
2. Fashion editorials refer to photo-editorials with full-page photographs on a particular theme, designer and model with or without accompanying text.
3. Rebecca Arnold, 'Looking American: Louise Dahl-Wolfe's fashion photographs of the 1930s and 1940s', *Fashion Theory* 6.1, 2002, 46.
4. Fredric Jameson, *Postmodernism, or, The Cultural Logic of Late Capitalism* (Durham, NC: Duke University Press, 1991).
5. cf. Luís Trindade's chapter in this volume, and see: José Rebelo, *Formas de legitimação do poder no Salazarismo* (Lisbon: Livros e Leituras, 1998), 346.

6. Madalena Braz Teixeira, *A moda do Século 1900–2000* (Lisbon: Museu Nacional do Traje, 2000).
7. *Flama* and *Modas e Bordados* (*M&B*) are the magazines extensively examined in Ines Brasão's chapter in this volume.
8. Tereza Coelho and Maria da Assunção Avillez, *A Moda em Portugal nos Últimos Trinta Anos* (Lisbon: Edições Rolim, 1987).
9. Ibid.
10. 'O primeiro vestido Dior aqui, fui eu: a "toile" e o tecido. Era carissimo, mas nunca gostei do que nao era bom' in Tereza Coelho and Maria da Assunção Avillez, *A Moda em Portugal nos Últimos Trinta Anos* (Lisbon: Edições Rolim, 1987).
11. Ready-mades were not available until the late 1960s.
12. Tereza Coelho and Maria da Assunção Avillez, *A Moda em Portugal nos Últimos Trinta Anos* (Lisbon: Edições Rolim, 1987).
13. Cf. Ines Brasão's chapter in this volume.
14. Alexandre Melo and Fernanda Câncio, 'Cenas da vida mundane. Do pós-guerra aos nossos dias' in *Panorama da Cultura Portuguesa no Século XX* (Porto: Edições Afrontamento, 2002), 326.
15. Ibid., 323.
16. In Porto, for instance.
17. Cristina L. Duarte, *15 Historias de Habitos, Criadores de Moda em Portugal* (Quimera, 2003), 13.
18. Alexandre Melo and Fernanda Câncio, 'Cenas da vida mundane. Do pós-guerra aos nossos dias', in *Panorama da Cultura Portuguesa no Século XX* (Porto: Edições Afrontamento, 2002), 324.
19. Conversation with Aida Duarte, 22 January 2015 in Lisbon, at the restaurant in the Faculdade de Farmácia da Universidade de Lisboa. Aida Duarte is currently an associate professor in the Department of Microbiology and Immunology at the University of Pharmacy in Lisbon. During the 1970s she was a young woman and student at the university.
20. Cristina L. Duarte, *15 Historias de Habitos, Criadores de Moda em Portugal* (Quimera, 2003), 14.
21. Angela Mcrobbie, *Postmodernism and Popular Culture* (London: Routledge, 1994), 31.
22. Dick Hebdige, *Subculture: The Meaning of Style* (London: Routledge, 1979), 17.
23. Paula da Costa Soares, 'Portuguese fashion design emerging between dictatorship and fast fashion', *Fashion Theory* 15.2, 2011, 225–38.
24. Ibid., 231.
25. Ibid.
26. See Ana Marta Gonzalez in *Identities Through Fashion: A Multidisciplinary Approach*, edited by Ana Marta González and Laura Bovone (London: Bloomsbury Academic, 2012).
27. Elizabeth Wilson, *Adorned in Dreams* (London: Virago Press, 1985), 174.
28. See Luís Trindade, 'Os excessos de abril', in R. Cordeiro Gomes and I. Margato (eds), *Literatura e Revolução* (Rio de Janeiro: UFMG, 2012).
29. Here I am comparing the 'Long 1980s' with what historians usually refer to the 'Long 1960s' as a period that combined social transformations and political rebellion. See Arthur Marwick, *The Sixties: Cultural Transformation in Britain, France, Italy and the United States, c.1958–c.1974* (Oxford: Oxford University Press, 1998).

30. 'Duas ideia basicas: surprender a transformaçao quotidiana do mundo na viragem do seculo, afirmar a imagem de juventude que domina, cada vez mais, essa transformaçao'.
31. Tereza Coelho worked at the weekly magazine *Expresso*, later as director of the magazine *Livros*, part of the newspaper *Indipendente*, and in 1987 she published a book called *Fashion in Portugal in the Last 30 Years* (*A Moda em Portugal nos Ultimos Trinta Anos*) which represents one of the rare texts about Portuguese fashion history; Maria Elisa Domingues was also a journalist, and a TV presenter. In 1973 she worked in *Radiotelevisão Portuguesa* as an announcer.
32. M.E. Domingues, letter to the readers, *Marie-Claire*, 1 November 1988, 11.
33. Ibid.
34. It is worth mentioning that one of the first manifestations of this neo-nationalism based on national consumer goods was the book called *A Causa das Coisas* (1986) written by Miguel Esteves Cardoso which talked about the '*coisas*' (things), referring to old and forgotten products once familiar in the daily life of many Portuguese.
35. About 'pastiche', see Fredric Jameson, *Postmodernism, or, The Cultural Logic of Late Capitalism* (Durham, NC: Duke University Press 1991), 21.
36. I am referring to the rise and the affirmation of a middle-class culture, the democratization of the public sphere, the rise of consumerism in the context of European integration. See Trindade, 'Os excessos'.
37. Helena Torres, 'Viva Portugal', *Marie-Claire*, 1 October 1988, 20–7.
38. Ibid., xii.
39. We are in 1988.
40. See Cris Shore, *Building Europe: The Cultural Politics of European Integration* (New York: Routledge, 2000). His main focus is to investigate what role culture plays in the process of European integration and in which way it is appropriated as a political instrument for the construction of Europe.
41. Antonio J. Araújo, 'A cultura de direita em Portugal,' Malomil web blog (2014), http://malomil.blogspot.pt/2014/01/a-direita-portuguesa-contemporanea.html [accessed 31 January].
42. The *Kapa* magazine was founded in 1990 with capital from Valentim de Carvalho and Attorney Luis Nobre Guedes SOCI, along with personality Paulo Portas. In Kapa, Miguel Esteves Cardoso (MEC) had a leading role; the magazine was his dream since the foundation of *The Independent*.
43. Araújo, 'A cultura'.
44. This trend of nationalist neutralization still survives nowadays in Catarina Porta's project 'A Vida Portuguesa' [The Portuguese Life]; a chain of shops offering only Portuguese products with a strong traditional character. Here too, most of the goods go back to the time of Salazarism and keep their old-fashioned style which attracts buyers to its retro charm.
45. Arnold, 'Looking American', 46.
46. Ibid., 11.
47. 'Fashion editorials' refers to photo-editorials with full-page photographs on a particular theme, designer or model, with or without accompanying text. They are the product of a mutual relationship between the photographer and the stylist who collaborate throughout the entire process.
48. Arnold, 'Looking American'.

49. Glenn Adamson and Jane Pavitt, *Postmodernism, Style and Subversion 1970–1990* (London: Victoria and Albert Museum Edition, 2011), 19.
50. Elisabeth Wilson, *Adorned in Dreams* (London: Virago Press, 1985), 63.
51. William J.T. Mitchell, *Landscape and Power* (University of Chicago Press, 2002), 2.
52. Here, the colonial imaginary represented seems very different from that expressed through the 'beauty contests' (Miss Portugal) of 1971–5, in which women from the colonies were invited in order to contribute to the idea of creating a 'bigger Portugal' as Marcos Cardão states in 'O Charme discreto dos concursos de beleza e o luso-tropicalismo na década de 1970', *Análise Social* 208, *XLVIII* (3°), 2013; he argues that the parades organized around these events represented the diversity of Portuguese territory, highlighting the Portuguese attributes which were distinguished from the ones which celebrated African tradition. Within this context, colonial fantasies functioned as mediation and cultural translation, and marked presence in a parade that choreographed the difference with the best-known African artefacts of the Portuguese. These contests, as forms of popular entertainment, reflected the vulnerability and the uncertainty of re-imaginig the Lusitanian community in post-colonialism.
53. Ibid., 246.
54. Eugenia Paulicelli and Hazel Clark (eds), *The Fashion of Cultures, Fashion, Identity, and Globalization* (Oxford: Routledge, 2009), 1.

CHAPTER 12
CONSUMING THE PAST AS A TELEVISUAL PRODUCT: GENDER AND CONSUMPTION IN *CUÉNTAME CÓMO PASÓ/TELL ME HOW IT WAS*
Abigail Loxham

Introduction

In 1975 when Franco died and Spain's transition to democracy began, postmodern cultural forms came to the fore as a response to this newfound liberation and as a means of exploring alternative expressions of cultural identity that had been repressed for so long under dictatorship.[1] This political interregnum marked a break, a rupture, and a chance to reject the past in a way that the arrival of modernity in Spain had been judged to fail at, forced as it was to conform to the continuing norms of dictatorship. With this rejection of the past came a rejection not only of history but also of memory. Paradoxically this radical cultural expression of postmodernity found an unexpected parallel project in the conservative ambition of politicians who assumed that it was through a rejection of the past that the country's (and by implication their) political future would be assured.[2] What this produces in the social life of Spain is a curious mix of conservatism and liberalism; the political will to move swiftly to stable democracy required a display of distance from the ideology of the previous regime while it retained some of its structures and supports in order to ensure this peaceful transition. With the dawning of the new millennium a more restrained appraisal of the transition can be discerned, and with it a desire to construct a narrative of the past which remedies the rupture represented by transition, and the postmodern politics of culture that typified it, by exploring the culture of amnesia that was constitutive of these conservative politics and the liberating aesthetic moment. Through the depiction of gender and consumerism I explore the presence of the politics of memory in popular television, paying attention to the ways in which the construction of a long running television drama seeks to both distance itself from serious political debates with regard to a violent past while simultaneously establishing a putative continuity with the regime that perpetrated this violence and the culture of present-day Spain. One of the main ways in which it enacts this continuity is through its representation of the social lives of Spaniards in the late 1960s and early 1970s. Cultural responses to this period have certainly not been lacking but popular culture and television has only recently been taken seriously as a critical component in the formation of responses to the recent Spanish past.[3]

Drawing on material from the emerging fields of Spanish television and media studies and Spanish cultural studies alongside a textual analysis of early episodes (set between 1968 and 1971 and aired between 2001 and 2004) of the popular television drama series

Cuéntame cómo pasó/Tell Me How it Was, I elucidate a link between representations of gender, domestic life and consumer culture, and wider ideological accounts of Spain's problematic relationship with modernity. The persistent tension discerned between continuity and rupture – Spain's particularity and its globalizing progress, and the desire to forget the past while allowing it to persist in the present – is traced through the representation and development of the three generations of female characters in the family at the heart of this popular television drama. I work through connections made between consumer culture and television and television's contemporary representation of a social history of this period – concerned with the memories of everyday life rather than national politics on a macro scale. Patterns of gendered consumption from the 1960s and 1970s are linked, in this series, through a concern with the past and an equivalent tension between progress and nostalgia which Spanish society in the twenty-first century is in the process of navigating. Television is pivotal in this relationship as a material denominator of progress in the period represented and because of its articulation of this relationship to media production and its history in the present. One of the major new consumer arrivals in Spain at this time was the television: between 1966 and 1969 the percentage of Spanish homes with a television set more than doubled.[4]

Consumer culture and television are frequently understood to be a measure of society's entry into the modern world, and for Spain this has tended to be considered as more complex than in other Western democracies, at best achieving a 'tarnished modernity'.[5] The reasons for this are tied to the ideological inconsistencies between the fascist dictatorship and those that would have been assumed to underpin a modern (liberal) capitalist society. There were certainly areas in which Spain's resistance to modernity was more marked than others: 'In gender relations Spain remained far adrift from developments elsewhere in Western Europe'.[6] Economic change brought a degree of social advancement that created a contradictory role for women for whom changing material conditions were at odds with their domestic duty, not to mention their legal standing:

> through the 1960s women remained at the epicenter of tensions between the competing demands of their official domestic role and the regime's growing need for an enlarged workforce. Women who were too young to experience the restrictions of the 1940s and 1950s were among the first to seek salaried employment in large numbers, [...] Henceforward, women would participate increasingly in the industrialization process and in the production of the goods and services that would in turn make their domestic responsibilities less arduous.[7]

Tatjana Pavlović's interdisciplinary survey of economic advancement and emerging consumer culture in Spain during the period 1954–64 describes it as a move 'from autarky to technocracy'.[8] Significantly she detects an equivalence between this increased prosperity and an apolitical approach to history in its promotion of 'a mood of acceptance that carried over to today's arguably apolitical democracy and a postmodern blend of amnesty and social amnesia gelled in the "pact of oblivion" (*pacto de olvido*) 1975–78'.[9]

Another example of the continuity that the show delimits as an attractive feature resides in this apolitical approach detected by Rueda Laffond's extensive and insightful work on Spanish television. He locates the appeal of the show in the apolitical attitudes of the patriarch, Antonio, but also in the growing affluence that the family enjoys: 'Hasta 1975, Antonio se ha incrustado, en silencio aquiescente, en los dispositivos de control social y de bienestar material relativo del tardofranquismo./Until 1975 Antonio is embedded, in tacit agreement, in the modes of social control and relative material comfort of late Francoism'.[10]

Exposure to the new medium – albeit through the controlled output of state sponsored channels – opened up Spanish homes to alternative possible modes of being, in line with increased possibilities for consumerism brought by material goods. During this period the Spanish economy flourished: 'The rate of growth (6.9 per cent of GDP per annum in 1960–75) was one of the highest in the world and even stronger in certain sectors of industry, as well as in services and tourism.'[11] These alternative modes of being challenged the status quo and the structure and operation of the Spanish family much like the advent of consumerism in America several decades previously which raised a 'set of contradictory responses and expectations, laced with anxieties over the sexual politics of leisure and middle-class ideals'.[12] The representational tensions that arise in the series are explored in relation to the changing material fortunes of the family and frequently the challenges to the patriarchal structure that these bring about. A desire for progress confronts a regime with deeply rooted conservative values and the resulting ambiguity is developed by the show's different characters and voices resisting and defending patriarchy and maintaining the drama's ambiguous political project. The politics of the show are frequently read as being rooted in a wider conservative project that aims to sanitize the past. Its appeal to domesticity and the formal approach that encourages conviviality through its use of humour, the high production values that enable recognition among the older viewers and a transgenerational content that has been seen to foment a similarly intergenerational appeal among its viewers all point to a continuity between then and now which effaces some of the brutalities and violent policies of the 'then' of the diegetic time and contributes to this highly selective revision of the past.[13] Television historiography has become more commonplace since the series first aired and challenges to this conservative tendency might be discerned in some of these more recent and equally popular productions such as *Amar en tiempos revueltos* (TVE1, 2005–) *La Señora* (TVE1, 2009–) or *Temps de silenci* (TV3, 2011–).

Television, gender and memory in *Tell Me How it Was*

The early twenty-first century in Spain has been dominated by its concern for – or perhaps even obsession with – memory. It seemed that the dawning of the new century provoked a concern for the unwritten history of the troubled twentieth century to be revisited. The impetus for this re-evaluation of a recent and contested past emanates, in the main, from grassroots movements and is driven by Spaniards whose family members disappeared during or following the Civil War and whose whereabouts are unknown.[14,15] At times the discourses of memory that attempt to redress the balance and question the strategies of violent discourse that have eliminated these stories in turn enact their own strategies of exclusion with regards to the popular – in this case televisual – narration of this troubled past. This particular television drama stages a desire to re-imagine everyday life, to reclaim domestic histories and incorporate them into a newly imagined (national) narrative of the past. This focus on the family and the domestic creates a degree of what Paul Julian Smith calls 'ideological ambiguity'.[16] Smith's analysis establishes many of the arguments from which I intend to develop a reading based on the place of television in the creation and consumption of gender and its relation to memory, not least of these would be the 'intimate relation of television with national history and identity'. And the 'new possibilities of meaning and subjectivity' offered by television's formal specificities. The terms of television's performance and the ways in which these alternative subjectivities might be formulated and understood, as Smith describes, can be seen in relation to the development and redefinition of gender roles in the national memory of the period. Perhaps most importantly, Smith's innovative work in this area allows for television in Spain to be taken seriously as a cultural product worthy of scrutiny as well as an agent in the country's redefinition of itself and understanding of its relationship to the past and in particular 'its focus on the family as a locus for the historical change that most closely connects the period depicted in the programme with the current conditions in which the show is produced and consumed'.[17] It is an approach which owes much to Karen Lury's evaluation of the reasons for studying television in 'addressing the encounter between viewer and text – recognizing this as offering opportunities to both escape from and return to the individual everyday'.[18] To dismiss these pleasures entirely is to fail to account for their basis in affective connections to the desire for a shared past, affective connections that might eventually play a part in a more serious ethical reappraisal.

In 2001, after an initial rejection and several years of attempts to commission this series, the producer, Miguel Ángel Bernardeau, and writers Patrick Buckley and Eduardo Ladrón, persuaded RTVE that their television depiction of late dictatorship Spain through the lives of a working-class family in one of the newer *barrios* of Madrid would have widespread popular appeal. In doing so they enabled production of one of this century's most popular televisual products in Spain. At the time of writing the programme is in its fifteenth series and its place as a canonical television text now seems assured. Its success must be credited to a combination of factors: the presence of established Spanish stars (of both big and small screen); the intergenerational appeal; the rise in popularity of nostalgia and retro,[19] high production values and attention to detail as well as propitious time-slot (Thursday evenings at 10.00 pm). The series is broadcast on the state-owned main television channel in Spain (TVE1). It is a family melodrama, centered on the Alcántara family who live in a working-class neighbourhood in Madrid, San Genaro, and it runs for seventy minutes an episode. It recreates a recent and difficult period in Spain's history, the first series beginning in 1968 and the most recent episodes set in 1981. Viewing figures attest to its popularity: by the time the fourteenth series aired, 63 per cent of Spain's population had seen at least one minute of the show. It regularly reaches at least 30 per cent of the market share; the third episode of the first series achieved a 33 per cent share of the audience (there were four national channels competing for this audience as well as the autonomous community channels).

To begin in 1968 is to allow the makers of the series to reflect the greater freedoms and economic prosperity enjoyed by Spaniards in the period of *tardofranquismo* (late Francoism) or *dictablanda* (soft dictatorship) and to avoid the more contested period of violence and economic penury of the postwar years. Coupled with an industrial revolution that sees Spain's urban centres grow at the expense of a dying agrarian economy (an urban–rural dichotomy that is a narrative mainstay of this television series given that the Alcántara family is the first generation to have left their village – *pueblo* – for the city), television as both the creator of modernity and its best representation coalesce. As Mercedes Alcántara says of the television set in the first episode, 'Es un lujo y nosotros nunca hemos tenido lujos' (it's a luxury and we've never had luxuries). To focus on the progress brought by the advent of increased consumerism within Spain offers television the opportunity to glorify its own history as a marker of progress but also to concentrate on Spain's claims to modernity as exemplified by the rhetoric of the late dictatorship. The regime's discursive attempts to claim Spain's status as a modern nation can also be located in a twenty-first century discourse of recuperation. This mediation through cultural forms resists a wholly negative view of the past by admitting some of its problematic elements but makes claims to a popular and unifying memory, sustained by television, 'It [*Cuéntame*] gathers the family around the TV to talk about our shared past'.[20] This might be true, but the series, in a reflection of contemporary Spanish culture, negotiates a tricky path between glorification and redemption of that past and condemnation of it in keeping with Spain's 'uneven' embrace of modernity as containing both rupture and continuity. The depiction and development of the female characters in this series and the use of the domestic space and the place of the television within it, contributes to an exploration of what Glen Creeber refers to as the 'personal nature of history': it seeks 'to analyse the minutiae of the past so that history itself increasingly became a self-reflexive, interpretative and subjective experience.' A strategy that he refers to as a 'politics of the everyday'.[21]

Nowhere was this tension between advancing modernity – epitomized by increased consumerism – and the values of Francoism more apparent than in the Spanish home and the role of women within it:

> Women of the time were caught in the conflicting demands of domesticity and the work place, provincial loyalties and the celebration of national mobility. The complex interplay of motherhood and sexuality, household chores and wage income, traditional economizing and frivolous consumption imply an evolving process of conflict resolution – both internal and external. As the epitome of modernity and progress, TV became a rhetorical figure for that contradiction.[22]

Consumption and Gender Post-Transition

Cuéntame depicts this tension through a self-conscious staging of the consumerist moment exemplified here in consumer objects, feminized domestic duties (an emphasis on food preparation and setting and clearing the table in keeping with the family mealtimes that are central to each episode); female fashions; and even feminized gestures and bodily markers of propriety.[23] In the case of *Cuéntame* material goods become the museum pieces that mark progress but also bind the series firmly to its 'period', and redouble its position both as authentic purveyor of memory and critical representation of a national past, tightening those affective links through more banal representations of memory that can be foregrounded thanks to the show's high production values and meticulous attention to *mise-en-scène*. In what follows I scrutinize the textual devices through which the series (in these early episodes) sustains and foments this dichotomous approach to memory, staging the tensions of the period through economic progress, increased consumerism and the alternative subject positions that these suggest for women in the period. Anecdotal and journalistic accounts of the series suggest that the central role of the family and its television viewing habits is mirrored by the show's audience and that its title echoes the intergenerational narrative provoked by a televisual reflection on the nation's past. Such accounts understand the series' value as a mobilizer of family memory encouraging the younger generation to investigate silenced public and private memories.

'La llegada del futuro'/The arrival of the future: *electrodomésticos* and automobiles

In episode sixty-eight, 'La llegada del futuro'/The arrival of the future (13 November 2003), the series demonstrates that in relation to Spain's past the television might become an acceptable archive of its own history and the history of consumption by which it is indelibly marked. The episode opens with archive footage of an unattributed exhibition of futuristic consumer goods announced by a couple of glamorous women with futuristic garb and gravity-defying hairstyles, underlining the futuristic aesthetic. The next shot is of a vehicle resembling a spacecraft with the word *futuro* emblazoned on the front, a series of innovative design prototypes follows accompanied by contemporary music. This is the structure of each episode, the archive footage opening and establishing the theme for each chapter. In this example the imagining of the future from within the past underscores the show's status as memory text. It demands a degree of engagement with the pleasures of nostalgia at the same time as it assumes an informed, empathetic but distant relationship to the histories it evokes.[24]

This contradiction is mirrored in the tensions embodied by Spanish broadcast media's global approach to modernity and Spain's insistently parochial vision of itself; a version of national identity which television in this epoch supported. The representation of the three generations of women in the Alcántara family enacts this temporal dynamic between the glorification of Spain's autochthonous identity and the progress brought by consumerism (also judged to be a reason for national pride), and the hankering after a truly Spanish way of life embodied by the rural and a lack of consumerism.

In this important relationship with the present, the three generations of the Alcántara family exemplify three generations whose experiences of Spain are vastly different. To a degree they are metonymic of the current generational battle over memory that plays out in contemporary media as grandchildren and children of the generation that lived through civil war and dictatorship are involved in gathering and preserving accounts of the period that has gone so long without being publicly, or privately, aired. Mercedes Alcántara (Ana Duato) is established as the character who holds the family together – she exemplifies moral virtue and developing independence mediating between the traditional feminine role embodied by her mother Herminia (Maria Galiana) and the more progressive one as portrayed by her daughter Inés (Irene Visedo Herrero). The encroaching modernity is seen to be creating a different kind of feminine role, one that, if the character of Mercedes is representative, must now negotiate a role outside the home while assuming all responsibility for domestic tasks as well. Furthermore, the increased freedom that her independent economic status delivers is a far cry from autonomy, given that legally women still ceded all their material possessions and financial property to their husbands on marriage. The narrative does not efface these details, when Mercedes requires a bank loan to open her boutique she must be accompanied by Antonio to authorize the loan. This is not merely symbolic either, the episode in which this takes place shows Mercedes negotiating with her husband and cajoling him into an acceptance of this apparent violation of the patriarchal structure to which his family, as good Spanish Catholics, must adhere.

Attempts to recuperate and redeem a contested past (or to 'escape to a return to the individual everyday') must also engage with the divisive and repressive politics of the regime and the effect that these had on everyday life in the domestic sphere. The complicated negotiation with the family patriarch mirrors the shifting politics of the regime upheld by the ultimate patriarch, Franco. By situating the television as a central agent of innovation, change and modernity in Spain, the series grapples with the use of the media by the regime to control the opinions and the actions of Spaniards.[25] These ideologically driven programmes were also charged with assuring the newly materialistic middle classes that Spain was becoming a newly modern nation at the same time as it perpetuated the ideology of national distinction, typically rooted in family and the gendered divisions within it.

This dual function becomes apparent from the moment the television set arrives in the Alcántara household in the first episode of the series. 'Antes de que tuviéramos televisión todavía se hablaba en la mesa, bueno hablaba mi padre los demás respondíamos' (Before we had a television we used to talk around the table, well my father talked and the rest of us responded'). The scene reinforces this patriarchal control: Antonio complains that his daughter Inés hasn't arrived home in time to have dinner with the family. When she does arrive he berates her for the tightness of her skirt, a skirt that we have just seen her lengthen by several inches before entering the family home. Mercedes defends her daughter saying 'es la moda' (it's fashion) but Herminia takes Antonio's side, 'Hay modas y modas' (There's fashion and fashion), a sentiment swiftly reinforced by Antonio, 'Sí hay modas y modas, las modas como Dios manda y las otras' (Yes, there's fashion and fashion, fashion as God intends it and the rest). This first episode establishes, often heavy handedly, the values and customs of the pivotal cast members, los Alcántara/the Alcantaras. The patriarchy is represented by Antonio here, a stand-in for the ultimate patriarch, Franco, and unshifting in his authority in the home. The attitudes voiced by other members of the family point unambiguously to an emerging resistance to these patriarchal values and allow the series to retain these competing views, simultaneously upholding and contesting patriarchy.

The voiceover (of the adult Carlos) that distils the narrative of each episode into a, frequently anodyne, lesson is more prevalent in this first episode as it is tasked with setting the stage for the new series. It reminds the viewers of the distance from this period in history but implores them not to forget how recent it actually was. 'Y no es que haya pasado tantos años pero lo que ocurre es que hemos cambiado tanto' (It's not that this is so long ago but that we have just changed so much). This establishes continuity and grants the series its status as repository of memories through which, as the title suggests, we might see how *things were*. Small details, such as the length of Ines' skirt and the argument between Toni and Antonio about what to listen to on the radio in the same episode, deliberately diverge from the greater political issues of the day in order to establish the domestic politics of the show as foregrounding the repressive politics of the regime. This is a day-to-day existence mediated by the new television set and dominated by the economic vicissitudes of the time and their impact on family life, that predicates progress in gender relations on the success of the nationalist government at the same time as it excludes a threat of feminism – not yet labelled as such – and equality for women as a non-Spanish idea. A more radical version of equality between the sexes is introduced by Inés who, in order to live in the way that she desires, has to leave the mainland and go and live on Ibiza, an island coded as *hippy* and *foreign*, and when her parents visit her there (Episode sixty-five, 'Paraisos y purgatories', 23 October 2003) their way of dressing and mode of deportment is at odds with the island's usual residents. Female autonomy was similarly designated as foreign and dangerous, as the series explores through the arrival of the contraceptive pill (from France) and the unhappy marriage and corrupted family unit represented by Antonio's brother, Miguel (Juan Echanove), who has been destabilized by the foreign ideas of his French wife and their life on the 'wrong' side of the Pyrenees. The threat to the chastity of the good Catholic daughter, Inés, also comes in the form of the English student, Mike, a representation of the foreigners that were increasingly arriving to Spain's coastal regions. Tourism was one of the principal reasons for this improved economic position, but of course the virtue of the good Catholic daughter had to be protected from these outside influences. *Cuéntame* reflects this contradictory stance identified by Justin Crumbaugh 'of a regime that was shamelessly courting foreign investment and promoting consumerism at home after having defined itself as the guarantor of antimaterialist spiritual integrity'.[26]

In the first four series of *Cuéntame* the encroachment of consumer culture is of significant material benefit to the Alcántara family, apparently because of the freedom it affords to the women in the family – a generational relationship that reinforces the temporal progression from the 'then' of the diegetic space to the 'now' of the viewing time.

Progress as embodied by material goods and the struggle to attain them is one of the means by which the series establishes its claims to urban modernity and underscores the tensions between home space, coded as feminine, and city space, until now the domain of the men. Significantly, this is explored through the material accumulation of the family contrasting the domestic consumer goods with the male acquisition of the automobile. After the arrival of the television the tide of progress cannot be stemmed and a washing machine (feared and then embraced by Herminia) is bought and paid for in instalments ('Amistades peligrosas', 25 October 2001). The premise of domestic revolution that these advances threaten, and the concomitant threat to familial stability, is approached both humorously – confusion as to how the machine works and where to put the detergent – and through a more serious narrative reflection on the state of the home and the nation (the one always bound to the other according to the Falangist dogma).

This spatial divide between male and female habits of consumption – domestic labour aided by the washing machine and the sewing machine contrasted with the command of the city that is enabled through car ownership for the men – demonstrates the more problematic side of female consumption; it is frequently tied to fashion and femininity as the regulation of feminine interests extends to their role outside the home. Mercedes in particular is liberated by the technological advances of the new *electrodomésticos* and, when she purchases a sewing machine, her part-time home-based employment, a feminine task and duty to supplement the income of the household, soon becomes a potential main source of earnings as her own designs are noticed; in series three she opens her own boutique in the local neighbourhood to showcase and sell her sartorial creations. The tensions that this changing family dynamic introduces into the household are one way that the show creates and sustains narrative tension over the course of these early seasons. The moment of transition to a proper consumer culture epitomizes some of the criticisms that have been levelled against its representation as a wholly liberating moment. The example of domestic labour that is the family's source of income and which allows for their acquisition of the television demonstrates the fluidity of the women's position as producer and consumer, dictated by class and economic position. This is clearly a sanitized depiction that also plays to the staging of the 1960s and 70s in the attention to sartorial detail incorporated narratively through Mercedes' boutique. In a series that admits numerous ambiguities, part of the pleasure to be found for the spectator is interpretative, and it also reminds us of the problems of female consumption at a time when the emerging middle class was negotiating its role and finding a space in urban centres that encouraged their role as consumers at the same time as ideological rules and economic imperatives marginalized this consumption and the means required to participate in it.[27]

The automobile is another marker of success and – literally in this case – mobility, but this time it is the male members of the family that, initially, benefit from greater accessibility to cars in the form of the SEAT 600.[28] The latent but insistent challenge to patriarchy that develops as the series progresses comes about through growing access to these new consumer goods. In the first episode of the fifth season (episode seventy-six, 'El año de la crisis'/The year of crisis, 22 April 2004) Mercedes learns to drive and the boundaries between male and female spaces are steadily eroded. This growing level of female independence is likened by the voiceover to access to the contraceptive pill and his turn of phrase complicates claims to gender equality that this economic prosperity might have enabled: 'las mujeres empezaron a no tener bastante con tomar píldoras anticonceptivas ahora se lanzaban a conducir coches. Lo que nos faltaban; mujeres conductores' ('Women were not content with taking contraceptive pills now they threw themselves into driving cars. Just what we needed, women drivers!'). The mobility that consumer culture brought to Spain with the car had been exclusively male until this challenge to their status as family chauffeur. This is further evidence of the woman leaving the confines of the domestic space – already a working woman, Mercedes expresses a potential for a practical liberation from her husband. That this is compared to the sexual liberation brought by the (still illegal) contraceptive pill demonstrates the limitations imposed upon women at this time. The humorous effect that the tone of this statement attempts to evoke is supported by the subsequent episode initially, as Mercedes is causing chaos on the roads when out with Antonio. Nonetheless, as is typical of the style of the show, progress is nudged in tentatively as she passes her test, contrary to her husband's expectations and (unexpressed) desires.

These formal techniques and narrative conventions function to domesticate the threat from outside (both historically and in terms of memory as it is experienced in the contemporary domestic setting). For Franco, and many aspects of today's political elite in Spain, the perpetuation of the myth of a prosperous and united country was to designate any threat to this as a dangerous manifestation of alterity, anti-Spanish and therefore ultimately dangerous.[29] The television set serves a dual function within the series and I would argue the series has a similarly dichotomous role in terms of its reception in the present. This dual function is tied to the status of television as 'a material object as well as a relayer of messages'.[30] In fact if the series is to successfully fulfil its contradictory function – to suggest a continuity of national identity and a progression of gender roles in the home – then it needs to establish the sense of progress that the material object brought into the home while selectively distancing itself from the progressive politics and new ideas that were part and parcel of this arrival. During each episode we consume adverts and entertainment television along with the family, as meal times become a spectacle of family viewing. Foreign ideas also arrive into the home through this box in the corner and hint at the possibility of alternative roles for women. When these ideas are seen to be too outlandish or to represent a threat to the established order of the home, they are designated as anti-Spanish, a feature consistent with the institutionalized attitude to feminist ideas during the period.[31] Allowing the foreigner into the home is a trope identified by Pavlović in her survey of contemporary literature surrounding the arrival of television, identifying 'the rising use of the trope of invasion to describe the relationship between spectators and images'.[32]

Conclusion

Describing the British series *Life on Mars*, Amy Holdsworth points out that 'the idea of home is a shifting site', one that evokes a nostalgic yearning but also a rejection based on the notion that we have progressed. This is precisely the shifting dynamic of *Cuéntame* – it is an 'example *of* but also reveals *how* television becomes significant for our sense of change and continuity'.[33] The series raises and explores notions of consumption, gender and progress which at time seem at odds with its perceived operation in the present: to neutralize the past and transform it into another consumer product along the lines of nostalgic consumption. As a text which foregrounds the changing status of men and women in society, and which is forced to do so as a result of the changing social structures of Spain in the years that it represents, it contributes to the re-imagining of Spain as progressive and European while struggling to reflect the modernization and changing gender roles as unproblematic. The voiceover that ends each episode reminds us of material progress but frequently contrasts that with the steady erosion of a certain set of ideals and values which seem to epitomize Spain as a place which is afforded this cultural distinction precisely because of its 'traditional' adherence to certain codes of gendered behaviour. Spain occupies a contradictory and complex position with regard to the advent of modernity and the relationship between social and cultural advancement and advancing consumer culture. Mediated representations of history, memory and gender both embody these contradictions and problematize their mediation.

A long running television drama which as it develops must engage with the vicissitudes of its viewers, network pressures, ageing actors and the altered political and societal circumstances into which it is received proves a valuable textual reference for unpicking the relationship between the consumer society that television is an agent of and the gendered consumer that it addresses. In Spain the ethics of memory complicate this representational capacity and in this negotiation there are moments at which the desire for continuity and redemption results in a conservative and newly commoditized version of the gender roles and the society that it depicts. Where it is most useful is in its reproduction of the everyday and its recognition of those everyday patterns of consumption is worthy of depiction and more importantly as a trigger for other avenues of mnemonic work. The everyday proves a legitimate site of study because it is the place from which we are allowed a degree of continuity, the home and the domestic past is a safe place from which to begin to make memories, hence the title of the series; it stresses the imperative to discussion of quotidian events as a precursor to a narrative concerned with serious political events. The strong link between consumption and modernity which is also grafted onto the development of television as the consumer object par excellence in terms of its commercial capacity (specifically through advertising) but also the transmission of ideological expressions of that society makes this a worthy object of study. If we question the notion of rupture that theorizations of modernity assume as integral to the development of society, then we are able to relate the past more effectively to the present, a relationship long denied in Spain.

Notes

1. Kathleen Vernon and Barbara Morris, *Post-Franco, Postmodern: The Films of Pedro Almodóvar* (Westport, CT: Praeger, 1995). Jo Labanyi, *Postmodernism and the Problem of Cultural Identity* (Oxford: Oxford University Press, 1995), 396–406.

2. I am aware that it may seem that these are two parallel forms of amnesia contrary to Paloma Aguilar's argument that it was a deliberate, vertically imposed and entirely politically motivated. See Paloma Aguilar, *Memory and Amnesia: The Role of the Spanish Civil War in the Transition to Democracy* (New York, Oxford: Berghahn, 2002). I would argue that while the effects may have been similar, the motivations were different and that the postmodern amnesiac tendency observed in (some) cinema, art and literature was a perceived rejection of the values of conservative politicians whose rejection of the past was a self-serving avoidance of blame and the advancement of personal careers. By the same token there was of course a period of intense reflection and memory became a trope of another body of cultural production, but these works did not provoke a debate in the public sphere, nor were they a spur for or a reflection of political and legislative change in a way that works in the twenty-first century can claim to be.

3. Helen Graham and Alejandro Quiroga, *After the Fear Was Over? What Came After Dictatorships in Spain, Greece, and Portugal* (Oxford: Oxford University Press, 2012).

4. R. Gunther, J. Ramón Montero and A. Mughan, *The Media and Politics in Spain: From Dictatorship to Democracy* (Cambridge: Cambridge University Press, 2000), 36.

5. Tom Buchanan, *How 'Different' Was Spain? The Later Franco Regime in International Context* (Basingstoke: Palgrave Macmillan, 2007), 85.

6. Ibid., 94.

7. Anny Brooksbank Jones, *Women in Contemporary Spain* (Manchester, New York: Manchester University Press, 1997), 77–8.

8. Tatjana Pavlović, *The Mobile Nation: España cambia de piel (1954–1964)* (Bristol: Intellect, 2011), 3.

9. Ibid.

10. Carlos Rueda Laffond, '¿Reescribiendo la historia? Una panorámica de la ficción histórica televisiva Española reciente', *ALPHA*, 29, 2009, 90–1.

11. Buchanan, *How 'Different' Was Spain?*, 86.

12. Lynn Spigel and Denise Mann, *Private Screenings Television and the Female Consumer* (Minneapolis, MN: University of Minnesota Press, 1992), ix.

13. Abigail Loxham, '*Cuentame como paso/Tell me how it was*: Narratives of memory and television drama in contemporary Spain', *European Journal of Cultural Studies* 2015, 7–8.

14. Carolyn Boyd, 'The politics of history and memory in democratic Spain', *The ANNALS of the American Academy of Political and Social Science* 617.1, 2008, 133–48. Francisco Ferrándiz, 'The Intimacy of Defeat', in Carlos Jerez Farrán and Samuel Amago, *Unearthing Franco's Legacy: Mass Graves and the Recovery of Historical Memory in Spain* (Notre Dame, IN: University of Notre Dame Press, 2010), 304–25. Paul Preston, *The Spanish Holocaust. Inquisition and Extermination in Twentieth-Century Spain* (London: Harper Press, 2012). Joan Ramón Resina, *Disremembering the Dictatorship: the Politics of Memory in the Spanish Transition to Democracy* (Amsterdam: Rodopi, 2000). Aguilar, *Memory and Amnesia*.

15. It is difficult to reconcile the serious accounts of genocide and torture committed in the name of Spain and the defence of the nation with entertainment television. Furthermore, to untangle accounts of history and memory from accusations of manipulation, truth and authenticity when the stakes are so high complicates discussions of popular culture in relation to accounts of historical memory and the past's recuperation. In this chapter I intend neither to dismiss nor belittle the serious and ethically complex accounts of memory which are of immediate importance to the lives of those generations who experienced the war and whose families urgently undertake a process of exhumation and mourning. Nonetheless the

popular representation in evidence on television cannot be entirely divorced from these more serious interventions in the country's memory culture.

16. Paul Julian Smith, *Television in Spain: from Franco to Almodóvar* (Woodbridge: Tamesis, 2006), 17.
17. Paul Julian Smith, *Spanish Practices. Literature, Cinema, Television* (London: Legenda, MHRA and Maney Publishing, 2012), 21.
18. Karen Lury, 'A response to John Corner', *Screen* 48.3, 2007, 372.
19. A tendency identified in US culture by Paul Grainge, 'Nostalgia and style in retro America: moods, modes, and media recycling', *Journal of American and Comparative Cultures* 23.1, 2000, 27–34. Elizabeth Guffey, *Retro: the Culture of Revival* (London: Reaktion Books, 2006) and in relation to this series by Anna Corbalán, 'Reconstrucción del pasado histórico: nostalgia reflexiva en *Cuéntame cómo pasó*', *Journal of Spanish Cultural Studies* 10.3, 2009, 341–57.
20. Lisa Abend and Geoff Pingree, 'Franco Lives Again – on Spanish TV', *Time*, 2007.
21. Glen Creeber, *Serial Television Big Drama on the Small Screen* (London: British Film Institute, 2004), 14.
22. Pavlović, *The Mobile Nation*, 89.
23. This is in keeping with a conceptualization of 'period television' understood as 'the mode of displaying a period', from which 'the television archive communicates a more intimate access to many-layered memory'. See Prudence Black and Catherine Driscoll, 'Don, Betty and Jackie Kennedy on *Mad Men* and periodisation', *Cultural Studies Review* 19.2, 2012, 188–206.
24. A form of nostalgia which has parallels with Svetlana Boym's conceptualization of 'restorative nostalgia'. Svetlana Boym, *The Future of Nostalgia* (New York: Basic Books, 2001), 41.
25. Manuel Palacio, *Historia de la Televisión en España* (Barcelona: Editorial Gedisa, 2005), 84–5.
26. Justin Crumbaugh, *Destination Dictatorship. The Spectacle of Spain's Tourist Boom and the Reinvention of Difference* (New York: State University of New York Press, 2009), 4.
27. This tension between production (as female labour) and emerging female consumption finds parallels in Angela McRobbie's work on 1980s Britain: 'such social changes along with the intensification of consumption and the apparent access of ordinary people to wide ranges of consumer goods should not be used as an excuse to ignore the limits of consumption and to dismiss the work and wage needed to be able to participate in consumption': Angela McRobbie, *In the Culture Society: Art, Fashion and Popular Music* (London: Routledge, 1999), 37–8.
28. The make and model of the car is representative of Spain's advancing modernity during this period according to Pavlović, *The Mobile Nation*.
29. Stanley Payne, *The Franco Regime 1936–1975* (Madison, WI: University of Wisconsin Press, 1987), 231–2.
30. David Morley, *At Home with Television* (Durham, NC: Duke University Press, 2004), 310.
31. Lorraine Ryan, 'A case apart: the evolution of Spanish feminism', in Rebecca Pelan (ed.), *Feminisms Within and Without* (Galway: Women's Studies Centre, National University of Ireland, 2006), 56–67.
32. Pavlović, *The Mobile Nation*, 93.
33. Amy Holdsworth, *Television, Memory and Nostalgia* (Basingstoke: Palgrave Macmillan, 2011), 109–10.

CHAPTER 13
AUDIO-VISUAL CONSUMPTION IN THE GREEK VHS ERA: SOCIAL MOBILITY, PRIVATIZATION AND THE VCR AUDIENCES IN THE 1980s
Ursula-Helen Kassaveti

This chapter examines the accelerating consumerism in Greek society following the victory of PASOK (Panhellenic Socialist Movement) in the October 1981 elections. A political party, temporarily promoting Keynesian economics, supported the middle class of the period and their increasing need to find new symbolic material to make sense of their changing lives. New hard goods, such as the VCR (video cassette recorder), disrupted the established audio-visual order and broke down the monopoly of the two national television channels. Seeing that VCRs had gained great popularity, especially in lower- and middle-income households, Greek film producers turned to direct-to-video films that were circulated in the thriving video library circuit. Through its generic variety, this short-lived video production appealed to many different audiences of that period, providing us with an example of the audio-visual consumption habits of 1980s' Greece. The goal of this chapter is to illustrate the rise of consumerism and the subsequent individualistic consumption within the special sociopolitical conditions appearing under PASOK's governing in the 1980s and to explain the focus shift of the audio-visual culture to domestic entertainment through the production and consumption of direct-to-video films of various genres and, in most cases, of the form of *pastiche*. As the local direct-to-video film industry produced c. 1,100 direct-to-video films within five years, it enables us to put forward a hypothesis concerning the taste of the Greek audience in relation to social mobility trends. As a conclusion, the chapter addresses issues of gender as an exemplary instance of domestic entertainment practices appealing to different audiences. Furthermore, through an investigation of the anthropological notions of gender in Greece, the direct-to-video representations could also be seen as a sign of the reconfiguration of traditional gender expectations and the advancement of a conservative society in terms of politics as well as ethics, which takes its first steps into postmodernity.

After the '*Allagi*': changing life, changing habits

Greece's post-war history is marked by specific periods of booming consumerism. The reshaping of large urban centers like Athens, following the arrival of more than 218,200 internal immigrants[1] in the years following 1955, led to what can be described as an asymmetrical and false urbanization.[2] This development was extensively supported by the boom in tourist and construction industries as well as the incoming flow of remittance from European and overseas immigrants.³ Especially in the 1960s, Greek society experienced, for the first time, a huge wave of consumption⁴ that followed a slow, delayed and problematic industrialization process. This boost in consumption was encouraged by the petty bourgeoisie who saw an opportunity to improve their living standards, followed by the dictatorship of 21 April 1967, when a new era of 'prosperity and mass consumption'⁵ was introduced.

Focusing our attention on social mobility after the restoration of democracy and the second wave of consumption in the 1980s, it is important that we understand the degree to which the socialist political party known as PASOK stood for a departure from the conservative postwar political strategies and the dictatorship (1967–74) and how it put an end in the nearly fifty-year-old dominance of the Greek Right. Within this historical context, the party's campaign catchphrases such as 'national independence', 'socialist transformation' and 'popular domination' played a pivotal role in Greece's postwar history, especially from 1981 to 1989. Based around the charismatic authority of its leader and future prime minister, Andreas Papandreou, PASOK's politics were a clear example of a populist⁶ political agenda that even though it provided Greece with newly-introduced quasi-hopeful institutions, i.e. the founding of ESY (National Health System) or the educational reformation in 1982, which affected all fields of social life, it also challenged what was perceived as actual socialist politics. The governing programme of PASOK, the 'Contract with the People' as it came to be known, can be understood as taking place in a contested space between a new-Keynesian economic model,⁷ showcased in the rise of 'non-privileged' Greeks' income, and the retrenchment of such politics that followed, when the government failed in fulfilling its main economic policies.

The tremendous growth in the numbers of public sector employees, growing from 15.4 per cent in 1951 to 21.3 per cent in 1983⁸ signified a process of transformation for certain social classes in Greece. It asserted that the 'ideology of the *upwards channel*', if we could use Poulantzas'⁹ phrase, would constitute one of the main desiderata of the 'non-privileged'. As part of this process, becoming a party member was a solid strategic move towards securing a post in the public sector. Spourdalakis¹⁰ contends that the geometrical increase of PASOK party members in 1984 up to 250,000, 70 per cent of which became members after the party's win in the national elections in 1981, is characteristic not only of the period's unemployment statistics but also of PASOK's primal intention of employing people who supported the movement. In this context, the 3 per cent rise¹¹ in the real income of the public sector employees relieved the lower- and middle-class strata of Greek society. Against this background, the Greek middle-class endorsement of PASOK became formative of a new way of life and serving as 'the backbone of *Allagi*',¹² as the party promoted social inclusion and advancement through a populist framework.

It should be noted that within this constantly changing social arena, PASOK's constitutional changes also began to affect some other aspects of Greek society, especially our cultural knowledge concerning gender and power. What is actually common in the cultural notions of gender and sexuality in social anthropology is that they are initially overcharged with a multiplicity of meanings and functions, especially in the Mediterranean Europe.[13] Especially, when it comes to rural Greece, anthropologists like Friedl[14] argue that still in the 1960s traditional patriarchic patterns – female subordination in contrast to a given male supremacy, stemming from the pre-capitalist period, were prevailing in the Greek society. Handman,[15] on the other hand, has asserted that Greek peasant women possessed a negative force, as a form of resistance against male subordination and Dubisch has argued that women were in no case some 'negligible part of the social system'[16] in which men are the leading force, but they own their personal strategies and targets.

However, some minor changes began to take place as early as 1922:[17] the constant presence of women in the Greek workforce, and their progressive economic independence and their participation in the educational institutions (high school, university), led to professional careers and the subsequent shrinking of the expanded family. In 1979, for the first time in Greek history, women could also join the army service and the police force. Furthermore, PASOK's government promoted some radical changes in family law. Starting from 1 January 1983, with the new constitutional amendment of Law 1329/134, gender equality was established: equal rights and equal obligations for spouses, consensual divorce and the abolition of the dowry. Alongside the establishment of women's clubs in Athens and other parts of Greece and the publication of women's journals, such as *O Agonas tis Gynaikas* (*Woman's Struggle*), the need for the redefinition of the 'other' and the fluid construction of gender roles introduced new occasions on which queer identities appeared to assert equal treatment.

It is important that we understand the degree to which the gay community asserted, in the late 1970s, its rights in a society acknowledged as 'explicitly retrogressive'.[18] AKOE (Apeleytherotiko Kinima Omofylofilon Elladas – Queer Liberation Movement) was founded in Athens in 1976 by Lukas Theodorakopoulos, who was also the publisher of *Amfi* (*Bi*) magazine. The same year, Christos Roussos, a nineteen-year-old man, killed his lover because he wanted him to work as a transvestite. Filmmaker Giorgos Katakouzinos, inspired by the true facts, shot in 1982 his film *Angelos*. In the meantime, the Greek transvestite Betty Vakalidou, also known as 'Betty', became the main character in a film by Dimitris Stavrakas (1979) and also in her autobiographical book (1980). In this new decade, trans Paola published her queer magazine *To Kraximo* (*The Caw*) while releasing her first poetry book *Saltarisma* (1985) on 'Odos Panos' publishing house in 1985.

Video practice and consumption as an 'index of identity'

From 1974 to 1987, the improvement of living standards combined with growing self-employment and the informal economy led to an expected increase in private consumption. Moreover, it showed a steady increase of approximately 2.91 per cent per year[19] and indicated the need for the further satisfaction of the consumer. As a product of urbanization, the Greek middle class was prone to consumerism and used it as a means for social advancement, all the while trying to adopt the lifestyle and habits of the upper class – especially its consuming habits, including designer clothing, expensive cars and luxurious housing, which, for instance could be a mimicry of American or European consuming trends, as represented in various soap operas or television serials. Thus, in the 1980s, the petty bourgeoisie had a more active role in the formation of a material culture of the Greek 'affluent society',[20] rather than an intellectual one. It is clear that increased consumption helped in acquiring that role, which traditional restricted social mobility used to make it seem inaccessible. In this light, Tsoukalas[21] also observes that the capitalist system maintains its equilibrium due to lower/middle-class consumption.

Myrizakis,[22] having investigated the infiltration of contemporary domestic technology in Greek households in the early 1980s, asserted that the financial status of the household members is firmly associated with the process of modernization of domestic hardware fuelled by the quick rise in the national per capita income. Urban centres also tended to excel in the acquisition of luxury electronic devices (e.g. electric fridge), alongside 'cultural goods', like the radio, television and telephone, all of which were perceived as transmitters of modern culture.[23]

In the early 1980s, the VCR, one of the newest luxurious domestic appliances, became a focal point[24] within the domestic entertainment framework, while complementing the television. ICAP's research survey in March 1987, carried out in 2,000 households across the country, mapped out the implications of the growing interest in VCRs: in September 1986, only 10 per cent of Greek households had a VCR.[25] By March the next year, this figure had risen to 18 per cent, encouraging an attempt at systematic video production and distribution, and the emergence of video clubs all over Greece. However, VCRs and the subsequent appearance of video rental libraries are not a Greek-only phenomenon. Greece was just one more case of a turn to domestic entertainment in a vast catalogue of similar phenomena to other countries.[26] At the beginning of the 1980s, the European video market, particularly in the United Kingdom, grew at a surprising rate[27] and underwent harsh criticism after a series of articles published in British tabloid the *Sun*.[28]

However, unlike in the United Kingdom, video-recorders took Greeks by storm and they actually established a flowering domestic direct-to-video film market that was popular from 1985 to 1990. In this sense, the last years of the 1980s extend our understanding of the privatization of leisure activities in Greece: this market is synonymous with movies shot with a video rather a film camera, while the editing was done in a video control unit. Typically, their screening time was c. ninety minutes and, after their final processing, they were distributed in the format of VHS exclusively via video libraries (or video clubs) for rent and mainly for private screening.

VCR, surpassing TV as the predominant technological form, 'assumes a position of dominance over the flow of screen' as an interference in its here-and-nowness, Cubitt argues,[29] which not only seizes precious time from the television flow but it can be considered as a device which produces pleasure and meaning, which in turn constitute subjectivities.[30]

Furthermore, video practice can be seen as the result of the symbolic reconstruction of VCR's primal function as a simple playback and recording medium. Embracing all aspects of the cultural commodities' industry, it operates as a 'component acquisition'.[31] In the wake of the 1980s, the lower and upper middle class, having experienced the beneficial effects of PASOK, were inclined to consume goods targeted at the 'beautification of the self', while at the same time hard goods, such as television sets and refrigerators, responded to leisure and home improvement needs – within and against[32] that background, consumerism really appears to be 'a mentality, behavioral motivation and individual action, as well as commercial institutions and a defining feature of society at large'.[33] A brand new perfect cosmos of technology is born of the production and consumption of exotic commodities, which transcend our previous technical knowledge and its value system. A luxurious imported commodity reveals how complex relations between technology, social interaction and consumption (as the holistic arena where identity is constructed) could be, as it constitutes 'the most valid index of identity'.[34]

Respectively, Giles[35] demonstrates that it was already in the beginning of the twentieth century that the commodification of the home in relation to gender positions and practices was established. Although it has been noted by Bowden and Offer[36] that all consumer durables during the interwar period in Europe and the USA were gender neutral and 'offered similar satisfaction to both men and women', it is important to emphasize that gender practices within the domestic setting should be 'regarded as most significant for the transformation of consumer culture',[37] which also has an impact on domestic practices. Although men appear as owners of the domestic appliances and 'domestic expenditure' lies in the hand of husbands,[38] women become involved in the decision-making about 'self-worth & identity', acquiring the 'cultural capital required to function as effective housewives'.[39]

Still, the VCR constituted a liberated form of expression, even if it had its commercial aspects. It is necessary to consider that, from their early beginnings, Greek radio and TV (established in 1938 and 1968 respectively) were always perceived as linked to and moulded by the political situation, characterized by a high degree of centralization[40] and frequent interventions by junta or the two major parties in Greek politics: PASOK and the right-wing ND (New Democracy). Their daily programme's profile promoted the higher art forms, such as theatre and cinema (including auteur films from Europe, the USA or the former Eastern Bloc); viewer ratings, however, were low, since the State-run television failed to develop an informal, everyday manner of communication so as to reflect the new ideological and aesthetic criteria emerging with consumerism at that time.

The deregulation of the audio-visual field after 1989 marked a turn of the dominant political line from the left to the right side of the spectrum and established a more neo-liberal strategy[41] through the promotion of privatization and the advancement and modernization of market mechanisms. The Greek media firms evolved rapidly into a dynamic sector with connections across the entire spectrum of the Greek economy. A step towards postmodernism, which is closely linked, according to Jameson, to 'the emergence of this new moment of late, consumer or multinational capitalism'.[42]

Consumption and Gender Post-Transition

Direct-to-video film genres: five years of fun, sadness and laughter

The VCR and the direct-to-video films in Greece proved themselves to be a challenging rival of the popular and auteur cinema of the 1980s. The political and social changes which Greece underwent in the period 1965–75 were affecting the Greek film industry, which boomed in the 1960s but then faced a decline until the mid-1970s, a period marked by the entry of TV in the life of the average Greek, and a drop in production and quality of the films produced.[43] This led to a fall in box-office sales and the closing of many cinema venues in Athens and in other regions. Despite efforts made at the end of the 1970s towards its rejuvenation by focusing on comedy as the dominant genre, popular Greek cinema in the mid-1980s faced problems similar to those of the 1960s and 1970s.[44]

When direct-to-video films emerged, popular cinema's production was diminishing and what was actually left from the New Greek Cinema's (NEK) tradition operated prohibitively for the Greek audience, which wasn't interested in the elaborate and 'difficult' readings of NEK's auteurs, like Theo Angelopoulos et al. This situation could be regarded as the reflection of a deeper contrast between highbrow and popular culture, meaning the different perceptions the Greeks held about the dominant cultural system of the time[45] and, especially, the big gap between the 'culture of the intellectuals', bearing influence from abroad, and the popular response from the lower classes.[46] The latter could be characterized as the ones who are keen to produce material culture and discard any complex cultural activity – Bourdieu argues that 'popular taste applies to the schemes of ethos, which pertain in the ordinary circumstance of life and so perform a systematic reduction of the things of art to the things of life'.[47] And direct-to-video films appeared to be that 'thing of life', bringing its spectators close to the different dimensions of their changing habitus.

An attempt at periodization and description of the commercial features and generic variety of the Greek direct-to-video films leads us to the distinction of three periods in their evolution, in terms of internal and external structure, outer form and inner content[48] (see Table 13.1). From 1985 to 1986, filmmakers embarked on their first tentative steps within the new format, identified by generic exploration, and the establishment of direct-to-video film personas, such as the Roma character Tamtakos, and subject-matters (i.e. adultery) directly transferred from the concurrent film production. The two years from 1986 to 1988 could be summarized as the golden age of the Greek direct-to-video-film.

This period is characterized by generic stability, the emergence of a local star-system and a burst of direct-to-video film companies.[49] In the last years until 1990, low budgets were held responsible for the direct-to-video films' cheap and kitsch aesthetics, examples of which could also be traced in everyday life.[50] Homogenized and poor quality products took the place of the former generic richness of the medium and actually worked as a *pastiche*[51] – a blank unsuccessful imitation of a genre or a formula, or a 'blank parody'. This operated as a clue to the country's transition to the postmodern era, especially due the deregulation after the arrival of free satellite TV (RAI, SKY, etc.) in 1988 and private TV channels (MEGA CHANNEL, ANT1, etc.) in 1989, which collided with a parallel shift towards a neo-liberal strategy and financial and social modernization.[52]

Table 13.1 Greek direct-to-video films produced from 1985 to 1990

	Greek Direct-to-Video Films
1985	77
1986	199
1987	366
1988	242
1989	202
1990	30
	1,116

Source: O.-E. Kassaveti (2014), *I Elliniki Videotainia (1985–1990). Eidologikes, Koinonikes kai Politismikes Diastaseis* (Athens: Asini), D. Koliodimos (2001), *Lexiko Ellinikon Tainion: Apo to 1914 eos to 2000* (Athens: Ekdoseis tou Genous).

It should be noted that the Greek direct-to-video film industry embraced older[53] and younger[54] Greek popular professional filmmakers. Also, older Greek popular cinema actors and actresses from the 1960s and 1970s[55] acted alongside a younger generation of actors and actresses of the 1980s. Standing beside them is the new generation of actors and actresses,[56] young professionals and sometimes amateurs.

Direct-to-video film comedies adopted the subject matter and conventions of the older Greek popular cinema, already known by the audience. Two major film genres, comedy[57]/romantic comedy[58] and melodrama, occupied a privileged place within the Greek direct-to-video film industry. Some filmmakers depart from the standard popular film genres and shot adventure or martial arts films, plus a few musicals alongside video-taped theatrical plays and soccer matches.

Apart from the direct-to-video market, older Greek, American, Turkish and Indian popular films were distributed by Greek video production companies, while newer films from the NEK and post-NEK tradition were released in the video format, aiming mainly at connoisseurs of cinema. In addition, it should be noted that the Greek auteur films' representations in some cases were closer to the European tradition, where nudism, representations of sexual acts and queer identities appeared on the screen and sometimes constituted symbols of sexual repression or even allegories on politics (such in the case of filmmaker P.P. Pasolini). However, the direct-to-video audience usually preferred simplistic narrations,[59] based a new renegotiation of older ones, also characterized by conservatism.

Putting forward a hypothesis: VCR spectatorships

What mainly constitutes the strength of this class-specific audio-visual consumption is apparently its power to produce popular pleasure among its spectators. It is suggested by

Fiske[60] that the social allegiances which are formed by subordinated people evoke popular pleasures that operate as an antidote to sociopolitical power – a power to control and to punish. Popular culture establishes its most important characteristics, relevance and productivity, through a process of constant battle between the power-block and the subordinate who seek to reject hegemony and denote their everyday life with an aesthetic or system that reflects their constant struggle – the struggle of change.[61]

DeCerteau was also correct in noting that 'the operational models of popular culture [...] exist in the heart of the strongholds of the contemporary economy', developing at the same extent the concept of culture as an elaborated terrain within conflictual relations between the weak and the poor.[62] Adjusting the direct-to-video films to their own needs, the ascending lower class identified itself with what was handy at the time but also adaptable to their exponential needs. Thus, VCR appeared as a major contribution to the construction of everyday representations and the circulation of meanings in 1980s Greece.

What can actually be discerned when examining the genre variety of the direct-to-video films of the 1980s is a vague indication about the gender aspects of domestic consumption of the era, as there has never been any quantitative research carried out. However, taking the sociopolitical and cultural ramifications of the period into consideration, alongside the incomparable domination of comedy, some inference can be drawn out, especially when it comes to female, male and child audiences.

The circulation of the first Greek video-films in the mid-1980s provided a new outlet for women's entertainment. During that decade, Ann Gray[63] mapped out the implications of technology operating in the domestic environment and the examined way gender played an active role in family decision-making regarding what was going to be watched. In Gray's research, the acquisition of a piece of domestic technology such as a VCR encouraged women's liberation from male domination of the remote control. Even if they were not as technically minded as men, women seemed to familiarize themselves with the VCR operating procedure on a regular basis, while they actually used the available generic categories for their selection of tapes for hire.

This actually leads us to the hypothesis that the re-emergence of older popular Greek film genres such as melodrama,[64] which apparently seemed old-fashioned and highly standardized in the swinging and fancy 1980s, did not take place due to a demand for an almost obligatory variety of direct-to-video genres. In fact, it was already in the 1960s, and throughout that decade, that the conservative Greek melodrama addressed the concerns of women alongside their position within the traditional patriarchal structures (female subordination in contrast to a given male supremacy) via a schematic treatment. However, comedy was usually the genre to articulate narratives whose main characters were liberated upper-middle class women. Some Greek film comedies of the late 1970s and early 1980s[65] could be seen as forerunners of the very significant changes described above, infiltrating comedy with some new trends concerning gender issues.

The Greek direct-to-video melodrama also constituted a domestic market, which targeted a female audience. This is definitely supported by the circulation of older Greek melodrama films of older decades and the huge trend of re-releases of older Indian and

Turkish films of the Yeşilçam[66] tradition in the VHS format, which were also very popular in Greek suburban cinemas and open-theatres in the 1960s and the 1970s.

The Greek direct-to-video melodrama films were almost exclusively shot by the playwright and filmmaker Makis Antonopoulos who believed that the impact of films such as *Love Story* (1970) had survived throughout the decades. His direct-to-video 'love-stories', such as *Horis Avrio* (1989), articulated a series of pessimistic narratives about mutual love between incompatible males and females. Although some female characters appear to be independent and working freelance in the 1980s, they are still tied to the same patriarchic structures as they appeared to be in the older Greek melodrama genre of the 1960s.

Promoting marriage as the ultimate goal of modern heterosexual couples could also be seen as the perpetuation of heteronormativity[67] and the marginalization of non-heterosexual practices. This is also indicative of the significant role which marriage plays in Greece, as 'familism [...] is the most important orientation in Greek life'[68] and it seemed that it still was, despite the emerging feminism and queer identities. In any case, queers are supposed to bear a 'moral stigma', lack a 'full humanity' and cannot form a family.[69]

Seen in this light, melodrama unsuccessfully tried to illustrate the desperation of inter-class conflicts in a modern world dominated by capitalism and consumerism, while it raised no ideological issues, as class barriers had already been broken. Having lost its valuable ritual[70] palliative function,[71] a function which suited large parts of the post-Second War World audience and provided them with hopeful allusions for their life and further survival, the Greek direct-to-video melodrama films strived to align themselves with real-life and institutions in modern Greece.

Furthermore, the screening of soap operas, like *Dallas*, on the two national Greek TV channels of the 1980s (ERT-1 and ERT-2) made direct-to-video melodramas central to the everyday audio-visual consumption of female audiences and had already been very popular, at least according to Nielsen's weekly spectatorship ratings. In addition, they were heavily promoted by the channels themselves.[72] *Dynasty*, another successful soap opera in Greece, had hit the first positions of the weekly TV stats, when its broadcast stopped and was planned to rebroadcast the following year. ERT-2's delay in buying the fourth season of *Dynasty* led Joy Video,[73] one of the many direct-to-video film and distribution companies in Greece, to buy the screening rights of the soap opera. The international financial strategy of *Dynasty*'s American production company, Metromedia, seemed to dictate such a move, since all their products had to be promoted firstly to film and video promoters and, secondly, to public television.

Although only one out of ten of its spectators were VCR owners,[74] the *Dynasty* tapes for hire were really popular in the video libraries, and they were heavily promoted in special VHS magazines. In any case, as Annette Kuhn argues, the popular narrative forms of melodrama, soap opera and Brazilian *telenovelas*,[75] as textual systems, are motivated by female desire, representations of wealth and intriguing heterosexual relationships and spectator identification, aimed at female audiences.[76] In Greece's instance, an acquaintance with older narrative forms of popular romance, such as the

Consumption and Gender Post-Transition

1950s–60s melodramas, may have allowed older women spectators, apart from younger ones, to watch soap operas as well as *telenovelas*. Drama as a realistic text, with its simplistic existing patterns of narratives aimed at different types of female personalities, tends to adapt to the expectations of women spectators who use it in order to produce popular pleasures.[77]

Male audiences' interests were captured by the martial arts and adventure direct-to-video films. Undoubtedly influenced by the vast American box-office successes of the genre,[78] which also circulated in the Greek video clubs, their numbers were relatively smaller than those of the video comedies and melodramas of the era. Usually exemplifying the vices and the glory of a single male character within a Manichean cosmos, they offered impressive representations of the struggle of a male hero to restore the disturbed narrative equilibrium. Despite the video filmmakers' attempts to shoot a decent direct-to-video action-adventure films,[79] the low budget greatly differentiated these works from their respective Hollywood counterparts.

At this point, we should put forward another argument about the audio-visual consumption of the Greeks, one that is a departure from a series of traditional and conservative representations of the 'other', towards more flexible and bold explorations in a vast market, which should include all genre categorizations, like hardcore sex films – which were by then only circulated in sex cinemas. The release of the latter on videocassettes to rent made them easily accessible for anyone (even teenagers) who wanted to watch them and found going to sex movie venues a taboo activity. Moreover, a link between the release of 1980s popular films about the 'other' in association with the rousing interest of some intellectuals (i.e folklorist Elias Petropoulos or author Leonidas Christakis,) and the queer community in the previous decade,[80] led Aloma, a Greek trans and president of the Greek trans community, to direct a series of hardcore direct-to-video pornographic films: *Ta Megala Kamakia Ton Travesti* (*Transvestites*), *To Spiti Tis Madame Aloma* (*Madame Aloma's House*) and *Oi Vlahoi Protimoun Travesti* (*Peasants Prefer Transvestites*) in 1989.

Even though hardcore sex tapes were being hired in the video clubs of the period, the Greek production companies mainly released films which were distributed by the foreign sex industry. Aloma's direct-to-video hardcore films were certainly aimed at male and also queer audiences, while becoming the first Greek direct-to-video venture to be produced by a member of the queer community. Despite their sketchiness and the amateur acting of their casts, they were more progressive than the first funny representations of queer stereotypes in the Greek popular cinema of the previous decades and their orchestrated moral panic,[81] also seen in video-films, such as *Oi Omofylofyloi* (*The Homosexuals*) by Giorgos Tsolakos in 1988. All the above examples could probably be seen as a faint sign of the audio-visual reconfiguration of traditional heterosexual masculinities, transcending the crystallized notion of Greek gender roles and to be empowered in the following decades (gay parade, LGBT festivals etc.).

Last but not least, children were represented by the release of dubbed Japanese *anime* series from video distribution companies, such as Joy or Gioconda Video. The first had circulated one of the most popular Japanese *anime* characters, Kagemaru Ingano, also known as 'Ninja Boy', and the latter a series of Taiwanese films with ninja kids, widely known as *Ta Mikra Ninjakia* (*The Little Ninjas*).[82] These became an inspiration for the direct-to-video pseudo-adventure films starring Chris Sfetas, a martial arts wonder-boy who starred in many films of this genre, alongside popular stars of the era, such as Sotiris Moustakas or Sotiris Tzevelekos, and other children of his age. Films like *Ta Mikra Ninjakia* and direct-to-video karate flicks with Sfetas might be seen as an alternative means of educating small children about their gender identity – the construction and development of masculinity values, as reflected through sports, muscular power and self-esteem.[83] In the case of the Greek family, *Kavounidi*,[84] examining family and employment in suburban Athens in the early 1980s, also suggests that the aim of marriage isn't simply the birth of children, but a struggle for the latter's successful social integration through the teaching of values.

To sum up, video films didn't only appeal to different audiences, but could import some new notions on gender, especially introducing video tapes with hardcore, mature queer subjects, in a country that in the previous decades had concealed its different subcultures and gender identities, On the other hand, some direct-to-video representations of women literally proved that female subordination hadn't ever ceased to exist and the struggle against patriarchal codes had a long way to go. Still, soap operas on videotape subverted this meaning and produced a new reading for Greek women, while children also found in the 'ninja' videotapes an educational means and perhaps a model for masculinity.

Conclusion

The fond regard in which the 1980s decade is held in Greece is not merely rooted in nostalgia for the eternal images of people hollering at the triumphant victory of the socialist party of PASOK in 1981 and the emergence of *Allagi* as its main sociopolitical project. The high standing of the 1980s in the Greek collective memory actually stems from the fundamental change in the perception of consumption and domestic entertainment in Greece based around VCRs and the Greek direct-to-video films of the 1980s. The rise of the lower and middle class, anxious to find a new social index to describe their newly-acquired economic status, credited to PASOK's strategies, associated VCR consumption with consumption per se. Disappointed by the everyday audio-visual narratives provided by popular and auteur cinema and public television, the Greeks turned to new audio-visual material for the means to describe this radical change in social life. The nearly 1,000 direct-to-video films, mostly based on a set of older narratives, mirrored the events of that time, accounting for their popularity which can be summarized in Fiske's quote: 'For a text to be popular it must "utter" what its readers wish to say, and must allow those readers to participate in their choice of utterances.'[85] Allowing for a repertoire of genres, the Greek direct-to-video films attracted different audiences, addressing issues of gender identities in a conservative society on the verge of transformation: showing a definite preference for romantic narratives, female audiences were keen on direct-to-video melodramas and popular soap operas, such as *Dallas* and *Dynasty*. Males turned to action-adventure films and also hardcore flicks, and kids to imported dubbed *anime* series. However, the five-year life of direct-to-video films, up until deregulation, recorded the jolts and major issues in terms of politics and social life of the new era, leading towards postmodernism. The VCR's life ended at the end of the 1980s when a set of scandals was revealed – the largest of which being the infamous 'Koskotas' scandal'[86] – in which many members of the government were found to be involved. Seen in today's light, their post-humous popularity could be a more-than-insignificant recorded change of the 1980s' 'structure of feeling', as defined by Raymond Williams.[87] And presumably, it was.

Notes

1. Bernard Kayser, *Anthropogeografia tis Ellados* (Athens: EKKE, 1968), pp. 107–13.
2. Silia Nikolaidou, *Koinoniki Organosi tou Astikou Horou* (Athens: Papazisis, 1993), pp. 118–22.
3. Grigoris Gizelis, Roxani Kaftantzoglou, Afroditi Teperoglou and Vasilis Filias, *Paradosi & Neoterikotita stis Politistikes Drastiriotites tis Oikogeneias. Metavallomena Shimata* (Athens: EKKE, 1984), p. 17.
4. Vasilis Karapostolis, *I Katanalotiki Syberifora stin Elliniki Koinonia (1950–1975)* (Athens: EKKE, 1984).
5. Kostis Kornetis, *Children of the Dictatorship. Student Resistance, Cultural Politics and the 'Long 1960s' in Greece* (New York, Oxford: Berghahn), p. 12.
6. Dimitris Haralambis, 'Anorthologika Periehomena enos Typika Orthologikou Systimatos', in X. Lyrintzis, X. Nikolakopoulos and D. Sotiropoulos (eds), *Koinonia kai Politiki. Opseis tis Tritis Ellinikis Dimokratias 1974–1994* (Athens: Themelio, 1996), pp. 289–311. Haralambis (1996) argues that PASOK's populism wasn't based on the market's laws, but on state interference, which resulted in the perpetuation of clientele politics. Angelos Elefantis, *Ston Asterismo tou Laikismou* (Athens: O Politis, 1991). Elefantis (1991) also describes PASOK as the 'loudspeaker of petit-bourgeois ideology'.
7. Michalis Spourdalakis, *PASOK. Domi, Esokommatikes Kriseis kai Sygentrosi Eksousias* (Athens: Exandas, 1988), pp. 288–93.
8. Konstantinos Tsoukalas, *Kratos, Koinonia, Ergasia sti Metapolemiki Ellada* (Athens: Themelio, 1987), p. 250.
9. Nikos Poulantzas, *Les classes sociales dans le capitalisme aujourd'hui* (Paris: Éditions du Seuil, 1974), p. 312.
10. Spourdalakis, *PASOK*, p. 296.
11. Giannis Voulgaris, *I Ellada tis Metapoliteysis (1974–1990). Statheri Dimokratia Simademeni apo ti Metapolemiki Istoria* (Athens: Themelio, 2002), pp. 161–3.
12. Konstantinos Tsoukalas, *Taksidi sto Logo kai tin Istoria. Keimena 1969–1996* (b') (Athens: Plethron, 1996), pp. 161–2.
13. Efthymios Papataxiarchis and Theodoros Paradellis, 'Eisagogi. Apo ti Skopia tou Fylou: Anthropologikes Theoriseis tis Syghronis Elladas', in E. Papataxiarchis and T. Paradellis (eds), *Taftotites kai Fylo sti Syghroni Ellada. Anthropologikes Proseggiseis* (Athens: Alexandreia, 1994), p. 44.

14. Ibid., p. 50.
15. Marie-Elizabeth Handman, *Via kai Poniria. Andres kai Gynaikes s' ena Elliniko Horio* (Athens: Kastaniotis, 1987), p. 104.
16. Jill Dubisch, 'Koinoniko Fylo, Syggeneia kai Thriskeia. Anaplathontas tin Anthropologia tis Elladas', in E. Papataxiarchis and T. Paradellis (eds), *Taftotites kai Fylo sti Syghroni Ellada. Anthropologikes Proseggiseis* (Athens: Alexandreia, 1994), pp. 104–5.
17. Gizelis, Kaftantzoglou, Teperoglou and Filias, *Paradosi kai Neoterikotita*, p. 86.
18. Kostas Yannakopoulos, 'Cultural meanings of loneliness: kinship, sexuality and (homo)sexual identity in contemporary Greece', (*Journal of Mediterranean Studies* 18.2, 2010), pp. 267–8.
19. Koula Kasimati, *Erevna gia ta Koinonika Haraktiristika tis Apasholisis – Meleti II. I Morfologia tis Defteris Apasholisis* (Athens: EKKE, 1998), p. 38.
20. Gizelis, Kaftantzoglou, Teperoglou and Filias, *Paradosi kai Neoterikotita*, p. 49.
21. Tsoukalas, *Kratos, Koinonia, Ergasia*, p. 259.
22. Giannis Myrizakis, 'I Dieisdisi tis Syghronis Technologias sto Elliniko Spiti kai i Stasi ton Ellinidon Miteron apenanti sti Syghroni Technologiki Ekseliksi kai tin Pyriniki Energeia', (*Epitheorisi Koinonikon Erevnon*, 53, 1984), pp. 55–73.
23. Gizelis, Kaftantzoglou, Teperoglou and Filias, *Paradosi kai Neoterikotita*, pp. 84–5.
24. According to the National Statistic Service of Greece (*Ethniki Statistiki Ypiresia Ellados*), the first VCRs for domestic use were imported en masse to Greece in 1979 (1,501 devices), but after two years imports reached 20,651 devices. In 1986 alone, VCRs imports reached a peak with 209,957 units, gradually decreasing from that point to the end of the decade. Also, during the period from 1986 to 1989, 2,082,363,817 blank videotapes were imported to Greece, a number to be reduced to one third of the total by 1989 when only 565,759,901 were imported.
25. *Eikones TV*, May 20–6 1987, 133, p. 187.
26. The USA came first in 1972, where video devices like the Cartrivision, a video recorder with excellent capabilities, had already served as a wonderful excuse to stay at home and enjoy.
27. John Ellis, *Visible Fictions: Cinema, Television, Video* (New York: Routledge & Kegan Paul, 1992), p. 270.
28. John Martin, *Seduction of the Gullible. The Truth behind the Video Nasty Scandal* (Plymouth: Stray Cat Publishing, 2007). This resulted in a wave of moral panic surrounding the 'video-nasties', usually horror, gore and porn films, which were banned from all the video libraries of the country with the accusation of corrupting youth.
29. Sean Cubitt, *Timeshift: On Video Culture* (London & New York: Routledge, 1991), p. 5.
30. Ibid., p. 4.
31. Vasilis Karapostolis, *Simbiosi kai Epikoinonia stin Ellada* (Athens: Alexandreia, 1987), p. 138.
32. Frank Trentmann, 'Beyond consumerism: new historical perspectives on consumption', *Journal of Contemporary History* 39.3, 2004, p. 376. Trentmann refers to P. Stearns' model of consumption, which describes the emergence of consumerism in Europe in two stages. The first one focuses on 'dress and household items', while the second, which begins as early as the mid- to late nineteenth century, is marked by the 'profusion of goods and leisure, the proliferation of retail outlets, and the spread of consumerist values into different social spheres as diverse as childreading and pornography'. However, in modern societies, this model has been transcended by the bare reality and appears to be 'a mentality [...] as well as commercial institutions'. About Stearns, see Peter N. Stearns, *Consumerism in World History. The Global Transformation of Desire* (New York: Routledge, 2001).

33. Trentmann, 'Beyond Consumerism', p. 377.
34. Karapostolis, *Simbiosi kai Epikoinonia*, p. 138.
35. Judy Giles, 'Class, gender and domestic consumption in Britain 1920–1950', in E. Casey and L. Martens (eds), *Gender and Consumption. Domestic Cultures and the Commercialisation of Everyday Life* (Basingstoke: Ashgate, 2007), p. 18.
36. Susan Bowden and Avner Offer, 'The technological revolution that never was: gender, class, and the diffusion of household appliances in interwar England', in V. de Grazia and E. Furlough (eds), *The Sex of Things. Gender and Consumption in Historical Perspective* (Berkeley, CA, Los Angeles, Oxford: University of California Press, 1996), p. 246.
37. Elizabeth B. Silva, 'Gender, class, emotional capital and consumption in family life', in E. Casey and L. Martens (eds), *Gender and Consumption: Domestic Cultures and the Commercialisation of Everyday Life* (Basingstoke: Ashgate, 2007), pp. 141–59.
38. Giles, 'Class, gender and domestic consumption', p. 19.
39. Ibid., p. 19.
40. Stylianos Papathanasopoulos, *I Tileorasi kai to Koino tis* (Athens: Kastaniotis, 2000), pp. 42–3.
41. Ibid., p. 44.
42. Fredric Jameson, 'Postmodernism and consumer society', in H. Foster (ed.), *The Anti-Aesthetic: Essays on Postmodern Culture* (Washington: Bay Press, 1983), p. 125.
43. Chrysanthi Sotiropoulou, *Elliniki Kinimatografia 1965–1975. Thesmiko Plaisio – Oikonomiki Katastasi* (Athens: Themelio, 1989), pp. 155–7.
44. Orsalia-Eleni Kassaveti, *I Elliniki Videotainia. Eidologikes, Koinonikes kai Politismikes Diastaseis* (Athens: Asini, 2014), pp. 72–3.
45. Grigoris Gizelis, *To Politismiko Systima. O Simeiotikos kai Politismikos Haraktiras tou* (Athens: Grigoropoulos, 1980), pp. 60–82.
46. Gizelis, Kaftantzoglou, Teperoglou and Filias, *Paradosi kai Neoterikotita*, p. 49.
47. Pierre Bourdieu, *Distinction: A Social Critique of the Judgement of Taste* (Cambridge, MA: Harvard University Press, 1994), p. 5.
48. Kassaveti, *I Elliniki Videotainia*, pp. 32–4.
49. Liana Kanelli, 'Krach sti Videogora', (first published in *To Vima tis Kyriakis* and republished in *Ta Theamata*, 1988), p. 22.
50. Panayis Panagiotopoulos, 'Kitsch', in V. Vamvakas and P. Panagiotopoulos (eds), *I Ellada sti Dekaetia tou '80. Koinoniko, Politiko kai Politismiko Lexiko* (Athens: To Perasma, 2010), pp. 267–71.
51. Fredrick Jameson, *To Metamoderno i i Politismiki Logiki tou Ysterou Kapitalismou* (Athens: Nefeli, 1999), pp. 52–6.
52. Maria Komninou, *Apo tin Agora sto Theama* (Athens: Papazisis, 2001), p. 180.
53. Popular filmmakers Odysseas Kosteletos, Kostas Karagiannis, Apostolos Tegopoulos, Nikos Foskolos, Omiros Efstratiadis and Giannis Dalianidis, whose name was a synonym for the old Greek popular film production, made a huge comeback in the direct-to-video film market.
54. In this instance, filmmakers, such as Vangelis Fournistakis or Kostas Bakodimos and scriptwriter Giorgos Mylonas, a video-film director himself, have been known from the 1970s popular cinema.
55. That is, Kostas Hadjihristos, Giannis Gionakis, Rena Vlahopoulou and Nikos Xanthopoulos.
56. That is, Stamatis Gardelis, Pavlos Evangelopoulos, Panos Michalopoulos, Christos Callow and Vina Asiki, Kaiti Finou, Lila Kafantari and Sofia Aliberti.

57. With subject matter such as adultery and infidelity or funny underdogs trying to survive in the PASOK era (*Gia mia houfta touvla*, 1989). Furthermore, it presented certain characters, such as high-school students (*Akros koufo kollegio*, 1987), clergymen (*O Papa-Faganas*), gypsies (*O Teleytaios Gyftokratoras*, 1988), army officers (*Commandos kai Vlimata*, 1987), private detectives (*O Anoihtomatis*, 1987) and juvenile delinquents (*Batsoi Poulane tin Iroini*, 1989).

58. *Radiopeirati, Agapi mou*, 1988.

59. Arthur Asa Berger, *Narratives in Popular Culture, Media, and Everyday Life* (Thousand Oaks, CA, London: Sage, 2010), p. 10.

60. John Fiske, *Understanding Popular Culture* (London, New York: Routledge, 1991), p. 49.

61. Ibid., pp. 56–8.

62. Michel DeCerteau, *The Practice of Everyday Life* (Berkeley, CA, Los Angeles & London: University of California Press, 1988), p. 25.

63. Ann Gray, *Video Playtime. The Gendering of Leisure Technology* (London & New York: Routledge, 1992).

64. Thomas Schatz, *Hollywood Genres. Formulas, Filmmaking, and the Studio System* (New York: McGraw-Hill, 1981), pp. 223–6. A film genre, which was very tenuously related to the equivalent 1950s' American Hollywood generic model revolving around family and race issues in the postwar age.

65. *Oi Fantarines*, 1979 and *O Teleftaios Andras*, 1982 or comedy direct-to-video films, such as *I Drakaina*, 1987.

66. Nezih Erdoğan, 'Narratives of resistance: national identity and ambivalence in the Turkish melodrama between 1965 and 1975', in D. Eleftheriotis and G. Needham (eds), *Asian Cinemas: A Reader and Guide* (Edinburgh: Edinburgh University Press, 2006), p. 232; Savas Arslan, 'High Yeşilçam II: genres and films', in S. Arslan, *Cinema in Turkey: A New Critical History* (New York: Oxford University Press, 2010), pp. 125–200. Yeşilçam, the popular Turkish cinema of the late 1950s until the 1970s, became a decisive factor in advancing the Greek melodrama genre. The popular Turkish melodramas, which were actually another generic category inspired by Indian cinema and traditional Turkish theatre, do not differ much from the Greek films in terms of cinematograpic style, female and masculine character types and plot settings.

67. Kostas Yannakopoulos, 'Istories Sexoualikotitas', in K. Yannakopoulos (ed.), *Sexualikotita. Theories kai Politikes tis Anthropologias* (Athens: Alexandreia, 2006), p. 33.

68. Peter Loizos and Eythymios Papataxiarchis, 'Introduction. gender and kinship in marriage and alternative contexts', in P. Loizos and E. Papataxiarchis (eds), *Contested Identities. Gender and Kinship in Greece* (Princeton, NJ: 1991), p. 3.

69. Peter Loizos and Eythymios Papataxiarchis, 'Gender, sexuality, and the person in Greek culture', in P. Loizos and E. Papataxiarchis (eds), *Contested Identities. Gender and Kinship in Greece* (Princeton, NJ: 1991), pp. 227–8.

70. Rick Altman, *Film/Genre* (London: BFI, 2002), pp. 59–61.

71. Aglaia Mitropoulou, *Ellinikos Kinimatografos* (Athens: Papazisis, 2006), p. 31.

72. 'Apopse Dallas kai Syzitisi', *Mesimbrini*, 12 February 1982, p. 13.

73. D. Golema, 'Meta 8 Mines i Dynasteia', *Ta Nea*, 16 October 1985, 27, 'Giati i Dynasteia metakomise sto Video', 17 November 1985, *Ta Nea*, p. 19.

74. 'Plokamia, Mafia kai Kassetes', *Eikones TV*, 1–7 April 1987, p. 87.

75. Thomas Tufte, *Living with the Rubbish Queen. Telenovelas, Culture and Modernity in Brazil* (Luton: University of Luton Press, 2000), i.e. *Sinhá Moça/Mikri Kiria* (1986) or *Malu* (1986), which were broadcast on Greek public television in the late 1980s.

76. Annette Kuhn, 'Women's genres: Melodrama, soap opera and theory', in C. Gledhill (ed.), *Home is where the Heart is. Studies in Melodrama and the Woman's Film* (London: BFI, 1987), p. 339.
77. Ien Ang, *Watching Dallas. Soap Opera and the Melodramatic Imagination* (Oxford: Routledge, 1989), p. 20.
78. i.e. *Rocky*, 1976 or *Rambo*, 1982.
79. In extreme instances, some adventure direct-to-video films were shot in cosmopolitan Greek islands, such as Kos (*Kos, to Kynigi ton Paranomon*, 1986) or even on Mount Olympus (*Olympos, Thanatos stin Katoikia ton Theon*, 1986).
80. A year after the release of *Angelos*, popular filmmaker from the 1960s, Vangelis Melissinos, directed the film *E . . . kai loipon!/To Soutien tou Baba mou* (1983), a loose adaptation of Edouard Molinaro's *La Cage aux Folles* (1978).
81. Popular comedy representations included the 'twink' stereotype or a transvestite, who were rejected by men and befriended by women and mainly ridiculed for their sexual orientation. Their sexual preferences served as an example to avoid, especially for children, as their morale was low.
82. *Lucky Seven*, 1986.
83. Sherry Ortner, 'Einai to Thiliko gia to Arseniko O,ti i Fysi gia ton Politismo?', in A. Bakalaki (ed.), *Anthropologia, Gynaikes kai Fylo. Keimena ton S. Ortner, M. Strathern and M. Rosaldo* (Athens: Alexandreia, 1994), pp. 99–107. As Ortner notes, 'woman associates herself with the structurally inferior domestic space and is held responsible for the crucial operation of her babies' transformation' to civilized human beings.
84. Jenny Kavounidi, *Oikogeneia kai Ergasia stin Athina* (Athens & Komotini: A. N. Sakkoulas, 1996), pp. 59–60.
85. Fiske, *Understanding*, p. 146.
86. Entrepreneur Yorgos Koskotas arrived in Greece from the USA in the late 1970s. He became an administrative officer in Trapeza Kritis (Creta Bank), of which he became the main owner, while he extended his financial activities within the publishing and football arenas. Shortly before the end of the 1980s, it was discovered, mainly after the attack of older publishers, such as Kitsos Tegopoulos (*Eleytherotypia*) that Koskotas had embezzled more than 80 billion drachmas, while he claimed he had cooperated with PASOK's government. He was arrested in the USA, where he served his sentence until 2001.
87. Raymond Williams, *The Long Revolution* (New York: Broadview Press, 2001), pp. 64–5.

CHAPTER 14
REVISITING THE GREEK 1980s THROUGH THE PRISM OF CRISIS[1]
Panagiotis Zestanakis

On 8 July 2012, I passed by a detached house in Maroussi, an upper-middle class suburb in Athens. Ioanna, then sixty-five and retired, was previously a well-paid employee at the Bank of Greece and mother of two teenagers in the late 1980s. She had agreed to assist my research project entitled 'Lifestyles, Gender Relations and Social Spaces in 1980s Athens' with an interview.[2] Since she spends most of her summertime in Syros, an island close to Athens, we needed to have three phone conversations to arrange an interview meeting. During these conversations Johanna posed the following question at least twice: 'But what kind of history can you write about the 1980s? It was a period of prosperity, an era of abundance! It was a golden age!'

Ioanna's objection is understandable. In Greece, from the 1990s to the present, oral history has been mainly used by historians focusing on turbulent periods, such as the experience of occupation or the civil war years.[3] Consequently, many interviewees felt astonished at my invitation to speak about everyday life issues during the 1980s such as changes in consumption habits, gender relations and cultural geographies.

In general, before the recent economic crisis, the 1980s were considered as a period of stability and relative affluence. After the political changeover of 1974 the country consolidated democratic stability, experienced noticeable economic growth, gained full participation in the European integration project and improved its public infrastructure.[4] Consumption standards improved. Modern, expensive technological products (such as VCRs) appeared in the living rooms of lower and middle class households.[5] In Athens, the reorganization of entertainment politics was further associated with conspicuous consumption; something evident in the popularization of expensive entertainment practices (e.g. going out to bouzoukia halls and drinking imported drinks, such as whisky).[6] Gender relations also changed. Albeit the patriarchal family remained the main organizational social unit, premarital relations that were quite common at least since the 1970s experienced further diffusion. Indicatively, in 1991, one in three female students of the University of Athens stated that they had had sexual relations before adulthood while according to a similar survey this percentage was only 17 per cent in 1981.[7]

The climate of optimism was evident.[8] Opinions on the 'happy go lucky 1980s' survived until very recently. A survey held a few months before the beginning of the current financial crisis showed that 36 per cent of the respondents saw the elections of 18 October 1981 as the most crucial turning point in post-dictatorship political history. The same respondents viewed Andreas Papandreou as the most important politician of the Third Hellenic Democracy (1974 to the present) and PASOK's (Panhellenic Socialist Movement) first term in office (1981–5) as the most successful in the post 1974 period.[9]

And then the crisis came. Detailed quantitative data cannot be analytically presented here,[10] but very briefly, in 2011 Greece had the second highest unemployment rate in the European Union, 18.4 per cent, after Spain.[11] The Greeks, who previously had experienced an 'economic miracle' based on credit expansion, the construction of public works and a real estate boom, saw the consumerist certainties of the previous decades disintegrate.[12] To use historian Antonis Liakos' words, if *Metapolitefsi*[13] represented 'a fluid, temporal place encapsulating expectations, disenchantments and feelings of nostalgia', the crisis represented a cause for dislocation of many of the certainties which this temporal place had been associated with.[14]

So, how do the Greeks see the 1980s now? Imagining the public sphere as a discursive space in which individuals and groups congregate to discuss matters of mutual interest,[15] this chapter reflects on (re)valuations of the 1980s in the contemporary Greek public sphere. The analysis focuses on the period before the double elections of 6 May and 17 June 2012; the 'double electoral earthquake' that radically altered the Greek political map.[16] The chapter attempts to show how perceptions of the current crisis were shaped in part by comparisons with a more optimistic, affluent and safer recent past focusing on two points; first, on debates on the emergence of a lifestyle media industry after the mid 1980s, its growing influence in the 1990s and the 2000s and its decay in the years of the crisis. The second part problematizes the conceptualizations of 1980s' 'prosperity' claiming that this 'prosperity' should be examined not only in association with the diversification of consumption opportunities but also as a consequence of the then limited anxieties about everyday safety. Furthermore, the chapter interrogates how the crisis brought to the fore new questions on perceptions regarding gender identities, placing particular emphasis on participatory web cultures. I perceive gender in terms of performativity, namely construed as an identity tenuously constituted in time through a stylized repetition of acts, which have to be conceptualized.[17] Furthermore, taking into account that, as communication scholar Julia Wood has argued, media are among the most pervasive and powerful influences on how gender is re(seen) in contemporary societies, and also that memory represents an engendered terrain, this chapter interrogates the potential remoulding of the interconnections between changes around the perception of gender norms and identities in a very recent past, and memories from the transformation of the Greek mediascape in the last thirty years.[18] More specifically, the crisis saw a shift regarding the relations between masculinity and conspicuous consumption: lifestyle discourses as a dominant component of the post-late-1980s mediascape are often criticized in various media. Commitment to such discourses is often discussed as promoting the feminization of men and as advocating 'corruptive' and 'undesirable' performances of masculinity. Thus, as we will see later in more detail, the 'effeminized consumer man' of the 1990s and the 2000s is discussed as a negative historical protagonist of the last thirty years.

I draw on three different primary sources. First, from oral interviews conducted in Athens between January and August 2012.[19] Secondly, the chapter relies upon evidence originating from mainstream media, such as newspapers and magazines. Thirdly, taking into account the claim that electronic and social media constitute an important, active part of our everyday experiences that are crucial in the emergence of new testimonial cultures and in the formation of public history, the chapter is based upon 'webnographical' research findings.

Traditional and social media are here addressed as supplementary. According to media scholar Henry Jenkins, we are currently living in a condition of convergence culture where individuals are affected simultaneously by traditional and new, participatory media.[20] Furthermore, as media scholar Stig Hjarvard argues, contemporary societies are 'mediatized'. Media become an integrated part of institutions like politics, work and religion as more and more of these institutional activities are performed through interactive and mass media.[21] Inevitably, formation of memory politics does not stay untouched by these developments. The proliferation of cheap access to digital technologies and the popularization of social and participative technologies have increasingly enabled both the mediation and mediatization of individual memories.[22] Expanding the analysis beyond mainstream media's 'official public sphere', I argue that the reconceptualizations of the 1980s cannot be fully examined without taking into account the representations originating from 'unofficial culture'.

Speaking about lifestyle when lifestyle is dying

The 1980s were a period of affluence and growing privatization for the Greek media industry.[23] The emergence of new media promoting 'lifestyle' was one of the main developments of the period between the late 1980s and the late 2000s. In the Greek context, contrary to its international sociological definition, the term 'lifestyle' refers to particular sets of discourses that were promoted by the cultural industry in the 1980s, especially by popular magazines mainly addressed to young audiences such as *Cosmopolitan*, *Playboy* and *Click*. Such representations took hold in the 1990s on private TV channels and experienced great success until the beginning of the recent economic crisis. Lifestyle discourses, usually advocated by journalists born after 1960, promoted conspicuous consumption, sexual liberalization and increased participation in the growing economies of pleasure. Furthermore, these discourses illustrated specific goods, services and experiences, such as branded clothes, jewellery, clubbing, expensive sports, travel abroad and regular change of seductive sexual partners as synonyms of modernity, Westernization and better quality of life. Although it is hard to estimate the appeal of cultural products that have been described as 'gnawing' vectors of lifestyle, the periodicity of discourses provides quantitative evidence of the fact that such representations experienced considerable success in recent decades.[24]

As I have already mentioned, from 2008, the Greek crisis radically changed the economic situation. Described as the most severe version of the tough crises that affected many European countries, it attracted international scientific and journalistic interest.[25] Briefly, in April 2010 the national debt was downgraded to junk-bond status and Prime

Minister George Papandreou announced that Greece had to resort to the European Union and the International Monetary Fund. Until the 2012 double elections, the crisis can be divided into three phases: the first tallies with the period 2008–9 and was characterized by the development of an illusion of immunity. The next stage runs across the last months of 2009 and first ones of 2010 when most Greeks realized the extent of the recession. The third stage started in the first months of 2011 and lasted until the double elections. During this stage, discourses about austerity monopolized the public sphere along with anti-German sentiments and stereotypes, which came to the fore after decades of oblivion.[26]

Since my research project started in November 2010, its progress went hand in hand with a deepening crisis that decimated advertising expenditures and saw the breaking down of the lifestyle media industry.[27] In January 2013, Antonis Lyberis, owner of 'Lyberis Editions', one of the most prestigious lifestyle media enterprises in Athens, announced the closure of his company due to debts. Petros Kostopoulos had taken a similar decision just a few months before. The collapse of these enterprises attracted public interest. In particular, the seizure of IMAKO, Kostopoulos' company, was described as a 'symbolic funeral' of lifestyle discourses and their influences and as the end of a 'corruptive itinerary' that started in the 1980s.[28]

According to most of my interviewees, the influence of lifestyle discourses was noticeable in the 1980s and vast after the early 1990s. Their success was based on various factors; innovating a saturated mediascape, lifestyle magazines were different from previous media.[29] In terms of layout, they were printed on big coloured pages including rich photographic material and reproducing the graphic design of successful titles such as the British *Face*, the French *Actuel* and the Finnish *City*.[30] Representational politics that had been proven successful in various countries not only of the 'mediatically advanced world' (e.g. the United Kingdom) but also of the European periphery (e.g. Finland and Spain), were introduced in the Greek mediascape. Such interactions show that mediascape formation took place through complicated processes committed to that of parallel modernities, providing another interesting example of cultural interactivity among peripheral countries.[31] In the case of Greece and Spain, whose late-modern cultures were determined through events that took place in the 1981–2 period, media modernization a few years 'after the fear was over' provides evidence that democratization was experienced as a process implying the modernization and radicalization of representational politics.[32] *Click*, a magazine title openly critical of the intense politicization of the first post 1974 years and the subsequent penalization of mass culture, and definitely the most discussed title in the crisis years, claimed *Ajo Blanco*, whose *segunda etapa* experienced significant success in late 1980s Spain, selling around 50,000 copies on a monthly basis, as a source of inspiration.[33] *Click*'s radical representational politics have been stamped in the memory of some of my interviewees such as M.A., a female university student and private sector worker in the late 1980s: '[*Click*] was a revolution [… *Click*] was speaking more openly on sexuality and was depenalizing pleasure. […] *Click* codified the slogans we were using. [Our] lines. Suddenly [our lines] became emblems'.[34]

Webnographical research findings provide further evidence of how Greeks dealt with the recent collapse of the lifestyle industry. Indicatively, here I use some testimonies from the forum of www.bourdela.com, a website that at the beginning of 2013 had more than 130,000 registered users, 'clones' included. Although the website is devoted to paid sex services, it includes many threads on various topics such as politics, sport, science and religion. Most users are men.[35]

A thread entitled 'Kostopoulos, Kostopouloi, I alloiosi ton charaktiristikon tou Ellina' (Kostopoulos, Kostopouloi, the alienation of the features of the Greek man) is interesting. It was initiated on 16 December 2011 and up until 16 September 2014 included 1,596 posts.[36] In the thread, the 1980s are often described as an era of frivolity, when the Greeks got spoiled and became accustomed to living beyond their means. The expansion of consumer credit and the diffusion of new banking products such as fast cash advance loans, no deposit car finance and credit cards are discussed as alienating and corruptive practices. Furthermore, the diffusion of such practices that were promoted by lifestyle discourses is discussed as alienating for an abstractly defined 'right' performance of Greek masculinity, which certainly has to be characterized by continence and industriousness. The biological connotations of the first post are quite characteristic. 'Kostopoulos. PASOK's curse that maimed [the] Greek man's DNA. After PASOK [the party] of Andreas [Papandreou] and Kostopoulos came into power the grafter and reflective Greek man was transformed into the scummy, noov person of nowadays [...] Street-toughness, fart, illiteracy and PASOK [...] For this reason we went morally, politically, socially and economically bankrupt.'[37]

The long conversation that follows is organized around two major axes. The first one resonates with the initial post downgrading the active role of audiences in the reception process and arguing that the representational politics of the 1980s distorted the previous performances of Greek masculinity that are described as authentic and superior. The systematization of male interest in issues that were previously considered as 'designed' for females, such as fashion trends and beauty care practices, is described as a negative development. Divested from its masculinity, the man alienated by the 'lifestyle' is profiled as effeminate. Consequently, the years following the late 1980s are discussed as a 'corrupting' period.

This point echoes the remark by historian Efi Avdela about gender politics during the Greek crisis. According to Avdela, unemployed men are often perceived as lacking a primary feature of their male identity; as women are more often economically inactive, such men are characterized as effeminate since in Greece masculinity is associated with diligence.[38] In the extracts above we can see a pertinent characterization. Performances of masculinity associated with conspicuous consumption and interest in practices often conceived as addressed to women, such as beauty care, are described as incompatible with the identities of the 'man-fighter' and the 'man-provider'.

Users adopting the second approach describe lifestyle as an attractive set of discourses introduced from abroad, but the subjects' possibilities in negotiating these are not discounted, nor is the dimension of selective choice discarded. The emergence of lifestyle discourses is addressed as part of a broader process; the systematization of cultural contacts between Greece and Western Europe in a period of transition regarding media and representational politics. The following post is representative:

> I remember that the magazines were sold at the kiosks [...] Nobody bought these titles at gunpoint. I also remember – because I was young and I used to buy lifestyle magazines as a teenager – nobody advised us to take loans to give ourselves airs or to sell our grandmothers' fields in the village to [buy] better cars. In any case, the magazines showed us a way of life but we were not obliged to follow this path. [...] Sometimes we were buying these magazines to see a piece of ass or to see if any new clubs had opened.[39]

Although most of these users avoid taking a black and white approach and sometimes attempt to historicize the phenomenon, occasionally through their personal experiences, feelings of chagrin and being let down are frequently expressed in the posts. Taking into account that most of the posts were sent in the politically turbulent period between December 2011 and April 2012[40] during which Kostopoulos' company finally went bankrupt, such texts reflect the users' difficulties in reconciling with a painful process of disenchantment in the decay of the concept of the 'prosperous' 1980s. As we will see, this process has emerged as a highly conflicted issue, used for various purposes during the crisis.

Memories from a 'period of prosperity'

Since 2010, many Greeks have responded to the intervention of the International Monetary Fund and the European Union into the country's domestic affairs with disappointment and anger. Labour unions and opposition parties organized impressive demonstrations. In one of them, in May 2010, three bank employees were burned alive during riots. Many Greeks felt 'betrayed by the political system', which was often pinpointed as responsible for cultivating illusions of well being after the mid-1980s. Various dividing lines emerged: the main division was between those claiming that the implementation of the so-called memorandum politics represented the less painful solution if Greece wanted to avoid an irregular bankruptcy, and those who argued that this type of politics was a shameful intervention in the internal affairs of Greece. New borderlines overlaid the major pre-existing political division between the left and the right and were organized around issues such as the uses of populism or differentiations between cultural and social performances of left-wing politics.[41] Such transcendences were clearly detected in the *kinima ton plateion* (movement of squares) – a Greek version of the Spanish *movimiento de los indignados* where protesters from the left coexisted quite harmoniously with protesters belonging to the far right.[42] Stereotypes from the 1940s came again to the fore and hate speech emerged as a dominant component of a mediascape characterized by growing polarization.[43] The governments that signed the memoranda were characterized as 'Tsolakoglou governments' after Georgios Tsolakoglou, the first prime minister of the collaborationist government during the occupation of Greece in the Second World War.[44]

Presumably these conditions contribute to the fact that most of the interviewees described their life experiences in the 1980s by using positive terms. In the interviews, foci of nostalgia about the 1980s are formed in two axes: first, around consumption. Across both gender and age, many informants argued that although some imported commodities such as cars or electronic equipment were very expensive in the 1980s, the overall situation was better insofar as basic goods and services such as food or public transport were cheaper; the latter became more expensive in the years that followed the integration of the country into the Eurozone. Such narrations perhaps mirror the strengthening of Euroscepticism since late 2009: only 26 per cent of the Greeks trusted the European Union in May 2012 compared to 56 per cent in November 2009.[45]

Occasionally, nostalgia for the 1980s is constructed in terms of retrofuturism, namely around a fascination for images and potential perspectives of the future. Images of a better quality of life flourished after 1981; a year that seems to represent a milestone.[46] In the interviews, the fascination with the future is often organized around memories of the modernization of consumption choices. These memories reproduce narrations detected in traditional and new media of the same period. For instance, in March 2011 the lifestyle magazine *Nitro* hosted a big tribute to the prosperous nightlife of 1980s and 1990s Athens.[47] Tributes to the 1980s were published in various webpages and blogs in the same period.

Some of my informants who experienced the cultural transition of the 1980s as youngsters still seem seduced by its reconfigurative dynamics. In this case, retrofuturism seems to be associated with the challenge of Europeanization. Facts such as the radical renovation of the mediascape and the generalized cultural extroversion provided new experiences for consumers. Images of a better quality of life flourished; even if they did not materialize in the years that followed, their impact is evident in the descriptions of some interviewees, such as P.K. or K.Z., two university students, a male and a female respectively, from upper-middle class Athenian families. In this case, nostalgia did not originate from satisfaction about the actual quality of cultural life but rather coalesced around expectations about the future and the Europeanization of the Greek capital's cultural life. The designation of Athens as the first European Capital of Culture in 1985 emerges as an event of pivotal importance:

> In the years 1981–85 Greece really lived [in] a period of affluence. [. . .] I remember the summer when Melina [Merkouri] organized the cultural capital and we were going from one theatre to another. [. . .] It was an absolute optimism.[48]

> I went to The Cure. [. . .] There were some concerts in Athens. [. . .] I had seen big names such as Ray Charles. Many artists. And I owe it to this decade.[49]

In such narratives we can see an interesting challenge about the relations between masculinity, femininity and retrofuturism. As retrofuturism is often associated with the concept of technological progress and technology is often considered as a preferential area for men, expectations of retrofuturism may be more likely in men's interviews. In some interviews, retrofuturism is associated with the perspective of cultural enrichment and modernization. In this respect, retrofuturism is significant in narrations by women as well as by men.

Memories from a 'period of safety'

The second axis rests on everyday safety. Since 2005, Athenians have believed their city to be the most dangerous European capital.[50] In fact, fears about the rise of crime in Athens go back to the late 1970s if not earlier. At any rate, Athens in the 1980s was not a crimeless place. On the contrary, in the early 1980s the popular press often represented the city as 'Chicago in Progress'.[51] Additionally, almost 1,000 robberies took place in Greece in 1991.[52] These public anxieties are not mentioned in the interviews. On the contrary, narrations describe Athens as an almost absolutely safe place. Four interviewees with different sociocultural backgrounds provide indicative descriptions which confirm this: T.P., a male high-school student born in the late 1960s; G.P., a male civil engineer born in the early 1940s; E.A., a female aesthetician born in the mid-1950s and E.P., a female private sector employee born in the mid-1960s. In the 1980s, they were living in Aghia Paraskevi, an upper-middle class district; Pagrati, a middle-class central neighbourhood; Exarchia, a central neighbourhood widely known for its student life and as an anarchist quarter and Kallithea, a lower-middle class area.

> I felt very safe. I was walking around Athens at 3 a.m. or 4 a.m. and I never felt threatened... In the summertime – we were living on the first floor – I was sleeping on the balcony. [...] Today, I couldn't even think about it.[53]

> [In the 1980s] Athens was definitely safer [than today]. My house in Lagonissi[54] has been robbed three times. [...] Then the doors were open.[55]

> There was no fear regarding security. You could walk around any time. And I am a chicken...[56]

> I never felt any sense of insecurity. [...] We were living in a raised ground-floor [...] We were sleeping with the door unlocked and the windows open.[57]

To use Svetlana Boym's term we can potentially locate expressions of 'restorative nostalgia' here.[58] According to Boym, the rhetoric of restorative nostalgia is not organized around the past but rather values obtaining a hyper-chronic status. Safety seems to emerge in such a concept in the narrations as highlights of everyday unsafety before the early 1990s seem to have retreated to the margins of the interviewees' memories. Furthermore, these narrations implicitly refer to the advent of immigrants in Athens from the early 1990s by linking them to the emergence of sentiments of insecurity and fear. Such sentiments seem to be widespread among women and men. This universality may echo a wider shift in the organization of urban geographies of fear: such geographies are not formulated only around local topographies of fear that may reproduce regional perceptions of engendered spatial hierarchies. Rather, they are rearticulated within more flexibly organized globalized emotional geopolitics.[59] As for perceptions of the advent of immigrants, it seems that the crisis functions, if not as a 'biographical turning point', namely as a historical moment that leads the subjects to different interpretations of past and present events, at least as a version of a 'fateful moment'; a moment when the subjects have to deal with the consequences of an event that radically affected their consumerist certainties, interrupted their pleasant routines organized around expansion of prosperity and provoked a multi-level shock.[60] Immigrants, who had rather marginal roles in the organization of the pre-crisis economies of pleasure, emerged effortlessly as a scapegoat. Thus, race relations appeared as one of the axes around which the narrations about the crisis were revolving.

Focusing on Athens, some interviewees distinguish between the 'peaceful' period prior to the early 1990s, when many immigrants began to settle in the city, and the years after. As anthropologist Alexandra Bakalaki has noticed, the systematic representation of immigrants as dangerous and the subsequent introduction of modern anti-theft technologies in the 1990s satisfied the need of Greeks to feel well-off, civilized and part of the Western, developed world.[61] In a sense, in the Greek narrations we can detect expressions of nostalgia for the last historical period before the introduction of security technologies that set limits between public and private space. As we will discuss, this kind of nostalgic memory emerged as a crucial political stake in the 2012 elections.

Figures for crimes committed by immigrants have increased by 1.11 per cent in 1990, 3.22 per cent in 1995, 6.44 per cent in 2000, 12.84 per cent in 2005, 16.38 per cent in 2006 and 19.78 per cent in 2007.[62] Immigrants are overrepresented in crime statistics not least because the crimes in which they usually take part, such as burglaries, are more likely to be reported. However, this rate of increase seems too large to be accounted for by simple misrepresentation or the vagaries of the statistics. Hence, there seems to be an association between immigrants and the rise in criminality. At any rate, the fear of crime exceeds the 'real' statistical possibilities of victimization and has to be perceived as the culmination of various factors affecting quality of life, such as housing conditions, the amount of corruption, the quality of policing or the extent and visibility of drug use.[63] This claim seems to be corroborated by the geographical details included in the interviews. These narrations echo Janoska et al.'s point that debates about spatial organization, inequality and gentrification issues abound in societies in crisis and with fragmentary capitalist expansion.[64] In this respect, some interviewees focused on degraded areas of the city centre; not those affected by contemporary gentrification trends,[65] but rather in the once middle-class districts such as Patissia, Kipseli and Victoria, whose identity changed radically during and after the 1980s as many of the residents of these areas moved to the suburbs.[66] Consequently, these areas, full of buildings constructed in the first postwar decades, offered affordable accommodation to immigrants.

As we can see in the descriptions of V.P., a female 63-year-old old middle-class hospital worker resident in Patissia in the 1980s, and of T.P., a male 43-year-old motorcycle merchant living in Aghia Paraskevi who frequented the city centre as a teenager after 1985, the memories of 'the safe 1980s' are organized around comparisons between a safe then and an unsafe now. Safety and unsafety are here constructed in terms of bipolarity. By perceiving change as a synecdoche of transitional dynamics[67] rather than as a moment of radical and total juncture and taking into consideration that people tend to organize memories around highlights of change and rupture[68] such narrations establish a 'borderline' covering a period of some years in the early 1990s.

> V: Regarding fear the next decade was worse.
>
> Author: What do you mean by saying fear?
>
> V: They started to steal, to kill people. [...] You were afraid to walk in the street, even in the daytime. In the 1990s I was more afraid. [...] I remember that after 1991–1992 they snatched my bag just outside my home. Things became dodgier.
>
> Author: Do you remember such incidents in the 1980s?
>
> V: I would say no. [...] Then many foreigners came and everyday life became more dangerous.[69]
>
> T: [In the 1980s] there were some seamy areas [...] but [only] up to a point. Even in the dodgier area about what could you be afraid of? To get mugged? OK, let's say that you got robbed. Not a chance then of what happened [to a guy] that they killed for a camera. Not a chance![70]

Current events affected the formation of the narrations. Although it is hard to define the precise terms of the interactions between representations of criminality by politicians, the influences of media and the formation of individual memories, influences seem obvious. The murder of a family man by two Afghani immigrants in central Athens on 10 May 2011 gives to T.P. grounds to make a comparison between the 'peaceful' 1980s and the 'dangerous' now.

Such comparisons reproduce contemporary narrations and tend to mirror a generalized demand for authenticity that favours black and white explanatory schemes. Indicatively, a few months before the 2012 elections, the then president of the Conservative party and prime minister until January 2015, Antonis Samaras, argued that the Greeks had to reoccupy their cities, which had been conquered by the immigrants.[71] A pertinent narration is detected in a text hosted on the webpage of 'Golden Dawn', a far-right organization established in the early 1980s that emerged as a major political contender during the crisis years, getting 6.97 per cent of the votes in the general elections of June 2012.[72] 'Golden Dawn' claims that immigrants are mainly responsible for economic crisis and high unemployment rates. Furthermore, issues of everyday safety play a key role in its political agenda. Based on a simplistic scheme distinguishing between the 'innocent' Greeks and the 'barbarous' immigrants, 'Golden Dawn' has emphasized the downgrading of quality of life in central Athens.

In 'Golden Dawn's' communication strategy the early 1990s are defined as a key moment dividing a safe 'before' from a dangerous 'after'. A nearly anonymous text entitled

'Anamniseis apo mia periohi pou den einai pia I idia' (Memories from a district that is not the same any more) uploaded on the party's webpage in late 2012 reflects this communicational choice. The text is signed by 'Korina', a member of the party's local branch in Ano Liosia which is a working-class suburb. Among other details, it seems unorthodox that a female narrator pays attention to the existence of vacant lots for football, thus the gender of the author rather emerges as an extra question. At any rate, using highly sentimental tones and focusing on Aghios Panteleimonas, an area with many immigrants widely discussed in the media, 'Korina' describes the 1980s as the last period when the centre of Athens was a safe place to live in.[73]

> We lived the last decade when we could play hide and seek, hunting, cops and robbers etc. When we wanted to play football we could still find some vacant lots. We were going out with our bikes and it was not that dangerous. [...] I was going out at night, sometimes until very late. [...] People were going out, did not lock themselves in their homes after dark. [...] Now everything is different. After the late 1990s. No kids in the squares, no elderly people sitting on benches. [...] Immigrants are everywhere.[74]

The text is accompanied by a photo, which shows seven children running carefree on a pavement. The photo was supposedly taken in Athens during the 1980s. As anthropological research has shown, the main difference between photography and representational practices, such as painting, is that, in pressing the camera's button, the photographer mechanically records what was happening at that moment including accidental happenings.[75] In this case, attempting to profit from photography's capacity to act occasionally as a 'medium of delusion',[76] 'Golden Dawn used a photo with details that gave away that the picture was *not* taken in Athens. The children are blond rather than the typical Greek skin-colour that tends to be darker. Moreover, the big pavement, paving and house entrances do not fit with the crowded centre of Athens. Looking for the original source of the photo using the reverse image search engine 'TinEye' I found that it was taken in 2008 by the photographer Jen Lemen in Alexandria, Virginia. Almost ironically, Lemen is actively involved in human rights, placing special emphasis on issues related to helping immigrants who are caught in migration loopholes (see Figure 14.1).[77]

We could make two assumptions; one is that the writer and the webpage's moderators paid limited attention to the photograph accompanying the text. But there are so many details conveying that the photo was not taken in Athens that it is hard to believe all of them as being accidentally overlooked before uploading. Potentially this negligence can be interpreted as extra evidence of the strength of the belief that the 1980s was a period of bliss: so much so, that meticulous evidence is not required. Contrary to the dominant line that usually associates the 'prosperous 1980s' with the broadening of consumption opportunities, this bliss is rather defined as a synonym of limited anxieties about crime in public spaces.[78] In this discourse the early 1990s emerge as a signifier of postmodernity with all its negative and fissiparous tendencies. Another clue indicating that the cultural construction of the 'great 1980s' was an inflexible representational nexus without negative

Consumption and Gender Post-Transition

Figure 14.1 Photo showing children running carefree on a sidewalk. The photo, which accompanied a text on the safety of Athens in the 1980s, published on Golden Dawn's website in 2012, was originally taken on 22 June 2008 by the photographer Jen Lemen in Alexandria, Virginia.

connotations is that it currently operates as a multilevel process resonating more than historiographical trends or scientific priorities. On the contrary, as this case clearly shows, black and white explanatory schemes of the recent past present political purposes and a wider pursuit for authenticity.

Conclusions

Kostis Kornetis recently examined the (re)conceptualizations of the Spanish *transición*, arguing that renegotiations of turbulent moments of the recent past emerge as an open, conflictual question in societies in crisis.[79] In Greece, as in Spain, only a few years interposed between the transition to democracy and the beginning of the 1980s when socialist governments took power. Despite inevitable highlights of political conflict in Greece, the 1980s represent a period of optimism, prosperity and smoothing over the traumatic experiences of the past. In a sense, 18 October can be perceived as the Greek version of the Spanish 23F, namely as the historical moment after which a return to authoritarianism was not likely any longer.[80] Many people believed that better days were to come and indeed many Greeks exceeded their income and consumption opportunities in the 1980s.

This chapter has explored how the 1980s are perceived though the prism of the current economic crisis, by placing special emphasis on the complex relations between productions of historical narrations about the 1980s and the logistics of the recent crisis. As we saw, the renegotiations of the notorious prosperity of a period which was until very recently seen as one of the most fruitful in contemporary Greek history demonstrate strains that are implying intense debates and political disputes; the cultivation of systematic interest in conspicuous consumption since the 1980s is discussed as alienating and incompatible with desirable performances of masculinity; the challenge of cultural convergence with the West as a pleasant experience implying noticeable retrofuturist dynamics; and the advent of immigrants in the early 1990s described as an unpleasant development that affected people's sense of security, especially in Athens. In terms of gender, the scepticism (and perhaps the derision) of performances of masculinity that emerged as recognizable referents in Greece between the 1980s and the beginning of the crisis perhaps reflect a wider shift towards more macho performances of masculinity and a wider critique of the gradual 'metrosexualization' of the mediascape in recent decades.[81]

If there is a 'truth' in how 'great' were the 1980s, we have to ferret it out somewhere in between the pre-crisis deification of the period and today's disdain. New media smooth the way for the production of alternative narrations of the past by creating new historical representations that professional historians who are focusing on forms of public history have to take into account. Furthermore, they provide useful information on how perceptions of gender identities have been transformed since the beginning of the crisis. In our case, it is hard to deny that these descriptions, as well as the interviews used here, voice a particular view from the prism of a country in crisis. Narrations reflect a juncture of insecurity, confusion and fear. So, the crisis is rarely itself presented as the basis for the formulation of conclusions. Surely the representations of the past that are being produced during the extraordinary times we are still living in will be a gripping topic for future historians who will have fascinating, even purely propagandistic, material about the representations of the 1980s to take advantage of. And, taking a risk in sounding didactic, we, namely, the social scientists who are studying Greece of the 1980s today, have to keep in mind that we are examining not only a historical period, but a political weapon as well.

Notes

1. This chapter has a long history. Some preliminary ideas were presented at the Social History Annual Conference in Leeds in March 2013. More developed versions were presented at the lecture series of 'Cariatide: asociación Argentina de cultura helénica' and at the Catholic University of Uruguay in June 2013 in Buenos Aires and Montevideo respectively. I would like to thank Jerónimo Brignone, María Eloísa González Damián, Susana Mangana Porteiro, Gonzalo Oleggini and Amilcar Peláez for generously giving me opportunities to discuss ideas contained in this chapter in South America. I would also like to thank Efi Avdela and Dimitra Vassiliadou for commenting on previous versions of this chapter, the volume's editors for their remarks and the photographer Jen Lemen for permitting me to republish her photo here. Of course, I am alone responsible for the analysis and shortcomings herein. This chapter is based on research conducted for my PhD research project 'Lifestyle, Gender Relations and New Social Spaces in 1980s Athens', which has been supported by the Greek State Scholarships Foundation (2010–14) and by an LLP European Commission Grant (2012–13).

2. I.Z., interview with author, Maroussi, Athens, 7 July. In order to protect the privacy of interviewees, I use here only the initial letters instead of their full names and surnames. One interviewee (M.A.) asked me to use anonymized initials for her name and surname. The altered initials used here are selected by her.
3. See indicatively: Polymeris Voglis, *Becoming a Subject. Political Prisoners During the Greek Civil War* (New York: Berghahn, 2002); Loring M. Danforth and Riki Van Boeschoten, *Children of the Greek Civil War. Refugees and the Politics of Memory* (Chicago: University of Chicago Press, 2012).
4. Stathis Kalyvas, George Pagoulatos and Haridimos Tsoukas, 'Introduction', in Stathis Kalyvas, George Pagoulatos and Haridimos Tsoukas (eds), *From Stagnation to Forced Adjustment. Reforms in Greece, 1974–2010* (London: Hurst & Company, 2012), 2.
5. For this development see Ursula-Helen Kassaveti, *I elliniki videotainia (1985–1990). Eidologikes, koinonikes kai politismikes diastaseis* (Athens: Asini, 2014).
6. Tryfon Bampilis, *Greek Whisky. The Localization of a Global Commodity* (New York: Berghahn Books, 2013), 109–52.
7. David Close, *Ellada, 1945–2004. Politiki, koinonia, oikonomia* (Thessaloniki: Thyrathen, 2006), 335–6.
8. For particular quantitative data see Christina Varouxi and Amalia Frangiskou, 'Attitudes and values', in Dimitris Haralambis, Laura Maratou Alipranti and Andromachi Hadjiyanni (eds), *Recent Social Trends in Greece, 1960–2000* (Montreal: McGill Queen's University Press, 2004), 669–75.
9. Giannis Mavris, 'Tomi sti metapoliteysi to 1981', *Kathimerini*, 30, 2007, http://www.kathimerini.gr/308896/article/epikairothta/politikh/tomh-sth-metapoliteysh-to-1981 [accessed 10 September 2014].
10. For this issue see analytically: Stella Zambarloukou and Maria Kousi, (eds), *Koinonikes opseis tis krisis stin Ellada* (Athens: Pedio, 2014)
11. Rates were higher in women (22.3 per cent instead of 15.5 per cent for men) and people aged less than 25 (43.5 per cent). I cite the data as republished in Efi Avdela, 'To fylo stin (se) krisi i ti symvainei stis "gynaikes" se halepous kairous', *Synchrona Themata* 115, 2011, 9.
12. Dimitris Dalakoglou and Antonis Vradis, 'Introduction' in Dimitris Dakakoglou and Antonis Vradis (eds), *Revolt and Crisis in Greece. Between a Present Yet to Pass and a Future Still to Come* (Oakland: AK Press, 2011), 22.
13. About the term, see the Introduction to this volume.
14. Vaggelis Karamanolakis and Ioanna Papathanasiou (eds), *Metapoliteysi. Saranta chronia meta* (Athens: ASKI, 2014), 14. The book contains a discussion among scholars, including historian Antonis Liakos.
15. Gerard A. Hauser, 'Vernacular dialogue and the rhetoricality of public opinion', *Communication Monographs* 65.3, 1998, 86.
16. See analytically: Giannis Voulgaris and Ilias Nikolakopoulos (eds), *2012: O diplos eklogikos seismos* (Athens: Themelio, 2014). Briefly, the Panhellenic Socialist Movement (PASOK) lost almost 70 per cent of its support between 2009 and 2012. In the same period, the radical left-wing coalition SYRIZA multiplied its political power by seven. Golden Dawn, a far-right party, evolved into a major political contender. The latter development will be discussed in detail in the last section. For SYRIZA see Michalis Spourdalakis, 'The miraculous rise of the "phenomenon" SYRIZA', *International Critical Thought* 4.3, 2014, 354–66.

17. Judith Butler, *Gender Trouble* (New York: Routledge, 1990), 179.
18. Julia T. Wood, *Gendered Lives. Communication, Gender and Culture* (Boston, MA: Wadsworth, 2006), 256–83. For the relations between gender and memory see Selma Leydesdorff, Luisa Passerini and Paul Thomson (eds), *Gender and Memory* (New Brunswick, NJ: Transaction Publishers, 2005).
19. The interviewees were living in Athens in the 1980s, or at least for much of the decade. The main criterion for their selection was their relation with the 'novel' lifestyles (interest in modern technologies, alternative entertainment trends, novel media etc.).
20. Henry Jenkins, *Convergence Culture: Where Old and New Media Collide* (New York: New York University Press, 2006).
21. Stig Hjarvard, 'The mediatization of society: a theory of the media as agents of social and cultural change', *Nordicom Review* 29.2, 2008, 105–34; Stig Hjarvard, *The Mediatization of Culture and Society* (London: Routledge, 2013).
22. Jean E. Burgess, Helen G. Klaebe and Kelly McWilliam, 'Mediatization and institutions of public memory: digital storytelling and the apology', *Australian Historical Studies* 41.2, 2010, 149–65.
23. Thimios E. Zacharopoulos and Manny E. Paraschos, *Mass Media in Greece: Power, Politics and Privatization* (Westport, CT: Praeger, 1993).
24. The magazines of publisher Petros Kostopoulos, the TV shows of journalist Themos Anastasiadis and the TV series of actor and director Christophoros Papakaliatis are some characteristic examples of such discourses.
25. For a recent example see Mariangela Paone, *Las cuatro estaciones de Atenas. Crónicas desde un país ahogado por su rescate* (Madrid: Libros del KOSLL, 2014).
26. Giannis Voulgaris, 'I krisi eiche ti diki tis istoria', *Ta Nea*, 26 January 2013, http://www.tanea.gr/opinions/all-opinions/article/4784709/?iid=2 [accessed 25 September 2014].
27. For analytic data see Afroditi Grammeli, 'Dramatiki meiosi tis diafimistikis dapanis', *To Vima tis Kyriakis*, 6 September 2012, http://www.tovima.gr/media/article/?aid=473606 [accessed 20 September 2014].
28. Indicatively see Dora Pavlidou, 'Kataschesi stin IMAKO', *To Vima tis Kyriakis*, 21 February 2012 http://www.tovima.gr/media/article/?aid=444800 [accessed 25 September 2014]; Gazzetta.gr, 'Telos epochis gia IMAKO-Kostopoulo', 21 February 2012, http://www.gazzetta.gr/media-cafe/article/item/267609-telos-epohes-gia-imako-kostopoulo [accessed 28 September 2014], especially the readers' comments below the article.
29. My use of the term 'mediascape' follows that of Arjun Appadurai, 'Disjuncture and difference in the global cultural economy', *Theory, Culture, Society* 7.2, 1990, 298–9. According to Appadurai mediascapes refer both to the distribution of the electronic capabilities to produce and disseminate information (magazines, newspapers, television stations, film production studios, etc.) which are available to a growing number of private and public interests as well as to the images of the world created by these media.
30. Gioula Eptakili, Ilias Maglinis, Margarita Pournara and Dimitris Rigopoulos, 'Lifestyle: I zoi itan daneiki', *Kathimerini*, 16 May 2010, http://www.kathimerini.gr/393570/article/politismos/arxeio-politismoy/lifestyle-h-zwh-htan-daneikh [accessed 2 October 2014].
31. Brian Larkin, 'Indian films and Nigerian lovers: media and the creation of parallel modernities', *Journal of the International African Institute* 67.3, 1997, 406–40.
32. Helen Graham and Alejandro Quiroga, 'After the fear was over? What came after dictatorships in Spain, Greece and Portugal', in Dan Stone (ed.), *The Oxford Handbook of Postwar European History* (Oxford: Oxford University Press, 2012), 502–25.

33. Jose F. Beaumont, 'Ajoblanco cumple 15 años', *El Pais*, 31 October 1989 http://elpais.com/diario/1989/10/31/sociedad/625791608_850215.html [accessed 30 September 2014]; 'Eurosexy', *Click*, October 1988, 54–61.
34. M.A., interview with author, Kessariani, Athens, 9 August 2012.
35. For more information on the website's profile see Alexa.com, 'Site overview: bourdela.com', http://www.alexa.com/siteinfo/bourdela.com [accessed 1 October 2014].
36. Bourdela.com, 'Kostopoulos, Kostopouloi neoellines. I alloiosi ton charaktiristikon tou Ellina', http://www.bourdela.com/forum/index.php?topic=136668.0 [accessed: 30 September 2014].
37. Post #1, user: jstar [accessed 2 October 2014]
38. Avdela, 'To fylo', 13–16.
39. Post #16, user: str81977. For another interesting narration see post 86, user: Gregory35 [both accessed 2 October 2014].
40. Indicatively, on 23 April 2012 the thread counted 991 posts.
41. Nikolas Sevastakis and Giannis Stavrakakis, *Laikismos, antilaikismos kai krisi* (Athens: Nefeli, 2012), 65; Antonis Liakos, *I epistrofi tis kokkinoskoufitsas. I aristera kai pos na ti skeftoume se krisimous kairous* (Athens: Nefeli, 2014), 35–9.
42. Media scholar Vassilis Vamvakas has described the 'movement of the squares' as a performance of 'revolutionary conservatism', namely as a form of routinized protest organized within a tolerant, democratic regime, so, an activity without real risk for the protesters. Vassilis Vamvakas, *O logos tis krisis. Polosi, via, anastochasmos stin politiki kai dimofili koultoura* (Thessaloniki: Epikentro, 2014), 95–101. In my opinion, in the 'squares' we can spot an interesting new form of protest where internet-age political radicalism met with more 'established' political performances as such activities were systematically screened by traditional media channels. One of the results of the new performances of community was the advancement of familiarity between left-wing and right-wing radicalism (at least at the level of an antigovernment theatricality organized in part for media consumption).
43. For this phenomenon see Gina Moscholiou, 'Mia via ochi kai toso politiki' in Xenia Kounalaki, Paschos Mandravelis, Michalis Mitsos, Gina Moscholiou and Tassos Pappas, *I via* (Athens: Polis, 2012), 121–48.
44. Such discourses are kept alive in the present, although not as strong as in the 2011–12 period. For a recent example see Giorgos Delastik, 'Ta aischi ton Tsolakoglou', *Iskra*, 31 March 2014, http://www.iskra.gr/index.php?option=com_content&view=article&id=15850:-qq&catid=81:kivernisi&Itemid=198 [accessed 30 September 2014]. This article was initially published in the newspaper *Prin tis Kyriakis*, 30 March 2014 and then republished in iskra.gr, a website of the then left platform of SYRIZA. As SYRIZA decided to sign a new memorandum in summer 2015, most members of the left platform abandoned SYRIZA in August 2015 creating a new political party named Laiki Enotita (Popular Unity). Laiki Enotita got 2.86 percent of the vote in the general elections of September 2015.
45. Data from the *Regular Eurobarometer Survey*, 82 (2014), 1–4. In late 2014 only 23 per cent of Greeks trusted European Union, the lowest percentage among the member countries.
46. Indicatively: M.A., interview with author; G.Z. (2012), interview with author, Pagrati, Athens, 23 March 2012.
47. Niki Hagia and Loukas Melos, 'Athens' Best: ola osa edosan lampsi stis meres kai tis nychtes tis Athinas ta teleytaia 25 chronia', *Nitro* (March 2011), 90–8.
48. P.K. (2012), interview with author, Kolonaki, Athens, 13 May.
49. K.Z. (2012), interview with author, Filothei, Athens, 29 June.

50. 'Ayxisi egklimatikotitas kai anasfaleias stin Attiki', *Express*, 15 March 2012, http://www.express.gr/news/ellada/577068oz_20120315577068.php3 [accessed 10 September 2014].
51. Sophia Vidali, *Elenchos tou egklimatos kai dimosia astynomia. Tomes kai asynecheies stin antiegklimatiki politiki*, volume b (Athens: Sakkoulas, 2007), 826.
52. Ioanna Mandrou, 'Katakoryfi ayxisi tis egklimatikotitas', *Kathimerini*, 19 August 2012, http://www.kathimerini.gr/466005/article/epikairothta/ellada/katakoryfh-ay3hsh-ths-egklhmatikothtas [accessed 10 September 2014].
53. T.P., interview with author, Ilissia, Athens, 12 March.
54. A prestigious seaside resort approximately 30 km southeast of Athens.
55. I.P., interview with author, Pagrati, Athens, 16 February 2012.
56. E. A., interview with author, Exarchia, Athens, 21 March 2012
57. E.P., interview with the author, Chalandri, Athens, 11 August 2012.
58. Svetlana Boym, 'Nostalgia and its discontents', *The Hedgehog Review* 9.2, 2007, 13–14.
59. For these developments see Rachel Pain, 'Social geographies of women's fear of crime', *Transactions of the Institute of British Geographers* 22.2, 1997, 231–44; Rachel Pain, 'Globalized fear? Towards an emotional geopolitics', *Progress in Human Geography* 33.4, 2009, 466–86.
60. Anthony Giddens, *Modernity and Self-identity: Self and Society in the Late Modern Age* (Stanford, CA: Stanford University Press, 1991), 113. The term 'biographical turning point' has been employed by the sociologist Gabriele Rosenthal, *Erlebte und erzählte Lebensgeschichte* (Frankfurt am Main, New York: Campus, 1995)
61. Alexandra Bakalaki, 'Locked into security, keyed into modernity: the selection of burglaries as source of risk in Greece', *Ethnos: Journal of Anthropology* 68.2, 2003, 209–29.
62. For analytical data see Ioanna Tsigkanou, Ioulia Lambraki, Ioanna Fatourou and Evangelos Chainas, *Metanasteysi kai egklimatikotita. Mythoi kai pragmatikotita* (Athens: National Center for Social Research, 2010), 78 (Table 1).
63. Christina Zarafonitou, 'Criminal victimisation in Greece and the fear of crime: a "paradox" for interpretation', *International Review of Victimology* 16, 2009, 277–300.
64. Michael Janoschka, Jorge Sequera and Luis Salinas, 'Gentrification in Spain and Latin America – a critical dialogue', *International Journal of Urban and Regional Research* 38.4, 2014, 1234–65.
65. For this issue see Georgia Alexandri, 'Reading between the lines; gentrification tendencies and issues of urban fear in the midst of Athens' crisis', *Urban Studies* 52.9, 2015, 1631–46.
66. For this phenomenon see Thomas Maloutas, 'The archaeology of the decline of the city centre: residential location choices of affluent groups', in Myrto Tsilimpounidi and Aylwyn Walsh (eds), *Remapping 'Crisis'. A Guide to Athens* (Winchester: Zero Books, 2014), 26–42.
67. Kostis Kornetis, '1968, 1989, 2011: reconsidering social movements, "moments of change" and theoretical framing over time', *Historein. A Review of the Past and Other Stories* 13, 2013, 57.
68. Stephan Feuchtwang, 'Mythical moments in national and other family histories', *History Workshop Journal* 59.1, 2005, 179–93.
69. V.P., interview with the author, Patissia, Athens, 6 January 2012.
70. T.P., interview with author.

71. 'Antonis Samaras: prepei na anakatalavoume tis poleis mas', *Naftemporiki*, 29 March 2012, http://www.naftemporiki.gr/story/387960/a-samaras-prepei-na-anakatalaboume-tis-poleis-mas [accessed 1 October 2014].

72. Comparatively, 'Golden Dawn' got 0.29 per cent of the votes in the general elections of 2009. On the development of Golden Dawn during the crisis years see Antonis A. Ellinas, 'The rise of Golden Dawn: the new face of the far right in Greece', *South European Society and Politics*, 18.4, 2013, 543–65. Golden Dawn maintained its influence in the last elections getting 6.28 per cent and 6.99 of the votes in the general elections of January 2015 and September 2015, respectively.

73. Xenophobic rhetoric has been also reproduced by journalists and intellectuals without relationships with far-right politics. Indicatively, in 2013 a pertinent apostrophe in a speech by Kiki Dimoula, a poet who had won the European Prize for Literature four years before, caused havoc in the media. Dimoula stated that she found unpleasant the fact that many immigrants were occupying the benches of Kipseli, a densely populated Athenian neighbourhood, denying access to elder Greek locals.

74. Korina, 'Anamniseis apo mia periochi pou den einai pia i idia', 25 November 2012, http://www.xryshaygh.com/index.php/enimerosi/view/anamnhseis-apo-mia-periochh-pou-den-einai-pia-h-idia [accessed 20 September 2014].

75. Konstantinos Kalantzis, 'Optikos politismos kai anthropologia', in Eleanna Gialouri (ed.) *Ylikos Politismos. I anthropologia sti chora ton pragmaton* (Athens: Alexandria, 2013), 198–203.

76. Robin Kelsey and Blake Stimson (2008), 'Photography's double index (a short history in three parts)' in Robin Kelsey and Blake Stimson (eds), *The Meaning of Photography* (New Haven, CT, London: Yale University Press, 2008), xx. This book is published by Sterling and Francine Clark Art Institute (Williamstown, Massachusetts) and then distributed by Yale University Press, New Haven and London.

77. Jen Lemen, personal communication with author on Facebook, 12 December 2014.

78. Although 'Golden Dawn' has been critical of contemporary feminist politics, denying any claims of gender equality, the autonomous presence of women in urban public is evaluated as important since the party's rhetoric associates it with the successful accomplishment of maternal duties. For Golden Dawn's view on women's position see Evgenia Christou, 'I gynaika kai o syncronos kosmos', 30 April 2012, http://isxys.blogspot.com/2012/04/blog-post_30.html [accessed 20 February 2015].

79. Kostis Kornetis, '"Is there a future in this past?" Analyzing the 15M's intricate relation to the transición', *Journal of Spanish Cultural Studies* 15.1–2, 2014, 1–16.

80. For the representations of 23 February in Spain see Francisca López and Enric Castelló (eds), *Cartografías del 23F. Representaciones en la prensa, la televisión, la novela, el cine y la cultura popular* (Laertes: Barcelona, 2014).

81. This critique has been extended towards wider trends in urban (youth) cultures. Indicatively, in 2013, Panagiotis Hadjistefanou, a journalist, creative director for the magazine *The Berlin Agenda* and then sympathizer of SYRIZA, argued that hipsterism should be rather perceived as a lifestyle adopted by middle- and upper-class consumers who sympathize with far-right politics and defined the phenomenon as 'hipsteronazism'. See Panagiotis Hadjistefanou, 'Hipsteronazismos', *To Kouti tis Pandoras*, 2 December 2013, http://www.koutipandoras.gr/article/100339/toy-p-hatzistefanoy-hipsteronazismos [accessed 12 May 2015].

INDEX

Abella, Rafael 10
Acção Católica Portuguesa (Portuguese Catholic Action) 86
Acção Médica (journal) 74, 77, 78
Actas Luso- Españolas de Neurología y Psiquiatría (psychiatric journal) 64
O Agonas tis Gynaikas (Woman's Struggle) (journal) 243
Aldevaran (Thomopoulos) 156
Almeida, São José 132
Almodóvar, Pedro, *Pepi, Luci, Bom* 155, 156–7
    commodifying marginality 162–3
    gender/pleasure/frivolity 164–5
    irreverence 158–9
    movida career 157
    post-politics 160–2
    subculture documentation 159–60
Ama, revista de las amas de casa (magazine) 138–9, 140, 141–2, 143–4, 149
    political socialization, 1975–80 144–5
Amar en tiempos revueltos (TV production) 229
Americanization
    consumption and gender 14–16
    Greece 14–16
    Portugal *see* Portugal
    Spain *see* Spain
Amor a todo gas (film) 63
Amphetamines 69
Amytal (drug) 70
Andreu, Rafael 144
Angelopoulos, Theodoros 155
Anti-Authoritarian Chóros (Dimitris) 159
António, Lauro 129
Apacergil (drug) 68
The Apartment (Wilder; film) 69
Appadurai, Arjun 85–6
Araújo, Antonio 216
Archivos de Neurobiología (psychiatric journal) 64
Arregi, Rikardo 50–1, 52
Arvelos, Edith 123
At the Beach (Urbain) 103
audio-visual consumption *see* Greece, audio-visual consumption, 1980s
Auslander, Leora 3
Avdela, Efi 261

Bakalaki, Alexandra 265
Bakshi, Ralph 130

Bardot, Brigitte 90
Barros, Valentim de 124
Barthes, Roland 91–2
Basque youth culture, 1960s
    Baserri Gaztedia (youth group) 46
    Basque language, stereotypes 46–7
    Catholic youth groups 48, 51
    cinema 48 9
    economic development 44–5, 47
    education provision 44–5
    Euskal Abesti Berri Jaialdia (music festival) 53
    Ez Dok Amairu (music group) 52–3, 54
    foreign influences 49–50, 54
    ideal woman, promotion 44
    key issues 43–4, 54–5
    leisure networks, Church 46
    leisure time activities 48–9
    male breadwinner family model 45–6
    modern music 49
    modern songs in the Basque language 52–4
    new generation 47–52
    OARGUI (network) 46
    traditional activities 51–2
    traditional dancing 48
    ye-yé movement 6, 49, 54, 96
    young girls, late 50s and early 60s 44–6
    youth association activities 51–2
    youth culture 49–51
    Zeruko Argia (journal) 49–50
    see also Spain
Baudrillard, Jean 59, 65, 79, 165
The Beatles 95, 96
Bernardeau, Miguel Ángel 230
Bertolucci, Bernardo 130
Betavida (drug) 70
Birmingham School of Cultural Studies 3, 166
Borowczyk, Walerian 133
Botto, António 123
Bourdieu, Pierre 104, 114, 163
Boym, Svetlana 264
Breakfast at Tiffany's 90
Brennan, Timothy 85
Buckley, Patrick 230
Buñuel, Luis 156

Cabral, Sarsfield 87, 96
Calcibronat (drug) 75
Câmara Pereira, Frei Hermano da 124

Index

Cardoso, Miguel Esteves 215
Castro, Helen Gray de 215
Catembe (film) 125
Cesariny, Mario 89
Christakis, Leonidas 250
Chronas, Yorgos 176
cinema
    Basque youth culture, 1960s 48–9
    post-authoritarian *see* Southern Europe, cinema, post-authoritarian Spain and Greece
La ciudad de los muertos 63
Clomiazol 70
Clorpromacin/Closerpil (drugs) 72
Coelho, Tereza 213–14
Coimbra Médica (journal) 74–5
Connell, W 4
consumer behaviour, 1960s *see* Portugal
consumerism, 1960s *see* Spain
consumption and gender
    Americanization 14–16
    and consumerism 3–4
    current research 2
    definitions of gender 4–5
    model 'Mrs Consumer' 8–9
    postmodernity transition 13–14
    structure of study 17–18
    temporalities' entanglement 16–17
    testing ground 1
    transitology revisited 9–13
Corfu Club Med 106
El Crimen de Cuenca (Míro) 155
Crumbaugh, Justin 147
Cruz, Braga da 61
Cruz, Carlos 197–200, 203
Cubitt, Sean 244
Cuéntame cómo pasó (Tell Me How it Was) *see* Spain, television, *Cuéntame cómo pasó* (Tell Me How it Was)
Cunha, Paulo 129

Dancin' Days (Brazilian *telenovella*) 203–5
de la Iglesia, Eloy 155
DeCerteau, Michel 248
Deplix (drug) 65–6
Dichter, Ernest 65
Dimitris, E. 159
Dionísio, Mário 194–5
El Diputado (de la Iglesia) 155
Distovagal (drug) 66, 67, 69
do Vale, Madame 210
Domingues, Maria Elisa 197–200, 203, 214
Dúrcal, Rocío 64
Dynasty (soap opera) 249

Eco, Umberto 167
Eikones magazine 109, 111, 112

Elias, Norbert 113
Elle (magazine) 213–14, 215, 216–17, 219, 220
Emmanuelle (film) 131

fashion magazines, 1980s *see* Portugal
The Feminine Mystique (Friedan) 63, 68
Fernández, Francisco Alonso 72
Ferro, António 122
Fiske, John 251
Flama (journal) 85, 87, 89, 90, 94, 95, 96
Fogaça, Júlio Melo 124
Foucault, Michel 105
Franco regime 60, 61, 62–4, 137–8, 140–2
Friedan, Betty 63, 68
Friedl, E. 243
Fritz the Cat (Bakshi) 130
Furlough, Ellen 3

Gabriela, Cravo e Canela (*telenovela*) 196
Garcia, Jordi Gracia 6
Giles, Judy 245
Goffman, Erving 75
Gonçalves, Manuela 217
Goncalves, Mário 89
Graham, Helen 7, 166
Gray, Ann 248
Grazia, Victoria de 2, 3, 8, 85, 91, 98, 139
Greece
    AKOE/*AMFI* 173, 184, 243
    Americanization 14–16
    audio-visual consumption, 1980s
        children 250–1
        cultural changes 242–3
        direct-to-video film genres 246–7
        key issues/conclusion 241, 251–2
        melodramas/soap operas 248–50
        political context 241–2
        post-*Allagi* 241–3
        practice/consumption, index of identity 243–5
        public sector growth 242
        VCR spectatorships 247–51
        women's roles 243
    cinema, post-authoritarian *see* Southern Europe, cinema, post-authoritarian Spain and Greece
    male sexualities, post-1960s
        all-male public places 178–80
        andres/adelfes distinction 175, 176, 178, 180, 181–2
        class/gendered differences 176–8
        conceptualizations, 1950s–1970s 174–5
        consumerist masculinities 181–3
        emergent gay movement 173
        heterosexual/homosexual, distinction 181, 183–4

key issues/conclusion 173-4, 184-5
poniroi 175, 177, 184
Western conceptualizations, emergence 180
PASOK 241, 242, 251, 261
postmodernity transition 13-14
prosperity of 1980s, and current crisis
   crime figures 265
   economic situation, changes 259-60, 262-3
   everyday safety 264-8
   Golden Dawns communications 266-8
   key issues/conclusions 258-9, 268-9
   lifestyle discourses 259-62
   nostalgia for 80s 263-4
   pre-crisis view 257-8
   restorative nostalgia 264-5
reflexive mediterranization 37
seaside recreational practices, postwar-1974
   beach tourism 105-7
   contested worlds 103
   ecological sustainability 110
   hedonism, conflicting attitudes 112-13
   key issues/conclusion 103-4, 113-14
   pedagogies of the sea 107-9
   socialization 110-12
   structuralism 104
   symbolic struggles 109-10
   territorial segmentation 109-10
   theoretical considerations 104-5
temporalities' entanglement 16-17
transitology revisited 10-13

Handman, Marie-Elizabeth 243
Harvey, David 105
Heidegger, Martin 104
Hepburn, Audrey 89-90, 92
Hjarvard, Stig 259
Houlbrook, Matt 178
housewives in transition, 1959-80 *see* Spain
Huntington, Samuel 10

Iberian consumerism, 1960s *see* Portugal, consumerism, 1960s; Spain, consumerism, 1960s
Immoral Tales (*Contes Imoraux*) (film) 133
The Indolence of the Fertile Valley (Panayotopoulos) 156
Ioannou, Yorgos 177
Iriondo, Lourdes 52-3

Jameson, Fredric 245
Jenkins, Henry 259
Jornal do Médico (journal) 74, 75, 77
José, Herman 200-1, 205

Karalis, Vrasidas 158
Karina, Anna 133

Kaufman, Jean Claude 113
Kavounidi (video drama) 251
Kennedy, Jackie 89
Kornetis, Kostis 121
Kostopoulos, Petros 260
Kramer vs. Kramer 204
Kuhn, Annette 249

La muerte de Mikel (Uribe) 155
Labanyi, Jo 166
Ladrón, Eduardo 230
Laffond, Rueda 229
Lamas, Maria 87-8
Lambropoulou, Dimitra 176
Landa, Mariasun 50
Lanfant, Marie-Françoise 103
Leal, Paul 123
Lefebre, Henri 105
Liakos, Antonis 258
Life on Mars (television series) 236-7
Limpo, Bertha Rosa 93
Lisboa, Irene 123
Lopes, Fernando 197
Lury, Karen 230
Lyberis, Antonis 260

Maçã (apple) (fashion chain) 211-12, 221
McNamara, Fabio 160
McRobbie, Angela 2
O Mal-Amado 127-8
male sexualities *see* Greece, male sexualities, post-1960s
Maravilhas, Ana 210-11
Marcuse, Herbert 3
Marie-Claire (magazine) 213-14, 215, 216
Marwick, Arthur 5, 7-8, 126, 139
media censorship abolition, Spain 129
Medina, Alberto 166
Mello, Pedro Homem de 124
Meratran (drug) 70
Messerschmidt, James 4
Midnight Cowboy (Schlesinger) 125
Ta Mikra Ninjakia (The Little Ninjas) 251
Miró, Pilar 155
Modas e Bordados (M&B) 85, 87-8, 89, 90, 96
Modesto, Maria Lourdes 93
Moniz, Egas 124
Monroe, Marilyn 90
Montalbán, Vázquez 62
Monteiro, Cáceres 87, 96
Monteiro, João César 127
Monteiro, Sttau 204
Morais, Ana Bela 125
Morcillo, Aurora 63, 142
Mourão, António 95-6
Moureau, Jeanne 88

Index

Mozos, Manuel 122
Múrias, Beça 87
Myrizakis, Giannis 244

Nikolaidis, Nikos 156
Nozolino, Paulo 216
The Nun (*La Réligieuse*) (Rivette) 133

Obrador, S 72
Omnacilina (drug) 74

Pacts of Madrid 139
Paliatín (drug) 69–70
Panayotopoulos, Nikos 156
Pantagruel (recipe book) 93
Papadogiannis, Nikolaos 156
Papandreou, Andreas 242, 257
Papandreou, George 260
Pasolini, Pier Paolo 130–1, 132
O Passeio dos Alegres (TV show) 200–1, 205
Pavlovic, Tatjana 6, 62, 228
Pepsodent advert 92
Pereira, José Pacheco 124
Pérez, Jorge 64
Perich (*La Vanguardia*) 72, 73 *Fig.*
Peristiany, Jean G. 32
Petropoulos, Elias 250
Pina, Luís de 128
El Pisito (film) 63
Pitt-Rivers, Julian 32
Pons, Obrador 104
Portugal
    Americanization 14–16
        consumer behaviour, 1960s 85
        consumerism 62–3
    cinema, 1974–1976
        censorship abolition 128, 129–30
        colonial wars, effects 122–3
        controversies/rollback 132–4
        eroticism and revolution 128–31
        Gulbenkian Golden Generation 127–8
        hegemonic/subordinated masculinities and femininites, conflict 122–5
        homosexualities 123–4
        homosexuality and revolution 131–2
        key issues/conclusions 121, 134
        Marcelist Spring 125–7
        outside influences 126–7
        poverty images 125
        women filmmakers 125–6
    consumer behaviour, 1960s
        American/European lifestyles, interest 89–90
        cultural consumption changes 95–7
        domestic appliances 91–2
        emancipation of women 96–7
        Estado Novo 86, 88, 98
        family routines 92–3
        hygiene/asepsis 92
        key issues/conclusion 85–6, 98
        male/female homosexuality, criminalization 88–9
        masculinization of women 89
        physical education/outdoor activities 86–7
        private lifestyle changes 90–3
        reception of new consumption pattern 97–8
        retail changes 94
        supermarkets/malls 93–4
    consumerism, 1960s
        American consumerism 62–3
        consumer demand 61–2
        economic development 61
        gender advertising, modernization 74–7
        key issues/conclusions 59–60, 79–80
        National Catholicism 60
        national community aims 60–6
        pro-family measures 61
        psycho-pharmaceutical drugs 59
        Salazar regime, *Estado Novo* 60–2
        scientific morality of sexuality 77–8
        tourist trade 62
        women's organizations 60–1
    fashion magazines, 1980s
        editorials 216–21
        haute couture 210–11
        key issues/conclusion 209–10, 221–2
        memory and national identity 213–16, 222
        modernity 210, 217
        popular fashion, emergence 210–13, 221–2
        safe values 217–21, 218 *Fig.*, 219 *Fig.*, 222
        stereotypical past 214–15
Manobras de Maio (May Manoeuvres) 212
Mocidade Portuguesa Feminina (Portuguese Female Youth) 86
Movimento de Acção dos Homossexuais Revolucionários (MAHR) 132
National Costume Museum 212
Portuguese Textile Association 212
postmodernity transition 13–14
Radiotelevisão Portuguesa (RTP) 193–204 *passim*
Salazar regime 60–2
Secretariado do Cinema e da Radio (Secretariat for Film and Radio) 133
television, 1976–1983
    Brazilian *telenovelas* 198, 199, 203–5
    cultural legitimacy/home entertainment 195–6
    figures/content 194–5
    imagined societies 200–5
    key issues/epilogue 193–4, 205
    post-revolutionary television 194–7
    television culture, development 197–200

Index

temporalities' entanglement 16–17
as testing ground 1
transitology revisited 9–13
El proceso de Burgos (Uribe) 155
prosperity *see* Greece, prosperity of 1980s, and current crisis
Psathas, Dimitris 112

Quaggio, Guilia 166

Radcliff, Pamela 10, 138
recreational practices *see* Greece, seaside recreational practices, postwar–1974
Redondo, Helen 211
reflexive mediterranization *see* Greece
Rentzis, Thanasis 156, 159
Rivette, Jacques 133
Rocky Horror Picture Show 159
Rodrigues, Amália 96
Römhild, Regina 37
The Rugs are Still Singing (Nikolaidis) 156

Salazar, Anna 211, 212, 213, 217, 221
Salazar regime 60–2
Saló (Passolini) 132
Sampaio Tavares, Abel 77–8
Santos, Almeida 132
Sarmento, Olga Moraes 123
Saura, Carlo 156
Schuster, Mel 159
seaside recreational practices, postwar–1974 *see* Greece
Sedeño, Ascensión 145–6
The Seduction of Modern Spain (Morcillo) 6, 142
Sena, Jorge de 132
La Señora (TV production) 229
Sierra, Consuelo Álvarez 63
Silva, Fernando Matos 127
Singer (machines) 91
Smith, Paul Julian 160, 230
The Sound of Music (film) 96
Southern Europe
 cinema, post-authoritarian Spain and Greece
 commodifying marginality 162–3
 disillusionment 154
 films of the period 154–6
 gender/pleasure/frivolity 164–5
 gradual cooption 165–6
 homosexual component 155–6
 key focus/conclusions 156–9, 166–7
 non-violent movements 153–4
 post-politics 160–2
 power transfers 153
 sexual/gender/consumer practices 154
 social concern/subversion 154–5
 subculture documentation 159–60

transvestism 165, 167
 see also Almodóvar, Pedro, *Pepi, Luci, Bom*; Zervos, Nikos, *Drakoulas*
consumption and gender in 2
post-authoritarian societies (1960s) 5–8
as testing ground 1
transitology revisited 9–13
Spain
 Americanization 14–16, 62–3
 Basque youth culture *see* Basque youth culture, 1960s
 cinema, post-authoritarian *see* Southern Europe, cinema, post-authoritarian Spain and Greece
 consumerism, 1960s
 American consumerism 14–16, 62–3
 balanced male, images 70–2
 burnout/*surmenage* 69–70
 consumerism increase 63
 consumerism in books/fiction/films 63–4
 economic expansion 62
 female emotional discontent 65–8
 Franco regime 60, 61, 62–4, 137–8, 140–2
 gender advertising 75
 gender/sex ambiguities 72–3
 key issues/conclusions 59–60, 79–80
 male pathologies of lifestyle 68–73
 psycho-pharmaceutical drugs 59
 psychotropic drugs 64–5
 Democratic Women's Movement (MDM) 147
 Flora Tristán Association 148
 Franco regime 60, 61, 62–4
 housewives in transition, 1959–80
 American influences 139–40
 behaviour models 141–2
 economic liberalization 140
 family planning/sexual liberation 144
 Franco regime 137–8, 140–2
 heterogeneous women's organizations 147–8, 149
 key issues/conclusions 138–9, 149
 Model Mrs. Consumer 139–42, 149
 neighbourhood movement 147
 political socialization of women 144–5
 rights of women 143–4
 social protests 147
 Spanish Housewives' Association 145–6
 transition era 138
 women's movement responses 146–8
 media censorship abolition 129
 Movida madrileña (The Madrilenian scene) 149
 National Catholicism 140
 Opus Dei Roman Catholic organization 142
 pact of oblivion, (pacto de olvido) 228–9
 Popular Allianz (AP) 144

279

Index

postmodernity transition 13-14
RTVE 230
Seminary for the Sociological Study of Women 147
Spanish Association of University Women 147
Spanish Communist Party 144, 147
Spanish Housewives' Association 145-6
Spanish Socialist Workers' Party (PSOE) 144
television, *Cuéntame cómo pasó* (Tell Me How it Was)
   arrival of the future (*La llegada del futuro*) 232-6
   consumerism, increased possibilities 229
   electrodomésticos and automobiles 232-6
   emerging consumer culture 228-9
   gender and memory 229-32
   key issues/conclusion 227-8, 236-7
   narrative of the past 227
temporalities' entanglement 16-17
touristification, 1950s-70s
   contact zones and gender roles 30-4
   employment and emancipation 30-2
   ethnographic conceptualization 31, 32, 34
   existing gender roles 30
   gender roles as attraction 29
   hegemonic masculinity 33
   hispanization/mediterranization 34-7
   homosexuality, responses 33-4
   key issues/conclusion 29-30, 37-8
   masculinity notions, challenges 30-1
   numbers 29
   otherness representation 34-6
   reflexive mediterranization 36-7
   sexual and moral behaviour 32-3
   transnational communication 37
   travel guide stereotypes 34-6
   women's employment patterns, challenges 31-2
transitology revisited 10-13
TVEI 229, 230
Union of the Democratic Centre (UCD) 144
O Spangorammenos (play) 1
Stearns, P.N. 63, 70
Súarez, Adolfo 129
Sun newspaper 244
Surmontil (drug) 68

Tachidromos (magazine) 108, 111
O Tal Canal (TV show) 201, 205
Tarrow, Sidney 147

Teixeira, Judith 123
television, 1976-1983 *see* Portugal
television, *Cuéntame cómo pasó* (Tell Me How it Was) *see* Spain
Telles, Cunha 127
Telva (magazine) 142, 143
temporalities' entanglement 16-17
Temps de silenci (TV production) 229
The Siege (*O Cerco*) (Cunha) 127
Thomopoulos, Andreas 156
Thornton, Sarah 163
Todos se han ido (Vintró) 63
Tojal, Manuela 217, 219, 221
Torres, Alberto Fernández 158
Torres, Helena 214
Touring Club of Greece 106-7
The Tourist Gaze (Urry) 104
touristification, 1950s-70s *see* Spain
transitology revisited 10-13
Três dias sem Deus (Virgínia) 125-6
Tsolakos, Giorgos 250

Ude, Fernando Álvarez Ude 68
Urbain, Jean-Didier 103
Uribe, Imanol 155
Urry, John 104, 113

Valium 75
Vasconcelos, Mário Cesariny de 124-5
Veijola, Soile 104-5
Velloudios, Thanos 176
Vintró, María Mercedes Ortoll 63
Virginia, Bárbara 125-6
A Visita da Cornélia (TV programme) 195-6, 197
Vitorino, Virginia 123-4
Voulgaris, Yannis 173

Warhol, Andy 159
Waters, John 159
Webb, Darren 105

Zervos, Nikos, *Drakoulas*
   career 156-7
   trangressive/irreverent nature 158
   commodifying marginality 162-3
   gender/pleasure/frivolity 164-5
   post-politics 160-2
   subculture documentation 159-60
Zorba (film) 96

www.ingramcontent.com/pod-product-compliance
Ingram Content Group UK Ltd.
Pitfield, Milton Keynes, MK11 3LW, UK
UKHW021837220426
470268UK00007B/221